VIRTUAL AME   S

*New Americanists*

*A Series Edited by Donald E. Pease*

# VIRTUAL AMERICAS

Transnational Fictions and the Transatlantic Imaginary

*Paul Giles*

Duke University Press   Durham and London  2002

Printed in the United States of America on acid-free paper ∞
Typeset in Scala by Keystone Typesetting, Inc.
Library of Congress Cataloging-in-Publication Data
appear on the last printed page of this book.

*To Nadine*

*and to our friends*

*in Oregon*

# CONTENTS

*Everything's comparative.*

—*Lambert Strether in Henry James,*

THE AMBASSADORS, 1903


*an outline broken by refraction,*

*a distortion in the mirror of being, a wrong turn*

*taken by life, a sinistral and sinister world*

—*Vladimir Nabokov, introduction to*

BEND SINISTER, 1963


*every image in every mirror is only virtual,*

*even when you expect to see yourself*

—*Don DeLillo,* THE BODY ARTIST, 2001

# PREFACE

Shortly before leaving Oregon in 1994, after working there for seven years, I wrote an article entitled "Reconstructing American Studies: Transnational Perspectives, Comparative Perspectives," which was subsequently published in the December 1994 issue of the *Journal of American Studies*. The essay came about partly out of a sense of frustration with certain ways the Americanist field was being conceptualized at that time in the United States, although this frustration was aggravated rather than ameliorated when I returned to England and witnessed the very different but often quite formulaic ways American literature and American studies were still being taught, not just in the United Kingdom but throughout many parts of Europe during the 1990s. This book, then, represents an attempt to establish some kind of transatlantic dialogue among different conceptual approaches to this Americanist field, in the hope of opening up new critical perspectives neither circumscribed entirely by a politics of location nor commensurate, either explicitly or implicitly, with the boundaries of the nation state.

Because *Virtual Americas* represents the culmination of several years' work, a number of the chapters have been published in earlier forms elsewhere. My interest in Thom Gunn's poetry goes back a long time, and Chapter 7 draws on material from two earlier pieces: an article in the summer 1987 issue of *Critical Quarterly* entitled "Landscapes of Repetition: The Self-Parodic Nature of Thom Gunn's Later Poetry," and "From Myth into History: The Later Poetry of Ted Hughes and Thom Gunn," an essay that formed part of the 1997 collection edited by James Acheson and Romana Huk, *Contemporary British Poetry* (Albany: State University of New York Press). I am grateful to Thom Gunn for pointing out a couple of factual inaccuracies in the latter piece. The Melville chapter is based on a contribution to *The Cambridge Companion to Melville*, edited by Robert S. Levine (Cambridge, England: Cambridge University Press, 1997), and I am glad to acknowledge how my approach to Melville benefited from Bob's admirable editorial skills on that occasion. The first chapter also reworks ideas first explored in an essay entitled "Two-Way Mirrors: British-American Literary History and the Ideology of Exchange," published in *Research in English and American Literature, 14: Literature and the Nation*, edited by Brook Thomas (Tübingen: Gunter Narr Verlag, 1998). Different versions of other chapters first appeared in various academic journals: "Narrative Reversals and Power Exchanges: Frederick Douglass and British Culture" in *American Literature* 73 (Dec. 2001); "Double Exposure: Sylvia Plath and the Aesthetics of Transnationalism," *Symbiosis* 5 (Oct. 2001); "From Decadent Aesthetics to Political Fetishism: The 'Oracle Effect' of Robert Frost's Poetry," *American Literary History* 12 (winter 2000); "Virtual Eden: *Lolita*, Pornography, and the Perversions of American Studies," *Journal of American Studies* 34 (Apr. 2000); "Virtual Americas: The Internationalization of American Studies and the Ideology of Exchange," *American Quarterly* 50 (Sept. 1998). I am grateful to the editors of these journals—Houston Baker Jr., Richard Gravil, Gordon Hutner, Richard Gray, and Lucy Maddox, respectively—for their assistance and advice.

Other parts of this book enjoyed their first airing in more informal settings. Part of the concluding chapter was given as a lecture on "Cyber-pastoral" at the European Association for American Studies conference in Graz, Austria, in April 2000. In Chapter 4, I draw on ideas discussed in a lecture entitled "The Surrealization of American Studies" presented at the Institute in American Studies, Dartmouth College, in June 2000. A much earlier version of Chapter 8 was presented at the International Pynchon Seminar held at King's College, London, in May 1998.

I am especially indebted to friends and colleagues who took the time to offer valuable suggestions on particular sections of the manuscript. Andrew Taylor, now at University College, Dublin, read the section on Henry James; Kasia Boddy, of University College, London, commented on the Pynchon chapter; Clive Wilmer, my colleague at Fitzwilliam College in Cambridge, shared with me his enormous expertise on Thom

Gunn. The two readers for Duke University Press also made observations that were perceptive and incisive and at the same time supportive, the kind of feedback every author should welcome. I am very grateful as well to Don Pease for his long-standing interest in and generous support for my work, and to Reynolds Smith at Duke University Press for helping at the end to bring this book into being.

Cambridge, England
October 2001

# Virtual Subjects:
## Transnational Fictions and the
## Transatlantic Imaginary

The focus of this book is on ways in which representations of the United States have been deflected from mythic to what I call "virtual" phenomena in literary works of the modern era. In particular, I consider the implications of this process of displacement for the construction of fictional forms of nationalism. My main concern here is with points of intersection between the United States and Great Britain, looking at ways American writers from Herman Melville to Thomas Pynchon have compulsively appropriated and reinvented aspects of English culture to advance their own aesthetic designs. Conversely, I also examine projections of American culture in the writing of British subjects such as Thom Gunn, as well as pseudo-British characters like Nabokov's Humbert Humbert, to elucidate ways mythic versions of American identity in the middle of the twentieth century arose partly through narratives of dislocation and alterity. One purpose is to shed light on established versions of British cultural nationalism at this time through a kind of reverse projection, as if a film were run backwards. Another is to suggest ways that conceptions of national identity on both sides of the Atlantic emerged through engagement with—and, often, deliberate exclusion of—a transatlantic imaginary, by which I mean the interiorization of a literal or metaphorical Atlantic world in all of its expansive dimensions.

I discuss in more detail later in this chapter what I mean by the critical process of virtualization; however, an initial definition might involve the way it works to hollow out cultural formations by looking at them from a comparative angle of vision. It is as if the observer were seeing native landscapes refracted or inverted in a foreign mirror. Webster's dictionary defines "virtual focus" as "a point from which divergent rays (as of light) seem to emanate but do not actually do so (as in the image of a point source seen in a plane mirror)"; a "virtual image," accordingly, is "an image (as seen in a plane mirror) formed of virtual foci."[1] Such mirror images deprive the objects reflected of their traditional comforts of depth and perspective, illusions by which their claims on natural representation are traditionally sustained; instead, these objects are flattened out into replicas of themselves in a process of aestheticization that highlights the manifestly fictional dimensions of their construction. By examining the cultural narratives of the United States from this position of reflection and estrangement, a position through which American fictions are brought into juxtaposition with those of other countries, it becomes easier to appreciate the assumptions framing these narratives and the ways they are intertwined with the construction and reproduction of national mythologies. To virtualize America is not only to denaturalize it, but also to suggest how its own indigenous representations of the "natural" tend to revolve tautologously, reinforcing themselves without reference to anything outside their own charmed circle.

The interaction of American writers with Europe is an old and extensive topic, but my interests here are somewhat more limited and specific. I am concerned above all with how certain texts represented themselves (or were subsequently represented) as being symptomatic of a certain kind of national identity. It is the mapping of text onto a kind of national grid, along with the transnational interferences and reversals that emanate from such theoretical superimpositions, that is the focal point of this book. When Frederick Douglass asks "What to the Slave is the Fourth of July?" the significance of his oration derives, obviously enough, from its juxtaposition with an implied narrative of national independence and liberation. When Henry James inspects his old haunts in *The American Scene* (1907), he is deliberately playing off embedded memories of American institutions and landscapes against the oblique, indirect impressions of a "restless analyst" long since uprooted from his native territory.[2] In both cases, these Americans are looking at their country from the outside: Douglass has been alienated by race, with his sense of displacement compounded by extensive involvements with British abolitionists, and James has marginalized himself through the experience of exile.

Such forms of alienation—structural alienation, as it were—work to undermine one commonly held belief about the relationship between literature and national identity: that theoretical inquiries into it are invariably circular, as the latter always manifests itself "naturally" in the former. To "demand" a national literature would be "absurd," declared the *Ladies' Home Journal* in 1854, because "whatever is naturally peculiar in our character, views, and modes of life, does and always will exhibit itself without any assistance from us."[3] Ann Douglas, in the introduction to her account of Manhattan in the 1920s, *Terrible Honesty* (1995), similarly argues that America is "a special case," imbued with "a national psyche," and she claims that to "say otherwise is . . . to ignore plain fact"; hence, the plain facts heaped up in her compendious study are supposed in themselves to testify to the "special" nature of the American experience.[4] What is at issue, however, is not the idea of cultural difference itself, but the means and efficacy of identifying it and the purposes to which such identifications are put. My argument here is not that America is not, in certain ways, different; rather, it is that by reconsidering national formations from a position of estrangement, writers like Douglass and James situate themselves to illuminate the nation's unconscious assumptions, boundaries, and proscribed areas. These are the assumptions that tend to remain latent or unexamined in studies of a national culture that are generated wholly from the inside or that lack a comparative dimension. Authors such as Douglass and James, or Frost and Nabokov, denaturalize what is supposedly familiar and consequently reveal the strange and sometimes sinister components that go to make up formations of a "national psyche." The relationship between literature and national identity, in other words, is not symbiotic or natural, but, at its extreme circumference, highly paradoxical, involving the backward projection of epistemological limits from a vantage point beyond their boundaries.

From a practical point of view, there are various difficulties inherent in any attempt to describe American literature and culture from a comparative standpoint. One of the most obvious involves what we might term, to misquote Clifford Geertz, thin description. There are, of course, whole swathes of American experience that do not feature prominently in the more recognizable categories of national mythology and that consequently are underrepresented in academic approaches to the United States, especially as these are practiced abroad. Whereas "major" figures in "major" urban centers can be placed relatively easily, large areas of the social landscape are much less well-known, and this can lead to some odd disjunctions in comparative accounts of American culture between the etiolated realm of myth and local or experiential perspectives. Questions of class and other forms of internal hierarchy, in particular, can too easily be glossed over by an outsider's distantly synchronic gaze. Though it would perhaps be invidious to single out particular examples, Barbara Eckstein has suggested that the "mythic westering" theme, with its inherently decontextualized emphasis, seems to have enjoyed a longer intellectual life abroad than within the United States itself, where the idea has been subjected to all kinds of critical interrogation from scholars concerned with differential equations of race, gender, and power.[5] Similarly, the tendency toward abstract uniformity and interchangeability in American suburbia—defended eloquently by Philip Fisher in a recent essay as a Cartesian form of "democratic social space"—remains aesthetically unfamiliar to the centralizing geography of many European analysts, too prone to ask traditional questions about which might be "the real Main Street."[6]

Linked with this concern about material thinness is the second frequent complaint about comparative approaches: that they tend implicitly to reinforce existing identities by simply playing off national mythologies against each other. The most famous paradigm in Britain for this kind of organicist, idealized treatment of American culture is D. H. Lawrence's *Studies in Classic American Literature* (1923), which brazenly hails "the old American classics" as introducing "a new voice," "a new experience," capable of breaking through the tired conventions of European writing.[7] Similar views of American literature as harboring an oppositional romanticism have continued to resonate through twentieth-century British criticism; for instance, Malcolm Bradbury's *The Modern American Novel* (1983), which takes its epigraph from Lawrence's *Studies*, sees New World culture as riven by a perpetual mood of apocalypse, a cataclysmic series of "threats to survival," which appear to render the more mundane nuances of historical change and development relatively inconsequential.[8] In the British context, this flattened version of "Americanness" promulgated by readers like Lawrence and Bradbury has characteristically operated through a stereotypical binary opposition, counterpointing the radical proclivities of American culture with what the authors took to be the more genteel liberal humanism of the English tradition.

In a more recent reconsideration of this problem, however, David Damrosch has usefully theorized the method of comparative literature as "inherently elliptical in nature." For Damrosch, the crucial aspect of comparative literature is its capacity to modify our perception of each particular area under analysis. By reimagining London "within a Copernican universe of many centers of gravity," he observes, we come to see the capital of England as "one focus of an ellipse, or more precisely as one focus for many different, partially overlapping ellipses, each with a second focus elsewhere." In this way, he argues, the "comparatist's elliptical perspective . . . can alter our picture of British literary geography": just as we read texts from Ireland or Australia differently by juxtaposing them with the forces of colonial empire, so we also come to see the canonical traditions of British literature in an unfamiliar light by relating them to these alternative geometries.[9] Consequently, this critical endeavor to read British and American literatures in parallel overlaps with current theoretical efforts in English studies to redescribe "an island's literature," in Regenia Gagnier's phrase, as "a complex and interactive anglophone culture."[10] To relate British culture to its American counterpart, then, is by definition to open up wider questions about the definition and status of literatures in English.

It is in this kind of ideology of exchange that estranged perspectives on particular cultures can appear at their most revealing. Rather than seeking simply to transcend national boundaries in the name of a universalist humanism or a benevolent multiculturalism, I am interested in what happens when different national formations collide or intersect with each other. In an essay on the "globalization" of literary studies, Paul Jay has suggested that we might "usefully complicate our nation-based approach to the study of English, not by dropping the nation-state paradigm but by foregrounding its history and its function *for* the nation-state," to examine ways literature has been instrumental in consolidating or interrogating forms of national identity.[11] From this point of view, the various crossovers between British and American literature might engender double-edged discourses liable to destabilize traditional hierarchies and power relations, thereby illuminating the epistemological boundaries of both national cultures. America, that is to say, introduces an element of strangeness into British culture, just as British traditions, often in weirdly hollowed out or parodic forms, shadow the democratic designs of the American republic.

Strangeness, as Zygmunt Bauman has written, holds up a quizzical mirror to the philosophical limits of liberal pluralism by its intimation of that which cannot, ultimately, be transformed or reconciled. In Bauman's words, "It is not the failure to acquire native knowledge that constitutes the outsider as a stranger; it is the existential constitution of the stranger which makes the native knowledge unassimilable."[12] From this angle, it might be possible to write another kind of history of American literature, one more concerned with a dialectic of familiarity and alterity, domesticity and estrangement. This would examine literature's relationship to the nation in quite different contexts, substituting the awkward, sometimes discontinuous processes of transition between global and local for that more settled sense of affiliation between writer and environment that has guided so many traditional accounts of America's (and Britain's) "homemade world."[13] The point here is that national histories, of whatever kind, cannot be written simply from the inside. The scope and significance of their narrative involve not just the incorporation of multiple or discordant voices in a certain preestablished framework of unity, but also an acknowledgment of external points of reference that serve to relativize the whole conceptual field, pulling the circumference of national identity itself into strange, "elliptical" shapes.

Studies of national culture as an entity in itself have suffered from an increasingly uncertain theoretical base since the 1960s, as the intellectual fortunes of structuralism have declined along with the historical polarizations of the cold war. The anthropological effort to map out particular academic areas, to codify cultures through all-encompassing modes of binary opposition—New World versus Old World, center versus margin, and so on—gradually lost analytical credibility as more reflexive critiques of origin disenfranchised any such claims to universalism or "objective" methodology. As Guenter H. Lenz observed in 1991, writing under the sign of poststructuralism: "The recent critical reflections in anthropology as well as in literary and cultural criticism make any attempt to interpret a culture, particularly American culture, 'as a whole' a futile and politically very dubious undertaking, if by 'unity' and 'wholeness' we still have in mind something like a consistent structure or even a dialectical unity."[14] Arjun Appadurai similarly has written about how the "area-studies tradition" in its classic forms depended on a certain "isomorphism" between geographical space and cultural specificity that has been impossible to sustain intellectually in "a world of disjunctive global flows."[15] The area studies model endorsed most frequently by American studies has involved the attempt to encompass a particular bounded territory—characteristically, a nation, but also smaller variants of the nation space, such as a region or a city—and through this enabling circumscription to treat that space allegorically, as emblematic of a particular kind of identity.

One of the purposes of this book, however, is to argue that a genealogy tracing associations between "virtual Americas" and a more general idiom of dislocation and estrangement might help to locate an alternative kind of American studies, one predicated openly on division and disjunction rather than that mythic integrity and interdisciplinary coherence that gave the subject its methodological rationale during its nationalist heyday of the 1950s and 1960s. These "myth and symbol" versions of Americanist scholarship were excited above all by the prospect of grasping the culture of the United States as an organic whole.[16] As Bill Readings observed, one key function of universities at this time was to reproduce as symbolic capital the substantial economic capital invested by the nation-state, a situation that led to various efforts to reimagine American cultural history according to paradigms of convergence and consensus.[17] One classic point of reference for this generation of Americanists was Crèvecoeur's images of transmutation and fusion, whereby "individuals of all nations are melted into a new race of men." Another was Henry Adams's testament to the World's Columbian Exposition at Chicago in 1893; for Adams, "Chicago was the first expression of American thought as a unity," and so, he suggested, "one must start there."[18] It is important to emphasize here the close proximity of religion and nationalism as narratives of cohesion; indeed, in the work of critics like Perry Miller these discourses famously overlapped, with Miller undertaking to analyze the New England Puritan experience as synecdochic of American culture as a whole. Miller and the other Americanists in the generation after the Second World War were significantly influenced by "systematic" critics like Northrop Frye, himself a Christian cleric, whose essay "The Archetypes of Literature" (1951) proposed a number of "classifying principles" for works of literature according to their relationship with various aspects of human custom and ritual.[19]

Such universalist, integrationist concepts now are often seen as a way of masking entrenched power relations; in Miller's case, of course, the way his focus on Harvard-trained intellectuals limited the scope of his inquiries has been exposed clearly enough. Far from inscribing a mythically inclusive America, Miller was actually mythologizing a socially exclusive one. To deconstruct the forces of nationalism by which a scholar like Miller was motivated is, however, not necessarily to rationalize them away entirely. Raymond Williams used to describe ideological structures as "residual," "dominant," or "emergent," with "residual" signifying a legacy from "some previous social formation" that still continues to exercise power in the dominant culture. In these terms, as Fredric Jameson and others have noted, the idea of a nation as a mythic totality continues to constitute a powerful residual discourse, in the way Williams observed that certain kinds of "religious meanings and values" can subliminally carry an affective and ideological charge, even when their function as a legislative or coercive force has diminished.[20] In his work on how "the new international" is reconfiguring the boundaries of civil society, Derrida similarly wrote in 1993 that "nationalisms of native soil . . . have no future," because they are supported merely by the ghosts of transcendent spirit: "There is no nationality or nationalism that is not religious or mythological, let us say 'mystical' in the broad sense."[21] Nevertheless, as Derrida went on to suggest, the *Geist* of nineteenth-century idealism connotes both spirit and specter, evoking the shades of a ghostly nationalism that will not quite disappear. In the light of such conceptual homologies between national and religious identity, it is no coincidence that at the end of the Victorian era Adams should have turned to nationalism as a substitute for religion; indeed, in his famous image of the "Dynamo and the Virgin" he seeks to conflate the two, imagining the dynamo, as displayed at the Chicago Exposition, to be a "symbol of infinity" and coming to see "an absolute *fiat* in electricity as in faith."[22] Adams's metaphor echoes the analogy in Ernest Renan's seminal essay, "What Is a Nation?" which appeared just a few years before, in 1882, where the skeptical Renan foreshadowed Adams in construing the nation as "a soul, a spiritual principle," a centrifugal force in this increasingly scientific and agnostic age.[23] With a typically late Victorian sense of anxiety, the idea of the nation is deployed here instrumentally, as a source of social containment and as the philosophical substitute for a religious teleology that is feared lost.

As Eric Hobsbawm has observed, it is unlikely anyone would attempt to write the history of the twenty-first century using the kind of nationalist apparatus that was popular during the nineteenth-century "age of revolution" and subsequently.[24] The ways national frontiers were rendered ever more fluid during the latter part of the twentieth century by the traversals of peoples, capital, and technology are obvious enough. Derrida noted that the speed of changes in "techno-tele-media apparatuses" toward the end of the twentieth century left many aspects of particular national cultures profoundly disturbed by these "new rhythms of information and communication," rhythms that have appeared to threaten the social independence as well as the economic autonomy of nation-states.[25] Not coincidentally, studies of "globalization and the world-system" burgeoned around the turn of the millennium, with Immanuel Wallerstein, to take just one example, declaring that "holding on to national or to ethnic or any other form of particularistic culture" could only be "a crutch" in the face of global development.[26] Appadurai has also developed what he calls "a theory of rupture" that sees the new internationalizing dynamics of electronic media and mass migration as eroding stable relationships between geographical locations and cultural imaginaries.[27] In this sense, there is an urgent need for the partitioned world of area studies, as traditionally conceived, to come to terms with the burgeoning forces of globalization.

There are, however, several crucial factors that these versions of globalization as rupture seem to ignore. One is the spectral argument put forward most compellingly by Derrida: the manner in which nationalism customarily encompasses certain residual and affective strains, the way communities become attached emotionally and psychologically to particular forms of civic organization, just as they remain under the influence of religious paradigms long after ceasing to believe in their spiritual efficacy. Another is how this curiously abstract "dream of the globe constituted as a single, integrated market place" tends to overlook class and other forms of material difference, differences that, as Paul Smith argues, continue to be mediated in one way or another by the regulatory power of the nation-state.[28] Jameson, in fact, maintains that "the state can still be a positive space," a "place of welfare and social legislation" offering a potential site of resistance to the circulations of multinational capitalism. He accordingly conceives of the relationship between "national situations" and transnational networks as involving complex "dialectical reversal" and a "never-ending series of paradoxes," whereby national identities are granted a contingent, strategic value even while their symbolic power is being radically hollowed out.[29] For many reasons, then, to acknowledge the increasingly uncertain trajectory and status of the nation is by no means to relegate it automatically to the level of what Masao Miyoshi calls "a nostalgic and sentimental myth." In the face of transnational corporations, suggests Miyoshi, globalization has simply superseded the old notion of a "shared community," so that we are left with a postnational scenario where "Cable TV and MTV dominate the world absolutely."[30] But surely it is manifestly untrue, even absurd, to claim that cable television and MTV enjoy this kind of world dominance. It would be more accurate to say that these processes of transnationalism have introduced harsh frictions and disjunctions between the flows of global capital and the residual force of a national imaginary, frictions that are played out within a cultural as well as a political framework. Accordingly, the field of area studies at the beginning of the twenty-first century finds itself in an odd intellectual position. On the one hand, it is obliged, like theology after 1860, to chart the radical problematization and potential disenfranchisement of its own theoretical assumptions; but on the other hand, again like theology, it finds itself dispersed into more amorphous modes, whose significance emerges from radical disjunction or aestheticization rather than through any inner logic or ultimate source of coherence.

From a materialist perspective, then, the sharp antagonisms associated with increasingly permeable boundaries of national identity produce a more complex and challenging terrain than older models predicated on relatively stable, reified understandings of any given national mystique. In the unpredictable world of capitalism in the twenty-first century, the "imagined community" of a nation-state appears as a constraining or limiting factor to circumscribe the more utopian, global pretensions of neoliberalism, rather in the way that regionalist cultures of the late Victorian era tended to act as a check on the centralizing tendencies of the national metropolis.[31] In the twenty-first century, neither Britain nor the United States is in a position to lock out the impulses of globalization, any more than Sarah Orne Jewett's rural Maine could lock out the dynamics of industrial capitalism at the end of the nineteenth; nevertheless, their situation as imagined communities crucially involves a capacity for interference and alterity, for pulling these larger, systemic loops out of shape. Whereas area studies during the cold war era specialized in defining the exceptional, antithetical elements within different regions of the world, such oppositions no longer appear plausible in the contemporary global framework. Thus, American studies today cannot continue to operate in the same old way, simply promulgating the virtues of particular kinds of identity politics as they emerge from the confines of the nation-state. Instead, the subject must play off what is inside a framework defined as "American" against what is outside it, thereby illuminating the ways specific local conditions and cultural landscapes reconstitute transnational networks in different ways.

As a theoretical idea, virtualization is commensurate with some of the most familiar themes in American intellectual history. In "A World of Pure Experience" (1904), William James discussed all cognition as a form of "virtual knowledge," where the process of knowing involves "continuous transition" between prior categories and the experiences of the observer. Just as Emerson's transcendental impulse was predicated on an "unfixing" of established forms and a metamorphosis of opaque phenomena into translucent designs, so James's version of pragmatism turned on an "unsettlement" of established conditions and a displacement of epistemological certainty into more fluid, contingent modes of perception.[32] Virtualization in this Jamesian sense can be closely correlated with a metaphysical idealism where all terrestrial entities become shadowy harbingers of a more distant promise. James, of course, juxtaposed his own "tough-minded" pragmatism with an interest in varieties of religious experience; more recently, Mark C. Taylor has also written of virtuality, in its specifically electronic and digital forms, as a state with theological implications. Taylor associates virtual reality with a ghostly omnipresence, where the material and the immaterial interface with each other rather than being locked into intransigent oppositions. Under the influence of Baudrillard's descriptions of hyperreality and simulation, Taylor nominates Las Vegas as the celestial city of virtuality, where questions of originality and authenticity have been sublimated into an autonomous realm of aestheticization.[33] In this virtual domain, traditional ontological distinctions between original and replica, the godhead and its pale human imitation, have been eliminated.

The Las Vegas example brings into focus another way that American cultural traditions can be seen as linked to an idiom of virtuality: their mutual reliance on a discourse of capital. The erasure of boundaries symptomatic of an idealist metaphysics is reflected in the unobstructed circulations of a capitalist system propelled by the dynamics of trade and exchange. Through such market practices, objects are displaced from use into exchange value, opening up the prospect of a parallel world in which phenomenological integrity finds itself fractured and duplicitously recycled. During the classic phase of American studies in the 1950s, various scholars, most notably David M. Potter, linked the exceptional qualities of the United States to the characteristic of economic "plenty," the democratic manifestations of material wealth that were said to set America apart from the war-ridden world of Europe.[34] The point I wish to emphasize here is how these fictions of abundance can be seen as interwoven ideologically with doctrines of philosophical idealism, because both capitalism and transcendentalism function by conscripting empirical objects into cycles of exchange, by "virtualizing" natural phenomena into their shadow or replica. Moreover, this mythic form of apotheosis is complicit with the celebrated narratives of American pastoral, whose radical abstractions of complex into simple—city into country, artifice into nature, or whatever—are similarly dependent on an ideology of exchange, whereby one side of a particular equation is traded for another. This encompasses what Leo Marx has called "the ineluctably 'double' character of the pastoral figure's consciousness in these American fables," a doubleness he associates with "the Protestant conversion experience," whereby the fallen world is regenerated through an infusion of what Thoreau in *Walden* calls "higher laws."[35] The Protestant dynamics informing this sudden irruption of "grace" as "moral change" are underlined by William James in *The Varieties of Religious Experience* (1902), which contains two chapters on the significance of "conversion," identified here as the "high-water mark" of a human being's "spiritual capacity." While acknowledging that the impetus for such "shiftings of character to higher levels" might derive from either divine or psychological causes, James links this experience of "regenerative change" with "Protestant theology," and he describes various ways the phenomenon of conversion has influenced the development of American culture.[36]

In this sense, there are clear affiliations between the manifestly religious connotations of R. W. B. Lewis's *The American Adam*, published in 1955, and the implicitly Puritan teleology of Lawrence Buell's *The Environmental Imagination*, which appeared forty years later. Whereas Lewis identified the "Adamic" qualities of the "new" American landscape with a redemptive vision of cultural nationalism, Buell, working with a secularized form of Protestantism heavily indebted to Thoreau, locates within American pastoral an "aesthetics of relinquishment" based on a negative transfiguration of the accoutrements of gentility, a retreat from inherently corrupt systems of social manners into a more natural land-scape of revelation. Like Lewis, Buell tends to apotheosize this pastoral principle, thereby suppressing its contingent and material aspects; in-deed, Lewis's explicitly Christian dialectic of "innocence" and "experi-ence" is replicated in Buell's transcendent aspiration to withdraw from a world of anthropomorphic metaphor into a state of ecological purity.[37] Once again, a deep ethical burden is imposed on the pastoral idea. Buell's "ecocentric" theme proposes a benign universalism, a concern for the fate of the globe; but this barely masks the nationalist agenda of a dis-course concerned above all to redescribe nature in idealist terms, as a scene of cultural identification and source of moral value. Just as Lewis constructed "the authentic American as a figure of heroic innocence," intent on a "return to the primal perfection," so Buell aligns his national narrative with a purification, or "relinquishment," of worldly goods.[38] Such an ascetic, dematerializing impulse obscures the ways the pastoral relationship itself is incorporated, as Leo Marx noted, within a mode of exchange, where it is ironically bound to the metonymical formulas of transaction it is overtly opposing. For all of the oppositional force of his domestic politics, it is important to recognize that when Thoreau accounts for his hut alongside Walden Pond in commercial terms—"Two casks of lime, $2.40. That was high"—he is not only parodying the capitalist operation of America but also, implicitly, aligning himself with it.[39] Parody, like pastoral, works as a dialogical discourse, what Linda Hutcheon calls "a paradoxical structure of contrasting synthesis, a kind of differential dependence of one text upon another."[40] In this sense, both capitalist and pastoral formulas can be understood as centering around an ideology of exchange, the substitution of one object for its figurative corollary.

This is not, of course, to deny either the coruscating brilliance or the social effectiveness of Thoreau's iconoclastic style, nor simply to re-capitulate that too familiar critical move where a text that appears opposi-tional is said ultimately to be complicit with the culture that frames it. Rather, my argument is that, within the American cultural context, pas-toralism, transcendentalism, and capitalism constitute overlapping cir-cles, whose cumulative effect is tautologically to naturalize each other.

The matrix of capitalism does not undermine Thoreau's pastoral invective, but it forms its outer limit, the circumference beyond which it cannot move. Accordingly, the virtual dimensions latent in these networks of exchange are suppressed within a nationalist agenda where the relationship between geographic location and symbolic meaning comes to be seen as "isomorphic," in Appadurai's term, if not altogether natural.[41] Conversely, to foreground the virtual cartographies of natural identity is to interrogate the boundaries of what Emily Apter calls "a natural subject, honored by traditional fields of literary and area studies." It is also to examine the ways such identities might be understood instead as a "play of affects," a "performative mimicry," which consciously acknowledges (rather than suppresses) the differential power relations negotiated therein.[42]

What I am arguing, then, is that virtual dimensions are implicit in America's mythic construction of itself—through philosophical idealism, capitalist exchange, pastoral ideology, and so on—but that the effect of these mythic narratives is precisely to suppress those virtual lineaments that would illuminate the fictional, contingent condition of such national mythographies. A virtual America, therefore, would be a mythic America turned inside out. Potter, Marx, Lewis, and the other "myth and symbol" critics postulated a visionary explanation of America from a position firmly within the geographical and intellectual boundaries of the United States, thereby unconsciously suppressing the formation of those boundaries and reproducing critical assumptions that were made to appear homologous with the nature of the United States itself; but a subsequent redescription of American culture as a virtual construction would seek to position itself on these boundaries and, by looking both ways, to render the mythological circumference of the nation translucent.

Sometimes these grandiloquent versions of a mythic America are parodied directly by the virtualizing narratives I consider in this book. For instance, Nabokov's *Lolita* gleefully mimes the metaphors of Eden that were being promoted by critical works like *The American Adam* during the 1950s, although *Lolita* altogether traduces the romantic dissociation of authenticity from imitation on which the pastoral thesis outlined by Lewis and Buell depends. Instead, Nabokov invents a world where no categorical distinction can be made between original and copy, a world in which Humbert Humbert's idiosyncratic view of paradise operates as a kind of reverse projection of Lewis's established paradigm. One of the most disconcerting aspects of Humbert's sardonic vision, in fact, is the way it trains back a skeptical light on other invocations of a promised land besides his own. In Nabokov's virtual America, the compulsions of national identity become metamorphosed into an elaborate masquerade, the kind of masquerade that, as Apter suggests, has the effect of rendering colonial discourse "transparent to itself."[43] Similar images of masquerade occur frequently in the works of authors such as Melville, and again my argument is that, by situating his texts on a dividing line between Britain and the United States, Melville deploys a transnational perspective to empty out the more coercive aspects of cultural nationalism. Melville, that is to say, hollows out familiar political iconography and domestic assumptions by relocating his narrative perspective to the boundaries of national identity, from which liminal position his texts reinscribe U.S. practices as a mode of alterity while simultaneously comparing them to situations in alternative domains. Through this process of transposing authority into elaborate forms of masquerade, Melville effectively virtualizes the authority of the state, reimagining its jurisdiction as a form of theatrical play. We see this Janus-faced tendency most obviously when considering his representations of English naval law in Billy Budd.

On the face of it, of course, it might seem peculiarly backward-looking to focus on America's encounters with Europe—particularly with the old imperialist shadow of Great Britain—as an example of the transnational imaginary. Werner Sollors has specifically linked the modern "age of transnationalism" with linguistic diversity, with a "reexamination of American literature and history in the light of multilingualism," and Rob Wilson has suggested that the main theoretical impetus for reconceptualizing the United States as a region of "dematerialized cyberspace" has emerged from the Pacific Rim, from where America's interactions with Europe do not seem so significant as relations among the "Globloc" linking the United States with postmodern Japan.[44] Without at all seeking to deny the usefulness of these conceptual approaches to transnationalism, I prefer to resist the assumption sometimes made concomitantly, that the cultures of Britain and the United States should be symbiotically conflated into one hegemonic discourse which languages from other parts of the globe strive to decenter.[45] This seems too simplistic; over the course of the past two hundred years the literatures of England and the United States have enjoyed a mutually antagonistic as well as a mutually constitutive relationship, and to raise the specter of a transatlantic imaginary is to problematize the parameters of each national constituency. Indeed, one of the points I make in this book is that transnationalism has a specific history, often connected to developments in communications technology and the various metaphorical displacements associated with them, and that canonical American authors often appear in quite a different light if they are examined through the matrix of a transnational rather than a national narrative.

Back in 1852, for instance, Frederick Douglass saw quite clearly the advantages for American reformers in exploiting networks of "commerce" and exchange to facilitate the transmission of ideas across the confined spaces of isolationism and "mental darkness."[46] As I suggest, the subsequent valorization of American national identity in Douglass's work was crucially dependent on conjuring up a virtual image of Britain as a space he could both appropriate and, ultimately, reject. For Douglass, accordingly, the boundary between Britain and America operated as a mirror within which each culture could hold up for examination the power structures and presumptions of the other. *Lolita*'s projection of an idyllically homogeneous America similarly reflects back on the British class system, as epitomized by the Old World provenance of the novel's hero; likewise, the poetry of Thom Gunn implicitly mediates between alternative attitudes toward formal conventions and the regulation of sexuality. Consequently, to consider British and American literature in terms of the border between these two nations is to highlight various issues of race, class, and authority, issues that have helped to determine relations between these variant cultures. This is not the place to rehearse the theory of American literature as a postcolonial phenomenon, except to emphasize that the national identity of the United States emerged in the late eighteenth century out of a civil war within the British empire and to suggest how shades of this internal fissure had continued to haunt the cultural traditions of both nations over the course of the past two hundred years.[47] The literatures of Britain and the United States position themselves as the other's other, alter egos, the kind of cultural formation each might have become, but didn't.

The interaction between transnationalism and national identity is, then, a complex historical phenomenon as well as a pressing political issue. In her 1990 book published in English as *Nations without Nationalism*, Julia Kristeva associated transnationalism at the end of the twentieth century with various Enlightenment projects intent on redescribing relations between the universal and the local. In particular, she invoked Montesquieu's *esprit général* in contradistinction to the idealization of *Volksgeist*, the spirit of the people, that became established in the nineteenth century through Herder and Hegel. In this sense, Kristeva argued, the function of contemporary transnationalism involves stimulating and updating "discussion on the meaning of the 'national' today"; as a formal method of inquiry, transnationalism works to reveal the circumference of national formations and thus to empty out their peremptory claims to legitimacy. In this, it differs from the older critical styles of comparative literature, very popular in the age of Goethe and then again in the American academy of the 1950s, which were predicated ultimately on the notion of simply transcending national cultures, cultures it loftily viewed as parochial and intellectually irrelevant. Transnationalism, by contrast, positions itself at a point of intersection—Kristeva talked about "a transnational or international position situated at the crossing of boundaries"—where the coercive aspects of imagined communities are turned back on themselves, reversed or mirrored, so that their covert presuppositions and ideological inflections become apparent.[48]

It is this process of reversing and mirroring that brings together the historical and theoretical dimensions of this argument. To virtualize literary and cultural texts is to subject them to the kind of "reversible process" that is itself characteristic of digital technology.[49] Whereas conventional analogue transcriptions depend on a relationship between original and copy, digital effects can simulate a scene without any reference to an anterior event. This apparent breach in the compact between experiential and imagined worlds has troubled censors and state legislators, as we shall see, and its theoretical premises have also perturbed some academic critics.[50] Indeed, many of the negative appraisals of virtual reality, as the idea was formulated at the end of the twentieth century, have turned on its apparent projection of a metaphysical dualism: its assumption that, as Robert Markley puts it, "the universe itself is computable and that mathematics reveals its underlying harmony." Markley is right to point out that virtual reality, in its purely scientific form, reinscribes an opposition of spirit/matter that has "structured Western metaphysics since Plato," and this historical perspective usefully helps to indicate how some of the wilder claims for the emancipatory potential of cyberspace, as advanced by Sadie Plant and others, belong simply to the realm of millennial fantasy.[51] In the light of such forms of self-indulgence, it is not difficult to see why Donald Morton, writing from a specifically materialist and class-oriented point of view, should argue: "Cyberspace is a bourgeois designer space in which privileged Western or Westernized subjects fantasize that instead of being chosen by history, they choose their own histories."[52] Yet, as we have seen, the "logic of alienation" that Markley perceives as endemic to constructions of virtuality can effectively dislocate reified conceptions of race, class, and sexuality, rendering their institutionalized boundaries more visible and fluid through its parallel "logic of exchange."[53] The crucial point here is that virtual reality does not so much reinscribe an antithesis between mind and matter as negotiate spaces between them.

Hence, to virtualize culture is not to dematerialize it so much as to subject it to a process of dematerialization. The iconoclastic effect of virtual reality lies in its hybrid form, its tantalizing position in between the material event and its shadow. As we will see later, Thomas Pynchon's *Mason & Dixon* (1997) might be described as constructing a virtualized version of eighteenth-century America in the way it plays knowingly with a fictitious rhetoric of Enlightenment culture, displacing historical characters such as Benjamin Franklin and Thomas Jefferson into simulacra of themselves. The power of Pynchon's novel derives from the maps it draws between past and present, England and America, freedom and slavery. By emphasizing these cartographic processes, by comically acknowledging his text's simulated re-creation of the historical events that it mirrors, Pynchon's narrative compels readers to situate themselves in relation to the scenes represented. The "logic of alienation" that Markley finds in virtual reality betokens, in literary terms, an alienation effect where Coleridge's "willing suspension of disbelief" is never entirely allowed and systems are perceived as always susceptible of reversal. Virtual domains create, suggests Rob Shields, "a *crisis of boundaries* . . . between time zones and between spaces, near and distant."[54] This is exactly what we find in *Mason & Dixon*, where time and space are compressed and the reader's relation to the narrative is turned inside out.

In her work on the historical evolution of cybernetics, N. Katherine Hayles identifies three distinct periods in the development of artificial intelligence. "The first, from 1945 to 1960," she argues, "took homeostasis as a central concept; the second, going roughly from 1960 to 1980, revolved around reflexivity; and the third, stretching from 1980 to the present, highlights virtuality."[55] Hayles goes on to trace analogies between these scientific frameworks and their particular cultural moment. For example, homeostasis, which highlights similarities between humans and machines, can be said to intersect with the liberal humanist tradition of the 1950s; likewise, reflexivity, which emphasizes "how systems are constituted as such" and how "the observer can be taken into account," is correlated with the reflexive turn, the self-portraits in convex mirrors, that permeated literature and culture throughout the 1960s and 1970s.[56] These categories, admittedly approximate, might be applied to American studies as well. A work such as Lewis's *American Adam*, published in 1955, identifies the origins of America with certain kinds of liberal ideals associated with originality and authorship, while the reflexive deconstruction of this myth-symbol school—which arrived somewhat belatedly in American studies scholarship—duly critiqued the absence of ideological self-consciousness that the earlier "radical humanist tradition" fostered.[57] My suggestion, though, is that American studies may be passing, like Hayles's forms of cybernetics, from a reflexive into a virtual realm. What has become crucial now is not so much the position of the observer within the system, but rather what Donna Haraway calls the "situatedness" of the actual system, "where location is itself always a complex construction as well as inheritance." Instead of reflexivity—which simply displaces the same elsewhere and sets up an epistemological conundrum about the status of original and copy—Haraway proposes a virtualized notion of "diffractions," which effectively establish interference patterns among different systems and so force a renewed emphasis on position and relation.[58]

It is not difficult to see how this kind of "situatedness" would fit with an approach to the study of the United States in comparative terms. The key issue is not so much how American culture itself is constructed (as in the reflexive model) but how, within a transnational framework, American culture intersects with, modulates, and is in turn modulated by cultural practices in other parts of the world. McKenzie Wark has coined the term "virtual geography" to describe how spatial relations in the modern world have been affected by the principle of "telesthesia," perception at a distance, as mediated by a wide variety of instruments from the telegraph to the telephone and television. In this digital age, telesthesia's repositioning of a discrete object of analysis in terms of "relationality and mobility" threatens to introduce instability into what have traditionally been self-enclosed systems.[59] Just as the telegraph and telephone were once thought to connect mysteriously with other worlds, as Margaret Morse observes, so virtual landscapes evoke a parallel domain that offers the tantalizing prospect of "transformation." By presenting "Renaissance space turned inside out," the virtual mode abjures the familiar perspective of the vanishing point and other traditional forms of aesthetic and political organization, thereby offering the prospect of alternative ways of seeing.[60] In Pynchon's *Mason & Dixon*, to pursue that example, there is much emphasis on the science of astronomy, which might be described as a form of prototelesthesia, as the novel's eighteenth-century heroes train their telescopes on the stars to remap the contours of the Old World as well as the New. In this sense, *Mason & Dixon*, though set at the time of the American Revolution, offers a characteristically late twentieth-century view of intersections between national identity and technological development. Pynchon's novel is not just about the supersession of national identity as a principle—indeed, with its cameo portraits of the Founding Fathers, just the opposite—but it deals with the twists and turns of national identity, the ways British culture finds itself transformed by its American counterpart and vice versa.

To reconsider American literature and culture in a transnational context, then, is not to abandon the idea of nationalism, but to reimagine it as a virtual construction, a residual narrative rather than a unifying social power. In this aestheticized form, nationalism, like Christianity at the end of the nineteenth century, functions more as a signifier than as a signified, a discourse whose emotive valence retains a capacity to shape the direction of material objects and events even though its theoretical coherence has been emptied out. To talk of American studies in postnational terms may be premature, for the nation has not yet ceased to be meaningful as a category of affiliation and analysis; even Appadurai, though he describes the nation-state as being "on its last legs" and suggests that we "need to think ourselves beyond the nation" into a "postnational space," still acknowledges that the United States operates more like a "transnation," a "switching point" between different modes of affiliation and identification.[61] Other scholars have associated the *post* in "postnational" with the *post* in "postcolonial," suggesting that it signifies a process of transition through which one cultural formation is modulated into another, rather than indicating merely a supersession of the older national model.[62] All of these critical perspectives imply the paradoxical and often contradictory nature of the relationships between national and international domains, and the usefulness of a term like transnational, as opposed to postnational, is the way it acknowledges explicitly the necessity for Americanists to rearticulate their field dialogically and comparatively. To redraw the map of American literary history in this way is also, through an old postcolonial paradox, to rethink the contours of British cultural identity, to examine the various power plays that have traversed the liminal space of the transatlantic imaginary over the past 250 years. At the junction of two millennia, American and English studies, like those who engage in them, might be classed as virtual subjects, whose sense of identity emerges in various forms of paradoxical displacement and nostalgic misremembrance.

## 2

## Narrative Reversals and Power Exchanges: Frederick Douglass and British Culture

Over the last thirty years of the twentieth century, as issues of race and gender became more prominent in American culture, the first two autobiographies of Frederick Douglass—*Narrative of the Life of Frederick Douglass* (1845) and *My Bondage and My Freedom* (1855)—quickly became established as integral parts of the American literary canon. Although the genre of black autobiography has often been seen as, in William L. Andrews's phrase, "an act of self-liberation," a formal correlative to the quest for self-determination inscribed therein, one reason for the rapid institutionalization of Douglass's work was that his advocacy of "the cult of the self-made man" triumphing over adversity seemed to fit so comfortably with a much more traditional American ethic of individual virtue.[1] As Joseph Fichtelberg has observed, Douglass appears in many ways to present himself as a kind of black Benjamin Franklin, an exemplar of heroic self-reliance, striving "to embody the millennial ideals of an America foretold in the Declaration of Independence."[2] The purpose of this chapter is to problematize these critical homologies that yoke Douglass and an abstract idea of American nationalism by reconsidering his works in the light of their author's engagement with various aspects of British political culture. I argue that the melodramatic representations of violence in the 1845 *Narrative* are reformulated in *My Bondage and My Freedom* by a textual dynamic of self-contradiction, which works deliberately to disrupt indigenous perspectives of all kinds. This dynamic can be linked to the impact of Douglass's work of transnationalism, which he began to regard as a literary and discursive phenomenon as well as a social imperative. Nationalism for Douglass thus came to involve not so much a positive or universal ideal but, rather, a set of fluctuating contrary terms. I argue, accordingly, that there is a correlation between his aesthetic structures of ironic displacement and the epistemological paradoxes that frame his political career, such that his point of identification keeps shifting and power is represented as a material commodity to be recycled and exchanged.

In the early nineteenth century, Britain enjoyed a reputation among American abolitionists as the world's leading antislavery power. An alliance between British military forces and African Americans had formed during the Wars of Independence in the 1780s, when, out of its own strategic interest, Britain promised freedom to any rebellious slave who would rise up against the mutual enemy. Subsequently, leaders of the American reform movement came to venerate well-known British figures such as William Wilberforce and Thomas Clarkson, whose influence helped to bring about the abolition of slavery in the British West Indies on 1 August 1834.[3] That date is regularly commemorated in Douglass's speeches and writings; in 1861, for example, shortly after the outbreak of the American Civil War, Douglass looks back to what he calls this "sublime event . . . the one of all others most creditable to the age." He goes on to express the hope that the U.S. sectarian conflict will have the effect of "breaking the chains of every American slave, and placing America side by side with noble old England in the glorious career of Liberty and Civilization."[4]

It was in "noble old England," moreover, that much of the momentum behind William Lloyd Garrison's abolitionist movement was generated during the 1830s and 1840s. Garrison first visited England in 1833, when he struck up a firm friendship with George Thompson, president of the British Anti-Slavery League, who himself crossed the Atlantic in 1835 to campaign in Boston. Garrison subsequently attended the International Antislavery Convention held in London in 1840 and returned to the country for a lecture tour in 1846. Indeed, despite various differences of opinion—notably, over women antislavery delegates, to which the British were firmly opposed—Garrison at this time felt that his movement enjoyed more general support in Britain than back in the United States. "We owe Mr. Garrison our grateful homage," remarked Douglass in 1857, "in that he was among the first of his countrymen who zealously applied the British argument for abolition, against American slavery."[5]

As Douglass suggests, much of the impetus behind Garrison's early success in the United States came from his visible association with British emancipationists who had recently secured their famous victory in the Caribbean. Douglass's own hugely successful tour of Britain between 1845 and 1847 helped further disseminate antislavery principles among the British public—he and Garrison traveled together for several months in 1846—and when the *Narrative of the Life of Frederick Douglass* appeared in 1845 it quickly went through nine English editions.[6] Also influential in the cause of emancipation was the publication in 1842 of Charles Dickens's *American Notes*, with its Gothic view of the South as characterized by "brutal lust, cruelty, and the abuse of irresponsible power."[7] "I believe," said Douglass in a speech at Paisley, Scotland, in 1846, "that the notice of Dickens had more effect in calling attention to the subject, than all the books published in America for ten years." Douglass here flatters his audience, perhaps, by assuring them of the American "deference" toward British public opinion, as represented by "the writings of such men as Dickens, as well as by the public press."[8]

Douglass also benefited quite directly from his two years in Britain, because it was his English friends, led by Ellen and Anna Richardson of Newcastle, who raised the funds to purchase his freedom from Hugh Auld of Maryland in 1847. This transaction caused a certain amount of controversy among the American abolitionists, many of whom maintained that it constituted an implicit recognition of the "right to traffic in human beings" and was therefore, by definition, immoral.[9] For Douglass, however, this financial exchange was symptomatic of a more general shift in his political attitudes, which the time spent in Britain had helped to bring about: gradually, he came to think of the issues of slavery in pragmatic rather than apocalyptic terms. In London in 1846, he linked up with the Chartists William Lovett and Henry Vincent to launch publicly their new Anti-Slavery League, and the influence of Chartism can also be detected behind the direction of *North Star*, the newspaper Douglass began to publish from Rochester on his return to the United States in 1847. The paper's title echoes Feargus O'Connor's *Northern Star*, the leading Chartist publication of its time, and indeed, in his editorial columns Douglass specifically allies himself with the Chartists and calls enthusiastically for radical social reform.[10]

Douglass was indebted also to the assistance of Julia Griffiths, an Englishwoman he had met on his British tour, who moved to Rochester in 1849 to manage the accounts of the *North Star* and to provide assistance for his cause in various practical ways. Although Griffiths was an extremely capable businesswoman, who quickly reduced the paper's debt and doubled its subscription list, Garrison and his acolytes were as hostile to Douglass's association with her as to his link with the Chartists. In both cases, they saw a pernicious British influence deflecting his attention away from what they regarded as the spirit of moral perfectionism and Christian purity animating the abolitionist movement; Garrison, in fact, went so far as to call her a "double-and-twisted worker of iniquity."[11] In truth, Griffiths was very much a political pragmatist whose intellectual agenda was cast in a familiar mold of English empiricism and stout common sense. After her return to England in 1855, she contributed a regular column, "Letters from the Old World," to *Douglass' Monthly*, and here her themes revolved constantly around social activism and fundraising. "We are a practical people in dear, old England," she writes, "and judge a good deal of 'faith' by the works it brings forth."[12] Commenting in 1862 on the progress of the Civil War, Griffiths evokes even more clearly what she sees as the virtues of gradualism and compromise: "It is an old and trite saying 'that half a loaf is better than no bread.' President Lincoln and his party have done something to forward the onward march of freedom, although by no means as much as we could wish, and many who abuse his Government are ignorant of the fact, that he has abolished slavery in the District of Columbia."[13]

Although Griffiths's column appeared nearly a decade after their close collaboration in Rochester, it may not be too speculative to infer from its tone the marked influence that Griffiths exercised on Douglass in the early 1850s. His famous "change of opinion" on the U.S. Constitution, when he broke with the Garrison party by declaring that the Constitution "might be made consistent in its details with the noble purposes avowed in its preamble," was announced in May 1851; but when Douglass adds that this crucial shift in his political stance had "not been hastily arrived at," he is speaking the literal truth rather than just paying polite lip service to his former mentor.[14] Indeed, the first inklings of his new position appear in a *North Star* essay, "The Constitution and Slavery," published on 16 March 1849, where he avers that the U.S. Constitution, if construed only in the light of its letter and without reference to the opinions of those who framed it, should not necessarily be seen as a proslavery instrument.[15] Douglass's change of opinion, then, took place within two years of his return to the United States from Britain, and it occurred under the aegis of political influences about which Garrison and his friends were right to feel suspicious. Traditionally, Douglass's work is said to take a more nationalist turn in the 1850s, with the writer seeking to forge for himself, as Eric J. Sundquist puts it, a "more sophisticated 'American' identity."[16] In fact, though, we can perceive here a curious series of reversals, whereby Douglass's emerging patriotism is intellectually dependent on a reconceptualization of the slavery issue in transnational terms: it was the British political scene, rather than the spirit of American transcendentalism, that led him toward a reconciliation with the legal framework of the Constitution. It is true that abolition itself became more politicized in the United States during the 1850s, with Garrison's newspaper, *The Liberator*, coming to seem increasingly old-fashioned in a decade of critical legal and political debates about the status of slavery. But it is also true, as we can observe from Douglass's writing, that a sense of estrangement from American institutions impelled him intellectually and politically toward transnational perspectives in the middle part of his career. One might suggest, in fact, that Douglass began to deploy a transnational perspective in order to turn nationalism against itself, to demystify national identity as a reified idea so as to reconstitute it as a political symbol.

We can see this emerging process through a comparison of the first two autobiographies. The 1845 *Narrative* integrates its participant-observer within an Emersonian pattern of self-reliance, so that the African American search for an authenticating voice becomes incorporated in a New England tradition of the conversion narrative. This fits with the way Douglass's own voice is framed by the *Narrative*'s prefaces, written by Garrison and Wendell Phillips, which emphasize, in Garrison's words, qualities of "pathos and sublimity." By setting the "dark night of slavery" against a vision of sailing ships in Chesapeake Bay "robed in purest white," Douglass's text reinscribes a mode of transcendence that aligns it with the intellectual context of antebellum New England.[17] Russ Castronovo has argued that slave narratives in general tend to "ambiguate national narratives," creating a hybrid and radically unstable form that performatively foregrounds "the discursive configuration of American freedom"; but such "interruptions and gaps" are not so readily apparent in Douglass's 1845 *Narrative*, which fuses its African American and transcendentalist discourses to create a tautological structure where each side of the equation is valorized by reference to the other.[18] Douglass's recollections are legitimated by Garrison's preface, just as Garrison's preface is substantiated by Douglass's experiences, and this circular structure is replicated in the *Narrative* itself, where the text implicitly reproduces religious metaphors even as it seeks thematically to critique them. The voice of Douglass describes his own emancipation, for example, as "a glorious resurrection, from the tomb of slavery, to the heaven of freedom" (*N*, 65), but, as Gregory Jay has written, the recirculation of this Christian rhetoric ironically "works to preclude a wider study of slavery's historical dimensions."[19]

The point here is not, of course, to deny what Robert Stepto has called the "sheer poetry" of Douglass's *Narrative* but to suggest that the book's effort to embody a poetics of subjectivity renders its relationship with the object of analysis inherently ambivalent.[20] Douglass's work of the 1840s involves a conception of public performance that underlines its links with the popular genres of oratory and melodrama, where again the emphasis is on embodying pathos rather than alienating it discursively into narrative form. This, of course, served the political ends shared by Garrison and Douglass at the time; on his tour of Britain in the 1840s, Douglass frequently employed his cousin Henny to act out the role of female victim as an ancillary to his antislavery speeches, while also displaying ostentatiously a variety of whips, chains, and other tools of slavery to make manifest the violence of a system that often was described elsewhere in more euphemistic terms.[21] In these British lectures, Douglass drew heavily on Theodore Weld's *American Slavery As It Is Now* (1839), which features a scabrous account of life on the plantations; like Weld, Douglass wanted to disturb and provoke his audience, to make them understand how the "intemperance" of slaveholders, as Weld put it, tended to feed on the intoxicating nature of "arbitrary power," which "is to the mind what alcohol is to the body."[22] Dickens, in his chapter on slavery in *American Notes*, paints a similarly explicit scene of sexualized violence as he describes how he saw women "indecently compelled to hold up their own garments that men might lay the heavier stripes upon their legs."[23]

Yet, while the tone of Dickens's work revolves around disenchantment—the demystification of hypocritical American aspirations toward liberty—the peculiar strength of Douglass's *Narrative* lies in its delineation of a state in which power and obscenity become interwoven with each other and, consequently, mutually reinforcing. Whereas Dickens disavows obscenity, Douglass theatricalizes it, turning it into a form of lurid melodrama that oddly heightens its political effect. One of the most famous scenes in the *Narrative* is when Douglass represents himself as a child witnessing Captain Anthony stripping and whipping his Aunt Hester. He recalls being "terrified and horror-stricken at the sight," which he would never "forget . . . whilst I remember any thing" (*N*, 19, 18). As many critics have observed, Douglass's text appears to participate voyeuristically in what it calls this "bloody transaction," positioning the reader, like the child who hides in the closet, as an unseen witness to this abject event (*N*, 19). David Van Leer has written of how this seems to turn parts of Douglass's work into "a subtle form of pornography," and Deborah McDowell finds his accounts of slave life to be disturbingly complicit with the "record of black women's abuse" that they describe.[24] What I suggest, though, is that this episode, set in the very first chapter of the *Narrative*, establishes an image of power as the central criterion and reference point in Douglass's world. Power becomes the one thing he can never forget, the commodity that will be negotiated, recirculated, and exchanged in all of his later works.

The 1845 *Narrative*, then, wavers in tone between the illusions of transparency and sincerity, on which so much of the nineteenth-century sentimental tradition depended, and a much more melodramatic subtext.[25] This divided tone is commensurate with the way the text balances highbrow abolitionist sentiment against the kinds of salacious scenarios more typical of Victorian popular culture. Analyzing the reception of American antislavery orators in mid-nineteenth-century Britain, Audrey Fisch concludes that the "titillation" experienced by the audiences as they listened to accounts of "taboo subjects such as sexual abuse" would have been safely circumscribed by assumptions of English national and moral superiority, against which American society appeared as "an exotic and degraded Other."[26] In a classic double bind, therefore, the idiosyncratic force of Douglass's performance derived from the way his political agenda was interwoven with the compulsive nature of his story. Sensationalism and didacticism were, for Douglass, mutually reinforcing, not mutually exclusive. In *The Plague of Fantasies*, an exploration of the liminal relationships between fantasy and politics, Slavoj Žižek analyzes how ideologies contain contradictions they cannot afford overtly to acknowledge: "Ideology," he writes, "is the 'self-evident' surface structure whose function is to conceal the underlying 'unbalanced,' 'uncanny' structure." For Žižek, therefore, ideology comprises not a "harmonious" sum of constituent parts but a more heterogeneous compound of "partial elements": "Power thus relies on an obscene supplement. . . . As for the status of this obscene supplement, one should avoid both traps and neither glorify it as subversive nor dismiss it as a false transgression which stabilizes the power edifice (like the ritualized carnivals which temporarily suspend power relations), but insist on its *undecideable* character. Obscene unwritten rules sustain Power as long as they remain in the shadows; the moment they are publicly recognized, the edifice of Power is thrown into disarray."[27] In an ingenious reversal of dialectical logic, Žižek displaces ideological consistency into a cathexis of fetishism, where the part exceeds, and provides access to, the wider circumference of the whole.

The significance of Žižek's theory for a reading of Douglass's *Narrative* lies in how it enables us to understand the cumulative ideological effects of the text's radical inconsistency of tone and its continual shifts in position and perspective. Rather than approaching any sense of aesthetic equilibrium or philosophical resolution, the *Narrative* draws its resonance from a mix of multifarious elements chronicling the erratic nature of power struggles in society. The ideological force of Douglass's first autobiography, in other words, derives from the way it brilliantly brings together different conceptual categories—transcendentalism and African American politics, sensationalism and didacticism, power and obscenity—and binds them tautologically into its performative circuit.

In the 1855 autobiography, *My Bondage and My Freedom*, Douglass retrospectively discusses his alliance with Garrison's party during the 1840s and talks of his eventual resentment at being treated by them as a *"thing,"* a "piece of Southern *'property,'*" whose proper role was to retell the "facts" about plantation life while leaving the "philosophy" of abolition to others.[28] This 1855 work is distinguished from its predecessor by a more reflective style that balances representations of power with greater consideration of where that power comes from and whom it serves. Symptomatic of this difference is the author's representations of his birth: whereas the 1845 *Narrative* begins by stating baldly, "I was born in Tuckahoe" (*N*, 15), the 1855 text spends four paragraphs describing the "dull, flat, and unthrifty" characteristics of Talbot County before inserting its protagonist into the scene (*BF*, 140). The active voice more prevalent in the earlier text has been partially displaced into a world where the subject finds himself shaped by external circumstances.

*My Bondage and My Freedom* is introduced by James M'Cune Smith, a black medical practitioner from New York educated in Scotland at the University of Glasgow, whose opening essay bears the same relation to this second autobiography as do the prefatory pieces to the 1845 *Narrative* by Garrison and Phillips. Smith hails *My Bondage* as "an American book, for Americans, in the fullest sense of the idea," and he describes Douglass himself as "a Representative American Man—a type of his countrymen" (*BF*, 137, 132). Yet Smith also mentions how it was Douglass's "sojourn in England" between 1845 and 1847 that "awakened him to the consciousness of new powers that lay in him," and he emphasizes how the particular characteristic of this new work is its skill in "observing, comparing, and careful classifying" (*BF*, 130, 134). Comparison, indeed, is one of Smith's central concerns: he describes Douglass as moving from a "knowledge of the world . . . bounded by the visible horizon on Col. Lloyd's plantation" to a faculty that "enabled him to see, and weigh, and compare whatever passed before him"; Smith himself plays on this theme by comparing the oratorical powers of Douglass to those of "the younger Pitt" when he entered the British House of Commons (*BF*, 126, 128). In a footnote to his introduction, Smith also acknowledges the general contribution to Douglass's work of Julia Griffiths, who probably helped with the editing of this text and who might well have been instrumental in steering the author toward a style of popular nationalism suitable for the literary marketplace of the 1850s.[29]

The point to be emphasized, though, is that this style of popular nationalism, as it emerges in *My Bondage and My Freedom*, is dependent on a transnational, comparative consciousness. Sundquist has remarked on how the terms *bondage* and *freedom* relate paradoxically rather than dialectically to each other in this work, and the same is true of *nationalism* and *transnationalism*: only by moving outside the charmed circle of the nation can Douglass put himself in a position to redescribe its circumference.[30] Consequently, the rhetorical structure of *My Bondage* differs markedly from Douglass's earlier autobiography in its heightened self-consciousness about how its formulations are contingent on a particular angle of vision. Early in the narrative, for example, Douglass deliberately foregrounds the process of authorial interpretation by relating how "Several old logs and stumps imposed upon me, and got themselves taken for wild beasts." Extending this childhood personification into a lesson about allegory, he concludes: "Thus early I learned that the point of view from which a thing is viewed is of some importance" (*BF*, 148). Such a focus on the point of view runs throughout the text, with the narrator taking pleasure in disturbing preconceptions about what *bondage* and *freedom* might signify. Colonel Lloyd's plantation, for instance, is said to be endowed with an "almost Eden-like beauty," and Douglass writes of how he used to enjoy its picturesque scenery without being aware of its more sinister implications (*BF*, 162). Thus the illusion that holds these networks of slavery in place, as Douglass describes it, is a fiction of absolutism that would translate history into myth and suppress any sense of geographical relativism: "Every slaveholder," he says, "seeks to impress his slave with a belief in the boundlessness of slave territory, and of his own almost illimitable power" (*BF*, 310). John Carlos Rowe has written of how Douglass's narratives show the system of slavery in general trying to repress the arbitrary nature of its construction in an attempt to naturalize the status of its own authority, and, through this pattern of perspectival reversal, Douglass illuminates ways in which the domain of freedom expands and contracts according to the consciousness of the observer.[31] Hence the Lloyd plantation, "a little nation of its own," was "just a place to my boyish taste" (*BF*, 160, 166): being unaware of anything different, the youthful Douglass acquiesces in the slaveholder's fantasy of omnipotence. In *The Black Atlantic*, Paul Gilroy points to this "little nation" metaphor as an indication of how the slave plantation was no less an "archaic institution" than the modern state, but the more subtle suggestion put forward by Douglass is that nationalism, like freedom, remains a relative construction defined through a series of conjunctions and disjunctions in the mind of the observer.[32]

Hence Douglass does not simply represent his childish self as misconstruing the nature of freedom; he also, more radically, manipulates this persona to interrogate the nature of freedom and its inherent contradictions. *My Bondage and My Freedom* consequently adumbrates a peculiarly mixed-up world, where the two central terms become mutually constitutive. While the author talks of how the "order of civilization is reversed" on the plantation (*BF*, 151), he also registers this confusion of categories extending to other aspects of society. If the 1845 *Narrative* defines its world in terms of Manichaean polarities of light and darkness, the 1855 autobiography redescribes it through a paradoxical play of contraries, where one category slides discomfitingly into its antinomy:

"There is," he says typically, "a healing in the angel wing of sleep, even for the slave-boy" (*BF*, 150). Conceptually, this makes *My Bondage* more abstract and impersonal than the earlier work: by emphasizing that "Everybody, in the south, wants the privilege of whipping somebody else," Douglass shifts the focus of his invective away from particular slaveholders toward the plantation system itself (*BF*, 165). The more melodramatic violence of the earlier *Narrative* is also tempered in this 1855 work by an acknowledgment that African Americans, too, are not averse to wielding the whip: Uncle Isaac Cooper, who teaches the young Douglass the Lord's Prayer, "shared the common passion of his country, and, therefore, seldom found any means of keeping his disciples in order short of flogging" (*BF*, 165). By a similar kind of reversal, Douglass's "old master," Captain Anthony, is described as "not by nature worse than other men" but as someone who, like his chattel, "is the victim of the slave system" (*BF*, 171). Later the narrator plays verbally on the idea of subject, suggesting that the active subject also finds himself subjected unknowingly to external forces: "The slave is a subject, subjected by others; the slaveholder is a subject, but he is the author of his own subjection" (*BF*, 189). The elaborate pun here is reminiscent of other literary texts of the 1850s that deploy wordplay to illuminate the complex intersections of bondage and freedom. Ishmael's complaint in *Moby-Dick* (1851)—"Who aint a slave? Tell me that"—is reflected in Douglass's prognosis of slavery as a chain reaction, wherein he finds himself relating to the oxen as Covey, the overseer, relates to him: "Covey was to break me, I was to break them; break and be broken—such is life" (*BF*, 263).[33]

This is not, of course, to imply that *My Bondage and My Freedom* equates oxen and black workers, or that it relapses into the fatalism of Melville's more somber work. It is, though, to suggest that Douglass's text complicates its progressivist agenda by chronicling a world organized around an ideology of exchange. This places *My Bondage* in an oblique relation to other African American narratives written during this decade. Carla Peterson has discussed "African-American writers' gradual shift from slave autobiography to novel" during the 1850s and has noted how writers such as William Wells Brown switched from the mode of first-person to third-person narration to problematize "essentialized notions of black selfhood."[34] What is not so clear, though, is how such fictional refractions of the black self effectively impinge on the nature of the racial dialectic itself: in *Clotel* (1853), for instance, Brown's narrator envisions freedom and slavery as forms of "good" and "evil," "parallel lines" that seemingly will never "come to an end."[35] For Brown, freedom and slavery remain mutually exclusive categories that define each other through their perpetual opposition. For Douglass, however, these oppositions threaten to turn into paradoxical equivalences, because nothing appears to make sense except in terms of its contrary: it is, he points out, the very idea of "Liberty" that came to "torment" him with a sense of his "wretched condition" (*BF*, 227). The dilemma of *My Bondage and My Freedom* is that no category is allowed to remain syntactically unqualified: Douglass talks of ascending, not to the "heaven of freedom," as in his earlier *Narrative*, but "to the heaven of comparative freedom" (*BF*, 286). Indeed, there seems to be a conscious intertexual relation here with the first autobiography, as though Douglass in 1855 were seeking deliberately to qualify, if not altogether demystify, the celebrated legend of heroic self-emancipation that had become associated with that earlier representation of his life story, a story that had of course served as a model for much African American writing in the 1840s and 1850s. Typical in *My Bondage* is Douglass's use of the cagey parenthesis, as when he observes: "We were plotting against our (so called) lawful rulers" (*BF*, 309). Everything here is presented as provisional, as susceptible to reversal, and he records with a certain sardonic humor how his mistress, Mrs. Auld, would have acted just like him "in a reverse of circumstances" (*BF*, 228). In the same vein, he takes a grim pleasure in showing how things can work out contrariwise: he tells of how, after his work in the Baltimore shipyards, Master Hugh would "dole out to me a sixpence or a shilling, with a view, perhaps, of kindling up my gratitude"; but then he goes on to note that "this practice had the opposite effect," as "it was an admission of *my right to the whole sum*" (*BF*, 341).

The darkly comic undercurrent that runs through *My Bondage and My Freedom*, then, emerges from intellectual quarrels with a utopian-dystopian topos common to New England abolitionism and various forms of African American narrative. In the last chapter, Douglass dispatches his former abolitionist colleagues with a paradoxical flourish, as he declares axiomatically that "a man may 'stand up so straight as to lean backward' " (*BF*, 393). Similarly, he distances himself from the emphasis on racial purity that inspired the emigrationist attitudes of his political rival, Martin Delany; indeed, as Robert Levine has noted, Douglass remains remarkably quiet in his autobiographical narratives about interactions with his black contemporaries.[36] It is an illuminating silence, though, indicative of markedly divergent points of view. Rather than

Delany's vision of alternative worlds, the entire structure of Douglass's second autobiography is predicated on a kind of paradoxical loop, where the narrator moves through successive situations—Colonel Lloyd's plantation, the Auld household in Maryland, the association with Garrison—not to leave them behind but to acquire a better perspective on them. Douglass's narrative, in other words, moves forward only for the purpose of looking back. This movement leads to an ironic symbiosis between his conditions of bondage and freedom, an irony he himself points out toward the end of this book when he remarks: "There is nothing very striking or peculiar about my career as a freeman, when viewed apart from my life as a slave" (*BF*, 349). In this way, we are led to see the peculiar interest of *My Bondage and My Freedom* arising not from any simple rhetoric of emancipation but from its account of interactions and exchanges between very different kinds of society. The text positions itself on a dividing line between North and South, present and past, black and white, and it achieves its style of unexpected congruence and comparison from a capacity to look both ways.

For Douglass, then, the politics of abolition in the 1850s involved gaining both literal and metaphorical distance on scenarios of slavery so that he could refocus them in a different kind of light. Slavery, in his eyes, became associated with isolation and parochialism, with the perspective of the slaveholder who misrepresented his fiefdom as the world. If the plantation presented itself as "a little nation of its own," emancipation would necessarily involve a process of metaphorical transnationalism, or "exposure" as Douglass puts it in 1853, whereby the atavism of slave conditions would be shown up by their being placed in juxtaposition to other territories and different customs.[37] This is one of the reasons Douglass was particularly keen on a transatlantic imaginary. Throughout the 1850s, he frequently remarks on the "rapidity, safety and certainty" of the Atlantic passage, going so far in 1859 as to suggest that the improved transport system was "almost converting the two continents into one."[38] For Douglass, this advanced capability for travel crucially betokens a psychological and political mobility, through which existing practices might be placed in parallel with those of other cultures. The clearest exposition of this philosophy comes in his famous speech in Rochester in 1852, "The Meaning of July Fourth for the Negro":

> No nation can now shut itself up from the surrounding world and trot round in the same old path of its fathers without interference.

The time was when such could be done. Long established customs of hurtful character could formerly fence themselves in, and do their evil work with social impunity. Knowledge was then confined and enjoyed by the privileged few, and the multitude walked on in mental darkness. But a change has now come over the affairs of mankind. Walled cities and empires have become unfashionable. The arm of commerce has borne away the gates of the strong city. Intelligence is penetrating the darkest corners of the globe. It makes its pathway over and under the sea, as well as on the earth. Oceans no longer divide, but link nations together. From Boston to London is now a holiday excursion. Space is comparatively annihilated.— Thoughts expressed on one side of the Atlantic are distinctly heard on the other.[39]

From this point of view, cosmopolitan consciousness becomes in itself a political necessity. Douglass is not interested only in establishing links with like-minded people on the other side of the Atlantic; he is also concerned with how the very form of this transatlantic communication serves to ironize and displace indigenous assumptions. The prophetic, slightly breathless tone here might seem almost McLuhanite in its anticipation of a global village binding together both sides of the Atlantic. But in fact, *My Bondage and My Freedom* is not so much concerned with the annihilation of space as with its traversal, and so it is appropriate that toward the end of the narrative his trajectory leads him to discuss his "two years of semi-exile in Great Britain and Ireland" (*BF*, 389). Indeed, the whole of this narrative is, in some sense, about exile: from the "Eden-like beauty" of Colonel Lloyd's plantation (*BF*, 162), from a world of innocence into the harsh experience of slavery, from the South to the North. If Douglass's first autobiography turns on a quest for self-realization, his second represents alienation as the condition of all knowledge. *My Bondage and My Freedom* clearly presents Douglass as an American patriot but, equally significantly, as one of those "cosmopolitan patriots," in Kwame Anthony Appiah's phrase, whose understanding of national fictions involves a recognition of contingency and of the need to negotiate rather than obliterate material difference.[40]

These strategies of reversal were not, however, confined exclusively to textual practices. In fact, it was Douglass's uncanny ability to manipulate perspectives to demystify power relations that makes his work particularly interesting to consider in a transnational context. Ireland was the first country of the British Isles that Douglass visited, from September 1845 through January 1846, and his observations here not only provide insights into the relationship between Ireland and England but also, by extension, suggest how American racial struggle came to appear a dark reflection of other ethnic conflicts at this time. In terms of a transatlantic imaginary, the buildup to the American Civil War carries reverberations heard in British literature and culture during the 1840s and 1850s.

In his 1845 *Narrative*, Douglass mentions "Sheridan's mighty speeches on and in behalf of Catholic emancipation" (*N*, 42), thus implicitly linking the circumstances of Irish Catholics under British rule with the plight of slaves in the American South. This is a parallel reinforced by Garrison's preface, which sings the praises of Daniel O'Connell, "distinguished advocate of universal emancipation, and the mightiest champion of prostrate but not conquered Ireland" (*N*, 6). Douglass himself heard O'Connell speak in Dublin on 29 September 1845, and he subsequently wrote to Garrison that of all the speakers he had heard over the previous four years, "I have never heard one, by whom I was more completely captivated than by Mr. O'Connell."[41] A few months later, commenting on the miserable social conditions in Ireland, Douglass remarked that the poor Irish lived "in much the same degradation as the American slaves," adding, "I see much here to remind me of my former condition."[42] In his farewell speech to the British people, delivered in London on 30 March 1847, Douglass reinforced this parallel between the Irish and African Americans by citing O'Connell directly: "O'Connell once said, speaking of Ireland—no matter for my illustration, how truly or falsely—that 'her history may be traced, like the track of a wounded man through a crowd.' If this description can be given of Ireland, how much more true is it when applied to the sons and daughters of Africa, in the United States?"[43]

Douglass was by no means the only commentator of this time to draw an analogy between slavery, which was dividing the United States, and the Irish question, which was causing political strife in Britain. Dickens, in *American Notes*, remarks that Southern slave culture reminds him of the "ignorant peasantry of Ireland," and Thomas Carlyle, in a series of essays over many years, consistently equates the "degraded" Irish with that "sooty African" element that he saw as a threat to what he called "the Transatlantic Saxon Nation."[44] Much of Carlyle's vitriol stemmed from his antipathy toward the emancipation of slaves in the Caribbean. In

"Occasional Discourse on the Nigger Question" (1849), he compared the West Indies to "a Black Ireland," prophesying that economic poverty and a psychology of "servitude" would not be abolished so easily as its legal equivalent.[45] In "Shooting Niagara: And After?" (1867), he develops his ontology of "servantship and mastership" still further, describing "Swarmery" as a regrettable outcome of the American Civil War, where principles of order and authority had fallen by the wayside so that "three million absurd Blacks, men and brothers (of a sort) are completely 'emancipated.' "[46]

One of the things that most concerns Carlyle here is the indirect effect of the American Civil War on English society. In particular, he fears that the triumph of liberalism in the United States will help promote the cause of electoral reform in Britain, thus dealing another blow to the "Aristocracy," whom he sees as the country's natural governors.[47] In this sense, many of the divisions within British society—between England and Ireland, conservatism and reform, the North and the South—are mirrored in the literal outbreak of violence across the Atlantic in 1861. The American Civil War, in other words, can be seen as a virtual reflection of those implicit tensions and half-suppressed conflicts that had been accumulating in British culture throughout the middle part of the nineteenth century. Carlyle's own "Signs of the Times" (1829), with its disdain for industrialization and its nostalgia for a unity "in the whole fabric of society," was one expression of the kind of organic idiom that sought to repress divisions in the name of national identity.[48] Benjamin Disraeli's *Sybil; or, The Two Nations* (1845) similarly frets about "the condition of the main body" of the state and harks back to a monarchical medievalism in its efforts to overcome contemporary conflicts. (Divisive abolitionists who address antislavery meetings at Exeter Hall in London are specifically satirized in Disraeli's novel.)[49] Even more illuminating in this regard is Elizabeth Gaskell's *North and South* (1855), which again contemplates the "condition of England" through its cultural clash between the southern landscape of Helstone, "like a village . . . in one of Tennyson's poems," and the harsher values of Milton, in the northern county of Darkshire. Here the captain of industry, John Thornton, finds his business threatened by the development of international trade markets: "The Americans," he complains, "are getting their yarns so into the general market, that our only chance is producing them at a lower rate." Accordingly, he brings in "hands" from Ireland in an effort to keep wages low, thus provoking contempt for "them Irishers" from the Milton workers; but this move turns out ultimately to be counterproductive, as the "utter want of skill on the part of the Irish hands whom he had imported" becomes a "daily annoyance" to Thornton himself.[50]

One of the points to emphasize here is that around the middle of the century this "condition of England" question that so much troubled Victorian Britain came to be reconceived in transnational terms.[51] In *North and South*, Gaskell's vision of English unity, the annealing of conflict between northern and southern regions, involves suppressing the move by Irish laborers to deny English workers their fair wages, as well as suppressing the tendency of U.S. markets to undermine English industrial communities. John Thornton is represented as getting his comeuppance in this regard, as he is eventually ruined by his agent's placing trust in an American company "which went down, along with several others, just at this time, like a pack of cards."[52] In this new world of transnational communication, capital, like labor, has become subject to the fluctuations of international markets, but Gaskell, prizing a more traditional social stability and cohesion, extrapolates her organic version of England from the (partial) repression of transatlantic turbulence, thus exemplifying how the attempt to demarcate British culture at this time was uncomfortably shadowed and threatened by the specter of the United States. Indeed, divisions between the North and South of England, as represented in Gaskell's novel, disconcertingly mirrored those between the northern and southern parts of the United States: on both sides of the Atlantic, the industrial North found itself pitted against the more traditional South. If the clashes in Britain were less overt and violent, they nevertheless formed parallels that sometimes became inescapable. Gaskell, a friend of Charles Eliot Norton and a staunch supporter of the North during the American Civil War, saw clearly how the cotton famine in Manchester during the early 1860s was tied inextricably to events in the United States, and the many large meetings held in Manchester and Liverpool to discuss the American conflict would have served not only to engage British workers with the progress of the Civil War but also to remind them of their own long-standing quarrels with English conservatism. These were parallels that liberal members of Parliament such as Richard Cobden and John Bright were keen to reinforce, as they linked support for the northern states with pressure for further electoral reform in Britain.[53] Conversely, of course, conservative organs such as the London *Times* disparaged these reform movements on both sides of the Atlantic equally.

Questions of U.S. slavery sometimes evoke the shades of national exceptionalism, on the grounds that the condition of southern slaves is not a topic susceptible to consideration in analogous or parallel terms. Recounting her visit to England in *Incidents in the Life of a Slave Girl*, for example, Harriet Jacobs insists on sharply differentiating class oppression in Europe from racial oppression in the United States: "The most ignorant and the most destitute of these peasants," she argues, "was a thousand fold better off than the most pampered American slave."[54] On his own tour of Britain in the 1840s, as we have seen, Douglass deliberately employed various shock tactics in an attempt to break through what he perceived as a common tendency toward the genteel trivialization of slave culture, and throughout his career he always disliked rhetorical obfuscations of slavery—in such figures as "wage slavery"—claiming that such circumlocutions tended to debase the uniquely horrifying nature of the actual plantation experience. Conversely, as Catherine Gallagher has observed, nineteenth-century British writers such as William Cobbett often used phrases like "the white slave" metaphorically, to imply a larger sense of disenfranchisement or powerlessness. As a critic of industrial society, Cobbett's hostility to what he saw as the hypocrisy of abolitionists derived in part from what he considered to be their unformulated, inchoate conception of "freedom" as a theoretical idea.[55]

For Douglass, however, slavery always connoted the bitter struggle for mastery. He was concerned not with the metaphorical attenuation of slavery nor with its epistemological conflation with an abstract form of determinism, but rather with its material situation on a transnational continuum where the power dynamics underpinning the U.S. situation could be seen to manifest themselves in equivalent antagonisms elsewhere. Just as English writers like Disraeli and Gaskell refracted American conflicts in their work, so from Douglass's point of view the mutual hostility between the English and the Irish was a political mirror of internal racial conflicts in the United States. This is why he identifies with the Irish when he is in Britain: from this perspective, they appear as honorary blacks, engaged in a power struggle with the white oppressor. At a meeting in Dublin in 1845 to campaign for the repeal of the Corn Laws, Douglass is introduced by Daniel O'Connell as "the black O'Connell of the United States."[56] In London a year later, Douglass reaffirms his support for the Anti–Corn Law movement and declares that after its "complete triumph . . . the next great reform will be that of complete suffrage."[57] Nearly thirty years later, in 1872, he is still describing himself as "something of an Irishman as well as a negro," thereby implicitly aligning himself with George Odger, secretary of the London Trades Council, who a few years earlier had specifically compared discrimination against African Americans in the United States with discrimination against the Irish in England.[58] Racial stereotyping was quite common on both sides of the Atlantic at this time and, as if to emphasize Odger's point, an 1862 article in the supposedly humorous London magazine *Punch* suggests that "the Irish Yahoo" might be "the missing link . . . between the Gorilla and the Negro."[59]

Thus, we can see how Douglass's conception of freedom interacting symbiotically with a form of bondage, as outlined in his 1855 autobiography, is reproduced in his analysis of the various power exchanges in mid-nineteenth-century Britain and the United States. For Douglass, freedom remained a category that could be explicated only in comparative terms: liberty for one party tended to mean less liberty for another. This is one of the reasons his view of emancipation is always tinged with pessimism. Unlike Whitman, say, who welcomes the idea of freedom with an exuberant largesse, freedom for Douglass is much more a competitive phenomenon, involving a grim fight for survival. In fact, it would be truer to say that power, rather than freedom, is Douglass's main theme, because his work is at its most effective when determining how this power nexus works its way through society. What Douglass perceives from his immediate political encounters, contemporary historians such as Theodore Allen have considered more analytically, for Allen describes racial slavery in the nineteenth-century United States as "a system of social control" dominated and maintained by class interests, a matrix forming a "mirror" of the hegemony exercised by the British ruling class of this time over Ireland.[60] In a speech in Baltimore in 1865, Douglass himself sardonically compared the power relations between the English and the Irish in Britain to those between white and black Americans in the United States: "Wealth, learning and ability made an Irishman an Englishman. The same metamorphosing power converts a Negro into a white man in this country. When prejudice cannot deny the black man's ability, it denies his race, and claims him as a white man. It affirms that if he is not exactly white, he ought to be."[61] Six years later, in 1871, Douglass similarly noted with approval that various members of the "English royal family" were roundly hissed on a visit to Ireland. He called the incident "a very natural and genuine exhibition of the feelings of the Irish people," bearing in mind the "tyrannical and oppressive" nature of their governance.[62]

More or less concurrently, however, Douglass also sought to marginalize the Irish in the United States itself as "foreigners" whose values remained antipathetic to those of American democracy.[63] To some extent, this hostility emerged from what the African American community in general took to be the reactionary, proslavery tendencies of Irish American culture. Speaking in New York City in 1853, Douglass epitomized the tensions that existed between these two ethnic groups: "The Irish people," he observed, "warm-hearted, generous, and sympathizing with the oppressed everywhere when they stand on their own green island, are instantly taught on arriving in this Christian country to hate and despise the colored people. They are taught to believe that we eat the bread which of right belongs to them. The cruel lie is told the Irish that our adversity is essential to their prosperity."[64] However, it was not just the Irish who saw things differently when they reached the United States but also Douglass himself. Time and again, we see the angle of incidence and reflection in his work varying according to the particular position in which he finds himself in a competitive interethnic situation. Notwithstanding his sympathy for the downtrodden Irish in Great Britain, he complains bitterly in 1855 when Thomas F. Meagher, an Irish immigrant, is admitted to practice as an attorney in New York when African Americans are still denied access to the legal profession. Douglass's invective against the Irish here reaches vituperative proportions. Addressing white America, he complains of how "native born colored Americans" are treated worse in their homeland than Irish "aliens . . . the foreigners swarming in your midst, those who *fill* your jails, and alm-houses *as well as build them*."[65] Douglass's description of "swarming" foreigners is a curious anticipation of Carlyle's complaint a few years later about the "Swarmery" brought about by emancipated American slaves, and it suggests the ways that, not unlike Carlyle, Douglass remained philosophically skeptical about the ontology of freedom and about ways the virtues of self-reliance could ever be dissociated from a larger confluence of power relations. Among the Victorians, argues Stefan Collini, it was "Carlyle above all who put into circulation a particular conception of manliness as part of a larger vision of the place of bracing conflict and stoically borne suffering in a power-governed universe."[66] Despite the manifold differences in their political perspectives, it seems likely that Douglass, who prided himself on being "a man among men," looked at the world in a similar way.[67]

As Richard Hardack has argued, there are various reasons why Douglass's attitude toward the Irish American community remained antagonistic. The economic rivalry between two disadvantaged groups is one obvious explanation; Douglass's tendency to demonize the Catholic Church "as a force of evil" is another.[68] Coming from a Methodist background, Douglass shared many of the traditional nineteenth-century American prejudices about Irish intemperance and squalor; during his trip to Europe in 1887 he manifested equally conventional reactions against what he calls "the hollowness of the vast structure of the Romish church."[69] In this sense, Hardack is right to say that when Douglass warns against the establishment of a "black Ireland in America," made up of an "aggrieved class," he is betraying a covertly "nativist" streak, because the idea of Irish poverty appears in his eyes as a potential threat to that patriotic ideal in which he wants African Americans to participate fully.[70] One particular aspect of the Douglass persona brought to light by this nationalist agenda is his political support for the Republican Party, with which he affiliated himself in 1856. Priscilla Wald has remarked on the parallels between Douglass and Abraham Lincoln, who both recognized and effectively manipulated the U.S. Constitution as a political symbol during the 1850s, but it is important also to recognize that Douglass's sympathy for Republican values carried on long after Lincoln's death.[71] It was, for instance, quite in keeping with this Republican inclination that Douglass's most popular lecture during the Reconstruction era was a paean to rugged individualism, "Self-Made Men."[72] Indeed, one reason his third autobiography, Life and Times (1882, revised 1893), has not received so much attention from critics is that its homage to a cult of success and its clear dissociation of civil equality from social equality do not sit comfortably with the more popular image of Douglass as a champion of liberal reform.

The revised Life and Times in fact reprints part of this 1883 speech by Douglass on the "black Ireland" threat. Taken in this context, it is easier to understand the continuities between his paradoxical representation of emancipation in My Bondage and My Freedom and his view in the later work of how racial prejudice and oppression work like chain reactions. It is, therefore, possible retrospectively to reread his second autobiography in the light of his third, and so to see how the pessimism explicit by 1893 is already implicit in the paradoxical equations of 1855:

> Perhaps no class of our fellow-citizens has carried this prejudice against color to a point more extreme and dangerous than have our Catholic Irish fellow-citizens, and yet no people on the face of the earth have been more relentlessly persecuted and oppressed on account of race and religion than have this same Irish people.
>
> But in Ireland persecution has at last reached a point where it reacts terribly upon her persecutors. England is to-day reaping the bitter consequences of her injustice and oppression. (*LT*, 973)

This perception of how a social dynamic "reacts terribly" suggests a double-edged quality that goes against Hardack's more straightforward proposition of an unequivocal "anti-Catholic, anti-Irish American discourse" in Douglass's work.[73] Although Douglass to some extent shared a common African American antipathy toward the Irish, he also acknowledged that they too had been caught up in the chain of oppression and reaction. The tone here is fatalistic as much as aggrieved. Charles Darwin is mentioned briefly in *Life and Times* (939), and what we find in Douglass's later work is a more typically naturalist conception of force, rather than morality, as the ultimate arbiter of social ends. Recording his impressions of Europe on the 1887 visit, he talks of an "irrepressible conflict between European civilization and barbarism," and it is such a recognition of primordial struggle, epitomized by scenes of "heroic endeavor" and "desperate courage," that inflects all of his later writings (*LT*, 989).

This drift toward a naturalist framework is another reason for the relative unpopularity of *Life and Times* as an example of African American literature. Whereas Douglass's first autobiography, in particular, projects the natural world as an extension of the narrator's mind, a territory heroically to be conquered, his third autobiography moves sharply away from such anthropocentric conceptualizations of the environment. Gillian Beer has written of how "Darwin found the constant placing of man at the centre of explanation probably the most exasperating characteristic of providential and natural theological writing"; but Douglass's autobiographies shift intellectually from one mode to the other, for if the 1845 *Narrative* is set ultimately in a providential light, casting Douglass himself as a heroic representative man, the 1893 *Life and Times* is shadowed by a more discomfiting sense of alienation.[74] As Sundquist observed, writers of the 1890s tend to refract "the pervasive influence of social Darwinism on the structure and values of the American community" during this era, and Douglass's last book also carries this burden.[75] We see these pressures at work in Chapter 16 of *Life and Times*, when Douglass recalls a visit he paid to his former master, Thomas Auld, a few years earlier: "Our courses had been determined for us, not by us," he writes. "We had both been flung, by powers that did not ask our consent, upon a mighty current of life, which we could neither resist nor control. By this current he was a master, and I a slave" (*LT*, 876). In line with his familiar narrative strategy of refiguring and recontextualizing the past, Douglass sets Auld's situation in another perspective as he notes that their lives were now "verging towards a point where differences disappear" (*LT*, 876). The emphasis here on determinism and on life's "mighty current" would seem to betoken an impersonality markedly at odds with his earlier narrative performances, which were directed more toward the generation of empathy with his audience.

Nevertheless, Douglass's work is characteristically at its most incisive and compelling when dealing specifically with power struggles, that concatenation of energies that brings together, in a fatal double bind, the oppressor and the oppressed. Although the nature of these forces varies— more personalized and explosive in the early work, more abstract and systematic in the later—this focus on power as the prime source of identification and antagonism remains relatively constant. This is why Douglass's accounts of his stand-up fight with the overseer, Covey, and the whippings meted out to his Aunt Hester are the most intense focal points of his first two autobiographies; in the 1845 *Narrative*, especially, these events carry a cathectic charge, associated with the literalization of a violence that would otherwise remain vaguely metaphorical. Rather than seeing power as something to be transcended, these narratives envisage it as something to be exchanged; indeed, the crucial points in these texts are those at which the power balance is renegotiated, so that Douglass comes to appear as master of his own destiny rather than its slave.

The way Douglass manipulates authorial perspectives so as not to confine himself to any single point of identification is in keeping with the way he avoids conflating cultural positions with essentialist identities. Although Douglass may have shared Carlyle's conception of nature as a hazardous and violent terrain, he certainly did not share the Scotsman's view of social aristocrats as "natural" rulers. On the contrary, Douglass's work incorporates a sense of fluidity that makes it amenable to psychological and social mobility. Couching this mobility in negative terms, Peter Walker has suggested that Douglass's sense of selfhood was shaped as much by the absent white father as by the black mother, and that he was consequently tormented by a "hopeless secret desire to be white"; similarly, George Fredrickson has observed how "romantic racialists," such as Garrison—and, indeed, Emerson—tended to attribute natural characteristics to particular races and thus to see the mulatto as a "degenerate type."[76] For Douglass, though, the recognition of such hybridity facilitated his capacity to switch positions, to align himself sometimes with the black community and sometimes with the white establishment. In his later works, particularly, Douglass appropriated the conception of himself as a "divided man," in Walker's phrase, to project an equally refractory view of society as a site of conflict and contradiction.[77] Disdaining notions of black unity and ethnic solidarity, Douglass interpreted racial affiliation as a much more plastic quality, liable to metamorphosis and always modulated by the inflections of power. This is why his attitude toward the Irish keeps shifting: in England, he empathizes with the "black" Irish as a downtrodden race, but in the United States he finds that Irish immigrants have become part of the oppressive "white" regime.[78] It is not just the position of the Irish that changes, but also that of Douglass. Schooled in an aesthetic of paradox and reversal, he is concerned always with the fractious and divisive nature of hegemony and resistance, how one party strives to exercise control over another.

The key point here is that Douglass always insists on seeing cultures in terms of their mutual relations. Writing of the Irish situation in the nineteenth century, Terry Eagleton has observed that it is through "tropes" such as paradox, metonymy, and oxymoron "that the relationship between imperial Britain and colonial Ireland has to be read," since each country could "glimpse something of its own future in the glass of the other." A similar kind of dynamic applies, in Douglass's eyes, to the interaction between white and black America. Just as Ireland represented what Eagleton has called "a rebarbative world which threatened to unmask Britain's own civility," so the power structures of white America are shadowed, in Douglass's texts, by a series of parallel black discourses that do not so much directly oppose institutionalized assumptions as empty them out, flaunting their moral hollowness and naked self-interest.[79] By focusing on a nexus of power exchange, and by illuminating how established formulations are susceptible to reversal, Douglass elucidates a world in which entrenched systems of authority can be rhetorically displaced and defamiliarized.

Douglass's argument with Garrison, then, involved not just an intellectual dispute over the meaning of the U.S. Constitution but a fundamental disagreement about the nature and purpose of power. In 1832, Garrison wrote that emancipation would mean the freedom of slaves "to seek intellectual and moral mastery over their white competitors"; but when this passage subsequently appears on the masthead of *The Liberator*, the words "mastery" and "competitors" are replaced by the more emollient terms "equality" and "brethren."[80] The change in emphasis here is revealing. Whereas Garrison came to see political power as corrupt by definition, Douglass perceived it as a category to be appropriated for his own purposes. Whereas Garrison looked forward to a utopian day of deliverance, Douglass always thrived on antagonism and provocation. This is one of the reasons the Garrisonians were so perturbed by Douglass's relationship with Julia Griffiths: by flaunting his close friendship with a white woman, by famously parading down Broadway in 1849 with Julia on one arm and her sister, Eliza Griffiths, on the other, Douglass appeared to be spurning noble ideas of Christian brotherhood in favor of a merciless desire to beat white society at its own game.[81] What Douglass's works project above all is a view of society as a cycle of conflict, riven by power struggles between different racial and ethnic groups, all of whom seem inexorably bound to the Ixion wheel of domination and subordination. The reverse projections of transnationalism open up these perspectives in Douglass's texts, while also reflecting back across the Atlantic, for one disconcerting aspect in his depiction of internecine violence is the way it threatens to lift the lid on parallel divisions elsewhere. Douglass's narratives render with a brutal literalism the corporate and corporeal strife that, in the case of English writers like Gaskell, is kept discreetly under wraps or sublimated metaphorically into harmonious, if unlikely, reconciliations. By addressing the explicit violence between competing groups in American society, Douglass comments also on the implicit violence between competing groups in Britain. In this way, the intransigent, compulsive nature of his work can be located ultimately in its ruthless demystification of conventional metaphors to locate an atavistic force that underlies social convention and literary gentility, as well as in its incisive capacity to represent how such power functions within a broad cultural framework of conflict and exchange.

# 3

## *"Bewildering Intertanglement": Melville's Engagement with British Tradition*

In her introduction to a 1994 collection of critical essays, Myra Jehlen writes that in America "Melville has remained canonical through the whole period of canon-busting." According to Jehlen, new styles of literary evaluation may have found different things to admire in Melville, but have not sought to devalue his central "importance or brilliance."[1] Melville has not, however, enjoyed a similar prominence in the British critical domain as it has developed professionally since the Second World War. Whereas Hawthorne and, to an even greater extent, Henry James have evoked a great deal of admiration and explication in British circles, engagement with Melville's more bulbous and erratic texts has remained spasmodic. My purpose in this chapter is to suggest reasons for this comparative neglect, and to suggest that some of this discomfort may arise not so much from any simple antagonism on Melville's part toward the British tradition, but from the way he interacts with it in a perverse and parodic manner, turning its apparently legitimating structures inside out.

Melville's relative invisibility in the field of later twentieth-century British culture is all the more telling, given his cult status among various maverick thinkers in Britain around the end of the Victorian era. Hershel Parker, in fact, has suggested that the initial "revival of Melville's reputation was almost exclusively a British phenomenon," arising out of a general interest in the American author among various groups of artistic and political rebels, notably the pre-Raphaelites and, later, the Fabian socialists.[2] In the 1860s and 1870s, poets like Dante Gabriel Rossetti and

James Thomson were attracted to Melville because of the way his broad cultural iconoclasm seemed to be linked, at some vital level, with an ambience of sexual freedom, an issue that greatly concerned British radicals of this era. A few years later, Thomson's influence helped indirectly to generate an admiring circle of Melville acolytes in the provincial town of Leicester, guided by James Billson, a political and religious iconoclast who worked in the legal profession. In 1884, Billson wrote to the American author, "Here in Leicester your books are in great request . . . as soon as one is discovered (for that is what it really is with us) it is eagerly read and passed round a rapidly increasing knot of 'Melville readers.'" Another of this Leicester set, J. W. Barrs, was friendly with Henry S. Salt, described by Parker as the first "Melville scholar" because he published two diligently researched essays on the American writer in the *Scottish Art Review* of November 1889 and the *Gentleman's Magazine* in 1892.[3]

In cultural terms, Salt might be seen in many ways as the typical British champion of Melville's writing around the turn of the twentieth century. After a traditional upbringing, he returned to spend nine years as a master at his old school, Eton, before creating such a stir by his interest in rebellious figures like Shelley, Swinburne, and Thoreau that he was obliged to leave this bastion of educational conservatism. He then forged links with the Fabian Society and the newly emerging Labour Party, and became a proselytizer for causes such as vegetarianism and the Humanitarian League. He continued to publish widely on British authors whom he could cast as outsiders—William Godwin, Thomas De Quincey— besides vigorously promoting American authors like Emerson, Hawthorne, Poe, and Whitman, as well as Melville. He also developed friendships with other intellectuals who shared his recalcitrant tendencies: William Morris, George Bernard Shaw, Edward Carpenter, Havelock Ellis. Ellis himself corresponded briefly with Melville in 1890, when the pioneering psychologist was, as he put it, "making some investigations into the ancestry of distinguished English & American poets and imaginative writers, with reference to the question of race."[4] Salt also published in 1889 *The Life of James Thomson*, a work Melville was so eager to read that he purchased the book himself before Salt's own presentation copy reached him. Melville's own enthusiasm during the 1880s for the essays and poems of Thomson, whose "City of Dreadful Night" epitomized the Scottish poet's pessimistic view of modern mass culture, suggests that the influences between the American author and British culture at this time were reciprocal.

All of these bohemian characters in Britain looked to Melville as an emblem of authentic nature, as an untrammeled spirit who seemed to offer an exuberant alternative to the stuffy principles of Victorian society. A similar pattern was repeated, on a less intellectually self-conscious level, by maritime authors such as W. Clark Russell and John Masefield, who spoke in 1912 about Melville's "picturesqueness and directness," as well as by fantasists such as J. M. Barrie, who cherished *Typee* and *Omoo* as escapes back into the adventure world of boyhood.[5] These British enthusiasts were impressed by the way Melville's fictional heroes fail to accommodate themselves to the landlocked preoccupations of an insular society, and their nonconformist sympathies anticipate the line taken by the most famous British advocate of Melville in the early twentieth century, D. H. Lawrence. *Studies in Classic American Literature* (1923) evokes the spirit of the New World as a welcome escape from the repressive confines of British culture, iconoclastically celebrating Melville's "slithery" and "uncanny magic" and going on to describe him as "a futurist long before futurism found paint."[6] Lawrence's whole style of articulation involves something new, of course, but it is worth emphasizing that the provincial, antiestablishment milieu from which Lawrence himself emerged had been remarking on the qualities of Melville for some forty years.

A new edition of *Moby-Dick* in 1921, edited by Viola Meynell for the World Classics series, helped to direct attention more generally toward an idea of American primitivism that was often seen at this time as a welcome antidote to nineteenth-century bourgeois values. J. W. N. Sullivan, writing in the *Times Literary Supplement* of 1923, specifically differentiates Melville's "profundities" and "mystical" dimensions from the "perfectly clear-cut and comprehensible affair" that constituted the "world of the Victorians."[7] In *Aspects of the Novel* (1927), E. M. Forster similarly acclaims Melville's prophetic capacity to break through the "tiresome little receptacle" of social morality and to encompass larger, metaphysical forces of evil. Forster equates this confounding of materialism with Melville's modernist skills of elusiveness and indirection: "The essential in *Moby Dick*, its prophetic song, flows athwart the action and the surface morality like an undercurrent. It lies outside words." It is noticeable, though, that Forster's private commonplace book is considerably less vague on the sources of this obliquity, commenting specifically on "H.M.'s suppressed homosex."[8] A generation later, another sexual rebel, W. H. Auden, was to proffer an existential interpretation of Melville's sea novels: in *The Enchafèd Flood* (1951), Auden writes that the departure from land in *Moby-Dick* signifies "a commitment to a necessity which, however unpleasant, is at least preferable to . . . the meaningless freedom on shore." This psychological "necessity" involves a rupture of domestic conventions, and Auden's discussion of *Billy Budd* is one of the first to insist directly on how the motive underlying Claggart's hostility to Melville's cherubic hero is "homosexual desire."[9] In the same year, another self-consciously gay artist, Benjamin Britten, produced his operatic version of *Billy Budd* for the 1951 Festival of Britain.

In general, though, it is noticeable that British critics in the first half of the twentieth century tended to focus on Melville's earlier narratives— *Typee, Omoo, Redburn, Moby-Dick*—and to emphasize their romantic, atavistic energies. There was relatively little conception of how Melville's fiction might be intricately interwoven with issues of hierarchical authority and control, and it could be that his texts were considered acceptable to British readers as long as they could be said simply to embody "the stark forces of nature," as E. L. Grant Watson suggested in a 1920 issue of the London *Mercury*.[10] When, however, a later generation of scholars began unpacking more assiduously the cultural crosscurrents and undercurrents of Melville's work, British readers who were quite at home with the reflective ironies and social ambiguities of James and Hawthorne found themselves less comfortable with the more profane implications of Melville's aggressive irreverence.

This growing transatlantic divide in the reception of Melville's work during the middle years of the twentieth century was not helped by the propensity of many American critics at this time to underline links between the author and the "Young America" movement, to which he was introduced by Evert Duyckinck in 1846. With its vigorous promotion of American democratic values and its concomitant hostility toward what it saw as the more genteel, Anglophiliac style of Boston, Duyckinck's brand of cultural nationalism provided an obvious framework and impetus for Melville's early career as a writer. The first American edition of *Typee* appeared in 1846 in Duyckinck's Library of American Books series, published by Wiley & Putnam, and Melville's famous review of Hawthorne's *Mosses from an Old Manse* appeared in the *Literary World*, the magazine edited by Duyckinck, in August 1850. "Hawthorne and His Mosses" is the critical essay in which Melville's patriotic spirit is most apparent: describing England as "alien to us," he rebukes Washington Irving, among others, for his "self-acknowledged imitation of a foreign model" and urges American writers generally to abandon their "leaven of literary flunkyism towards England."[11] Melville's piece echoes the critical assumptions in Duyckinck's own review of *White-Jacket* in the same journal a few months earlier, where the editor praises Melville for the way he "tests all his characters by their manhood," a process he considers to be "thoroughly American and democratic" because it involves "no patronage" in its representation of ordinary sailors.[12] The hostility of Young America toward England at this time was exacerbated by the particular antagonisms that developed between the two countries in the mid-1840s over the Oregon Question: Melville's older brother, Gansevoort, was one of many who violently opposed British attempts to prevent the United States from incorporating the whole of the disputed Oregon Territory, and he urged on his countrymen the merits of a third war with England to finally expel the Crown from the North American continent.[13] It is sometimes forgotten that John L. O'Sullivan's term "Manifest Destiny" became famous in December 1845 after he had used it in a discussion of this American dispute with England over Oregon; indeed, as Robert W. Johannsen noted in 1997, "Anglophobia . . . has been a missing ingredient in most discussions of Manifest Destiny."[14]

Melville himself, however, never entirely endorsed his brother's chauvinism, and the complications in his representations of colonialism are implicit in even his earliest works. The first editions of *Typee*, despite Duyckinck's imprimatur, carry an appendix supporting the "liberal and paternal sway" exercised by Lord George Paulet over the Hawaiian people. Dismissing the popular American indignation against British imperial designs as misguided, it argues that Britain never had any intention of appropriating the Sandwich Islands for their own purposes. Melville's description of the Pacific Islanders as "depraved and vicious" and his hostility toward the American missionaries has the effect of vindicating Lord Paulet's "spirited and high-minded" intervention.[15] The author chose to eliminate this appendix, along with other expressions of "pro-British" opinion, when he prepared a revised American edition for Wiley & Putnam in 1849, although from a study of the author's manuscripts and annotations Hershel Parker believes it is "clear that he had meant everything he had said in the first edition of *Typee*."[16] All of this reinforces the notion that Melville never believed that issues of national politics and postcolonial emancipation were as straightforward as Young America liked to imagine. In this sense, the double-edged nature of *Typee* anticipates the metaphorically and conceptually elusive quality of *Moby-Dick* (1851), where one oblique reference to Oregon can be found in Chapter 42:

> . . . what knows he, this New England colt, of the black bisons of distant Oregon?
>
> No: but here thou beholdest even in a dumb brute, the instinct of the knowledge of the demonism in the world. Though thousands of miles from Oregon, still when he smells that savage musk, the rending, goring bison herds are as present to the deserted wild foal of the prairies, which this instant they may be trampling into dust. (194)

The narrative describes this "young colt" as "foaled in some peaceful valley of Vermont" (194), and Edward L. Widmer suggests this may be a "damning judgment" by Melville on the expansionist politics of Stephen Douglas, a native of Vermont and long-time hero of the Young America movement, who in 1845 had stated his desire "to drive Great Britain and the last vestiges of royal authority from the continent of North America." By seizing the Oregon Territory, proclaimed Douglas, the United States would "extend the limits of the republic from ocean to ocean."[17] Rather than being represented here as a triumphal movement west, however, the journey across the prairies is seen as a form of "demonism," something "savage," like Ahab's parallel quest for the inscrutable white whale.

These multifaceted, multidirectional aspects of style in *Moby-Dick* elicited a negative review from an uncomprehending Duyckinck in November 1851, leading Melville to cancel his subscription to the *Literary World* three months later. In the light of the author's pronounced skepticism about the politics of American exceptionalism in the last four decades of his life, it is one of the ironies of literary history that Melville's reputation as a figurehead of nationalism should have been reinvigorated some hundred years later by the critical readings characteristic of the cold war era, readings that pitted the individualistic energies of Melville's all-American heroes against the restrictive shackles of more traditional societies. In the wake of F. O. Matthiessen's *American Renaissance* (1941),

Melville became canonized as a romancer dedicated to exploring the possibilities of liberty, a writer prepared heroically to confront estrangement from the material circumstances of his corrupt world to aspire to an imaginative and putatively spiritual freedom; hence the title of Lawrance Thompson's 1952 work, *Melville's Quarrel with God*.[18]

While Matthiessen himself sought to align Melville and his other chosen nineteenth-century authors with the fabled promise of American democracy, C. L. R. James, in *Mariners, Renegades, and Castaways*, projected a utopian view of Melville's world as rooted in "the humour, the sanity, the anonymous but unfailing humanity of the renegades and castaways and savages of the Pequod," whose "heroism . . . consists in their everyday doing of their work."[19] For James, this dedication to equality and freedom epitomized an American spirit that stood in opposition to the perils of totalitarianism, represented in *Moby-Dick* by the figure of Ahab and in James's own American experience by his sequestration on Ellis Island awaiting deportation for alleged affiliations with the Communist Party, which is where he wrote his book on Melville in 1953. As a native of Trinidad who had come to England in 1932 before moving to the United States in 1938, James would have had every reason to be skeptical about the American commitment to a spirit of liberty; but he chose, as he put it, to take "in my stride the cruelties and anomalies that shocked me" and to keep his eye on higher ideals by emphasizing instead "the immense vitality, generosity and audacity of those strange people."[20] Yet in this way, as Robert A. Hill has observed, James came "close to subscribing to the Cold War mystique of Americanism" that was so prevalent in the years after the Second World War.[21] "The question of questions," ponders James in *Mariners, Renegades, and Castaways*, "is: how could a book from the world of 1850 contain so much of the world of the 1950s?"[22] Obviously enough, James's analogies can be seen from a later perspective as an extrapolation from the cultural politics of his own time, but they indicate especially clearly the way Melville's fiction tended to be understood in this postwar era within a specifically nationalistic framework. In *American Civilization*, James cites Wordsworth's famous preface of 1798 to the *Lyrical Ballads*, where the Lake poet claims to be speaking in the language of the common people, and James argues that Melville is performing a similar service in the name of what he calls the "average American worker of today."[23]

More recent work on Melville has tended to move away from this dualistic paradigm. The romantic antitheses pitting an egalitarian spirit against the restrictive shackles of the Old World, freedom against totalitarianism, have been undermined by questions about the extent to which such binary oppositions work simply to define each other. More generally, theoretical interrogations of the status of agency in Melville's writing have suggested how his fictional characters tend to find themselves pushing up against inherited social structures, rather than being in a position to objectify or transcend them. This question about agency quickly becomes an ontological one, involving imponderable issues about the meaning of origins; but, in a less abstract sense, a greater willingness to examine the ways Melville's fiction negotiates intertextually with the circumscribed genius of English literature has focused more attention on the extent to which the author's chosen field of inquiry involves not simply the narrower terrain of the United States but the more expansive circuits of North Atlantic culture in general.

Lawrence Buell has theorized these interactive movements as a form of postcolonial anxiety. Melville's art, Buell suggests, should be seen as embroiled within a "much more complicated transnational historical matrix" than the master narratives of nationalism or slavery that have become almost synonymous with American Renaissance texts over the past fifty years.[24] In this respect, Melville's early writing refracts the complications of the international scene as it appeared from the vantage point of the United States at this historical moment. As David M. Potter reminds us, to those living through the turbulent years of the late 1840s and early 1850s, when Melville was at his most prolific, it was mass immigration from Europe that was generally thought to be the biggest problem confronting the Union, not slavery.[25] Yet, if there are troublesome affinities between Young America's drive for cultural independence and the more rampant xenophobia of the Know Nothing Party, which was burgeoning at this time, there are also parallels between Melville's eventual rejection of Duyckinck's approach and his desire to encompass broader, less specifically nationalistic traditions in his writing. In light of the ways his writing reflects the complications of transnationalism, Melville might appear not so much a postcolonial writer as a post-postcolonial, a Janus-faced figure who finds uncomfortable parallels between markedly divergent cultures.

As with most American writers of his era, Melville's professional career was heavily involved with English literary models and professional paradigms. He himself undertook three expeditions to Britain during the first half of his life, each of which offered a different perspective on English culture. In June 1839, he sailed from New York to Liverpool on board the *St. Lawrence*, a trip that was to form the basis of his transatlantic comparisons in *Redburn*. On his second visit, though, the focus was more on London as a center of literary trade and commerce. It had been another London publishing company, John Murray, that had first brought the author into print, after Melville's brother, Gansevoort, then secretary of the American Legation in London, had taken the manuscript of *Typee* to England with him in 1845. Four years later, in October 1849, Melville decided to act as his own agent and left New York for London with a view to placing *White-Jacket* with English publishers. He succeeded in selling the novel to Richard Bentley, then spent several weeks touring London and Paris, before leaving Portsmouth to return to the United States on Christmas Day. On this trip, Melville also acquired a huge number of English books to take home with him: works by Ben Jonson, Beaumont and Fletcher, Samuel Butler, James Boswell, Sir Thomas Browne, Horace Walpole, Charles Lamb, Shakespeare, Marlowe, De Quincey, William Godwin, and others. He also took an opportunity to dine in Elm Court, Temple, describing in his journal how he "had a glorious time" in this "Paradise of Batchelors."[26] The story deriving from this experience, "The Paradise of Bachelors and the Tartarus of Maids," was to appear in *Harper's* in April 1855.

Finally, in October 1856, Melville sailed from New York to Glasgow on the first leg of his voyage to the Middle East, a pilgrimage that he was to recreate imaginatively some twenty years later in *Clarel*. It was on the outward leg of this journey that he renewed his acquaintance with Hawthorne, then American consul in Liverpool, an encounter that Hawthorne chronicled famously in his notebooks by remarking that Melville appeared to be suffering from "a morbid state of mind" and could "neither believe, nor be comfortable in his unbelief."[27] On his return trip, Melville passed through England again in April and May 1857, spending time admiring the Turner collection at the National Gallery in London before traveling north to sail home from Liverpool. On this final expedition, Melville's mood appears generally pensive and philosophical, and he ruminates in his journal on the Old World as a site of tradition and determinism. The tone is set on the initial voyage over to Glasgow, when Melville engages a passenger, one George Rankin, in a series of discussions about "fixed fate." It continues as the author wanders through Europe: he appears discomfited by the monuments of Italy ("Started for Appian Way. Narrow,—not like Milton's Way—not suitable to dignity &c."), but is more at ease among the collegial landscapes of Oxford, where he feels impelled to confess "with gratitude my mother land" and to acknowledge that he knows "nothing more fitted by mild & beautiful rebuke to chastise the sophomorean pride of Am[erica] as a new & prosperous country."[28]

Without seeking to delineate excessively causal relationships between life and art, I suggest that all of Melville's texts comprise, in some fashion, travel narratives. Obviously enough, the early books that describe voyages to the South Seas involve clashes between different cultures, and it is not difficult to relate this to a cross-cultural comparativeness, predicated on a "politics of nonidentity," where nationalist teleologies and traditions become problematized by theoretical confrontations between different cultures.[29] This, of course, is the classic site of postcolonial criticism, with its focus on the "join" or border that reconfigures essentialist identity as unstable hybridity: "Where, once, the transmission of national traditions was the major theme of a world literature," writes Homi Bhabha, "perhaps we can now suggest that transnational histories of migrants, the colonized, or political refugees—these border and frontier conditions—may be the terrains of world literature." Although this may be relatively clear in relation to Melville's earlier texts, the more difficult question concerns the ways these "dialogical or transferential" structures work their way into his later fiction.[30] In what ways does a continuing postcolonial encounter with the British empire come to frame, indeed in some ways define, the range of Melville's artistic ambitions?

*Redburn*, published in 1849, constitutes in many ways the most straightforward example of cross-cultural critique. Like Melville in 1839, Wellingborough Redburn crosses the Atlantic and lands at Liverpool, where he is confronted by "a confused uproar of ballad-singers, bawling women, babies, and drunken sailors." Melville's hero responds to this loss of the picturesque by relapsing into a kind of ironic nostalgia: "But where are the old abbeys, and the York Minsters, and the lord mayors, and coronations, and the May-poles, and Fox-hunters, and Derby races, and the dukes and duchesses, and the Count d'Orsays, which, from all my reading, I had been in the habit of associating with England? Not the most

distant glimpse of them was to be seen."[31] Through these comic defla-
tions, stereotypes are dismantled and Liverpool comes to seem more like
New York than Redburn has supposed. The same process of demystification also works in reverse: on his whirlwind visit to London, Redburn
assures the anxious Englishman, Harry Bolton, that not all "Yankees lived
in wigwams, and wore bear-skins." On the contrary, declares Redburn,
"New York was a civilized and enlightened town; with a large population,
fine streets, fine houses, nay, plenty of omnibuses; and . . . for the most
part, he would almost think himself in England; so similar to England, in
essentials, was this outlandish America that haunted him" (280). This
notion of America being "so similar to England, in essentials" is a theme
that runs through *Redburn*. The trajectory of the narrative is not so much
a linear quest as a disillusioning circle, where the protagonist ends up
where he began, in the knowledge that the promised land turns out in the
end to be only a chimera.

Relinquishing his fantasies of a pastoral England, Redburn is confronted instead with a statue of "four naked figures in chains . . . seated in
various attitudes of humiliation and despair" at the base of a pedestal
depicting Lord Nelson expiring in the arms of the goddess Victory (135).
In a strategy characteristic of Melville's hybridized idiom, his narrator
here begins to construct figurative analogies between different types
of slavery, juxtaposing the racial discrimination familiar to him from
nineteenth-century America with the social and economic slavery he
sees around him in England:

> These woe-begone figures of captives are emblematic of Nelson's
> principal victories; but I never could look at their swarthy limbs and
> manacles, without being involuntarily reminded of four African
> slaves in the market-place.
>
> And my thoughts would revert to Virginia and Carolina; and also
> to the historical fact, that the African slave-trade once constituted
> the principal commerce of Liverpool; and that the prosperity of the
> town was once supposed to have been indissolubly linked to its
> prosecution. (135)

One of the tendencies Melville takes from Emerson (and later from
Thomas Carlyle, whose work he read in 1850) is an intellectual proclivity
to run different objects or ideas into one another. This is the transcendental style of embracing disparate entities within one all-encompassing

arc; in Melville's case, though, these mirrors of similitude lack the meta-physical idealism with which they are endowed by Emerson, and are in fact more likely to betoken the mise-en-abîme of fate, where every object inescapably foreshadows the next. Thus in *Redburn*, the dominating posture of Nelson evokes the power relations of racial slavery, and this in turn is conflated in the narrator's mind with the oppressions of the class system as it manifests itself in Liverpool, whose "masses of squalid men, women, and children" (201) are bound under the yoke of British dominion. By affiliating American slavery of race with British slavery of class, Melville appears to project both of these power systems beyond the order of worldly empiricism into a realm where they become imbued with some shadowy, quasi-Calvinistic sense of fate.

Associated with this pessimism is a profound skepticism about the ways such power struggles become rationalized and naturalized in particular social contexts. *Mardi*, published earlier in the same year as *Redburn*, is a satirical allegory that once again uses the form of a voyage to subvert local pieties that have become reified and institutionalized through established custom. Like Swift in *Gulliver's Travels*, Melville deploys the travel narrative to diminish and ridicule the rulers who equate their own small domain with the size of the universe: "To the people of the Archipelago the map of Mardi was the map of the world."[32] Melville's extravagant tone here evokes a world of ironic pastoral, where mock paradises are no sooner glimpsed than exposed. In his quest for "Yillah," the narrator keeps coming across "sweet forms of maidens like Eves in Edens ere the Fall" (549), though he recognizes their prelapsarian status is no more valid than his own amiable inclinations toward divinity: "I now perceived that I might be a god as much as I pleased" (176).

Though hard going at times, *Mardi* is a comic narrative whose effectiveness has been generally underestimated, and its burlesque possibilities are seen to good purpose in the sections specifically reflecting the political antagonisms in Europe and America. King Bello appears as monarch of "Dominora" (England), a land dedicated to acquiring more territories; meanwhile, at the entrance to "Vivenza" (the United States) is found an arch bearing the inscription: "In this republican land all men are born free and equal. . . . Except the tribe of Hamo" (512–13). Of this republic in general, the narrator notes that "in the flush and pride of having recently attained their national majority, the men of Vivenza were perhaps too much inclined to carry a vauntful crest" (472), and he describes how this has brought about particular complications in their dealings with Dominora, engendering "a feeling akin to animosity" between the two nations. Nevertheless, the inhabitants of Vivenza relate to the citizens of Dominora as "sons to sires," and "though . . . Vivenza is now its own master, yet should it not fail in a reverential respect for its parent." King Bello, for his part, "should never forget, that whatever be glorious in Vivenza, redounds to himself" (519). On one level, these familial analogies serve to naturalize political conflicts, making them seem as inevitable as the cycle of the generations; but, through a formal double bind, Melville's analogical style works also to denaturalize these established authorities, which consequently find themselves travestied and traversed by unstable zones of comic parody.

Richard H. Brodhead describes *Mardi* as something like a "first draft of all [Melville's] subsequent works," and certainly it is not difficult to see how the author reworks these kinds of metaphysical conceits and figurative analogies in a more controlled way in *Moby-Dick*.[33] Here, once more, the idiom of the travel narrative trains a mobile, ironic light on the obsessive nature of primitive beliefs. Captain Bildad's Quaker infatuation with the Scriptures, which he has been studying for thirty years, is placed alongside Queequeg's devotion to Yojo, "his black little god" (68), whose apparently infallible predictions elicit an unflattering comparison on Ishmael's part with "ants worshipping a toad-stool" (81). Such chains of analogy again decenter and demystify the internal structures of belief in this fictional narrative, so that religious emblems become reduced to forms of crazed fetishism, akin to Ahab's futile passion for running down the white whale.

In biographical terms, the influence of English literature on the composition of *Moby-Dick* is well-known. Six months after beginning to write the novel, Melville started to reconceive its shape in light of his recent readings in Shakespeare and Carlyle. He greatly admired Shakespeare—though not, he insisted, the vacuous elitism that went along with the Bard's reputation, as indicated by "the number of the *snobs* who burn their tuns of rancid fat at his shrine."[34] Indeed, in the essay extolling the "power of blackness" in the "hither side of Hawthorne's soul," the very essay that campaigns fiercely against "literary flunkyism towards England," we find Melville seeking to reinvent Shakespeare as another exponent of "deep far-away things," with a putatively Calvinistic feeling for "dark characters" who find themselves "tormented into desperation."[35] Whatever the merits of this as a critique of the English dramatist, it is not difficult to see how *Moby-Dick* appropriates Shakespeare in an attempt self-consciously to grapple with what the author takes to be universal themes. The multilayered dramatic interludes and Shakespearean soliloquies, as well as the metaphysical speculations with which the text is larded, testify to Melville's desire to overcome a cultural "anxiety of influence" by projecting his novel beyond American provincialism into the "unshored, harborless immensities" of world literature.[36]

Carlyle's *Sartor Resartus*, which first appeared in 1833–1834, but which Melville borrowed from Duyckinck's library in July 1850, more specifically furnished Melville with a prototype for his playful, iconoclastic style in *Moby-Dick*. Carlyle's work, like that of Melville, establishes an inner structural dialectic between transcendence and irony, spirit and matter. Through this dialectic, philosophical inquiries into the "azure of Eternity" and the symbolic truths underlying "blind Custom" find themselves framed, if not circumscribed, by Professor Teufesldröckh's fussy discussions of clothes, editorial apparatuses, and other aspects of the familiar human world.[37] Yet Melville, like Carlyle, also takes on board the paradoxes of German Romantic irony, self-consciously manipulating his narrative stance to subvert the premises of empiricism, so as to create space for an infusion of spirit into the fractured world of "the terraqueous Globe" (114). Carlyle's chapter "Symbols," with its proposition that "the Universe is but one vast Symbol of God" (166), clearly prefigures Emerson's "Nature," published two years later. Of course, the thematic associations between Carlyle and Melville are less obvious than those between Carlyle and his good friend Emerson; typically enough, Melville was unsuccessful in his attempts to meet Carlyle in England in 1849. Yet it might be argued that the style and tone of *Moby-Dick* in many ways more closely approximate Carlyle's rhetorical manner than anything that Emerson wrote. For whereas Emerson's aphoristic and ecstatic language aspires mimetically to imitate his transcendental doctrines, Carlyle and Melville both choose playfully to balance their neoplatonic idealism against the voices of imperfect narrators, narrators who can act for the reader as conduits between familiar everyday circumstances and the more abstract regions of metaphysics. Ishmael, like Teufesldröckh, helps to maintain a comic tone that Emerson's writing generally lacks.

Melville's language, then, moves chameleon-like between epic and mock-epic, the idealistic and the aggressively deflationary. Part of his "slithery" quality, as Lawrence describes it, consists in traducing established conventions from English literature and culture by sliding them rhetorically into new, parodic forms. Through wordplay and metaphorical analogy, Melville demystifies the cherished icons of British civilization and reconfigures them in burlesque modes. In Chapter 25 of *Moby-Dick*, for instance, the narrator relates that the whale's sperm oil, "in its unmanufactured, unpolluted state," is used at royal coronations: "Think of that, ye loyal Britons! we whalemen supply your kings and queens with coronation stuff" (114). Again, the author uses the metamorphosing force of similitude for subversive purposes, introducing analogies that deprive petrified British customs of an authority that rests necessarily on a suppression of their more arbitrary attributes. It is, perhaps, hardly surprising that the whole of Chapter 25, dealing with this coronation oil, was omitted by Richard Bentley when he published the first English edition of the novel. (Melville always enjoyed tweaking the pretensions of British royalty: "Long live the 'prince of whales,'" he jokes in his journal after visiting Windsor Castle on 22 November 1849).[38] Later in *Moby-Dick*, Ishmael implicitly mocks the whole idea of the English Victorian novel through the way the mariners "humorously discourse of parlors, sofas, carpets, and fine cambrics" as they scrub the decks. This cleaning takes place after "an affair of oil," and the decks are rendered so "immaculate" that the sailors would "object not to taking tea by moonlight on the piazza of the forecastle" (428), as though they might be in a novel by Trollope or George Eliot. *Moby-Dick*, like the *Pequod* itself, is "pitched about by the most riotously perverse and cross-running seas" (221), intertextually arguing with traditional English manners, but gaining much of its satirical energy and philosophical depth from a rebarbative relationship with British models. In Chapter 69, the narrator argues openly with Samuel Johnson's staunch empiricism: "Are you a believer in ghosts, my friend? There are other ghosts than the Cock-Lane one, and far deeper men than Doctor Johnson who believe in them" (309). The "ghosts" here are not just spiritual specters, but also the shades of British history and tradition by which Melville, as a Young American author, finds himself spooked.

As John Carlos Rowe notes, one of the characteristic styles in texts of the "American Renaissance" is a strategy of defamiliarization, whereby "the very formlessness of American prose . . . evolves into a form in its own right." Classic American writings of this time self-consciously position themselves in a rebarbative and sometimes parodic relation to more established European genres. In this sense, there is always some circuit of commerce between "tradition and originality," Europe and America, involving a series of negotiations to which only the critical method of "comparatism" can do justice.[39] At the same time, however, Melville's peculiar capacity to hollow out the assumptions of institutionalized culture leads him to create in *Moby-Dick* a work of fiction where the sense of interiority is, as Leo Bersani notes, almost entirely abolished. For instance, as Bersani says, the philosophical idea of homoeroticism is introduced so easily into *Moby-Dick* precisely because, in psychological terms, so little is at stake; Melville's characters, unlike those of Gide or Proust, never engage subjectively with affairs of this kind, and this is why the experience of *Moby-Dick* for the reader is often one of puzzlement and alienation.[40] Although every kind of interpretive mode is made available in the novel, they all seem to manifest themselves in a belated and inconsequential fashion; even the idea of Providence becomes a jokey, aesthetic idea, orchestrated by "those stage managers, the Fates" (7).

Bersani understands this as a paradoxical attempt on the author's part to annul the "unrelenting analogical habit" on which *Moby-Dick*'s rhetorical manner is predicated. According to Bersani, Melville appears to suspend or frustrate every hermeneutic impulse, so that his text might aspire toward a style of utopian negation where any similarity with English prototypes becomes undermined and the novel is, quite literally, "incomparable."[41] But it is possible to look at these maneuvers in another way and to suggest that these radically demystifying analogies work self-consciously to promulgate an American cultural identity by disenfranchising the English heritage, rendering the assumptions of that older tradition transparent and aesthetically visible. It is, finally, impossible in this novel to transcend the boundaries of linguistic association: every stab at originality turns out to involve reduplication, every character who would be "free as air" finds himself "down in the whole world's books" (472). Yet it is the way these famous books are renegotiated, their well-worn assumptions opened up to revisionist scrutiny, that constitutes Melville's great challenge to the canonical imperatives of British culture.

One example of how these intertextual analogies operate can be seen in Melville's relation to Milton. After analyzing Melville's annotations in his copy of Milton's poetry, Robin Sandra Grey concludes that the American author "ascribes to Milton calculated, highly self-conscious interrogations of the divine scheme that Milton cleverly and often ironically camouflages by ascribing to the character of Satan." Melville did not follow Blake in believing Milton was of the devil's party without knowing it; on the contrary, Melville reads Satan in Book 9 of *Paradise Lost* as Milton's mouthpiece, as the snake quizzes the Divinity on why he keeps his worshipers "low and ignorant." "This is one of the many profound atheistical hits of Milton," concludes Melville: "A greater than Lucretius since he teaches under a masque, and makes the Devil himself a Teacher & Messiah."[42] Whatever the merits of this as literary criticism, it is highly illuminating in relation to the representation of Ahab, whose desire for revenge on the white whale is as anguished as Satan's quest in Milton's poem for vengeance against God. In this sense, *Moby-Dick* might be understood as a blasphemous reworking of *Paradise Lost*, a scenario in which the drive for revenge overwhelms any theological framework or moral restraint, connoting instead a philosophical demurral from the paths of Christian order and a transgressive flirtation with the darker powers of anarchy.

Besides censoring the section on how the ceremonial oil for royal coronations derives from the profane practices of whaling, the editor at the publishing house of Richard Bentley made a sizable number of other excisions when Melville's novel was first published in England as *The Whale* on 18 October 1851. (Melville had changed his mind about the title in September 1851, too late for Bentley, though not for Harper and Brothers in New York, who brought it out as *Moby-Dick* on 14 November.) The English edition omitted most of the supposedly indecorous references to the Bible; thus, farcically enough, "that's Christianity" became "that's the right sort," and "Providence" was recast as "those three mysterious ladies." Likewise, the "crucifixion on Ahab's face" was toned down, becoming the blander "eternal anguish in his face." Other alleged obscenities were simply omitted, including references to Nature "painting like the harlot," the "back parts, or tail" of the whale, and so on.[43]

Such editorial caution, however, failed to prevent *The Whale* from being harangued by English reviewers for its blasphemy and indecency. The anonymous contributor to *John Bull*, for instance, complained of "some heathenish, and worse than heathenish talk" in the novel, which was, he said, "calculated to give . . . serious offence." This writer was appalled that Melville "should have defaced his pages by occasional twists against revealed religion which add nothing to the interest of his story, and cannot but shock readers accustomed to a reverent treatment of whatever is associated with sacred subjects." Other English reviewers equated these moral transgressions with Melville's apparently wild and lawless rhetoric, a literary style of "eccentricity" (*Britannia*), "purposeless extravagance" (*Illustrated London News*), "rhapsody run mad" (*Spectator*). The London *Morning Chronicle* of 20 December 1851 epitomizes this early English reception of *The Whale*, with the reviewer associating the "strange contents" of Melville's epic with its willful rejection of Anglo-Saxon empiricism. The profligate author is said to display his "old extravagance, running a perfect muck throughout the three volumes, raving and rhapsodizing in chapter after chapter—unchecked, as it would appear, by the very slightest remembrance of judgment or common sense."[44]

Accusations of an aversion to judgment and common sense were also much in evidence in relation to *Pierre*, which appeared one year later, in 1852. The arguments began even before the novel was published, with Richard Bentley, stung by the commercial failure of *The Whale* in Britain, offering the author a substantially lower rate for his new work and also insisting on certain "alterations" (made either by Melville or "a judicious literary friend") to ensure that the book would be more acceptable to English audiences.[45] Melville refused these terms, and in fact, *Pierre* never found an English publisher; its pages were shipped across the Atlantic by the Harpers, and then bound and distributed in Britain by Sampson, Low, Son and Company. This circuitous approach would not have helped sales, but it is unlikely that *Pierre* would have done well in Britain anyway, as it almost entirely forgoes that "comfortable, good-humoured feeling" of roomy interiority, with its illusion of aesthetic transparency, which Henry James later associated with the endearing theoretical "*naïveté*" of English Victorian fiction.[46] On the contrary, the strategy of Melville's textual excursion involves appropriating the conventional apparatus of the English domestic novel while twisting its assumptions inside out, so that all the affective sympathy usually associated with this genre is lost. This, of course, is why readers have found it so difficult to engage with the narrative of *Pierre*; it appears to be a cerebral performance rather than a novel embodying, as in F. R. Leavis's "great tradition," "a feeling for value and significance in living."[47] In fact, all of Melville's work after *Moby-Dick* involves a process of emptying out and parodically twisting around experiential categories, so that the parallel lines that normally would relate narrative subject to referential object become twisted and crossed. Rather than finding themselves in a reassuringly familiar landscape, readers are confronted with scenarios where perspectives appear alarmingly reversed, as in a trick mirror: in Book 9, Pierre finds to his bewilderment that all the "immemorially admitted maxims of men begin to slide and fluctuate, and finally become wholly inverted" (165).

*Pierre* starts by parodying the ancient British convention of inscribing literary works to royalty. Just as in "old times authors were proud of the privilege of dedicating their works to Majesty," the author explains, so his own volume is proffered to "Greylock's Excellent Majesty," Greylock being "the majestic mountain . . . my own more immediate lord and king—[which] hath now, for innumerable ages, been the one grand dedicatee of the earliest rays of all the Berkshire mornings" (vii). Hershel Parker suggests some kind of link here with "Wordsworthian attitudes," and it is certainly true that oblique references to Wordsworth are to be found scattered throughout Melville's works: in the story "Cock-A-Doodle-Doo," which specifically parodies Wordsworth's "Resolution and Independence"; in *White-Jacket*, where the narrator comments sardonically on how "the business of writing verse is a very different thing on the gun-deck of a frigate, from what the gentle and sequestered Wordsworth found it at placid Rydal Mount in Westmoreland."[48] Throughout Melville's writing, we see an impulse iconoclastically to refract these inchoate aspects of American life by playing native idioms off against more seasoned models of English vintage; Melville engages with Wordsworth only to traduce ironically the English poet's paradigms of emotional attachment and empathy. Robert Weisbuch argues that Melville is the only American figure of this time who can be described as "essentially antagonistic toward the English romantic poets": in his copy of Hazlitt's *Lectures*, Melville made a marginal note describing Wordsworth as a "contemptable [*sic*] man (tho' good poet, in his department)," and Weisbuch perceives a similar kind of hostility in the way Melville responds to Dickens's work throughout the 1850s. In particular, he sees the fictional protagonist's refusal to compromise in "Bartleby the Scrivener," first published in 1853, as a way of "implicitly yet fiercely" attacking the more pusillanimous behavior of the characters in *Bleak House*, which had appeared in book form earlier the same year.[49] In Dickens, the victims of Chancery start out by challenging oppressive customs, but ultimately choose to acquiesce in the norms of social or familial values; in Melville's legalistic world, by contrast, the individual's right to dissent is not so easily gainsaid.

Yet Melville's intertextual dialogue with British culture is more complex than this series of oppositions might suggest. As *Pierre* demonstrates, the thematic direction involves not just antagonism but also equivalence. Only a few pages into the novel, the narrator briskly disposes of the binary opposition between "monarchical" Britain and "demagoguical" America (8) by describing how the aristocratic genealogies of England are no less circuitous and arbitrary than those of America:

> If Richmond, and St. Albans, and Grafton, and Portland, and Buccleugh, be names almost as old as England herself, the present Dukes of those names stop in their own genuine pedigrees at Charles II. . . . In England the Peerage is kept alive by incessant restorations and creations. One man, George III, manufactured five hundred and twenty-two peers. An earldom, in abeyance for five centuries, has suddenly been assumed by some commoner, to whom it had not so much descended, as through the art of the lawyers been made flexibly to bend in that direction. For not Thames is so sinuous in his national course, not the Bridgewater Canal more artificially conducted, than blood in the veins of that winding or manufactured nobility. (9–10)

Through Melville's favorite trope of reversal, the nouveaux riches in Old England are contrasted with "the hundreds of unobtrusive families in New England who, nevertheless, might easily trace their uninterrupted English lineage to a time before Charles the Blade" (10). This leads the narrator to conclude with a paradoxical and sardonic flourish: "Our America will make out a good general case with England in this short little matter of large estates, and long pedigrees—pedigrees I mean, wherein is no flaw" (11). The novel thus unravels the popular stereotype pitting English authenticity against American fakery, thereby constructing a heavily ironic framework for this American example of the family romance. As *Pierre*'s narrative unfolds, the claims of American landowners and capitalists to social legitimacy turn out to be no less self-serving than those of the recently created aristocracy in England, who strategically align their titles with English place-names in a bogus attempt to invest these new-fangled titles with some of the ancestral qualities of the land itself.

In *Pierre*, Melville empties out the form of the novel in the same way he empties out accustomed social hierarchies. As always, it is the radical disruption and dissociation of apparently congruent narratives that Melville's edgy, unsettling style works toward. This also, of course, carries important implications for the kind of text he writes. In Victorian England, the type of the novel was predicated on recognizable forms of social stability in terms of family situations, class positions, and so on. Melville's inversion of this genre, though, throws a scathing light on these cultural and fictional conventions through its radical self-reflexivity, its skeptical consciousness of the fabricated nature of its artistic prototype. Of Lucy Tartan, for example, the narrator admits: "It is needless to say that she was a beauty; because chestnut-haired, bright-cheeked youths like Pierre Glendinning, seldom fall in love with any but a beauty" (23). In this light, it is interesting that English writer John Fowles should have nominated *Pierre* as a model for his postmodernist novel, *The French Lieutenant's Woman* (1977), another highly self-conscious metafiction that both imitates and parodically critiques the premises of the Victorian novel. However, as Richard Gray observes, there is little that seems ludic or merely playful about *Pierre*, which generates more of a sense of anger and frustration at the way its "surface stratified on surface" is structured in something like an infinite regress.[50]

Yet *Pierre*, like the novel's hero, maintains an incestuous relationship with the tradition from which it would depart. *Pierre*'s theme of genealogical continuity and family relationships is mirrored in the book's intertextual structure, which reproduces standard motifs from domestic romances—the dark versus the light lady, and so on—as if to conform to the "family" structure of this particular genre. Though *Pierre* is written against the "countless tribes of common novels" (141), it is still doomed to imitate them, just as Ahab in *Moby-Dick* finds he cannot escape various forms of analogical similitude with the despotic kings of old England. From this perspective, the explicit rejection of Young America in *Pierre* involves epistemological as well as practical concerns. When the hero attempts to establish himself as an author in New York City, he comes into contact with idealistic "Apostles," whose devotion to "the sublimated categories of Kant . . . is the one great palpable fact in their pervadingly impalpable lives" (267). Pierre, however, fails to match their supposedly sublime originality; when he attempts authorship, he finds himself lying back in his chair "with the deadly feeling of faintness" (340). This is not, as has sometimes been suggested, merely an example of the mercenary literary marketplace of the 1850s compromising Pierre's artistic ambitions; it also signals a philosophical conflict between transcendentalist idealism coupled with Young America's romantic craving for originality on the one hand and "the coarse materialism of Hobbes" (265) on the other. Pierre finds that the material circumstances of his situation compromise his mental independence to such an extent that his dreams of authorship become frustrated. This deliberately inverts the traditional Puritan dualism that scorned Hobbesian materialism as a cynical attempt to drag down the freedom of the human spirit. Hence, in reacting against the Apostles, Melville's hero succumbs to an "anxiety of influence" that forces him fatalistically to acquiesce in the inherited customs of an older culture. It is this submissive aspect, moreover, that the imitative form of *Pierre* itself implicitly endorses.

One of the structural paradoxes of Melville's literary career, then, is that his sense of originality can construct itself only through various forms of deviance, where the author's styles of idiosyncratic transgression are pushed up against the institutional constraints of cultural stability and the continuities of canonical expression. Melville's most overt treatment of American experience as intertextual process occurs in his three diptychs, linked pairs of short stories, that directly compare particular scenes in Britain and the United States. "Poor Man's Pudding and Rich Man's Crumbs" juxtaposes the conditions of the "native American poor" with a description of how peasants fare under the system of aristocratic patronage in England, and "The Two Temples" compares Grace Church in New York City with the more worldly rituals of a London theater.[51] In the best-known of these diptychs, "The Paradise of Bachelors and the Tartarus of Maids," Melville constructs elaborate parallels between the Inns of Court in London, where bachelors in the legal profession enjoy rich feasts, and a snowy hamlet in New England, where "blank-looking girls" work at the paper mills (328). The comparative method here works through contrast, of course, but this contrast depends on prior analogies, as the narrator himself acknowledges: "Though the two objects did by no means completely correspond, yet this partial inadequacy but served to tinge the similitude not less with the vividness than the disorder of a dream" (326). Hence this juxtaposition becomes almost surreal, a mode of "inverted similitude" (327), where conceptual matrices of heaven and hell are superimposed on two quite different sets of circumstances, linked only by the accident of gender exclusivity. Furthermore, the image of these girls "all blankly folding blank paper" (328) seems to hint, in Melville's typically enigmatic fashion, at some kind of vacancy underlying these analogical designs of reduplication. While cognizant of the arbitrary nature of his "folding" or comparative method, the author nevertheless foregrounds such metaphorical construction of syntactic parallels as the condition of all knowledge.

"Poor Man's Pudding and Rich Man's Crumbs" extends this strategy of intertextuality into a more specifically political realm. Taking refuge in the "constitutionally damp" (292) house of the Coulters, representatives of the "native American poor" (296), the narrator notes that his countrymen "never lose their delicacy or pride; hence, though unreduced to the physical degradation of the European pauper, they yet suffer more in mind than the poor of any other people in the world" (296). Again, the story's thematic resonance turns on the intersections of similarity and difference: the narrator comments on how the Coulters' particular misery derives from their "keenest appreciation of the smarting distinction" between an American "ideal of universal equality and their grind-stone experience of the practical misery and infamy of poverty." The irony is, as he goes on to record, that the fact of such misery "ever has been, and ever will be, precisely the same in India, England, and America" (296). Although these material conditions resemble each other across continents, the interpretations of such conditions do not, and it is in the deviations from such parallelisms that we find the significance of Melville's comparative idiom. "Rich Man's Crumbs," the companion piece to "Poor Man's Pudding," shows how the poor live under the English system of aristocratic patronage, and it extends this analogical method outward still further by elaborating a simile between the London masses and "a mob of cannibals on some pagan beach" (298).

This "mob of cannibals" echoes the primitivist dimensions that appear frequently in the Pacific narratives of the 1840s, such as *Typee* and *Omoo*. Geoffrey Sanborn has written of how Melville's images of cannibals are used reflexively in these early works to signify what Western humanity is not: "Cannibalism is in this sense constitutive of humanity. Without the presence of some such image of inhumanity, humanity could never be anything more than a notion, an endlessly extensive and purely contentless act."[52] A similar logic can be applied to the author's equation of cannibals and Londoners in "Poor Man's Pudding and Rich Man's Crumbs": impoverished Americans, with their "delicacy" and "pride," will at least never be reduced to the level of English savages. As Sanborn goes on to observe, however, this sign of the cannibal in Melville's work is never uncomplicated, because it implies the imposition of "false names" on indigenous others by an estranged observer.[53] Just as the "cannibalism" that defines American humanity can itself be seen as a theatrical phenomenon, so the view of England that, by a reverse projection, helps to elucidate American national identity can itself be seen as a performative charade. In Melville, cross-cultural comparisons are forged through a series of textual regressions, where the reader is transported analogically from one society to the next. Such comparisons do not involve stable oppositions, however, but rather a series of mutually reflecting signs, two-way mirrors, where each side of the equation is contravened as well as constituted by its opposite.

This performative dimension makes it especially apt that the third of these diptychs, "The Two Temples," should play off Grace Church in New York City against a London theater where "the stately Macready" (311) is acting the part of Cardinal Richelieu. The phrase "the transatlantic temple" is applied to both of these edifices (309, 314), and the twinning of these institutions is worked out on a formal as much as a thematic level. Approaching the London theater, Melville's narrator records how it "was like emerging upon the green enclosure surrounding some Cathedral church, where sanctity makes all things still" (311). Through another process of comparison, the theater is represented as a house of glass where Macready's posture as a "mimic priest," self-consciously acting the part of Richelieu, is mirrored in the "rosy reflexes of these stained walls and gorgeous galleries" (315) that make up the theater's architecture. Reflexivity and transformation inform every aspect of the narrator's experience in this London emporium; he even meets a down-at-heel boy who, in honor of the fact that his "dad" has "gone to Yankee-land, a seekin' of his fortin'," stands the narrator a drink, thus proving how, in true fairy-tale fashion, a "ragged boy may be a prince-like benefactor" (314). Such magical transfigurations are contrasted with the more repressive atmosphere of Grace Church, where the protagonist is apprehended as a "lawless violator" (309) for infiltrating the precincts of this religious establishment.

All of these diptychs, turning on an axis of similitude and difference, represent five-finger exercises for Melville's major theme of the analogical interaction between British and American cultures. But the most elaborate consideration of how national identities become "snarled" occurs in *Israel Potter* (1855), where Melville takes a young American sailor imprisoned by the British during the War of Independence and shows how the calamities that befall him not only confuse his personal identity but also undermine the very notion of a sovereign state. After his capture, Israel is taken to England, where he finds himself so "metamorphosed . . . in all outward things, that few suspected him of being any other than an Englishman."[54] Subsequently, he meets up in Paris with Benjamin Franklin, who talks of employing Israel on a spying mission but then double-crosses and abandons his compatriot. As a cosmopolitan figure from the skeptical world of the Enlightenment, Franklin is portrayed as acting coolly toward Israel's more naïve and romantic involvement with his native land. Israel then establishes himself as quartermaster aboard Captain Paul Jones's American warship, which engages in confused conflict with an English vessel, the *Serapis*: "Never was there a fight so snarled. The intricacy of those incidents which defy the narrator's extrication, is not ill figured in that bewildering intertanglement of all the yards and anchors of the two ships, which confounded them for the time in one chaos of devastation" (120). As these two ships find themselves "manoeuvering and chasseing to each other like partners in a cotillon" (124), Israel makes "a rush for the stranger's deck" (132), thinking he will be followed by others from the American vessel. In the melee, however, the American *Ariel* departs, leaving Israel stranded once more among the English and forced to resume his role as an impostor.

According to F. O. Matthiessen, Melville set out in *Israel Potter* "to portray the tragedy of exile," with the novel implying "how much Melville had reflected on the American character."[55] But the tragedy here, if there is one, consists in the flimsiness of this abstract idea of "American character" that Israel clings to. In this narrative, the inchoate nature of the naval battle, in which "Israel is Sailor under Two Flags, and in Three Ships, and All in One Night" (85), reflects the muddled and arbitrary status of national identity and of patriotic allegiance more generally. Though the hero remains nostalgic for his homeland, Melville's novel also implies how much Israel's mental images are generated by simple sentimentality as he becomes "bewitched by the mirage of vapors" (165) accumulating around his dreams of America. In this light, all imagined associations with particular places or countries come to seem like romantic illusions. Working in his later years as a brickmaker in London, Israel yearns for the "agile mists" climbing the "purple peaks" (165) of his old New England home, and he paints to himself "scenes of nestling happiness and plenty, in which the lowliest shared" (166). But he also unmasks his own pastoral fantasies by coming to reflect on how slavery, considered in the term's broadest sense, should be considered a universal rather than a merely local or political phenomenon:

> Sometimes, lading out his dough, Israel could not but bethink him of what seemed enigmatic in his fate. He whom love of country made a hater of her foes—the foreigners among whom he was now thrown—he who, a soldier and sailor, had joined to kill, burn and destroy both them and theirs—here he was at last, serving that very people as a slave, better succeeding in making their bricks than firing their ships. . . . Poor Israel! well-named—bondsman in the English Egypt. But he drowned the thought by still more recklessly spattering with his ladle: "What signifies who we be, or where we are, or what we do?" Slap-dash! "Kings as clowns are codgers—who ain't a nobody?" Splash! "All is vanity and clay." (157)

Israel's plaintive "who ain't a nobody?" echoes Ishmael's famous "who aint a slave?" three years earlier. According to Carolyn L. Karcher, *Israel Potter* signifies how "questions of national identity and patriotism that loomed so large at the outset appear utterly irrelevant in the face of the desperate plight Israel shares with the English working class."[56] Wherever he goes, and whichever country he affiliates himself with, Israel cannot seem to escape the condition of thralldom. Israel's predicament is given metaphorical expression by an incident at Falmouth, on the South Coast of England, when he is recognized by an American, Sergeant Singles, who threatens to expose him as a traitor to both the English and the American cause. At this moment, the hapless exile finds himself "doubly hunted by the thought, that whether as an Englishman, or whether as an American, he would, if caught, be now equally subject to enslavement" (152). Again, this perplexing situation functions as a microcosm of the novel's wider pattern, where the whole idea of loyalty to a particular nation becomes hopelessly "snarled," lost in "bewildering intertanglement" (120).

One notion that becomes increasingly significant in Melville's later writing, then, is that of imposture or masquerade. This idea forms the basis for the "shadowy tableau" of "Benito Cereno," also published in 1855, where the representation of slavery in terms of self-conscious acting, role playing, and disguise works to defamiliarize that cultural institution, making it appear a caricature of itself and therefore reversible.[57] On the side of Captain Delano's ship in "Benito Cereno" there hangs a "shield-like stern-piece" comprising "a dark satyr in a mask, holding his foot on the prostrate neck of a writhing figure, likewise masked" (49). Such masks may connote the more impersonal aspects of power struggles in the ubiquitous interchanges of slavery, but they also imply the ways power seeks to mask or efface itself, a notion that becomes particularly obvious toward the end of this narrative. Such notions of masking have been associated by Louise J. Kaplan with modes of psychological perversion, where a series of false façades problematizes the boundaries between external demeanor and internal consciousness, ensuring that "nothing is ever as it first seems to be."[58] For Kaplan, the maneuvers of masquerade involve a dislocation of fixed reference, with the more customary teleologies of moral meaning held in suspension. From this point of view, part of Melville's challenge to Victorian cultural institutions involves a transformation of established social assumptions into elaborate masquerades, where authority is constituted through fetishistic paraphernalia or some inward, self-gratifying perversion rather than according to any coherent ethical imperative or metaphysical sanction. By shifting attention from the signified to the signifier, Melville extends his image of the masquerade into a disconcertingly political realm, reconstituting American culture, in the broadest sense of that term, within an aesthetic framework.

Jonathan Arac emphasizes how Melville, like Hawthorne, was developing at this time a theory of art and literature as being qualitatively different from the more mechanistic routines of the social realm. In this new romantic idiom, says Arac, the ability of the imagination to reconfigure and reorder material contexts was considered paramount.[59] Yet, I would argue that this aesthetic capacity in Melville never degenerates into rarefied transcendence or escapism, because the author's textual personae are continually involved in intertextual engagements that open up the prospect of differences, radical alterity, between American and British cultures. In Melville's eyes, the genius of American literature lies in its belatedness, its lack of originality or authenticity, its swerving away from the traditions of English literature. Consequently, the subversive qualities of the American idiom involve the ways it parodies or intertextually revises those cultural expectations associated with the British heritage. American literature, in other words, aestheticizes British literature, works to disenfranchise its moral underpinnings, while turning its conventions into forms of elaborate masquerade; consequently, British literature is made different by the advent of American culture, which opens up an alternative agenda, a world elsewhere. Similarly, by a reciprocal movement, this intertextual relationship with the Old World serves to aestheticize American culture itself, to reconceive social and political institutions in the United States as fluid and even chimerical phenomena, informed by the lights of the imagination rather than according to any kind of empirical or scientific knowledge. In this way, Melville's comparative style works to justify his aesthetic expenditures; it is these processes of cross-cultural mirroring that most revealingly backlight the strange and artificial masks endemic to any given set of social customs.

Masking again provides a subtitle for Melville's last full-length novel, *The Confidence-Man: His Masquerade* (1857), where the protagonist assumes a chameleonic series of disguises designed to ensnare gullible passengers on a Mississippi steamboat. When *The Confidence-Man* is read as an American national narrative, this quality of mutability tends to become related either to the frontier spirit of the American West or to a protean quality often claimed to be inherent in the tradition of the American novel; R. W. B. Lewis, for instance, linked Melville's protagonist with the individualistic heroes of Mark Twain, Ralph Ellison, and John Barth in the way they all resist traditional social hierarchies through their unfixed, protoplasmic aspects.[60] *The Confidence-Man* is, however, deliberately global rather than just regional or national in its orientation, with its metaphors always tending toward the universalist. To take just a couple of examples of this:

> The man in gray revealed a spirit of benevolence which, mindful of the millennial promise, had gone abroad over all the countries of the globe.

> Polite boys or saucy boys, white boys or black boys, smart boys or lazy boys, Caucasian boys or Mongol boys—all are rascals.[61]

Such abstracting impulses typify the way Melville's novel moves ascetically to strip away established social categories and forms of recognition. The focus modulates from the mannered to the primitivist, as when the narrator recounts the story of how "a grave American savan" at an evening party in London found himself "in a corner with the jackanapes," only to find subsequently "that the jackanapes was almost as great a savan as himself, being no less a personage than Sir Humphrey Davy" (64). This process of misrecognition works in two ways: the illustrious personage of Sir Humphrey is ironically reduced to a monkey-like figure, at the same time as the intellectual preconceptions and misperceptions of the "American savan" himself are made apparent. Throughout Melville's writing, there is a tendency to see the skull beneath the skin, as it were, the animalistic contours underlying the well-padded human frame. But this continual doubleness of perspective leads to a slippage in the act of identification, a slippage predicated in this book on the rhetoric of comparison, whereby objects are always explained in terms of already existing categories. Such cultural translations are exposed repeatedly as a mode of linguistic colonization often verging on absurdity: "When the duck-billed beaver of Australia was first brought stuffed to England, the naturalists, appealing to their classification, maintained that there was, in reality, no such creature; the bill in the specimen must needs be, in some way, artificially stuck on" (70).

This radical interrogation of the process of naming carries important implications for *The Confidence-Man*'s critique of American imperialism. "Indian hating" is described here as a form of "metaphysics" (144), a prejudice that the backwoodsman imagines to be "not wholly without the efficacy of a devout sentiment" (155). Like a self-reliant transcendentalist, the American backwoodsman convinces himself that divine nature itself will second and sanction his rapacious instinct: "nature all around him by her solitudes wooing or bidding him muse upon this matter . . . taking counsel with the elements, he comes to his resolution" (149). One purpose of Melville's novel, then, is to disrupt the tautological pattern whereby the narratives of American nationalism, Manifest Destiny, and metaphysical idealism work to reflect and validate each other. Rather than allowing these discourses simply to intersect analogically with each other to generate an organic vision of "American" identity, Melville's structural irony leaves them as stranded or disjointed signifiers that cumulatively hollow out the institutional rhetoric of nationalism. Demystification is one of *The Confidence-Man*'s crucial themes, and the various references throughout the book to exponents of a *via negativa*— La Trappe, Loyola, Augustine—reemphasize this virtualizing dimension. Melville's fictional travelers down the Mississippi River are also compared early in the narrative to pilgrims—"Chaucer's Canterbury pilgrims, or those oriental ones crossing the Red Sea towards Mecca in the festival month" (9)—and this not only illustrates the book's transnational inclinations but also anticipates the direction of *Clarel*, Melville's long poem about a pilgrimage to the Holy Land. Although this epic work was not published until 1876, nineteen years after *The Confidence-Man*, Melville was actually gathering material for *Clarel* in his own extended journey through the Middle East at the very time *The Confidence-Man* was going through the press, and there is more continuity between his last novel and his most ambitious poem than is often thought.

So much Melville criticism continues to be focused on his fiction of the 1840s and 1850s that it is sometimes difficult to remember how assiduously he kept reading and writing up until his death in 1891. One author we know Melville did study conscientiously after 1860 was Matthew Arnold: he bought Arnold's *Poems* in 1862, *Essays in Criticism* in 1869, *New Poems* in 1871, and *Culture and Anarchy* in 1883.[62] Arnold believed that culture should be guided by "Aristotle's profound observation that the superiority of poetry over history consists in its possessing a higher truth and a higher seriousness," and this doctrine of poetry becoming a substitute for religion in a faithless world would have struck a chord with Melville, particularly as he began to turn his own energies toward poetry rather than prose fiction.[63] Like Arnold, Melville saw poetry as an art dedicated not just to aestheticism in the narrow or decorative sense, but to aestheticism as embodying the highest form of philosophical truth. One poem by Arnold whose title Melville triple-checked in his own copy is "Austerity of Poetry," where Arnold describes the Muse as a "bride," but a woman whose ultimate value lies beneath her "sparkling" surface:

> Fair was the bride, and on her front did glow
> Youth like a star; and what to youth belong—
> Gay raiment, sparkling gauds, elation strong—
> A prop gave way! crash fell a platform! lo,
>
> 'Mid struggling sufferers, hurt to death, she lay!
> Shuddering, they drew her garments off—and found
> A robe of sackcloth next the smooth, white skin.
>
> Such poets, is your bride, the Muse! young, gay,
> Radiant, adorned outside; a hidden ground
> Of thought and of austerity within.[64]

*Clarel* itself shares this pietistic vision of an austere truth located "within." Melville's narrative chronicles a pilgrimage to the Holy Land by a variety of characters intent on deciphering spiritual mysteries that might lie hidden behind the terrestrial veil. Being agnostics who shared the late nineteenth-century obsession with the problematic status of divinity in an age of Darwinian science, both Arnold and Melville were keen to explore the functioning of religions across different cultures and mythologies.[65] As a comparative study, *Clarel* exemplifies the transnational method most characteristic of Melville's later style, uprooting its American heroes from their familiar territory and displacing them into the world of the Levant, where, as one of them puts it, "travel teaches much that's strange."[66] *Clarel* is thus a hybrid epic in more senses than one, as it negotiates the borders of faith and doubt, art and religion, America and the Middle East.

At the same time, much of the black humor that pervades *Clarel* derives precisely from its inversion of categories, its displacement of religion from a metaphysical into a heterodox or aestheticized phenomenon. The concept of "perversion" is often evoked here in its characteristically nineteenth-century sense of theological heresy; Rolfe, for instance, contemplates the "sad perversion" of the "Franciscan retinue," the dissipation of "Assisi's saint" into "Clouds of myth" (432–33). Similarly, when blithe Anglican cleric Derwent tells the American pilgrim Rolfe that he admires a Greek cross because "it has grace," the Englishman receives a dusty answer: " 'Attic! I like it. And do you?' / 'Better I'd like it, were it true' " (332). In Derwent's eyes, the idea of "grace" has slipped from a religious principle into a merely agreeable, "graceful" social and aesthetic custom. By contrast, the harsh, uncompromising aspects of Melville's epic poem signify his tortuous attempts to plumb other depths: "Alas, too deep you dive," says Derwent to Clarel a little later (347), echoing in reverse a remark Melville himself made back in 1849 in approbation of Emerson: "I love all men who *dive*."[67] Many critics have commented on *Clarel*'s "gnarled, and rugged" diction (Newton Arvin), the way its "ungainliness and irregularity in metre, rhythm, and stanzaic form" seem to be "deliberately sought" (Andrew Hook); and all this supports what Robert Penn Warren described as the "analytic" and "dialectic" qualities of the poem, its willingness to set unresolved contraries—faith and doubt, art and religion—against each other, rather than attempting, like Whitman, to resolve them into a unifying or "synthetic" vision.[68]

We know that Melville was reading Arnold's "Empedocles on Etna" while he was writing *Clarel*, and in his own copy of Arnold's *Poems* he marked heavily that section of the preface where Arnold justified excluding this poem from the 1853 edition of his works.[69] At the end of "Empedocles on Etna," the hero finds himself so overcome by "wrath and gloom" that he finds no alternative other than to jump into the volcano. Arnold, though, later came to think this ending unacceptable because it was one of "those in which the suffering finds no vent in action; in which a continuous state of mental distress is prolonged, unrelieved by incident, hope, or resistance; in which there is everything to be endured, nothing to be done."[70] This act of self-censorship can be seen as part of Arnold's conscious attempt to keep his work within the boundaries of Victorian society; this was not just for personal gain, but because he saw it as the responsibility of the intellectual at some level to guide and articulate the common values of society rather than just expressing the anguish of a solipsistic self. In *Clarel*, Mortmain, "the splenetic Swede" (286), shares some of Empedocles's misanthropic characteristics, but in general terms Melville was deeply ambivalent about what he described, in an 1885 letter, as this "prudential worldly element, wherewithall Mr. Arnold has conciliated the conventionalists."[71] From one angle, as Walter E. Bezanson observed, Melville seems to have little interest in the more optimistic, ebullient traits of Arnold's persona, his concern with public uplift and with the classical reconciliation of antagonistic forces; indeed, as Bezanson remarked, despite his heavy annotations of Arnold's verse Melville noticeably chose to ignore Arnold's "triumphant conclusions."[72] But on the other hand, Melville himself is "preponderantly an objective and dramatic poet," as Richard Harter Fogle argued, whose stylistic and thematic emphasis in *Clarel* is not "fully lyrical and subjective" but falls rather on "public objects, situations, and ideas."[73] Indeed, William C. Spengemann has suggested that it may be this very absence of an obviously recognizable authorial "personality" in Melville's poetry that has helped to alienate American readers from a work like *Clarel*. Unlike Whitman or Dickinson, Melville declines to provide the reader with a self-portrait, to project a poetic persona in a characteristically American romantic manner.[74]

The point here is that it would be an oversimplification to imply that Melville simply sought to transcend Arnold's neoclassical forms in the name of an uncompromising quest for artistic and metaphysical truth.

Rather, Melville imitates Arnold's impersonal style in the way he constrains the expression of subjectivity through an idiom of emotional distance and resignation. Arnold's poem "Resignation. To Fausta" was one of Melville's particular favorites—"admirable," he called it—and *Clarel* too is imbued with a stoical sense of resignation and loss.[75] Nor is this stoicism connected merely with epistemological anxieties. There is at times in Arnold's poetry a hint of the professional civil servant that he was, as for example in "Empedocles on Etna," when the protagonist's "mind" is said to have been

> trained
> By other rules than are in vogue today—
> Whose habit of thought is fixed, who will not change.[76]

This idea of superannuation, of discovering one's training and experience to be out of place, finds an echo in *Clarel*, where the characters seem to wander around in exile from a center they can never quite attain or bring into focus. Just as Empedocles feels that his proper era has gone by, so Melville's characters find the world no longer offering them a clear sense of purpose. Imagery of circling, of "roundabout" movement (429), recurs frequently in *Clarel*, and these spatial dislocations are commensurate with a more extended rhetoric of diffusion, where time itself seems to have become the burden. In this sense, the very length of *Clarel* becomes an integral part of the work's meaning; it is partly a poem about procrastination and boredom, about the slippage of the calendar from a divine chronology into a more passive, pessimistic sense of time relentlessly passing. The teleology of time has become secularized, turned into a matter of circuitous routine, something with which both Arnold and Melville, as government bureaucrats, were all too familiar.

This failure of regeneration in *Clarel* involves a disavowal of American exceptionalism as well as a withdrawal from religious transcendence. By transplanting his American romancers to Palestine, Melville shows how they too become fatally enmeshed in a world of corruption:

> Our New World bold
> Had fain improved upon the Old;
> But the hemispheres are counterparts. (401)

The pattern here is not unlike that of Hawthorne's last novel, *The Marble Faun* (1860), where again American intellectuals are transplanted to the global epicenter of a world religion—Rome, in Hawthorne's case—so that their Puritan consciousness can be examined within a larger comparative perspective. In this sense, Melville, like Hawthorne, tends to be interested in dialogues of one kind or another, with ways in which foreign categories impact on the domestic and familiar. "Hawthorne and His Mosses" is often cited as proof of Melville's admiration of Hawthorne's "mystical blackness," but what Melville admires more specifically is Hawthorne's capacity subtly to interweave "lights and shades," so that the two are played off tantalizingly against each other: "The Indian-summer sunlight on the hither side of Hawthorne's soul, the other side—like the dark half of the physical sphere—is shrouded in a blackness, ten times black. But this darkness but gives more effect to the evermoving dawn, that forever advances through it, and circumnavigates his world."[77]

For Melville, then, Hawthorne was both a compeer and an alter ego, a writer from a similar situation addressing similar concerns in a more socially conventional way. The metaphysical anxieties that manifest themselves overtly in Melville's texts can be seen to emerge much more obliquely in Hawthorne's. What Hawthorne was to Melville's early works, Arnold was to his later: a kindred intellectual spirit whose work he admired, but an author whose widespread social respectability (and, in Arnold's case, indeed, fame) derived partly from his refusal ultimately to undermine the coherence of his literary texts in accordance with his intuitions of skepticism. Arnold himself seems to have ignored Melville completely, although he did meet Hawthorne and described his "literary talent" as "of the first order, the finest, I think, which America has yet produced."[78] It is, perhaps, not surprising that Arnold should have made this judgment on Hawthorne, bearing in mind their mutual interests in the accommodation of Christian traditions to a national culture. One significant aspect of Melville's conception of masquerade, however, is the way it works explicitly to foreground disjunctions between social convention and the arbitrary nature of authority, disjunctions that the more demure narratives of Hawthorne and Arnold prefer to keep implicit and understated.

The culmination of these cross-cultural perspectives in the guise of masquerade manifests itself in *Billy Budd*, Melville's last work, and a narrative whose specific engagement with British culture has not been sufficiently recognized. Like *Clarel, Billy Budd* can best be understood as a transnational narrative whose foreign milieu illuminates by reversal the parameters of Melville's own national situation. All of the main characters in this story are English, and, as the long historical prologue makes clear, the context for this tale is the revolutionary climate of the late eighteenth century. Billy Budd finds himself transferred symbolically from America to Britain, from a ship called the *Rights-of-Man* to one by the name of *Bellipotent*, whose martial echo recalls King Bello, the allegorical King of England in Melville's *Mardi* some forty years earlier. Captain Vere's own name, meanwhile, is appropriated from Andrew Marvell's poem "Upon Appleton House," a panegyric to the English country house:

> Within this sober frame expect
> Work of no foreign architect . . .
> But all things are composed here
> Like Nature, orderly and near . . .
> This 'tis to have been from the first
> In a domestic heaven nursed,
> Under the discipline severe
> Of Fairfax, and the starry Vere.[79]

In keeping with this xenophobic outlook ("no foreign architect"), Melville's Captain Vere is said to be deeply perturbed about "the disruption of forms going on across the Channel," and he sees in the Nore Mutiny which threatened the British Navy in 1797 a disturbing memento of the French Revolution, akin to "the distempering irruption of contagious fever in a frame constitutionally sound."[80]

Several critics have taken the fictional narrative that unfolds within this framework to indicate the growing conservatism of Melville's later years, his discomfort with the violence that accompanies insurrection, his preference for the stable society advocated by Edmund Burke rather than the doctrine of individual rights put forward by Thomas Paine. Many of the earlier critical essays on *Billy Budd*, in fact, address the imponderable question of whether Vere was right to hang Billy, whether the tale should be seen as a reactionary endorsement of legal formalism or a liberal critique of its authoritarian assumptions. As Brook Thomas observes, however, this question has been framed in the wrong way. Rather than seeing Vere as tragic hero or nefarious hypocrite, it makes more sense to consider the internal logic through which different systems of government operate, and the ways the structural indeterminacy of Melville's narrative exposes law as an ambiguous and historically contingent process.[81] Justice in *Billy Budd* is acted out according to ideological directives; it does not reflect abstract or divine truths. This is why the story is subtitled *An Inside Narrative*: it deliberately plays with discrepancies between outward appearance and inward psychology, between the façades of authority Captain Vere must maintain and the subterranean tensions that constitute "the inner life of one particular ship" (54). Hence, of course, the motif of secrecy and concealment that runs through this narrative. Claggart's "ferreting genius," obviously enough, involves an ability to manipulate "wires of underground influence" (67), but the "secret currency" (65) circulating around Claggart is mirrored and validated by a sequence of images that envisions the ship's world as a multilayered and opaque phenomenon. Describing "the complicated gun-deck life, which like every other form of life has its secret mines and dubious side" (93), the narrator talks of the ship's "levels" as "so like the tiered galleries in a coal mine" (122), where what happens on one level is not necessarily evident to those on another plane. "War looks but to the frontage, the appearance," remarks Vere a little earlier (112), thereby implying those events behind the scenes to which he turns a British naval commander's highly trained blind eye.

There are several levels on which these tensions between blindness and insight in *Billy Budd* operate. The most obvious of these latent discourses involves repressed sexuality. Sexual attraction here becomes fictionally refracted into forms of disciplinary authority, with Billy perfectly cast in the role of masochistic innocent, not only unable to fathom Claggart's motives but even incapable of responding vocally to his charges; instead, Billy can only stand helpless "like one impaled and gagged" (98).[82] Taking up these disjunctions between "frontage" and rear sight, Eve Kosofsky Sedgwick's reading of *Billy Budd* projects this "queer" interpretation into the domain of Captain Vere's own relationship with the young hero, pointing out how "Vere's supposedly impartial motivations toward Billy Budd are also founded on a Claggart-like partiality as against which, however, they as well are imperiously counterpoised."[83] At his first sight of Billy, for instance, the Captain "had congratulated Lieutenant Ratcliffe upon his good fortune in lighting on such a fine specimen of the genus homo, who in the nude might have posed for a statue of young Adam before the Fall" (94); he subsequently recommends to the executive officer that Billy be promoted "to a place that would more frequently bring him under his own observation, namely, the captaincy of the mizzentop, replacing there in the starboard watch a man not so young whom partly for that reason he deemed less fitted for the post" (95). The rhetorical tone here strategically reflects the duplicitous cast of Melville's narrative, where eminently respectable façades cover, but can never quite conceal, more compulsive motivations.

This is why the court-martial and eventual execution of Billy are appropriately cast as elaborate theatrical performances. Vere takes care at the trial to position himself visibly above the other officers, and he skillfully suppresses his own affective involvement as Billy is publicly hanged, a moment at which the Captain's phallogocentric authority is consummated: he "stood erectly rigid as a musket in the ship-armorer's rack" (124). Vere's admitted rationale—to others, and perhaps to himself—is that he represents no more than an agent of that "martial law operating through us" (110), the impersonal system of justice through which good order is maintained in the British Navy. Yet Melville's text involves a reappraisal of this legal framework according to what is described in Chapter 11 as a kind of negative Calvinist theology, negative in the sense that it involves a Calvinist cultural urge to rip the protective veil off established social hierarchies, even if the specifically religious justifications for such iconoclasm are no longer seen as tenable: "In a list of definitions included in the authentic translation of Plato, a list attributed to him, occurs this: 'Natural Depravity: a depravity according to nature,' a definition which, though savoring of Calvinism, by no means involves Calvin's dogma as to total mankind. Evidently its intent makes it applicable but to individuals. . . . Civilization, especially if of the austerer sort, is auspicious to it. It folds itself in the mantle of respectability. It has certain negative virtues serving as silent auxiliaries" (75–76). Throughout this story, various kinds of "depravity" fold themselves "in the mantle of respectability," creating a narrative structure that oscillates uneasily between a familiar logic of social discourse and the more impenetrable conditions of absence and silence.

This negative Calvinism, along with the sexual subtexts, has the effect of defamiliarizing and radically undermining the fictions of British justice that *Billy Budd* recounts. Writing under the austere influence of Schopenhauer, his favorite philosopher during the last decade of his life, Melville in this story represents British justice as a kind of masquerade, an affective charade that manages to invest itself with an idea of impersonal truth. In a tone more fatalistic than oppositional, he implies that the visible emblems and external rituals of this culture depend on a suppression of libidinal investments and psychopathological forms of deviance, as well as on a positivistic rejection of the more obscure enigmas of metaphysical inquiry. *Billy Budd*, in fact, takes British culture and demystifies its assumptions in the light of American cultural perspectives. As such, it makes a fitting conclusion to a literary career in which Melville was continually reconfiguring British models within an American idiom. The multiple reports that conclude *Billy Budd*—the newspaper account in *News from the Mediterranean*, the elegiac poem from the foretopman—once again operate to dislocate the central narrative, to reposition it within the ironic framework of what Barbara Johnson calls the text's "snowballing of tale-telling."[84] It is noticeable that *News from the Mediterranean*, a British publication, circulates the fiction that Billy Budd was a foreigner: "Though mustered into the service under an English name the assassin was no Englishman, but one of those aliens adopting English cognomens." Claggart, by contrast, is represented as a loyal servant of His Majesty, thereby refuting, "if refutation were needed, that peevish saying attributed to the late Dr. Johnson, that patriotism is the last refuge of a scoundrel" (130). In this conventional kind of reportage, insurrection becomes associated automatically with what is foreign or alien. Melville's skill, though, lies in framing the plot of this novel within a matrix of estrangement, holding up the customs of English authority to the dark glass of comparative consciousness.

This is not to suggest that such comparative consciousness locates issues of "imperial" authority simply within an English context, any more than it associates the idea of America exclusively with aspects of "private conscience" (111). Indeed, Chapter 21 of *Billy Budd* mentions the similar case of "the U.S. brig-of-war *Somers*," where the American Captain Mackenzie put down a prankish rebellion led by Philip Spencer, son of the U.S. Secretary of War. Spencer was hanged in accordance with what is described here as "the so-called Articles of War, Articles modeled upon the English Mutiny Act" (113). There is a longer discussion of this affair in *White-Jacket*, but Melville's comparative method is designed not just to contrast reified notions of different national situations but to demonstrate how they complicate and interpenetrate each other's local autonomy and identity. In this instance, the author indicates how draconian methods of martial law found their way into the American Navy through the influence of English models. Hence the projection of *Billy Budd* into a British milieu fulfills one of the traditional responsibilities of comparative literary perspectives: to shed light back on the text's culture of origin. By reconstructing an imaginary version of British authority, Melville creates a virtual space to reflect on the growth and development of American culture.

The fact that Melville has become canonized as an advocate of American literary nationalism, celebrated for his work of the mid–nineteenth century and the anti-British sentiments expressed in "Hawthorne and His Mosses," represents one of the anomalies of cultural history. Undoubtedly Melville enjoyed a checkered relationship with the English public; though his work was first published in Britain, none of his books after *The Confidence-Man* were to find an English publisher. Yet, in the later and relatively anonymous part of his career, he was frequently accorded a more sympathetic public in Britain than in America. In the final years of his life, he maintained a correspondence with English men of letters such as W. Clark Russell, Henry Salt, and James Billson, whose openness and receptivity to the author's narrative designs foreshadowed the direction of the "Melville Revival" that was to become widespread in the early twentieth century. In addition, of course, Melville himself read voluminously in English literature, swimming through libraries and sailing through oceans like his most famous fictional narrator, and one consistent strand throughout his work is the desire to play off British and American idioms against each other, thereby relativizing the assumptions of both national cultures. Melville is often cast as someone who sought to escape from mundane social concerns into the more rarefied realms of art, but the power of his imaginative genius lies in its capacity radically to estrange established conventions, to re-create ethical and political ideas within an aesthetic mode.

This is the source of Melville's peculiar stylistic opacity and elusiveness, a quality remarked on by Andrew Delbanco, among others. However, it is not that Melville, as an exemplar of "classic American writing," simply transcends political ideas, nor even that he continues to view such transcendence as "a haunting possibility"; rather, his multifaceted prose takes pleasure in exploiting the residual forces of religion and nationalism, in negative or inverted forms, to contravene received idioms.[85] To say that Melville's "slithery" texts always seem to slide out from under the confining circle of American cultural and political narratives is not to imply the irrelevance of ideology to his work.[86] Rather, Melville's ideology metamorphoses itself into an aesthetic, virtual construction, susceptible of reversal, just as his aesthetics themselves are inflected by ideological concerns. To interrupt that circular process whereby Melville's fictions are understood in terms of their incarnation of a "classic" tradition of American writing is to acknowledge how the author's later work, in particular, reflects back on and distances itself from the agendas of cultural nationalism within which his reputation has so often been ensnared. Melville's cerebral voyages to other lands effectively complicated his outlook on American domestic politics, particularly the slavery issue. His texts tend not to be pliant receptacles for any kind of millennial rhetoric of freedom, neither in its nineteenth-century variants of Manifest Destiny or abolitionism, nor in relation to twentieth-century discourses of emancipation inflected by race and gender. From a British perspective, similarly, Melville's "riotously perverse and cross-running seas" effectively fragment established conventions into a duplicitous world of reflection, where they come to appear disconcertingly bizarre and at the same time oddly familiar, as in some crazy-mirror hall. Just as *Pierre* involves an unbalanced parody of the English genre of feudal property and familial propriety, so *Billy Budd* reimagines British justice as a self-gratifying phenomenon, an objectification of imaginative desires rather than a statement of more substantial truths.

Melville, then, uses a transatlantic mirror to virtualize both British and American cultures, to empty out their substantive dogmas and practices while reflecting, as through a glass darkly, their inherited forms and assumptions. Melville was adept at disorienting social orthodoxies, in catching cultures off-balance, as it were; thus it is hardly surprising that Joseph Conrad, a typically conservative convert to English values, should have criticized *Moby-Dick* for having "not a single sincere line in the 3 vols of it."[87] The author's ultimate achievement, however, was to reject separatisms and homologies of all kinds, and to forge a style of comparative cosmopolitanism where different cultures interact analogically with each other without ever being collapsed into the objects of some synthesized or monocular vision. In *Moby-Dick*, Ishmael records that the two eyes of the whale are so far apart that it "must see one distinct picture on this side, and another distinct picture on that side" (330), and he goes on to record his admiration for the "comprehensive, combining, and subtle" brain of the whale which enables it to "examine two distinct prospects" simultaneously (331). It is an image that epitomizes Melville's traversal of cultural space across the North Atlantic divide, space intersected by the "snarled" and intertwined cables of similarity and difference.

## 4

## "Changed and Queer":
## Henry James and the Surrealization
## of America

The surrealist movement has traditionally been understood as a marginal and recondite phenomenon, a footnote to the more prestigious modernist movements in the arts that flourished in the first four decades of the twentieth century. In the United States, particularly, both modernity in the more general and modernism in the more technical sense tended to connote an iconoclastic newness, a break with staid Victorian traditions. T. J. Clark has described the "purism" of modernism as involving an "emptying and sanitizing of the imagination," an escape from the superstitious inheritance of the past.[1] Devout modernizers such as the photographer Alfred Stieglitz identified the "spirit" of America both with a technological efficiency and with a transcendental significance that he and his circle believed to be associated at some profound level with the native "soil," one of the Stieglitz circle's favorite words, as Wanda Corn has remarked. This is why Stieglitz, despite admiring the provocative humor of Marcel Duchamp, thought that surrealist jeux d'esprit such as his infamous *Urinal*, exhibited at the 1913 Armory Show, could never fully encompass the utopian potential of the New World.[2] For Stieglitz, such dynamics were more fully expressed in such journals as *Camera Work* and *The Seven Arts*, or, a few years later, in classic treatises of cultural nationalism such as Waldo Frank's *Our America* (1919) and William Carlos Williams's *In the American Grain* (1925).

The formation of both American literature and American studies as academic fields of inquiry have remained heavily indebted to the models of national identity described in this modernist era. D. H. Lawrence's

*Studies in Classic American Literature* (1923), another key influence on cultural nationalism at this time, understands American culture as involving a radical simplification of aesthetic forms, along with a pastoral purification of corrupt European social values. Lawrence, like Stieglitz, conceives of a clean conceptual line joining an abstract idea to its physical embodiment, leading to a stylistic emphasis on the luminous rhetoric of allegory, in which objects become transparent to their own intellectual design. This, of course, anticipates the epistemology of American studies in its "mythic" phase, where American phenomena were thought to be endowed organically with teleological purpose; it also accounts for the widely influential nature of *Studies in Classic American Literature*, where, in the same exceptionalist way, the "classic" idiom of American writing is said to exemplify "an alien quality, which belongs to the American continent and to nowhere else."[3] Lawrence's introductory essay to this book is entitled "The Spirit of Place," and it epitomizes these associations between geographic location and cultural identity through its promotion of an archetypal modernist impulse to "purify the dialect of the tribe," as T. S. Eliot was later to describe it, to reveal a source of interiority that had become blurred and confused by the paraphernalia of gentility and social convention.[4]

The surrealists, on the other hand, focused not on interiority but on exteriority. Their concern was not so much with the "spirit" of place but with its more visible manifestations, particularly as these presented themselves in the form of random spatial juxtapositions. Philippe Soupault admired American culture for its skyscrapers and subways, its cinema and jazz, its manifestly zany and inchoate aspects; Duchamp, who moved from France to the United States in 1915, similarly praised New York City itself as "a complete work of art."[5] In structural terms, surrealist aesthetics were motivated by what Roger Shattuck has called a "principle of simultanism, in which all parts interpenetrate and interact through contrast and humorous conflict rather than by discursive logic or conventional perspective"; this emphasis on contradiction and incompatibility positioned humor itself as what Peter Nicholls calls "an antimetaphysical principle," a principle that was concerned radically to demystify what the surrealists saw as the pompous white elephants of cultural authority and tradition.[6] The legendary encounter on a dissecting table of a sewing machine and an umbrella, as visualized by Lautréamont, was extended into a structural principle of collage whose paratactic properties sought deliberately to defy rational and transcendental perspectives. Charles Altieri has written of how surrealism's emphasis on disjunction was designed to undermine the metaphysical implications of modernist idealism: by asserting the material provenance of categories that modernism characteristically preferred to represent figuratively, surrealism disavowed the idea of the creative mind as a spiritual force and instead reconceived it as a technological instrument, a mediator among what Altieri calls "incongruous surfaces and biological energies."[7]

One of the difficulties of discussing surrealism in an American context is that the movement has too often been understood exclusively through interpretations of its most prominent literary characters. There are various compelling reasons for this, among them the propensity of Maurice Nadeau, the most influential historian of surrealism, to canonize certain key figures, along with the tendency of most of the surrealists themselves to participate, ironically or otherwise, in cults of individual personality and self-promotion. These narcissistic proclivities were also bolstered by the dogmatic "manifestoes" issued periodically by André Breton and others during the 1920s. But to appraise the movement on the basis of Breton's "Manifesto of Surrealism" would be like judging modernist poetics exclusively on the basis of Eliot's 1919 essay "Tradition and the Individual Talent": it would be to place too much emphasis on a philosophical work that, although interesting in its idiosyncratic way, is narrowly conceived and far from universally relevant. More recently, scholars such as Robin Walz and James Clifford have moved away from this kind of hermetic approach and have attempted to recover what we might call a broader genealogy of surrealism. Clifford, examining surrealism from an anthropological perspective, writes of how its aesthetic forms of random juxtaposition mirror "a pervasive condition of off-centeredness" in an increasingly rootless world. Walz, meanwhile, argues that "the popular origins of surrealism have been neglected," and he is concerned to uncover the configuration of "surreal perspectives at the level of mass culture itself."[8] Walz consequently considers how the emergence of surrealist sensibilities in early twentieth-century France was shaped by formations of mass culture, popular entertainment, and technological gadgetry, all of which had the effect of dislocating the native cultural tradition, of disturbing its cherished relationship to the past. By the end of the twentieth century, surrealism had shifted into an upper-case register and had, as Walz observes, become safely institutionalized within the domain of official French culture; however, during that earlier period it was associated at a more amorphous level with the displacement of identity and with a certain incoherence in the representation of time and space. The advent of mass culture in France brought in its train a general sense of bouleversement, a mood of violent disturbance, which could be adequately mirrored only in the bizarre imaginations of those who were "surreal before the letter."[9]

This is the force of Man Ray's observation that "nobody and everybody" made Dada.[10] Dada was the anarchic forerunner to the artistic movement that subsequently became categorized as surrealism, and it even more obviously derived its manic force from an unscripted sense of iconoclasm and from the dynamics of an "esprit nouveau." The latter term was coined by Apollinaire, who in 1912 declared "machines, automobiles, bicycles, and airplanes" to be "masterpieces of the modern style."[11] A few years later, in 1917, Apollinaire also invented the term surrealism, first employing it in a program note that described Cocteau's ballet *Parade* as embodying "a kind of super-realism [sur-réalisme]."[12] *Parade* was performed on this occasion by the Russian Ballet under Serge Diaghilev, a troupe that gave many performances in London before the First World War, one of which, in April 1912, was seen by Henry James.[13] I am not trying to force a link between James and surrealism so much as to emphasize that James's twentieth-century work emerged from a cultural context that was responding with a mixture of perplexity, bravado, and resistance to the "shock of the new." One particular critique of modernism made most forcefully by Georg Lukács was its tendency to suppress processes of temporal change in the name of aspiring toward an aesthetic universalism where subjective consciousness might simply supersede the objects of history; for example, Lukács cites Henri Bergson as a modernist philosopher who went so far as to make "subjective time . . . identical with real time."[14] But for all of James's interest in these intuitive dimensions of Bergson's thought, his own writings never abjure the material world to this extent. Indeed, the idiosyncratic nature of James's oblique, off-center style derives partly from the way he represents consciousness as always, as it were, bumping into solid objects. The convoluted rhetoric that famously characterizes James's twentieth-century idiom implies a cultural landscape where relations are not direct or transparent and where frictions arise from potentially incongruous interactions between different mental and physical categories.

In this sense, James's late writing might be said implicitly to refract the conditions of a world on the edge of mass mechanization, conditions that were to form the basis of surrealist aesthetics a few years later. For example, the last novels of what F. O. Matthiessen was to call James's "major phase"—*The Wings of the Dove* (1902), *The Ambassadors* (1903), and *The Golden Bowl* (1904)—were written at the same time as the best-known works of Alfred Jarry, who is sometimes referred to today as a "pre-surrealist" writer, even though he died in 1907, well before the tenets of surrealism were identified or codified.[15] Jarry was a friend of Apollinaire, and his "pataphysical" universe, based on a world governed by exceptions rather than rules, subsequently became highly influential in surrealist circles.[16] Jarry's notion of pataphysics was inspired by a well-informed if eccentric approach to the developing physical sciences, and this manifests itself in his short novel of 1902, *Le Surmâle* (*The Super-male*), a story about a bicycling race that represents human bodies and machines as more or less interchangeable. At the beginning of *The Super-male*, the blank-faced hero, André Marcueil, takes a sardonic delight in ridiculing the traditional idea of romantic sentiments as "an impression of the soul" and in declaring the "act of love" to be "of no importance, since it can be performed indefinitely."[17] The way the sexualized human body here takes on the quality of an automaton might be seen as a correlative to the animism that is, as J. H. Matthews noted, a frequent component of surrealist imagery; in the mixed-up world of the surrealists, people assume the characteristics of inanimate objects and vice versa.[18] We find such animism prominently on display in James's *The American Scene*, an account of his return visit to the United States in 1904 and 1905 which was first published in 1907, where the New York skyscrapers are personified and start conversing among themselves. W. H. Auden in 1946 remarked that he knew no book "outside of fairy tales . . . in which things so often and so naturally become persons," and this transposition involves not just a picturesque form of anthropomorphism but the kind of "dislocative factor" that, as Matthews has suggested, was characteristic of the surrealist idiom around this time.[19]

Many of the most significant recent discussions of surrealism as an aesthetic and cultural practice have been influenced by the work of Walter Benjamin. Benjamin's 1929 essay "Surrealism: The Last Snapshot of the European Intelligentsia" describes how the revolt of Lautréamont, Apollinaire, and Rimbaud involves the dissemination of "a *profane il-*

*lumination*, a materialistic, anthropological inspiration," serving "to liquidate the sclerotic liberal-moral-humanistic ideal of freedom."[20] Benjamin's writing evoked, as Margaret Cohen has suggested, a kind of Gothic Marxism, whereby a culture's strange and marginal practices were seen as a rich field of social production and as forms of potential resistance to the established order.[21] Thus, Ross Posnock, for instance, specifically compares James to Benjamin in his discussion of what he describes, following Matthiessen, as James's fourth or "last phase": the works written between 1905 and 1913, including his prefaces to the New York edition and his autobiographies, *A Small Boy and Others* and *Notes of a Son and Brother*, as well as *The American Scene*. For Posnock, the dissonant rhythms evoked by the narrator of *The American Scene* prefigure the stance of the urban flâneur, who practices, in Benjamin's phrase, "the art of being off center," and who delights in deviations from standard forms. Indeed, Posnock talks of "James's mode of experimental flânerie in *The American Scene*," relating this to what he calls a "cosmopolitan nonidentity" shared by both James and Benjamin.[22]

Although this reading is illuminating in all kinds of ways, it does highlight also one of the more problematical aspects of Benjamin's appropriation by the American academy. Benjamin has become vulnerable not only to depoliticization, but also to being reimagined in relation to a liberal pluralism that is both historically and philosophically distant from the much more uncomfortably iconoclastic temper of his own work. For example, Posnock accommodates Benjamin's interest in paradox and heterogeneity to what he sees as James's commitment to contingency and antifoundationalism, so that *The American Scene* relapses into a version of "pragmatic fallibilism" linking Henry neatly with his brother, William James, whose lectures on pragmatism were also first published in 1907. Posnock emphasizes the Jamesian commitment to "contradictions and paradoxes" to dismantle the rarefied, formalist image of his work prevalent in the 1950s; but then he simply uses Benjamin to reinscribe James as a cultural nationalist committed to the American pragmatist project of "fluid nonidentity."[23] Formalist ambiguity may have become fallibilistic hesitancy, but the final critical product turns out to be very much the same. There is, of course, a long tradition in American criticism of appreciating James for his apparent commitment to intellectual flexibility: Ezra Pound in 1917 talked of his "life-long, unchangeable passion" for "personal liberty" and his hatred of "tyranny"; T. S. Eliot the following year made his famous comment about James's "mastery over, his baffling escape from, Ideas," and of his having "a mind so fine that no idea could violate it"; Richard Poirier, two generations later, wrote of how James's "later style was designed so that his favorites might indulge in the images and verbal exaggerations necessary to their illusion of freedom, their dream that they create the world they live in."[24] Poirier's version of Jamesian "freedom" is more cagey and provisional than that of Pound and Eliot, of course; but they all, like Posnock, cherish an image of James as an avatar of emancipation whose native genius involved the familiar American capacity for unsettling conventional categories and boundaries.

To emphasize James's commitment to an aesthetics of liberty and mobility, however, is fundamentally to romanticize his work to bring it into line with American traditions of democratic renewal. One thing Posnock's redescription of Benjaminian surrealism as ambivalence tends to occlude is surrealism's intellectual associations with the aesthetics of decadence at the end of the nineteenth century. If modernism involved an imaginative cleansing and "sanitizing" of the ghosts of the past, as Clark suggests, then surrealism, like decadence, cut the other way, testifying to the intractability of such ghosts; in decadent aesthetics, neither the corporeal human body nor the dense material of cultural traditions can so easily be dissolved.[25] This leads to the paradoxical scenario where decadent artists play ironically with categories that they are altogether unable to transcend. Just as the ludic imagination of the surrealists found itself colliding comically with an inert world of material objects, so their predecessors associated with the decadent movement envisaged a world haunted by ancestral inheritances that were not so susceptible of regeneration through the progressive forces of liberal pragmatism.

James himself had quite close contacts with this Aesthetic Movement at the end of the Victorian era. He met Oscar Wilde and Walter Pater fairly regularly during the 1880s and supported Wilde's nomination for membership of London's Savile Club in 1888, and the characterization of Gabriel Nash in James's novel *The Tragic Muse* (1890) is commonly thought to owe much to Wilde.[26] *The Tragic Muse* features a conflict between the worlds of art and public service, a conflict that speaks to the values of the Aesthetic Movement: Nick Dormer abandons his role as member of Parliament for the constituency of Harsh and also his forthcoming marriage to Julia Dallow in favor of pursuing his talents as a painter. By paralleling Nick's "perversities," as his sister calls them, with Peter Sherringham's erotic obsession with the actress Miriam Rooth, the structural function of James's text is to equate sex and art as alternatives to the bourgeois proprieties: Nick, we are told, "was conscious of a double nature; there were two men in him, quite separate, whose leading features had little in common and each of whom insisted on having an independent turn at life."[27] John Carlos Rowe has called *The Tragic Muse* a "protogay novel" because of this emphasis on a double life, and it is certainly true that it addresses implicitly the concept of "modern homosexual identity," which, as Elaine Showalter observes, was beginning to emerge in a formulated way during the 1880s.[28] Yet it is also clear that *The Tragic Muse* is not explicitly about homosexuality: as Sheldon M. Novick has remarked, James was never "out" to the general public, as we say now, in the way that Oscar Wilde and Arthur Symonds were, and in general terms he remained "a Victorian gentleman of conservative views."[29]

This is not to suggest that James's fiction is either sexless or entirely repressive in the old genteel sense. As John R. Bradley points out, given the author's own involvement with the Wilde and Symonds circles it is "inconceivable" that he could have remained unaware of his own "homosexual propensity," as Richard Ellmann delicately phrased it.[30] What it does suggest, though, is that James's concern is not with gay identity as such but rather with the sites of interaction between conventional and aberrant codes of behavior. In fact, James's work after 1890 is concerned more with the refraction than the consolidation of identities of any kind. His displacements of narrative perspective and his inclination to circle suggestively around inscrutable centers bespeak an author enamored of enigma and obliquity, seeking what he describes in the preface to *What Maisie Knew* as the "smothered rapture" of a vision whose very excitement derives from its suggestiveness and half-suppression.[31]

This is why to talk about issues of "disguise" in relation to James's stories of the 1890s such as "The Death of the Lion" and "In the Cage" can be misleading. "The Death of the Lion" came out in the first issue of *The Yellow Book*, which appeared in April 1894 and quickly attracted to itself a louche reputation, mainly due to its publication of Aubrey Beardsley's drawings. James's tale brings together the ostentatiously unworldly and the ostensibly vulgar in a teasingly uncertain combination, juxtaposing the sensibilities of reclusive literary master Neil Paraday, who "had succeeded in separating" from his wife, with the prying investigations of journalists who attempt to traduce the personality of the "lion" for their own commercial ends.[32] The world of the yellow press is portrayed here as fostering confusions about sexual identity: Dora Forbes, author of a gossip column entitled "The Other Way Round," is exposed as "the 'pen-name' of an indubitable male—he had a big red moustache" (116), and "Obsessions" is written by Guy Walsingham, who turns out to be a woman. The narrator complains of how "in the age we live in one gets lost among the genders and the pronouns" (144), but such bewilderment, rather than being merely a product of the popular press, is represented here as endemic to the whole society. Although the narrator would like to imagine a sharp antithesis between the perverse practices of the journalists and the straightforward integrity of Paraday, the burden of the tale is that there is more of an uncomfortable bond between them.

In this sense, James uses the gossip columnists in "The Death of the Lion" to signify how, within this world of mass circulation, identities of all kinds have been displaced into exteriorized realms of travesty and misrecognition, with the result that older Victorian notions of solid and consistent character have become less tenable. We might compare the representation of Paraday with that of Nick Dormer in *The Tragic Muse*, of whom we are told in the novel's 1890 version: "He only aspired to be continuous." In the 1909 New York edition, however, James made a slight but suggestive emendation, strengthening the phrase to read: "He only aspired to be decently continuous."[33] Decency was always a touchy business for James, and although he seemed a mite defensive at being associated with such a risqué enterprise as *The Yellow Book*, writing to his brother William and sister Alice that he published "The Death of the Lion" there simply "for gold and to oblige the worshipful Harland (the editor)," such alleged scruples did not prevent him publishing two more stories in the journal in July 1894 and July 1896.[34] Nor would he have been displeased with Lena Milman's essay, "A Few Notes upon Mr. James," which appeared in the October 1895 issue and which praised the formal qualities of his short fiction as a welcome antidote to those more staid triple-decker novels that represented mere "respectable monuments of British industry." For Milman, the aesthetic charm of James's tales lay precisely in their responsiveness to "elusive impressions"; rather than merely regarding a "short story as the cartoon for a possible novel," she said, James's verbal "pictures" preferred a technique of subtle indirection that eschewed the "grave moral teaching" characteristic of a Victorian temper.[35]

One way James's fiction of the 1890s anticipates the interests of the surrealists, then, is in its emphasis on split personalities. "In the Cage" (1898) represents one of the most extended treatments of this theme, with its portrayal of a post office clerk falling in love with an aristocratic man who sends telegrams that testify cryptically to his own clandestine life. Reality in this story manifests itself in the "safe sentiment" associated with the heroine's betrothed, Mr. Mudge.[36] The tale's "fantastic vision" (463), on the other hand, consists in "the queer extension of her experience, the double life" (386) through which the unnamed heroine glimpses an "alternate self" (469) who might lead a quite different life. Indeed, many of the characters in this tale seem to be endowed with alternate selves: Captain Everard enjoys a whole repertoire of false identities, and Mr. Drake, the servant who is forced to "separate" from his "loved friend" Lord Rye before the latter's marriage (491), provides a narrative counterpoint that is, as Rowe says, "explicitly homoerotic."[37] Again, though, "In the Cage" is less concerned with the identification of sexual psychology per se than with what Hugh Stevens calls the exploration of how "Victorian queer subcultures" function within a wider social and historical context.[38] For James, indeed, the most significant aspect of the Wilde trial and the other famous sexual scandals of the 1890s was the way they forced into general consciousness the idea of a disjunction between public and private selves. As a writer influenced by what Suzanne Nalbantian has described as the decadent strands of "perversity, paradox and perplexity," it was this very possibility of antagonisms between alternate realms that inspired James's transgressive imagination.[39]

The surrealists' fascination with divided selves was one reason for their interest in the various discourses of psychoanalysis, which were also beginning to emerge around the beginning of the twentieth century. For the surrealists, Freud's investigation of the world of dreams betokened not so much a quest for restorative health or medical normalcy but, rather, a revelation of ways that ghosts from the past might exist alongside present consciousness in a synchronic if uneasy juxtaposition. James's own ghost stories—notably, "The Turn of the Screw," first published in 1898—exemplify this line of association between mental disturbance and ancestral haunting, but perhaps his most self-conscious narrative expression of a dream state comes several years later, in his 1913 autobiography *A Small Boy and Others.* Here James describes how the "polished floor" of the Galerie d'Apollon in Paris, a location he knew well from childhood visits, manifested itself again years later in "the most appalling yet most admirable nightmare of my life." In this "dream-adventure," the hero finds himself pursuing around the gallery a "dimly-descried figure" that retreats before his "rush and dash." The memory is reconstructed by the narrator in an appropriately labyrinthine way, with the protagonist awakening with a start from sleep—but only, as he says, "the sleep within my sleep." The whole episode is, therefore, presented as an "immense hallucination," and it suggests again the ways James, particularly in the last few years of his writing career, sought to explore more than just attenuated forms of ambiguity or hesitancy.[40] The reader infers here a concern on the author's part with what seems to be the divided, incoherent nature of human psychology, while the grotesque and distorted shapes that make up this scene imply a sharp aesthetic response to the new circumstances of this post-Edwardian era. Whereas the works of the 1890s introduce the idea of a divided self as a recurring theme, then, James's later texts often internalize this principle of fragmentation as a formal component in the narrative.

The crucial point to emphasize here is the awkwardness of James's relationship not only with the Victorian legacy of moralism but also with the modernist impulse toward purism. In 1918, Charles Demuth, who was a close friend of Marcel Duchamp and whose painting was strongly influenced by his surreal style, produced a series of watercolors to illustrate "The Turn of the Screw," pictures that were not designed to be printed alongside the text but to be shown independently.[41] It seems entirely appropriate, however, that Demuth should have been attracted to this aspect of James, for he himself was looked on askance by Stieglitz and his acolytes for lapsing into what they took to be a visual style of vulgar materialism rather than attaining the transcendent purity appropriate to an indigenous American spirit. Paul Rosenfeld, for example, complained about Demuth's "grotesque and monstrous forms"; yet, it is just that sense of hybridity, of obstinate and inchoate forces colliding, that runs through Demuth's visualizations of "The Turn of the Screw" and another series he produced for "The Beast in the Jungle" a year later.[42] In the latter series, Demuth imagines James's characters as fantastically elongated, as contorted figures who have been twisted out of more familiar shapes, reflecting the way James's twentieth-century style was described by his own contemporaries as "perverse" (William James) or as "tantalizing" and "queer" (Frank Moore Colby). Despite Showalter's observation that "queer" as a term for homosexual had entered English slang by 1900, it would, of course, be misleading conceptually to equate Colby's use of the word in 1902 with the way it is used by Eve Kosofsky Sedgwick and her followers today.[43] Nevertheless, it is true that there is something in James that remains unassimilable to the conventions of the modernist project, and in this sense Michael Moon is right to say that James's transgressive idiom is nearer to the surreal style of David Lynch's films than to the much more ponderous cinematic narratives of Ismail Merchant and James Ivory.[44] However, the skill in James's surrealism turns on the way it wraps itself around and integrates itself within much more conventional narratives, so that Moon's exuberant iconoclasm should be qualified by recognition that James never openly flaunts such transgressive signs in the way an artist like Lynch does.

It might be argued, then, that the "tantalizing" quality of James's later work, in terms both of sexual psychology and national identity, lies not in any simple infraction of orthodoxy but in the way such orthodoxies are twisted and turned back upon themselves, so that generic boundaries of all kinds become susceptible to traversal. This is why James, though committed to what he called the "international" perspective in his writing, nevertheless returned compulsively to national identity as a site of character formation; he needed the formation of national identity to react against, because his work involves what he called the "highly civilized" business of breaking through these boundaries rather than simply acquiescing in them.[45] In his essay on Proust, Benjamin linked the "surrealist" tendencies of the French novelist to an implicit dialectic between resemblance and distortion, so that the reader "is constantly jarred by small shocks" as a "universe of convolution" disturbs the continuity of the acts of remembrance worked through by Proust's narrator; similar conflicts between resemblance and distortion haunt the field of James's vision, so that he should be considered ultimately neither an English nor an American writer, but someone who uses each category to problematize both.[46] William C. Spengemann has argued that in writers like James traditional demarcations of national identity or affiliation simply break down, so that it makes more sense to consider him under a generic term such as "literature in English"; but this is to privilege language itself as an idealist category, while placing less emphasis on the ways James plays with the material differences between nationalities and consciously trades off those conflicting expectations that alternative countries bring to bear.[47] James does not seek to transcend national identity so much as to traduce it; his texts portray the psychological and cultural transformations wrought in those who travel between different environments. Part of the pleasure of James's fictions derives from turning things around the other way, reversing the presuppositions of America by confronting them with Europe, and vice versa.

Hence James's famous international theme involves not an ethereal cosmopolitanism but a principled rejection of what is straight and straightforward. The traversal of national identity works in parallel with the traversal of other kinds of identity, so that James's fiction maintains a fine balance between the conventional and the aberrant. It is this more transgressive side of James that has been highlighted by much of the most interesting recent criticism; in particular, *The Wings of the Dove* has become a locus classicus for "queer" readings of James. The novel's perverse coupling of sex with death is epitomized in the way Merton Densher becomes increasingly enamoured of Milly Theale as her body is overtaken by consumption. The tortuous and inverted syntax that permeates the narrative—Milly, for instance, oxymoronically cherishes "the power to resist the bliss of what I *have*"—betokens the text's paradoxical mediation between possession and loss, where Densher is able to consummate his relationships with Milly and Kate Croy by losing both of them.[48] As Moon has observed, this reflects on Densher's loss of masculine mastery and on the process of exchange whereby he forfeits his "phallic status" to Milly's commercial power; but the obliquity of the narrative perspective—for Kate Croy, "nothing . . . would ever have been for her so direct as the evasion" (1.272)—also signifies a world where psychological and moral deviance is intertwined with the crossing of national boundaries.[49] While Milly's literary companion, Susan Shepherd, staunchly acts out the role of "one of her own New England heroines" (1.201), Densher, by contrast, is described as full of "foreign things" (1.92), a character so deracinated that "it was not given to those of his complexion, so to speak, to be exiles anywhere." James goes on: "His natural, his inevitable, his ultimate home—left, that is, to itself—was n't at all unlikely to be as queer and impossible as what was just round them" (2.365). The circuitous double negative here stylistically mimics the "queer and impossible" condition of Densher's subjectivity, where all that is transparent becomes opaque, where everything apparently indicating an "ideal straightness" (2.85) is twisted into the realm of perversion.

According to Mark Seltzer, this "style of deviation" in James can be related to an aesthetics of naturalism, where power can never be gainsaid, confinement is ubiquitous, and the narratives "typically provoke interest in what they censor and disavow." Because freedom is represented in these novels as an illusory impossibility, argues Seltzer, James contents himself with an "aestheticizing of power," assuming an ironic posture toward the engines of state and writing as if they might be reversible through acts of the imagination.[50] There is something to be said for this argument; we know James kept thirty-seven volumes of Zola in his personal library, and in a 1902 essay he discussed the French novelist's "rank materialism," while defending his use of the "supposedly 'improper.'"[51] For James himself, though, the "improper" was always something to be represented obliquely, and it is this predilection for a tantalizing, liminal space in between conflicting categories that differentiates James's writing both from the agendas of naturalism, where institutional forces become coercively all-encompassing, and from American pragmatism, where the evasion of established definitions typically involves a lofty transcendence of such institutional constraints. Rather than either the abrogation or the reification of power, James tends to favor its ironic suspension. In this, there is a conceptual affinity between *The Wings of the Dove*, for example, and the work of Georges Bataille, who writes in *Erotism*: "How sweet it is to remain in the grip of the desire to burst out without going the whole way, without taking the final step!"[52] Bataille has been described by Dickran Tashjian as "an apostate Surrealist" whose "radical materialism" challenged the programmatic views of Breton, but his materialism is perhaps nearer to that of James than is Zola's; it is materialism with a twist, materialism that takes a paradoxical delight in iconoclastically desublimating the rarefied realms of spirit.[53]

This surrealist strain in James's work differentiates it from many of the more orthodox directions of American writing. Contrast the duplicitous interplay between the law and its infraction, such as we find in James or Bataille, with the more self-reliant impulse of the contemporary American critic, Teresa de Lauretis, who demands that we should "really follow through the idea of a mobility of fetishistic or perverse desire by giving up the convenience of notions such as oscillation and undecidability."[54] De Lauretis, in the time-honored fashion of American romanticism, proposes an oppositional idealism that would simply break through the fetters of social and cultural restraint, thereby replacing the duplications of perverse oscillation with the singular authenticity of self-definition. This is useful as a cultural contrast, because it is, clearly, not what we find in a writer like Henry James. Within the terms of the American literary tradition, it is de Lauretis who writes in the traditional shadow of Emerson, whereas James appears as the more hesitant outsider. Queer theorists such as Moon and Sedgwick are right to point out the "suppressed thematic" of homoeroticism in *The Wings of the Dove*, but they do not emphasize how vital it is to the direction of this text that such currents remain suppressed: glimpsed partially and tantalizingly, perhaps, but always balanced off against, and gaining their sinister resonance from, a tangential relation with the more conventional powers of English society.[55] Rather than aspiring toward emancipation, James's deviant imagination always needed some kind of monumental establishment to play itself off against. In the first paragraph of *The Golden Bowl*, the Italian, Prince Amerigo, is said to find modern London "a more convincing image" of the grandeur of ancient Rome "than any . . . left by the Tiber," a phrase that positions London squarely as an imperial center, "the City to which the world paid tribute." Even in the antique shops of Bond Street, he imagines the objets d'art "tumbled together as if, in the insolence of the Empire, they had been the loot of far-off victories."[56] In this sense, *The Golden Bowl* is another example of an elliptical or postcolonial narrative, refracting assumptions of English hegemony through estranged forms of American consciousness.[57] James's fiction needs perpetually to cross these boundaries it establishes for itself, and his texts are transgressive in the way they take pleasure in moving across national as well as ethical frontiers.

Thematically, James's work emerges out of the late Victorian and early modernist era, when the identification of national characteristics was being consolidated rather than radically interrogated. His concern was not so much to scrutinize skeptically the whole range of national types as to foreground such essential differences, thereby dramatizing the ways character changes with environment. In his early travel essay, "Occasional Paris" (1877), he writes of how the task of the "cosmopolite" involves "comparing one race with another," but there is little sense as yet of James inquiring into the overall coherence or validity of national identity as a category of affiliation: "Nothing can well be more different from anything else than the English from the French," he says blithely.[58] Throughout James's long career as a novelist, therefore, the idea of transnationalism is associated not so much with a deconstruction of the whole idea of race and nation, such as we see emerging in *The American Scene*, but more with the possibilities of transformation, the passage from one state to another. (In the first decade of the twentieth century, the respective merits of life in the Old World and the New were a frequent topic for discussion in upper-class salons, with the United States generally held in these circles to be markedly provincial and inferior. Leo Stein, brother of Gertrude, wrote in 1902 to Mabel Weeks: "We have Am vs Eng. disputes all the time. The general theme is why in the name of all that's reasonable do you think of going back to America?")[59] In relation to this theme of metamorphosis, the James novel above all consecrated to what is called in its second paragraph "a deep taste of change" is *The Ambassadors* (1903).[60] Under the influence of Paris, Chad Newsome's New England character undergoes a "transformation unsurpassed," the "sharp rupture of an identity" (2.137), while his fellow countryman Lambert Strether subsequently finds himself made "strange" and "altered, in every way" by his foreign experiences. "He couldn't even formulate to himself his being changed and queer," the narrator continues; "it had taken place, the process, somewhere deep down" (2.75).

Changed and queer: on one level, this resonant phrase implies a subversion of the stable nature of moral character, but from another perspective it also suggests a radical metamorphosis in the conditions of art, a shift from Victorian realism to modernist abstraction. Strether gradually finds his received epistemological landscapes transformed into a more ambiguous and ironic scene, a world where he can no longer be sure of his ethical choices—indeed, can no longer be certain about how such ethical choices might be framed. "Everything has come as a sort of indistinguishable part of everything else," he remarks to Chad's sister (2.200); and later he complains: "I can't separate—it's all one; and that's perhaps why, as I say, I don't understand" (2.233). James himself described the novel as turning on the idea of "difference," difference from what was expected, and his strategic redescription of the trick perspectives in Hans Holbein's painting *The Ambassadors* reinforces this sense of rugs continually being pulled out from under the characters' feet.[61] The collapse of Strether's moral universe is also consistent with what Julie Rivkin has called the "ambassadorial logic" of the narrative, its proclivity for modes of substitution or secondary representation that supersede full moral presence, just as Mrs. Newsome appears in the novel only through the medium of delegates from Massachusetts who act in her place.[62] Consequently, the aesthetic consciousness in *The Ambassadors* manifests itself as analogical rather than logical, predicated on mutual relationships rather than discrete objects or categorical imperatives. When the flummoxed Strether tells Madame de Vionnet that "Everything's comparative" (2.120), he means that personal and cultural identity can no longer be compartmentalized in any self-enclosed or separatist manner, for they find themselves continually traversed by, and dispersed across, the constantly shifting shapes of a wider environment.

Thus, when William James criticized representations of character in his brother's later novels as merely "prismatic interferences of light, ingeniously focussed by mirrors upon empty space," he was actually responding sensitively to their idiom of abstraction and deviation, even though such qualities were naturally anathema to the allegiances of Harvard's "tough-minded" pragmatist.[63] The general sense of theater in *The Ambassadors*—all is "a scene and a stage," thinks Strether (2.253)— heightens this mood of displacement; so does the author's slide back into the more impersonal style of allegory, foreshadowed in his preface to the novel where he declares the idea "that people's moral scheme *does* break down in Paris" as "one of the platitudes of the human comedy," thus invoking in the reader a sense of déjà vu that, from the author's point of view, "had the great merit of sparing me preparations" (2.xiii–xiv). This leads us into the imaginative recreation of Europe as "a world of types" (2.53), with the action summarized in the last book as a "typical tale of Paris" (2.271).

In James's twentieth-century fictions, though, such stable allegorical typologies always tend toward a state of fracture and fissure. Indeed, this might be one way to distinguish them stylistically from his nineteenth-century works, where the allegorical equations remain more securely intact. The climactic scene in *The Ambassadors* takes place when Strether sees Chad and Madame de Vionnet together in their dangerous liaison on the river outside Paris, whereupon the aesthetic frame Strether has superimposed on the French countryside, as if it were an Impressionist painting, becomes rudely disrupted. Again, the hermeneutic drive in these narratives revolves around dislocation, traversal, turning things around the other way. Bataille writes of the erotic as involving the violation of a boundary or taboo, and there is an analogy here between the "irregularity" of adultery and the novelist's formal rupture of his Lambinet setting. James, in other words, participates in a literary correlative to adultery in the way he deliberately spoils his picturesque setting, just as the erotic designs of his characters are motivated by their desire to move to what Bataille calls "the other side of a façade of unimpeachable propriety."[64]

The surrealization of identity that becomes more prevalent in James's twentieth-century writing, then, involves taking a conventional framework or scenario and pushing up against it so that its limits and limitations become manifestly visible. By delineating the boundaries of a particular construction, James suggests how such boundaries can be seen as contingent or reversible. Just as *The Ambassadors* travesties its Lambinet model, so James works the process of despoilment in a similar way in *The American Scene* (1907), his valediction to his native land. Here the author repeatedly evokes allegorical types of American landscape, only to disavow the efficacy of their lineaments. Take his account of New England, in the first chapter:

> Why was the whole connotation so delicately Arcadian, like that of the Arcadia of an old tapestry, an old legend, an old love-story in fifteen volumes, one of those of Mademoiselle de Scudéri . . . why did most of the larger views themselves, the outlooks to purple crag and blue horizon, insist on referring to the idyllic *type* in its purity?—as if the higher finish, even at the hand of nature, were in some sort a perversion, and hillsides and rocky eminences and wild orchards, in short any commonly sequestered spot, could strike one as the more exquisitely and ideally Sicilian, Theocritan, poetic, romantic, academic, from their not bearing the burden of too much history.[65]

The dialectic here is between "Arcadian" myth and contingent "history," between the "idyllic type" and its inevitable "perversion." The departed shades of Puritan typology, which linger on the margins of James's text, find themselves confronted by material circumstances that will not conform to their etiolated designs. This dialectic works its way through *The American Scene*, characterizing it as a narrative of loss where idealized scenes are conjured up, only to be plaintively demystified. Always James establishes his aesthetic frame, centering on the "formal enclosure of objects" (62), and then he contrives to break that formal mold. Part of this pattern derives again from the temporal passages of modernity and the advent of change: visiting Harvard, James finds Cambridge still "faithful to its type," though his alma mater also appears to have undergone various kinds of "mutation," as it appears "in multiplied forms, with new and strange architectures looming through the dark" (57–58). It is, of course, this rebarbative spirit of transformation that propels the narrative dynamic of James's text, despite all of his retrospective sighing for the old familiar Boston of his youth.

Less obviously, perhaps, James flaunts the gap between narrative expectation and textual embodiment to problematize the status of his own spectatorial authority, thereby raising the question of what kind of inferences might actually be drawn about the substance of America from these pictorial representations of "the American scene." On Cape Cod, for instance, the narrator inserts himself into the picture in a self-conscious and self-reflexive way, anthropomorphically establishing an image that is no sooner epically inscribed than ironically desublimated: "Cape Cod, on this showing, was exactly a pendent, pictured Japanese screen or banner; a delightful little triumph of 'impressionism,' which, during my short visit at least, never departed, under any provocation, from its type. Its type, so easily formulated, so completely filled, was there the last thing at night and the first thing in the morning; there was rest for the mind—for that, certainly, of the restless analyst—in having it so exactly under one's hand. After that one could read into it other meanings without straining or disturbing it" (34). Reading meanings into the landscape in this way, the "restless analyst" comes up with a series of visualizations that perfectly epitomize what Robin Walz calls the more amorphous "surrealist imagination" that was prevalent before the formularization of surrealist aesthetics by Breton and his coterie.[66] James observes "a supreme queerness on Cape Cod" (35) and remarks on the "high, thin church" at Farmington "made as pretty as a monstrous Dutch toy" (43–44); he fantasizes about a "huge democratic broom" being "brandished in the empty sky" above Boston (55); he envisages the skyscrapers of New York "standing up to the view, from the water, like extravagant pins in a cushion already overplanted" (76). Stephen Spender, in calling the landscape of The American Scene "surrealistic," suggested it may have been a response on James's part to the brazen imagery of advertising so prominent in New York in 1904, although this kind of extravagant anthropomorphism also suggests on the author's part an element of willed bravura, an attempt creatively to appropriate material he finds distinctly alien.[67] Hence James's surrealist imagination functions here as a kind of aesthetic counterattack, as he attempts aggressively to disestablish naturalized objects by redefining them as artificial performances. Through his surrealist idiom, James seeks to reduce modern New York to a mere objet trouvé, which is why he talks of "the essentially *invented* state" of these urban landscapes (77). As we have seen, surrealism was generally hostile to the idealistic metanarratives of high modernism, and it sought not so much symbolic forms of order as provocative juxtapositions that might undermine the credibility of established frameworks. This is a motivation shared by *The American Scene*: by inscribing "reflecting surfaces, of the ironic, of the epic order, suspended in the New York atmosphere" (83), the narrative oscillates between the ironic and the epic, thereby building in a duplicity and belatedness that relay in a formally sophisticated way the processes of change portrayed here.

The narrator in *The American Scene*, then, is less a commentator than a mediator, a camera through whose lens aspects of twentieth-century America are made available to the reader. James consciously demystifies his own authority, representing himself less as a Victorian savant than as a displaced flâneur. On the cusp between Victorian and modernist understandings of national identity, James ponderously imagines "the alien presence" of immigrants in New York evoking as a riposte "the proper spirit of St. George" (138); yet he also, in a paradoxical reversal that verges on self-parody, inquires why the Italians he meets in the New World seem much less "agreeable" than their Old World compatriots, who "so enhanced for the stranger the interest and pleasure of a visit to their beautiful country" (128). By complicating his own category of the "Italian" in this way, James implicitly reflects on his inherited assumptions about national identity. As Patricia McKee observed, race and nation tended to be conceptually equated in the late Victorian era, but one of the peculiar charms of *The American Scene* is the way it travesties such identities, transposing them from metaphysical compulsions into contingent, externalized markers.[68] Sara Blair perceptively discussed the elements of "racial theater" in this book, the way its "racial figures . . . tend to hover between metaphor and historical fact"; however, this performative di-

mension is informed not only by James's earlier experiences as a dramatist but also by his surreal tendency to flatten out racial and national
types, denying them interiority and radically reinventing them as material phenomena. We know James read and admired Du Bois's *Souls of
Black Folk* in 1905, but "souls" are just what we do not have in *The
American Scene*.[69] The idea of "spirit" is demystified into a verbal cartoon,
as with the spirit of St. George, and the narrative as a whole parodically
resists those assumptions of immanent meaning that would enable it to
be recuperated as an allegory of national consciousness.

Michael Seidel calls the outlook of *The American Scene* "comparative
and double," because it epitomizes the "*chiasmus* or narrative crossing"
characteristic of an exilic topos of belatedness, revision, return.[70] Furthermore, as Philip Horne has noted, there is a parallel to be made
between the revisionary stance of this book and the retrospective method
of the prefaces to the New York edition, which James was also working on
in 1905 and 1906, and where he again looks back at his own past produc-
tions in the light of a lapse of time.[71] The whole of *The American Scene*, in
fact, is framed within a time-lapse idiom that creates the ironic spaces
for a complex, problematical response to the question James poses
openly in the book's third chapter: "What meaning, in the presence of
such impressions, can continue to attach to such a term as the 'American' character?—what type, as the result of such a prodigious amalgam,
such a hotch-potch of racial ingredients, is to be conceived as shaping
itself?" (121). This question is more than a rhetorical one, though, for
there is a curiously lopsided relationship in *The American Scene* between
the particular and the general, the part and the whole, and it is never clear
to James's narrator whether any particular "scene" can be classed as
characteristic of "American" identity. Apart from the complexities of ethnic hybridity, another facet of the twentieth-century United States that
perturbs James and makes him doubt his capacity to encapsulate it
within traditional typologies is the country's sheer geographic range and
scope. The opening up of the South and West, together with rapid population growth in those areas, blurs the plausibility of any organic "fit"
between James's putatively synecdochic account of the national scene
and the United States as a whole. For instance, the old friend of Longfellow and James Russell Lowell finds himself on less certain ground in
Palm Beach, Florida, where he is obliged to consult his *Baedeker* like any
other foreign tourist. The restless analyst depicts himself seeking con-

tinually to pin down the idea of America, but this unitary conception becomes harder to maintain the further away from New England he travels, and among the commercial hotels and cheap reproduction vases of Florida he is obliged to acknowledge wistfully that these paraphernalia have the effect of "qualifying at last your very sense of the American character" (450).

The American Scene thus hollows out its conception of the unitary subject and reconstitutes it as a figurative rather than literal entity. At various points toward the end of the book, James seems to invoke the word "America" in a purely circular way, as if the very act of repeating the country's name might magically impose on the landscape qualities not inherent in it. Slavoj Žižek has discussed how ideological classifications of this kind always tend to function in a self-reflexive manner, being held together not by observable evidence but by the skeins of reflexive fictions: "The crucial step in the analysis of an ideological edifice is thus to detect, behind the dazzling splendour of the element which holds it together ('God,' 'Country,' 'Party,' 'Class' . . .) this self-referential, tautological, performative element. A 'Jew,' for example, is in the last resort one who is stigmatized with the signifier 'Jew'; all the phantasmic richness of the traits supposed to characterize Jews (avidity, the spirit of intrigue, and so on) is here to conceal not the fact that 'Jews are really not like that,' not the empirical reality of Jews, but the fact that in the anti-semitic construction of a 'Jew,' we are concerned with a purely structural function."[72] Žižek's analysis of national identity as tautology corresponds precisely with the representation of "America" in The American Scene. The figure is evoked not to coincide with the country's "empirical reality," but to sustain, or perhaps to dramatize, the mythography of a nation coming into rude collision with the modern world.

In The Golden Bowl, James describes the illustrious object of his title as fatally flawed and cracked, betokening its failure ultimately to cohere with the experiential perspectives of its owners; in The American Scene, similarly, the titular object is flawed and fissured, with the narrator taking a poignant delight in demonstrating how the national object fails to cohere with its own symbolic designs. The West, for instance, proves even more resistant than the South to James's aesthetic categories, although we know he spent several weeks in 1905 traveling through what he thought of as the ruder parts of the country. He took the train through Kansas, Arizona, and New Mexico to a speaking engagement in Los

Angeles, before resting for a few days at Coronado Beach near San Diego. From there he traveled north, spending one night in Portland, before visiting his nephew in Seattle, from where he returned by way of St. Paul and Chicago to New York. However, the only mention of this expedition in *The American Scene* occurs as an aside in Chapter 3, when he is describing the scenery of the Hudson: "It is still vivid to me that, returning in the spring-time from a few weeks in the Far West, I re-entered New York State with the absurdest sense of meeting again a ripe old civilization and travelling through a country that showed the mark of established manners. It will seem, I fear, one's perpetual refrain, but the moral was yet once more that values of a certain order are, in such conditions, all relative" (146–47).

We know that James had originally planned a second volume to *The American Scene*, which would have focused on these Western regions, but it is not difficult to understand why it never emerged. In his notebooks and letters, James generally reacts to the West with a hostility that implies his intellectual as well as physical discomfort at these vast open spaces. The "great Middle West" he finds "an unimagined dreariness of ugliness" and "a single boundless empty platitude"; Milwaukee is a "desolation of dreariness"; San Francisco epitomizes a "poverty of aspect and quality."[73] Southern California provides, for James, the great exception to this general "Barbarism"; in "the charming sweetness and comfort" of Coronado Beach, he finds "a delicious difference from the rest of the U.S.," at least as far as the natural environment goes. "The days have been mostly here of heavenly beauty," he writes to his sister Alice, remarking that "no one had given me the least inkling I should find California so sympathetic." But the surprise expressed by James here is only the other side of this same coin, a more positive corollary to his sense of bewilderment when confronted by the "unspeakable" deserts of Arizona and New Mexico.[74] None of this landscape fits into his preconceptions; this is why he cannot write about it, cannot conscript it into his understanding of American national identity. The West renders him, literally, speechless; in a letter to Edward Warren from Chicago, he says: "I'm not pretending to write—I can't; it's impossible amid the movement and obsession and complication of all this overwhelming *Muchness* of space and distance and time." Similarly, to Jocelyn Persse he laments, "This country is too *huge* simply, for any human convenience."[75] At the very time James was traveling through this country, President Theodore Roosevelt, whom the author met at a White House dinner in 1905, was championing the idea of a rugged American masculinity by equating it with the "winning of the West"; for James, though, Roosevelt's notion of manhood was as problematic as his conception of statehood, and *The American Scene* declines to uphold either of them.[76]

Confronted with this new world of the West, James can only lapse into silence. Yet, as the author himself implicitly recognized, the shadow cast by this relatively uncharted territory contributes to the tone of reflection and irony that haunts the author's inscription of cultural fictions on his more favored East Coast. The lesson of the West, says James in *The American Scene*, is "that a sign of any sort may count double if it be but artfully placed" (147). Even Albany, New York, might be transposed from an unlettered frontier town to one boasting "the mark of established manners" (147) for a traveler entering it from the west rather than the east. Such an experience of the West consequently reinforces James's comparative consciousness, his recognition that particular aspects of the American scene come under a "sign" that is inherently duplicitous and that fluctuates according to the perspective of the observer. This in turn contributes to the cultural surrealism that hovers around James's invocation of America, his aesthetic telescoping of the New York skyscrapers into a fabulous pincushion, his intuitive grasp of their "essentially" *invented* state" (77). James's text is rent by this unresolved conflict between his lopsided surrealization of national identity on the one hand and a more traditional, essentializing quest for "the American spirit" on the other (102). Whereas the realist movement in American fiction at the end of the nineteenth century was associated with the identification and consolidation of a specific national culture, James's surrealist style flaunts the ideological discrepancies and potential sources of incoherence within such a nationalistic idiom.[77]

Žižek has written of "the paradoxical fact that the dimension of universality is always sustained by the fixation on some particular point," and it is this paradox, the unstable equation between the universal and the particular, that James plays with throughout *The American Scene*. He envisages America through the valence attached in his mind to particular locations—Cambridge, Harvard, Washington Square—but is forced to acknowledge that these landmarks can no longer extend their circumference into a synecdochic manifestation of the nation as a whole.[78] Deprived of this kind of symbolic expansiveness, the narrator in *The*

*American Scene* is thrown back on nonsequential perceptions and impressions; as in surrealist aesthetics, the debilitating collapse of a larger metanarrative referent leaves everything dependent on an iconoclastic, often highly idiosyncratic point of view. This angle of perception is foregrounded in *The American Scene* when James describes himself as viewing America through the "plate-glass" of a Pullman train (464); he is self-consciously witnessing his native land through a lens, a prism, through which, as he puts it, "every fact was convertible into a fancy" (68). Again, this leads to an idiom of radical exteriority that can be differentiated sharply from modernist conceptions of a naturalized "spirit" of place. For James in *The American Scene*, national identity remains a metaphorical rather than an immanent phenomenon: "It was thus at any rate," he says, "a question . . . of what one read *into* anything, not of what one read out of it" (68). Describing the "overwhelming preponderance" of the " 'business man' face," for example, the narrator deliberately eschews any representation of interior consciousness, noting: "I speak here of a facial cast and expression alone" (64). The theatrical images that run through this narrative betoken a world where density and interiority have been displaced into a series of endlessly reflecting surfaces, so that at the end of his journey the narrator's final attempt in his typological quest is to associate the Florida hotels with twentieth-century America more generally, where there is nothing "behind and beyond" the visible façade (406). America, in this apparition, has become a site of mechanical reproduction, where "multiplication, multiplication of everything, was the dominant note" (131), and where phenomenological identity has consequently taken flight.

This representation of Florida in terms of a pristine mechanical blankness serves effectively to empty out the romantic ideas associated with what James's narrator calls, in ironic quotation marks, "the 'old' South" (403). There is a double movement running throughout James's account of the American South, from Baltimore and Washington, D.C., down to Richmond, Charleston, and finally Florida. On the one hand, the narrator seeks self-consciously to make connections and equivalences, to re-inscribe the South within a map of national significance: describing himself punningly as "a constitutional story-seeker" (313), he talks of how in Washington "everything conduces to a single great representative image" (337), and all through his journey he keeps his eyes open for such "representative values and constructive connections" (307). Yet in the South, particularly, he also becomes aware of how such "pleasantly-playing reference and reflection" are dogged by a "spectre of impotence" (307). The South, where the "huge shadow of the War" remains "a ghostly presence" (310), hardly conforms to the narrator's "poor little array of terms and equivalents" (307). With its geographic and climatic differences and its continuing racial tensions, the South seems to shed "a certain sinister light on the general truth of our grand territorial unity" (305).

James is not content, however, simply to acquiesce in the received idea of regional differences. Rather than merely using the South to epitomize the problematic nature of federal cohesion, James also virtualizes the South to bring it into an imaginary relationship with the rest of the United States. By reconstituting the South within a mode of aestheticized relation, his narrative style of "reference and relation," James denies to the South that local independence so cherished by nineteenth-century political and literary regionalists:

> The solidity and the comfort [of the antebellum South] were to involve not only the wide extension, but the complete intellectual, moral and economic reconsecration of slavery, an enlarged and glorified, quite beatified, application of its principle. The light of experience, round about, and every finger-post of history, of political and spiritual science with which the scene of civilization seemed to bristle, had, when questioned, but one warning to give, and appeared to give it with an effect of huge derision: whereby was laid on the Southern genius the necessity of getting rid of these discords and substituting for the ironic face of the world an entirely new harmony, or in other words a different scheme of criticism. Since nothing in the Slave-scheme could be said to conform—conform, that is, to the reality of things—it was the plan of Christendom and the wisdom of the ages that would have to be altered. History, the history of everything, would be rewritten *ad usum Delphini*—the Dauphin being in this case the budding Southern mind. . . . We talk of the provincial, but the provinciality projected by the Confederate dream, and in which it proposed to steep the whole helpless social man, looks to our present eyes as artlessly perverse, as untouched by any intellectual tradition of beauty or wit, as some exhibited array of the odd utensils or divinities of lone and primitive islanders. (373–74)

This passage is worth citing at length because it illuminates so clearly the virtualizing method at work in this book. James situates himself on the boundaries of the Confederate South, looking in on a society that tried deliberately to resist such alienating perspectives. Whereas the South had attempted to rearrange the world in "harmony" with its own agenda, James realigns the region comparatively, setting it against the brutal "reality" of history, and showing how the world's response to this Southern idyll was one of "huge derision." The effect here is not dissimilar to that in Douglass's *My Bondage and My Freedom*, where the estranged, relativizing perspective of the narrator mocks Colonel Lloyd's attempt to turn his plantation into "a little nation of its own." James here uses a mordant humor to hollow out the pretensions of "the 'old' South" to local autonomy, and he deploys what he calls a "disprovincializing breath" (391) to turn the South, as it were, inside out, to suggest that from this cosmopolitan twentieth-century viewpoint its "reconsecration" of slavery appears no more plausible than the fetishistic beliefs of "primitive islanders."

By holding up a mirror to "the 'old' South" in this way, James comments implicitly on all systems of meaning arising out of the projection of circumscribed territorial boundaries. The cartography of the Old South works as a microcosm of the larger cartography of the United States, whose values again are revealed by the observer positioned on the nation's border to be highly contingent and susceptible of reversal. Just as James's "restless analyst" denies cultural integrity to the South, so he ironizes the efforts of the United States to forge for itself a romanticized version of identity based on the primacy of race or soil. In *The American Scene*, the construction of national identity is seen as a process of "immense fluidity" (401); the America on display forms only a shadow of the country to come, hence, any conclusions the analyst might draw are already "on the way to become quite other, and possibly altogether different" (402). This in turn renders the national prospect even more elusive and illusory. James, in other words, has no real "agenda" in the political sense as he revisits a country from which he has been absent for twenty-two years, and so to attribute to him a sentimentalized commitment to cultural diversity—to imagine him promoting "a society in which it is meaningful to live and to love," for example—is to engage in a forcible act of intellectual repatriation whereby James is conscripted to serve under the American national flags of pragmatism and romanticism.[79] The contours of *The American Scene* follow neither of these trajectories: the book is about the hollowing out of national identity rather than its replenishment, its tone is bilateral and self-mocking rather than involved on an empathetic level with questions of ethics or ethnicity. James's primary concern is with how the American scene is transformed in his eyes into just that: a scene, a performative landscape within which national identity has taken on the characteristics of a charade.

On the most obvious level, James attributes this displacement of inner identity specifically to the vulgar nature of the United States itself, with its characteristic lack of respect for privacy and individualism. More significantly, though, we see how the narrative formally mimes those very aspects of impersonality that it describes, implying that *The American Scene* itself becomes an aesthetic product locating itself within this field of mechanical reproduction. Though James the fusty critic often laments the progress of this new era, James the rigorous artist seeks to incorporate this mood of abstraction in the tone of his art. This is one important reason for the photographic imagery that permeates the book: he talks of "apertures" (168), "impressions" (89), "spectralities" (258); he calls New York City "phantasmagoric" (133); he describes the open plan of an American home as a "combination of the hall, of echoes and the toy 'transparency' held against the light" (168–69). Walter Benn Michaels has written of how, around the turn of the twentieth century, photography became associated with a style of automatism on the grounds that it was a machine rather than any individual person making the picture.[80] Far from seeing this as a threat to the imaginative integrity of his art, however, James exploits this mode of impersonality to render a photographic discourse in literary form: America, he aptly concludes, "registers itself on the plate with an incision too vague and, above all, too uniform" (454). Alvin Langdon Coburn, the American photographer whom James employed to provide illustrations for the New York edition of his work, subsequently recalled their tours together through prospective locations and observed: "Although not literally a photographer, I believe Henry James must have had sensitive plates in his brain on which to record his impressions! He always knew exactly what he wanted, although many of the pictures were but images in his mind and imagination, and what we did was to browse diligently until we found a subject."[81] In his guise as a verbal photographer, James's narrator in *The American Scene* similarly draws a line of extension between his optical gaze and the world he inverts or etherealizes but cannot entirely eviscerate.

It is also particularly telling that James should have chosen to draw on this new and unrecognized art of photography for the frontispieces to the New York edition, despite his long aversion to having his novels illustrated by more conventional means. The function performed here by Coburn's photographs is not so much to reproduce any given text in visual form as to empty it out, to interpose a layer of abstraction between narrative and reader, as if James, like a curator organizing a retrospective exhibition of his own works, were choosing to rehang his relatively realist fictions in more abstract, modernist frames. Coburn's works are, as James put it in his New York preface to *The Golden Bowl*, "images always confessing themselves mere optical symbols or echoes"; consequently, James saw his photography as an equivalent means of virtualizing the world of specific objects, thus refracting it into an aestheticized, reversible construction.[82] Nancy Armstrong has described how "photographic modernism" of the kind practiced by Coburn and others at the beginning of the twentieth century attempted to situate the art photographer as an "optical predator" who would wait to capture these visual qualities that might reveal an object's inner authenticity beyond the realm of superficial appearances; but she also writes of how photography at this time became complicit with a world of mass culture and mechanical reproduction that operated as a threat to modernism's attempt to relocate identity "on the other side of the image."[83] What is interesting about James in this context is how the photographs that he chooses for the New York edition reflect a landscape where consciousness can almost, but not quite, rearrange the world of inanimate objects to suit its own designs. To virtualize the landscape, as I suggested in the first chapter, is not so much simply to dematerialize it as to subject it to a process of dematerialization, and Coburn's photographs retain some of this tantalizing quality, suspended as they seem to be between the ghost and the machine. Rather than the idealized form of modernism that would dissolve material phenomena into a purely abstract state, James constructs a hybrid, surreal world where mind and matter, essence and accident come into collision with each other.

James's virtual America, then, involves not simply a physical detachment from his native landscape but also its reinscription through strategies of projection and screening. In this sense, the short story "The Jolly Corner," published one year after *The American Scene* in 1908, might be understood as a companion piece to that latter work, as this tale also revisits the United States through a memorial consciousness expressed in optical forms. At the center of the tale is an expatriate, Spencer Brydon, absent from America for "more than thirty years," who is now obliged to confront his alter ego and to imagine how things might have turned out differently had he stayed in his native land.[84] Again, this "ghostly life" (456) emerges through "shifting effects of perspective" (458), themselves dependent on an "optical reach" (459), a "presence encountered telescopically" (466), a "double eye-glass" (475). Returning across the Atlantic to a land from which he has been displaced, Brydon encounters "the differences, the newnesses, the queernesses," with "proportion and values" seeming to be "upside-down" (436). This idiom of inversion is commensurate with the optical and photographic imagery, the "concave crystal" (455), whereby the narrator's alternative persona is represented in "spectral" form: "The penumbra, dense and dark, was the virtual screen of a figure" (475). The story describes a sense of "stifled perversity" (452), of this "virtual" or ghostly realm being only partially accessible; this exemplifies the way James's virtual domain gains its resonance not from simply leaving behind the recognizable world, but from subjecting it to a much more subtle process of displacement.

The milieu of James's later work, which encompasses many such shadowy and divided characters, embodies that "paradoxical community" described theoretically by Julia Kristeva as "made up of foreigners who are reconciled with themselves to the extent that they recognize themselves as foreigners."[85] For Kristeva, the literal condition of exile presages a psychological revelation of the foreigner within oneself, inducing the stranger to confront all that is *unheimlich*, beyond one's familiar boundaries; she accordingly sees cosmopolitanism not so much as a universalist mode of enlightenment as a strategy of paradox and reversal, a means of stripping nations of their inherited sacral aspects. James's personae, like Kristeva's strangers, resist the comforts of cultural assimilation and take a more perverse pleasure in being strangers everywhere. This becomes analogous as well to the way James plays the discourses of English and American culture against each other, introducing forms of discontinuity and reversal that problematize the coherence of any imaginary, integral tradition. For James, therefore, transnationalism involves a mode not of transcendence but of transposition and transgression.

James's style of transnationalism, then, follows a logic of paradox more akin to the aleatory aspects of surrealism than to the universalizing impulses of high modernism. In their representation of the workings of chance, James's late novels oddly anticipate the predilections of the dadaists and the surrealists, who both liked the idea of chance, though for different reasons. For the more scabrous dadaists such as Tristan Tzara, chance worked as a welcome interruption to the normal order of things, bringing quite disparate entities into unexpected combinations; however, for those like Breton who considered themselves more bona fide surrealists, chance could be understood more redemptively, as a revelation of those hidden harmonies that the everyday world obscured.[86] This is why Henri Bergson's doctrine of the *élan vital*, a form of intuition working against the normal routines of logic, influenced the surrealists as strongly as it had James himself a few years earlier.[87] The plot of *The Wings of the Dove*, though, starts out with a more modernistic version of the uncanny, impelled by a curious scene in which Kate Croy, having met Merton Densher briefly at a reception, runs into him again six months later on the London Underground. Such an encounter might be considered in Bergsonian terms an intuitive rendezvous or spiritual symbiosis, but James's narrator here prefers to represent it as a "happy hazard," an "accident," a "chance" encounter (1.54). The apparent randomness of the incident introduces into James's apparently circumscribed and well-ordered world a sense of radical contingency, implying the invasion of a traditional social order by more amorphous modes of mechanical reproduction, where lives and encounters can be shaped according to those haphazard patterns engendered by the Underground Railway system rather than under the shadow of any higher purpose. Again, the cultural surrealism here works as a mode of desublimation, reshaping the teleologies of romance within the context of more hazardous twentieth-century urban landscapes.

In *The Ambassadors*, similarly, Strether's fateful encounter with Chad and Madame de Vionnet in the country outside Paris is ascribed by the reluctant protagonist to the unforeseeable mechanisms of chance: "Surface and sound all made for their common ridiculous good fortune, for the general invraisemblance of the occasion, for the charming chance that they had, the others, in passing, ordered some food to be ready, the charming chance that he had himself not eaten, the charming chance, even more, that their little plans, their train, in short, from *là-bas*, would all match for their return together to Paris" (2.259–60). This incident seems to lean more toward the Bergsonian mode in that chance is presented here as not only "charming" in the polite sense but also as carrying a sinister "charm" or magic spell of its own, as if it were the embodiment of an invisible hand of fate. Again, though, such an intrusion of apparent disorder into the protected circles of James's world implies that his narratives, for all of their elaborate formal architecture, are also driven by bizarre, random juxtapositions, rather than by, say, the methods of scientific probability that underwrite Zola's fictions. This is another example of how James's writing anticipates the surrealist conception of parataxis, manifested most obviously in plastic forms through the aleatory modes of collage, where events are framed within an idiom of epistemological and stylistic incongruity rather than through more traditional lines of causal sequence.

This structure of paradox and illogicality that characterized the surrealist movement in general has often been critiqued for its apparent rejection of ulterior meaning and political commitment. Jean-Paul Sartre in 1948 famously accused the surrealists of being confused and amoral, of flitting aimlessly between opposing points of view.[88] This would appear to heighten the natural friction between surrealism and American studies, as the latter has traditionally worked to allegorize cultural events as emblematic of a higher purpose, an idealized form of national identity. Such allegorizations have not depended specifically on foundational philosophies; indeed, as Frederick M. Dolan has observed, "the problem of acting without grounds" has itself assumed "the status of a national mythology," with the "tropes of self-creation and fictionalization" themselves testifying supposedly to an American national discourse of contingency, openness, and freedom.[89] The issue here is not the aleatory as such, but the equations that are made between specific objects or phenomena and the national symbolic. It is the process of allegorization, not the specific forms of allegory, that are at issue; however "America" is defined, American studies demands a translucent allegorical line between the object and its circumference, and it is that conceptual extension that the murkier elements of surrealism work to frustrate. In *Nadja* (1928), for example, André Breton describes his pleasure at visiting the Saint-Ouen fleamarket in Paris and "searching for objects that can be found nowhere else: old-fashioned, broken, useless, almost incomprehensible, even perverse."[90] Breton, as a surrealist, delights in both the random quality of this paraphernalia and in its refusal to be conscripted into any kind of ordered design or realm of the symbolic. By contrast, American studies, principally a method of conversion rather than perversion, would prefer instinctively to maximize the efficiency of its semiotic economy by making every cultural sign stand as a replica of ideal purpose.

This kind of philosophical disjunction exemplifies how the premises of surrealism have cut against the academic grain of American studies in various discomfiting ways. More traditional Americanists such as Philip Rahv and Clement Greenburg, writing from a relatively orthodox moral viewpoint in the 1930s and 1940s, tended to disparage the surrealists as nihilistic, decadent, and sexually deviant. Other metropolitan critics who looked at American culture from an institutionalized liberal perspective after the Second World War were scornful of the ways surrealism was becoming increasingly complicit with what they took to be the vulgar capitalist worlds of fashion and advertising.[91] But while these advocates of the liberal imagination postulated a highbrow version of American studies based on an exclusivist and often intensely moralistic conception of national identity, the aesthetics of surrealism, in their various forms, continued to enjoy wider popular appeal in the broad domain of American culture all through the twentieth century. Whereas modernism sought typically to identify an American national agenda within a context of utopian renewal, surrealism tended more to reflect the impure, inchoate nature of America's encounter with the conditions of change and futurity. Part of surrealism's general attraction lay in its uncanny capacity to mimic dramatic changes in the modern environment, to respond to increasingly unfamiliar landscapes with the production of apparently incongruous artifacts whose weird shapes epitomized a world in radical transformation. James Clifford has written of the implicit affiliations in twentieth-century culture between surrealism and ethnography, surrealism working to make the familiar strange, ethnography striving to make the unfamiliar comprehensible, but both turning on "a permanent ironic play of similarity and difference . . . the here and the elsewhere."[92] In this respect, it is not surprising that so many of those associated with the dadaist and surrealist movements between the wars were exiles or emigrés; the challenge of responding to a new and different culture ran in parallel with the more general surrealist project of addressing the strange and *unheimlich*.

The prevalence of transatlantic crossings among surrealists of this generation—Picabia, Duchamp, Man Ray—is obvious enough, and Wanda

Corn has recently sought to rewrite the early history of artistic modernism in the United States to acknowledge the many foreign voices who helped to shape American culture between 1915 and 1935.[93] In music, for example, the French-born Edgard Varèse, who came to New York in 1909, introduced discordant sounds into his compositions in an attempt to imitate what he took to be the startling modernity of his new American world. In *Offrandes*, first performed in New York in 1922, Varèse includes settings of poems by Picabia and Duchamp to reflect the bizarre world of advertising signs that he saw as characteristic of modern urban America. *Amériques*, his first major composition, was heard in the same year, and it became infamous for letting loose a wailing siren in the confines of its score; the title was in the plural, explained Varèse, because he was not concerned with America solely as a geographical location, but as "symbolic of discoveries—new worlds on earth, in the sky, or in the minds of men."[94] In this way, the iconoclastic form of Varèse's work can be seen as commensurate with his projection of America as the crucial site of modernity. In *Arcana* (1927) the composer follows other surrealist pathways by addressing the notion of hidden knowledge, envisioning a magic realm that might be unlocked by the arcane properties of alchemy, and by aligning America prophetically with the dynamics of transformation. Many of Varèse's other pieces—*Ionisation*, for instance, and *Hyperprism*, both from 1923—similarly suggest a process of scientific transformation, the prismatic reconfiguration of Old World values through the irregular perspective of the New.

For writers working directly under the sign of surrealism, this process of transatlantic displacement became symptomatic of an expression of internal foreignness, the duplicitous recognition of a perverse otherness within the self. As in Kristeva's theoretical model of strangeness, its emancipatory potential emerged not in a purely utopian fashion, but through the paradoxical inversion of what was only too familiar. Henry Miller claimed he "was writing Surrealistically in America before I had ever heard the word"; but it was the world of Paris that moved his imaginative earth "out of its orbit," as he puts it in *Tropic of Cancer* (1934), transposing its axis from the familiar locations of Brooklyn to the more bizarre vision of "a thick tide of semen flooding the gutters" in Montparnasse.[95] Miller's grotesque imagery was directly influenced by the films of Buñuel as well as by the paradoxical genius of Dostoyevsky, one of the acknowledged "patron saints" of interwar surrealism: "Dostoevski," wrote Miller admiringly, "was the sum of all those contradictions which either paralyze a man or lead him to the heights."[96] Miller's French counterpart, Céline—the two men knew and admired each other's work—follows a similar pattern of bouleversement in reverse, by representing America as his vehicle of liberation, the place where his suppressed sexual and scatological desires come to fruition. Céline's narrator in *Journey to the End of the Night* (1934) encounters an American woman in the lobby of the Opéra-Comique in Paris, and declares: "It was in the immediate vicinity of Lola's rear end that I received the message of a new world."[97] For the savagely repressed petit-bourgeois, such lovemaking offers a "profound and mystically anatomical adventure," and he vows, "while feeling and fondling Lola, that sooner or later I'd take a trip, or call it a pilgrimage, to the United States" (54). When he arrives there after the First World War, his eye for sexual adventures is still active: in New York, he lasciviously contemplates how "Major Mischief's daughter, a stunning young lady of fifteen, used to turn up in extremely short skirts after five o'clock and play tennis directly under the window of our office" (175).

On one level, according to Céline's narrator, America seems like "ecstasy" (177), a means of deliverance from the degrading toils of European corruption. It is important to recognize, though, that Céline's virtual America manifests itself as a literalization of those more atavistic instincts kept smothered back in his native country. Just as Paris operates for Miller as an inversion of his quotidian environment, so America turns Céline's world upside down and, through a characteristic surrealist paradox, reveals what it should have looked like the right way up. To strip away the protective layers of domesticity can be a disorienting as well as a liberating experience: now that his "petty habits" of home have disintegrated, he says, "I was sure of my individual nullity . . . close to nonexistence" (186). In the "jungle light" (176) of Broadway, he comes across an underground lavatory where men seem inspired by an "air of liberation and rejoicing . . . at the prospect of emptying their bowels in tumultuous company," and this "faecal grotto" (179) epitomizes Céline's aggressively scatological consciousness, where any kind of "poetry" is "squashed" by the mechanistic circuits of human existence (191). The narrator's spell in the Ford factory at Detroit, rather than indicting the destructive methods of American capitalism, more plausibly encapsulates this satirical perception of men as radically desublimated "machines" (204), performing their limited functions according to the habits of accretion. For Céline, it is this process of deracination that brings into focus these primordial scenes: "That's what exile, a foreign country is," explains the narrator, "long lucid hours, exceptional in the flux of human time, when the ways of the old country abandon you, but the new ways haven't sufficiently stupefied you as yet" (194).

One distinction between the cultural surrealism we see in Céline's text and the more canonical imperatives of high modernism lies in the former's propensity to flaunt, rather than attempt to conceal, the artificial nature of its metaphorical juxtapositions. This is the principle of collage transferred into a linguistic framework. When, for instance, Céline's narrator recounts how sitting down in the North African desert "would have made you swear by your bleeding buttocks that you were being forced to sit on a chunk of sun that had just fallen off" (140), the comic incongruity of the image—the literal impossibility of sitting on a piece of the sun—serves to emphasize the figurative, fictional nature of such constructions. This foregrounds an idiom of lack or absence that becomes a stylistic counterpart to the psychological and philosophical sense of alienation on which surrealism itself is predicated. In this case, the ludicrousness of the metaphorical juxtaposition introduces an element of burlesque that subverts the dignity not only of the narrator but of the act of meaning in general. Surrealism in this sense might be described as modernism's bad dream, a mechanism through which the arbitrary nature of its symbolic configurations are mockingly exposed.

From this perspective, it might be argued that there is more of a continuum between the idealistic leanings of high modernism and the burlesque proclivities of surrealism than is apparent at first sight. In a discussion of "Céline, Miller, and the American Canon," Raoul R. Ibargüen argued that modernist theory and practice, with its emphasis on the finely wrought capacities of the mythic and symbolic, tended to marginalize the more scabrous methods of surrealism.[98] This, of course, is true enough. Nevertheless, the kind of exchange of identities that we find in a writer like Henry Miller, where the infraction of syntactic and linguistic conventions becomes commensurate with sexual transgression and with the crossing of national boundaries, is replicated to a greater or lesser extent across a whole range of early twentieth-century writers: Joyce, Beckett, Hemingway, Fitzgerald, Stein, Crane, Eliot, Pound, Barnes. These cosmopolitan modernist writers tended to cherish exile as generating an alternative form of identity, to see it as what J. Gerald Kennedy calls "a site of rebirth"; however, the actual effect of their transatlantic displacement was often to problematize the idea of identity altogether.[99] This pattern manifests itself most obviously in Djuna Barnes's *Nightwood* (1936), a novel manifestly influenced by the aesthetics of surrealism. In Barnes's narrative, Robin Vote, an American in Paris, becomes "strangely aware of some lost land in herself," and, under the tutelage of Sade, embarks on a lesbian relationship with Jenny Petherbridge. Here we have the transmutations of gender—Robin is described as "a tall girl with the body of a boy"—mirrored in Barnes's opaque and riddling style, where it becomes difficult for the reader to figure out the various heterodox couplings in this obscure night world.[100] Yet this is not so different from Hemingway's *The Sun Also Rises* (1926), or, even more obviously, *The Garden of Eden* (published posthumously in 1986), where the discontinuities of exilic experience are seen as akin to the multiple prospects of bisexuality. Not belonging definitively to a particular race runs in parallel in these texts with not adhering definitively to a particular kind of gender, and this ambivalence constitutes one of the ways the more anarchic dynamics of surrealism threaten continually to undermine the teleological directions of modernism.

The modernist faith in exile as an intellectually enabling act, especially for the artist, was based on the fundamental assumption of countries being different. Sara Blair has observed that "leisured travel and disciplinary race thinking" became "the Siamese twins of Anglo-American culture" from about the 1870s, when tourists would visit foreign sites with the expectation of being able to define a particular land in terms of certain distinctive characteristics.[101] The popular notion of Paris as a cultural antithesis to the United States in the early twentieth century can be seen as a legacy of this way of thinking, and it also highlights the tension within modernism generally between an impulse toward impersonality and a more worldly stance of defamiliarization. The abstractions of modernism, in other words, are never immune from the more mundane aspects of inversion or parody. On one level, modernism's desire to fly by what Joyce's Stephen Dedalus calls the "nets" of "nationality, language, religion" impelled it toward the geometries of abstraction, whose universalist qualities could refine away the mere contingencies of local affiliation or (as in Joyce's case) transmute them into global significance.[102] Gertrude Stein's language, for example, is always straining toward an impersonality that would strip away appearances to their archetypal structure or essence: "a rose is a rose is a rose," "One's native land is one's native land." But the original quality of Stein's work emerges not so much from its neoplatonic aspects but from its sense of a cultural estrangement predicated on the faculties of paradoxical reversal and juxtaposition. Stein went to Paris because she thought its blank canvas, at least so far as her own history was concerned, would not impede her creativity in the way the more familiar (and therefore psychologically repressive) landscapes of America might have done. Stein declared that an American could never achieve such freedom in England, because the latter's history, culture, and language were too similar and recognizable; artistic creation, she claimed, therefore involved an "opposition" between cultures.[103]

It is this conception of representation as a form of "opposition," whereby a particular scenario is implicitly or explicitly turned inside out, that suggests modernism's latent affiliations with the more self-evidently anomalous characteristics of surrealism. According to Walter Benn Michaels, American modernist writers in the early twentieth century frequently engaged in a mystification of the idea of nationhood, equating the capacity to produce a native literature with membership of the American race, membership that could only ever involve a natural rather than an elective affinity. Despite the recent efforts to recuperate Henry James for an indigenous tradition of American pragmatism, this is clearly a form of "identitarianism" that *The American Scene* resists. Through the way it foregrounds the intensely problematic relationship between localized and abstract, specific and allegorical, James's text virtualizes the land it describes rather than seeing the work's success as bound up with the "achievement" of national identity.[104] In *The American Scene*, the narrator toys with the idea of presenting fetishized particulars, such as his beloved Cambridge, as emblems of America as a whole, but ultimately he withdraws gracefully from the promulgation of such grandiose designs. Striving manfully to rediscover the natural heart of his country, James ironically portrays himself as mortified to find it displaced into a virtual realm, a reconfigured artifice. One of the characteristics of cyberspace, according to Margaret Morse, is the way it demystifies any conception of objective perspective, creating an environment responsive to the observer and enunciating the world according to a subject's own projections.[105] James's transposition of his authorial eye into the lens of a camera in *The American Scene* anticipates such a style of narration mediated through mechanical means, where artistic representation becomes not a "spiritual" but a distinctly material phenomenon. This highlights the sense of plasticity common to the work of both James and the surrealists, who acknowledge, reluctantly or otherwise, the incapacity of the observer to play god, to move beyond his or her idiosyncratic perspective.

T. S. Eliot, writing just two years after James's death, praised his "capacity for keeping his mind alive to the changes in the world during twenty-five years."[106] Indeed, the extraordinary receptiveness of James's texts even to things their author did not sympathize with or fully understand constitutes one of the great charms of his late writing. James is, of course, a writer admired more traditionally for his formal, impassive qualities—the best American novelist of the 1950s, as Fredric Jameson sardonically described him—but in fact, during the last ten years of his life he experienced a disorienting relationship with the onset of modernity, and shades of this confusion manifest themselves in the surrealistic ambience of his later writings.[107] It is strange to think of James reading D. H. Lawrence, attending a lecture by James Frazer, visiting an exhibition of paintings by Matisse and Picasso, going to the cinema, chatting constantly to friends on the telephone; but in fact, during his final decade he did all of these things.[108] In his last essay, "The Question of the Mind," written in 1915 under the shadow of the First World War, he oddly welcomes the confusion and bewilderment the war has brought about, saying that "laying bare all our grounds and our supposed roots" may be "a very good thing for many of them, or may become so, and not a bad thing for any."[109] Far from wishing to bury his head in a comfortable domesticity, James saw these brutal, incoherent aspects of the modern age in the guise of an avenging angel ready to jolt the old established world out of its complacency. The surrealistic proclivities in James's representation of the United States anticipate this sense of confusion, perversely cherishing a disjointedness with which the national allegories of American studies are still far from comfortable today.

# 5

## From Decadent Aesthetics to
## Political Fetishism: The "Oracle Effect"
## of Frost's Poetry

Whereas the work of Henry James, with its self-consciously international dimensions, appears actively to invite comparative readings, the poetry of Robert Frost has more frequently been associated with a curmudgeonly, moralistic style of American patriotism. The purpose of this chapter, though, is to explore the ways Frost's peculiar brand of American modernism engaged in various forms of dialogue with the aesthetics of the decadent movement that was widely influential at the end of the Victorian era, particularly in England. We shall then see how strains of this "decadence" linger in Frost's laureate poetry of the cold war period, thereby casting disorienting shadows over his performative invocation of a national identity predicated on ritualistic embodiments of the common good. In this sense, Frost's eventual cultivation of what Pierre Bourdieu calls an "oracle effect," through which the poet self-consciously represented himself as a spokesperson for America, might be seen to derive not so much from the simple reproduction of native moral assumptions but, in a more sinister way, from the compulsion systematically to repress less homely forces. The axis of Frost's poetry, in other words, rotates on a deliberate strategy of diplopia, or double vision. From this estranged perspective, the internalization and circumscription of decadence in his early work can be seen as commensurate with what Bourdieu calls that "structural censorship" whereby a charismatic national figure seeks to map the parameters of the public domain.[1]

Although Frost was to become closely identified with the twentieth century, his intellectual roots lay further back, in the fin de siècle world of nineteenth-century culture. Frost himself was always rather older than one thinks: he was born in 1874, making him eighteen when Whitman died, twenty-five at the turn of the century, and thirty-nine when his first collection of poems, *A Boy's Will*, was published in 1913: hardly, by that time, a *boy's* will. He was forty-one by the time T. S. Eliot published the first version of "J. Alfred Prufrock" in Harriet Monroe's *Poetry* in June 1915, all of which makes him something of a displaced modernist, chronologically if not geographically. Definitions of American modernism itself are, of course, multifarious and contested, but Frost seems to have been influenced most obviously at the beginning of his public career by the injunction of his first benefactor, Ezra Pound, to "make it new." As Pound himself recognized, one of the most refreshing aspects of Frost's early work involved its deliberate movement away from stilted Victorian rhetoric and its appropriation of "the natural speech of New England" for poetic purposes.[2]

This is why Frost can still be understood as, in Frank Lentricchia's phrase, the "ordinary man's modernist," a writer concerned to ensure that twentieth-century revolutions in poetic language would become part of the wider common currency.[3] Over the past hundred years, there have been innumerable critical debates about the extent to which American writers similarly oriented toward a form of democratic realism—Ernest Hemingway, William Carlos Williams, and others—might be classified as modernists at all, despite their conscious attempts to integrate their popular and recognizably American styles with the aesthetic techniques of Gertrude Stein and others. In general terms, Marjorie Perloff is surely correct to point out that the formal characteristics usually attributed to modernism overlap so much with those of other taxonomies—realism or romanticism or postmodernism—that these terms in themselves have only a limited usefulness.[4] But such taxonomies do, perhaps, have a wider and more generic usefulness when seen in relation to the historical circumstances of specific eras. As a writer in America during the early twentieth century, Frost inevitably found his work engaged in dialogues with the inclinations of modernism, however much he personally may have reacted against such tendencies.

The oblique manner in which Frost positions himself in relation to this modernist impulse is in fact particularly self-conscious and revealing, because he is aware from the time he writes *A Boy's Will* of a need to reconcile quite different things. Suffering from an acute sense of existential dislocation, he also desires to be a representative American; speaking of isolation and alienation, his poetry nevertheless aspires toward social conformity and, in Mark Richardson's phrase, "cultural accommodation."[5] Accordingly, the peculiar charm and genius of Frost's work involves the ingenious production of a popular brand of modernism, a version that succeeds in bringing together the more disturbing qualities of high art with the familiar, reassuring aspects of commodity culture. Andreas Huyssen described modernism as generally constituting itself "through a conscious strategy of exclusion," working in a purist manner to avoid any contamination by the forces of mass culture; but Frost's poetry positions itself in a more inclusive manner to confound this opposition, as it paradoxically joins together the abstract and the orthodox, the deviant and the domestic.[6]

Nietzsche in 1888 distinguished between two types of artistic decadence. The first, epitomized in his eyes by Edmond and Jules de Goncourt and Richard Wagner, was an aesthetic imperative, a specific kind of style designed ostentatiously to reflect the internal or external compulsions of depravity; the second, much more covert, involved those works that appeared to lapse into decadence in spite of themselves.[7] Frost's poetry fits into both of these categories; his early writings, in particular, express a sense of decadence within recognizable artistic and generic patterns, whereas in his subsequent texts this decadence is more suppressed, overlaid with the burdens of modernity and social conscience. In *North of Boston* (1915), many of the narrative descriptions—in poems such as "Home Burial" and "The Black Cottage"—revolve around decay and ruin, as if to encompass the loss of New England's traditional landscapes and value systems. This, suggests Richard Gilman, was one of the historical functions of decadent aesthetics: to break up the philosophical complacency of Victorian positivism and to interrogate its effusive rhetoric of idealism.[8] Yet it is the manner within which such dissolutions are inscribed that emphasizes Frost's affiliations with the stylistics of self-laceration and entropy. We know that in his youth Frost was a keen reader of Victorian verse; he cited Tennyson's *Morte d'Arthur* as one of his favorite poems in 1894, the same year he arranged for his own first collection, *Twilight*, to be privately printed in Lawrence, New Hampshire. The five poems in *Twilight* really did describe the circumference of "a boy's will," evoking a sentimental yearning for romance characteristic of an adolescent heavily steeped in the mystique of late Victorian sentiment.[9] In "Summering," the protagonist's inner turmoil expresses itself in a languorous reverie of self-immolation:

> I would arise and in a dream go on—
> Not very far, not very far—and then
> Lie down amid the sunny grass again,
> And fall asleep till night-time or next dawn.

In "Twilight," similarly, the poetic voice turns in on itself, taking the shadowy environs of evening as a romantic correlative to its own world of anxiety and doubt:

> Why am I first in thy so sad regard,
> O twilight gazing from I know not where?
> I fear myself as one more than I guessed!

Traces of such misty, crepuscular landscapes can still be glimpsed in *A Boy's Will* nineteen years later. "Waiting," for example, is subtitled "Afield at dusk":

> What things for dream there are when specter-like,
> Moving among tall haycocks lightly piled,
> I enter alone upon the stubble field,
> From which the laborers' voices late have died,
> And in the antiphony of afterglow
> And rising full moon, sit me down
> Upon the full moon's side of the first haycock
> And lose myself amid so many alike.[10]

The "antiphony of afterglow" is reminiscent of the language of early Yeats, but the capacity to "lose myself amid so many alike" is more characteristic of Swinburne, whose narrative voices tend climactically to immerse themselves in, as his 1866 poem "Anactoria" puts it, "Thick darkness and the insuperable sea."[11] Given Frost's reputation for colloquial idiom, the diction of *A Boy's Will* often appears curiously archaic, including as it does such phrases as "O loud Southwester!" (11), "O'er ruined fences" (5), and "I am fain to list" (7). Equally musty are the mythological scenarios, such as that described in "Pan with Us," where the Greek god is represented "in the zephyr, pipes in hand / On a height of naked pasture land" (23).

It is true, of course, that the modernizing aspects of *A Boy's Will* enter into a spirited dialogue with this late Victorian rhetoric. In "Mowing," for example, the narrator specifically rejects the prospect of "easy gold at the hand of fay or elf," a "dream" he associates with "the gift of idle hours," and turns instead to the domain of tough-minded "fact" as "the sweetest dream that labor knows" (17). Yet this dialogue is, as always, a double-edged sword, because the dynamics of Frost's modernist realism retroactively embrace the legacy of Victorian sentimentalism even as they seek to discard it. Peter Nicholls has written of how the "masculinist" tone of literary modernism establishes a break with the more narcissistic, self-indulgent aspects of decadence, but in the case of Frost there is no clear-cut transition between one style and the other.[12] Decadence and modernism, abject self-abasement and virile self-assertion become mutually intertwined in something like equal measure.

One way of thinking about this conceptually is to consider Frost's intertextual relationship with Swinburne's poetry. Swinburne's work was generally an object of derision among the modernists, who castigated his attention to linguistic suggestiveness rather than phenomenological clarity as an example of artistic "morbidity," as T. S. Eliot put it, something excessively "feminine" and insufficiently "objective."[13] Male modernists, priding themselves on their purism, reacted strongly against the indeterminacies of gender and the ambiguities of sexuality in Swinburne's work, although, interestingly, female modernists such as H.D. tended to be more sympathetic to these explorations of androgyny and role-reversal.[14] Unlike Eliot and Pound, however, Frost admired Swinburne in the way he admired Emerson: as a worthy progenitor, whose aesthetic patterns he would want to internalize and reconceptualize for alternative purposes. "Itylus," said Frost, was "very lovely poetry," even if "Swinburne didn't *really* feel the least bit sorry about Itylus."[15] Just as Frost was intent on modulating Emerson's neoplatonic abstraction into his own version of pragmatism, so he was concerned to disrupt Swinburne's mellifluous masochism by interposing the sterner maxims of common sense. As he put it in a 1913 letter from England to John Bartlett: "The great successes in recent poetry have been made on the assumption that the music of words was a matter of harmonised vowels and consonants. Both Swinburne and Tennyson arrived largely at effects in assonation. But they were on the wrong track or at any rate on a short track. They went the length of it. Any one else who goes that way must go after them. And that's where most are going. I alone of English writers have consciously set myself to make music out of what I may call the sound of sense." This phrase "the sound of sense" is ambiguous and elusive, suggesting that Frost's proverbial wisdom functions not so much for what it says as for the way it sounds.[16] Its pertinence lies not in the aphorism's universal applicability—its ostensible raison d'être—but in its particular style, its simulacrum of closure, its manner of relating to the aesthetic designs that surround it.

On one level, this is simply to emphasize once again Frost's debt to William James and his strategic deployment of poetic language as a "momentary stay against confusion."[17] But my point is that this "tough-minded" persona is always engaging in dialogue with, and attempting to preserve itself from being smothered by, the more sinister charms of decadence, in the broad as well as the specific sense of that term. Indeed, it is this dynamic interaction between decadence and pragmatism that gives Frost's poetry its peculiar valence; one side of the equation would not be so effective without the other.

Sometimes this interaction takes the form of a directly intertextual argument with the fin de siècle, as with "Come In," published as late as 1942:

> As I came to the edge of the woods,
> Thrush music—hark!
> Now if it was dusk outside,
> Inside it was dark . . .
>
> Far in the pillared dark
> Thrush music went—
> Almost like a call to come in
> To the dark and lament
>
> But no, I was out for stars:
> I would not come in.
> I meant not even if asked,
> And I hadn't been. (334)

The direct antecedent here would seem to be "The Darkling Thrush," a lament for the old century published in December 1900 by Thomas Hardy. Frost knew Hardy's work well; he first mentioned it with approbation in a letter of 1894, and in another of his 1913 letters to Bartlett he declared Hardy to be "an excellent poet and the greatest living novelist here"—here, that is, in England.[18] The melancholy tone of "The Darkling Thrush" arises from his narrator's perception of a macabre incongruity between the "spectre-gray" landscape of winter, which he imagines as "The Century's corpse outleant," and the joyous "carolings" of a songbird:

> An aged thrush, frail, gaunt, and small,
>   In blast-beruffled plume,
> Had chosen thus to fling his soul
>   Upon the growing gloom.[19]

On the face of it, these two birds are represented quite differently: Frost's thrush is allegorized self-consciously as a harbinger of doom ("Almost *like* a call to come in / To the dark and lament"), whereas Hardy's appears more innocently "ecstatic." Yet the irony here, as so often in Hardy, is that the cry of joy is also a cry of anguish, for agony and ecstasy become intermingled and mutually reinforcing. Like Swinburne, Hardy constructed an aesthetic in which the fatality of pain and the raptures of pleasure came to be symbiotically entwined. As Richard D. McGhee observed, Swinburne and Hardy knew and admired each other's work, and were particularly close personal friends toward the later part of their careers, when they could, as Hardy put it in his *Autobiography*, commiserate "with each other on having been the two most abused of living writers."[20] Frost, later to become institutionalized as the doyen of Middle America, might seem an odd third party to such a disreputable circle; but he manages to keep the threats of dissolution and self-dissolution at bay only by a string of paradoxical negatives that embrace the luxurious darkness only, ultimately, to reject it. Indeed, it is noticeable that each of the final four lines in "Come In" involves a syntactic negative, as if this landscape of lamentation were being held irresolutely in suspension, balanced against an alternative vision of self-reliance.

In this sense, many of Frost's poems follow the pattern of "Come In" in the way they play themselves out on some kind of spatial or figurative "edge." John R. Reed has described "decadent style" as "an art of aesthetic algolagnia, a craft of exquisite self-tantalization" predicated on "the sustained tension of yearning caught between opposites," and the "edginess" of Frost's verse, no less than that of Swinburne and Hardy, epitomizes this paradoxical mediation between alternate possibilities.[21] As Frost himself put it in a 1917 letter to Louis Untermeyer: "All the fun is . . . saying things that suggest formulae that won't formulate—that almost but don't quite formulate."[22] The basis of Frost's art, that is to say, consists in a willful irregularity or deviance, a swerving away from those ready-made formulas that nevertheless continue to frame his transgressive enterprises. In the letter where he discusses Swinburne, Frost records his desire to interrupt Victorian euphony "by skillfully breaking the sounds of sense with all their irregularity of accent across the regular beat of the metre"; this notion of using an irregular instrument to break across the rhetoric of convention again suggests the extent to which a style of transgression was crucial to Frost's poetic designs.[23] Transgression, the crossing of a boundary, always involves an interplay between two discrete realms, and in Frost's case this reinforces a sense that his particular version of modernism was ironically enabled by the very framework of decadence that he was reacting against.

Given Frost's own roots in the nineteenth century, as we have seen, it is not surprising that he was interested in the art of the 1890s. He shared this sympathy not only with Ezra Pound—despite Pound's subsequent profession of contempt for that decade, his early poetry was heavily influenced by its aesthetic charms—but also with Edward Thomas, his close friend in Gloucestershire, who had inherited his book reviewing column in the London *Daily Chronicle* from the pre-Raphaelite poet Lionel Johnson.[24] What is different about Frost, however, is the way his texts integrate the uncomfortable forces of decadence within the purifying realms of American modernism. In this way, he inscribes a radically paradoxical notion of cultural identity that simultaneously proposes symbolic manifestations of an American national consciousness and, at the same time, problematizes that chimera of organic identity by drawing implicit parallels between the reification of national identity and the logic of fetishism.

There were many different strands to American modernism, of course, but one of its most common sources of energy involved a determination to reject the legacy of English culture as an inappropriate model for the representation of a brazenly new American world. Randolph Bourne and the *Seven Arts* writers set an Anglophobic tone around the time of the First World War that was to be followed in the 1920s by William Carlos Williams in his famous disagreements with T. S. Eliot about the nature and purpose of culture.[25] American writers of the interwar years were often uncomfortable both with English gentility and with the mystifications of obscurity that they tended to associate with the European avant-garde. For instance, in a 1937 review of Djuna Barnes's *Nightwood*, her novel written in exile and published the previous year, Philip Rahv wrote of how the Paris scenes represented "the shifting sands of decadence at its most absolute," evoking "an atmosphere of general mystification and psychic disorder . . . in which the reciprocal workings of social decay and sexual perversion have destroyed all response to genuine values and actual things."[26] Frost himself expressed similar impatience with what he saw as the self-indulgent aspects of radical art, criticizing in a 1931 interview "the extreme modernists . . . on the insane fringe of things" who "do not care whether their communication is intelligible to others."[27]

It was, in fact, during the 1930s that Frost came to be associated with a specifically conservative agenda, on account of his apparent dedication to quintessentially American scenes and values in his poetry, along with this apparent hostility to "foreign" ideas. The most famous expression of this nativist strain came in "Build Soil," his "political pastoral" read as a Phi Beta Kappa poem at Columbia in 1932, when he seemed deliberately to reject the international program of the Left by declaring "We're national and act as nationals" (320). Yet "Build Soil," with its conversation between two Virgilian shepherds about the relative merits of socialism and the marketplace, typifies Frost's contrary, elusive tendencies in that it is more about the staging of individualism as a political philosophy than an argument for "a one-man revolution" (324) on its own account. Frost delights here in the paradoxical business of making the private public, of broadcasting the virtues of solitude and retreat. His interest lies not so much in promulgating a specific ideology as in the ways such an ideology might be mythologized and recirculated.[28]

As so often with Frost, then, an overtly patriotic agenda tells only part of the story. The structural diplopia in his poetry entices us to read it for its rhetorical play as well as for its manifest content. While his poems successfully domesticate the more disruptive aspects of modernism, rendering them safe for middle-class consumption, this same dialectic also works in reverse, for we should recognize how his work simultaneously seeks "a further range" beyond such genteel assumptions to explore less familiar zones of psychological, sexual, and linguistic violence. This is not simply to reclaim the modernist or "dark" side of Frost as opposed to his reputation as a realist or sentimental poet, an academic strategy that has been practiced relentlessly since Lionel Trilling's praise for Frost's "terrifying" qualities in the *Partisan Review* of 1959.[29] More insidiously, it is to suggest that the popular, communal symbols in Frost's texts themselves become distorted by the forces of decadence, so that his poetic landscapes involve the surreptitious invasion of folksy scenes by an alien dimension that forces the reader to interrogate received notions of identity and normalcy. In recent years, Frost's poetry has become an enticing site for "queer" readings, because his pastoral imaginary has traditionally been so closely associated with the rhetoric of national identity that to unpack the bizarre paradoxes embedded in these textual structures is to challenge some of the notions of "heteronormativity," to use Michael Warner's term, embedded in American civil society itself. To discover, as Karen L. Kilcup does, "homosocial or even homoerotic" tendencies in his work is to read Frost from a deliberately provocative perspective, to move him out of that tautological straitjacket whereby his poetry is found to embody the homespun idealism of an indigenous American literary tradition, and to foreground instead within his writing the dynamics of metaphorical and libidinal exchange.[30] My argument, though, is that these transgressive readings can be related not just to an idea of psychological latency or textual vacillation, but, more specifically, to the transatlantic circumstances that framed Frost's field of composition. In this sense, the intertextual allure of decadence and the unregenerate culture of England form a material infrastructure within his poetry.[31]

"Birches," for instance, that canonical tribute to the moral vistas of New England, was in fact written back in the old country, at Beaconsfield in Buckinghamshire. The first reference to it appears in a letter to Bartlett on 7 August 1913, where the author lists it as "Swinging Birches," and the poem first appeared in the *Atlantic Monthly* for August 1915, only six months after Frost's return to the United States.[32] Exile and estrangement were, of course, familiar themes among the modernist writers, and—like Joyce recalling Dublin from Paris, or Eliot writing in London about the Mississippi River—it may be that Frost was able to construct a sharper image of native particularity through this condition of displacement. "We are very very homesick in this English mud," Frost wrote in a letter to Susan Hayes Ward in May 1913: "We can't hope to be happy long out of New England. I never knew how much of a Yankee I was till I had been out of New Hampshire a few months."[33] However, the virtual image of America projected in "Birches" does not operate through a mode of simple nostalgia, but rather, recapitulates formally that complex interaction between communality and defamiliarization that lies at the heart of Frost's multifaceted achievement.

On the face of it, the poem uses the homely image of a boy climbing a birch tree as a self-conscious figure for the tension between celestial idealism and earthly wisdom. Following Frost's typical pattern, the moralistic narrative works toward an aphoristic resolution, concluding that "Earth's the right place for love." On one level, the foregrounding of this pedagogical voice has the effect of directing the reader toward the intertextual referents implicit in his text. In his essay "Poetry and Happiness," Richard Wilbur points out that Frost's pastoral landscape is concerned dialectically to overhaul and reimagine in American terms the neo-platonic aspirations of Percy Bysshe Shelley's *Adonais* (1821):

> They click upon themselves
> As the breeze rises, and turn many-colored
> As the stir cracks and crazes their enamel.
> Soon the sun's warmth makes them shed crystal shells
> Shattering and avalanching on the snow crust—
> Such heaps of broken glass to sweep away
> You'd think the inner dome of heaven had fallen. (121)

As Wilbur explains this passage:

> "Many-colored." "Glass." "The inner dome of heaven." It would not have been possible for Frost to pack so many echoes of Shelley into six lines and not to be aware of it. He is slyly recalling the two most celebrated lines of Shelley's *Adonais*:
>
> > Life, like a dome of many-colored glass
> > Stains the wide radiance of eternity.
>
> Such a reminiscence is at the very least a courtesy, a tribute to the beauty of Shelley's lines. But there is more to it than that. Anyone who lets himself be guided by Frost's reference, and reads over the latter stages of Shelley's lament for Keats, will find that "Birches," taken as a whole, is in fact an answer to Shelley's kind of boundless neo-Platonic aspiration. . . . Shelley, spurning the Earth, is embarking on a one-way upward voyage to the Absolute. . . . Frost's answer to that is "Earth's the right place for love."[34]

This is helpful, to be sure, but it does not address the larger question of what the author hoped to gain by his strategy of teasing allusion and concealment. Are Frost's games of hermeneutic hide-and-seek an attempt to valorize the domestic pleasantries of American rural life by connecting them analogically with the classical monuments of Western civilization, as Emerson recommended in his essay "The Poet"? Certainly we get a feeling that the Shelley reference in "Birches"—and the allusion to Dante in this same poem, Frost's "pathless wood" picking up the "selva oscura" from the *Inferno*—were intended to be marked and annotated, just as Frost surely intended "After Apple-Picking" (1914) to be construed by the wised-up reader as a down-home version of *Paradise Lost*. Perhaps these overdetermined systems might derive from the codes of modernism itself; one thinks by comparison of Eliot's academic footnotes to *The Waste Land*, or Pound's manic Renaissance scholarship, or Joyce setting out (as he said) to keep the professors busy for a hundred years with *Ulysses* and *Finnegans Wake*. Yet the qualities of opacity and difficulty in these authors are more obvious than similar characteristics in Frost. In fact, the odd thing about a poem like "Birches" is the way the text itself appears to swing elusively between many different levels of possibility, inviting allegorical decipherment, but also sliding out from under any discomfiting connotation of transgression by its blithe façade of folksy innocence. In this way, one senses, as one does not sense in Emerson, some crucial disjunction in Frost between poetic object and analogical circumference. We know that Frost, who much admired Emerson, nevertheless conceived of his own natural world as misshapen and "oval" rather than, as in the Emersonian cosmos, "a circle round."[35] "Birches" appears to be a poem in this anamorphic vein, as it is concerned to mediate between opposing, antagonistic forces rather than to transcend or reconcile them.

The recognition of a duplicitous or paradoxical element in Frost's work goes back to the 1920s. Writing in 1924, Dorothy Dudley observed: "It is as if he said, 'There are my perverse words, but turn the piece around, while revolving you will see it shine.' "[36] Or, one might add, see it darken. In "Birches," we do not have to excavate far beyond the relative security of the Shelley/Dante echoes before we encounter something more like a weird dream landscape, where meanings are projected anthropomorphically on inert matter:

> When I see birches bend to left and right
> Across the lines of straighter, darker trees,
> I like to think some boy's been swinging them.
> But swinging doesn't bend them down to stay
> As ice storms do. (121)

The patterns here are of traversal and conflict: the birches bending across the lines of darker trees, the fiction of a youthful adventurer played off against the more "matter-of-fact" ice storms. A few lines later, though, the author develops an altogether stranger simile, linking the battered trees to a prospect of young women:

> You may see their trunks arching in the woods
> Years afterwards, trailing their leaves on the ground
> Like girls on hands and knees that throw their hair
> Before them over their heads to dry in the sun. (121)

The enabling pun here is on the word "trunks": tree trunks, but also the trunks of the girls' bodies. Although this parallelism may make sense in an abstract way, as Robert Crawford suggests, "the more we think about the simile the more it approaches the absurd." Its power lies not so much in any logical signification or rational common sense, but rather in its metamorphic capacity to transmute the trees into female forms. Thus the figurative landscape, as Crawford says, becomes eroticized, but eroticized in a peculiarly suggestive way. To some extent, this scene may be redolent simply of the pre-Raphaelite world of Edward Burne-Jones and the Rossettis, but Frost pushes this pastoral iconography past its conventional limits, with these "girls on hands and knees" intimating the kind of violent sexuality that Frost addressed explicitly only occasionally, most famously in his poem "The Subverted Flower," drafted in 1912 but not published until 1942.[37]

In "Birches," however, this suggestion of erotic violence is no sooner made than it is, of course, withdrawn:

> But I was going to say when Truth broke in
> With all her matter of fact about the ice storm. . . .

We are back to the poet's public, moralizing tone. The energy and the charisma of Frost's poetry seem to derive from the tensions of self-censorship, where a private, lyrical vision is transliterated roughly into the realms of public performance. Yet it is this innate violence, or restrained psychopathological deviance, that gives Frost's work its intense cathectic charge. He is, as Katherine Kearns has written, "a master of the sexual innuendo, which is always seemingly belied by the hearty voice that utters it"; his poems embody the "muted but undeniable notes of sadomasochistic desire" as they run the gauntlet between control and lust, between the aphoristic rigidity of moral order and the vagaries of corporeal appetite.[38] Hence the sadistic persona that emerged infamously from Lawrence Thompson's biography—the monster of vengeance, the man who desired to punish or even murder his enemies—forms an integral dimension in Frost's poetic personality. The antisocial extremism of poems like "Fire and Ice" (1920) or, in this example, "Beyond Words" (1947), testifies to a readiness to gouge out ethical sensibility, to substitute the dynamics of bestiality for the politer circuits of civic cooperation:

> That row of icicles along the gutter
> Feels like my armory of hate;
> And you, you . . . you, you utter . . .
> You wait! (393)

From this more overtly sinister perspective, we could return to "Birches" and infer its encompassing of rather more than a benign liberal humanist response to Shelley's *Adonais*, as Wilbur suggested. The poem, indeed, seems to oscillate between two radically conflicting horizons of possibility, of the kind described by Habermas in *A Theory of Communicative Action*, where he distinguishes between "lifeworld" and "system": the first a realm of mythic plenitude, where law and morality are equated; the second involving a more complex network of differential values, where national identity is a secular, legal mode of affiliation rather than a transcendental good in itself.[39] At one moment, Frost's poem seems to work on the level of mythic fable, extrapolating its folk wisdom from the activity of children and the timeless idyll of nature. At the next moment, its differential metaphors have introduced a jarring note of alienation, turning the established pastoral world into a realm of escapist fantasy, from which the narrator ultimately backs off by transposing himself into the voice of a ruminating, distant third person: "One could do worse than be a swinger of birches" (122). Well, one could indeed. By opting for the safe haven of impersonality, Frost ultimately shifts "Birches" from lifeworld into system, from the affective plenitude of myth to the more instrumental logic of social control. The manifold references in this poem to baseball and other forms of "play" add to this sense of Frost's world as an arena of elaborate internal systems, where meanings are generated according to the rules of the game.

Another way of putting this, one that doubtless would have been more recognizable to Frost himself, would be to recall the division between public and private spheres endemic to the culture of Ancient Greece.[40] The classical world made a categorical distinction between private domains of sexuality and the public realm of civic responsibility, and, again, it is possible to see the narrative of "Birches" working its way uneasily from one side of this equation to the other. In 1925, Gorham B. Munson wrote an essay in the *Saturday Review* praising Frost as "the purest classical poet in America today," a description with which the poet himself was so enamored that he invited Munson to write a book-length profile of his work.[41] This commission resulted in *Robert Frost: A Study in Sensibility and Good Sense*, published in 1927. Frost, as always, had his reservations about the finished critical product, but Munson makes an interesting analogy here between Frost's proverbial wisdom and that form of common sense, in the etymological meaning of that term, the sense held in common by a particular community: "Commonsense," he argues, "is a community of judgements, intellectual, emotional and practical, upon life. It is an exact balance demanding the utmost strenuousness to achieve and the perfection and harmony of our faculties. Good sense is a gift: commonsense must be deliberately arrived at, as witness the efforts of Socrates."[42]

Munson's description in this book of conscious parallels between classical paradigms and twentieth-century culture, of the kind that we find in the works of Eliot and Joyce, again suggests the influence of modernist principles on Frost's poetry. In his 1939 essay, "The Figure a Poem Makes," Frost in fact chose to describe himself as one of the "modern abstractionists."[43] On the face of it, this self-definition might seem somewhat surprising, but it underlines that Frost never intended his concern for local rhetoric to blind him or his readers to those more abstract virtues associated with his particular style of American modernist writing. Indeed, the poet's own concern to foreground these universalizing qualities in his work implies that he was trying to design a popular, bipartisan brand of American modernism that would not suffer from the fatal "parting of the ways" that Raymond Williams saw as characteristic of the parallel movement in English literature.[44] For Williams, English modernism in the early twentieth century had divided cataclysmically into an obscurantist formalism underwritten by traditional forms of cultural privilege—exemplified, above all, by the elitism surrounding the Bloomsbury circle—and, on the other hand, a tradition of social realism linked more directly to pressing concerns of economic survival and social class. This, however, is a dichotomy that Frost, "the ordinary man's modernist," set himself specifically to collapse.[45]

It is noticeable, for instance, that although Frost was always uncomfortable on a personal level with Eliot, the native Missourian who had gone to London to reinforce those social and artistic hierarchies that the American popular poet himself eschewed, he nevertheless recognized that he and Eliot were both "modern abstractionists," even if of a different kind. At a reception for Frost in London in 1957, the New England writer told Eliot that they had both "shot off at different tangents from almost the same pin wheel," and Eliot returned the compliment by making various remarks about Frost's "universality": "I think that there are two kinds of local feeling in poetry," said Eliot. "There is one kind which makes that poetry only accessible to people who had the same background, to whom it means a great deal. And there is another kind which can go with universality: the relation of Dante to Florence, of Shakespeare to Warwickshire, of Goethe to the Rhineland, the relation of Robert Frost to New England. He has that universality."[46] Eliot's critical approach here typifies the way Frost was made to appear intellectually respectable after the Second World War: he became gradually incorporated into the canons of modernism valorized by the "myth and symbol" Americanists of this era precisely because his concern for oblique formal questions enabled him to be recuperated as one of the "modern abstractionists." Frost's most famous poems did not, explained John Lynen in 1960, simply describe plain old snow on snowy evenings; they were also invoking that abstract quality of enigmatic blackness recognizable from the white whale in *Moby-Dick*, and from other scenes with metaphysical innuendoes in the established topographies of American literature.[47]

In this sense, Frost's engagements, however oblique, with the international dimensions of modernism served to shore up his reputation as a world figure. In the years after the Second World War, established American poets like Frost and Wallace Stevens looked to validate their intellectual credentials by engaging self-consciously with various cosmopolitan aesthetic practices, drawing on the legacy of an international modernism that by then had become, as Huyssen noted, "realigned with the conservative liberalism of the times."[48] In 1942, James Soby, a friend of Stevens and administrator at the Museum of Modern Art in New York, hailed "the beginning of a period during which the American traditions of freedom and generosity may implement a new internationalism in art, centered in this country." Warning that it "would be disastrous to apply rigid standards of nationalism to the arts," Soby nevertheless welcomed the way the 1940s had shifted the "center" of modernism to the United States, whose "native" practitioners could now enjoy the "broadening effect" of contact with artists driven into exile in America by the political situation in Europe. Around this time, then, the emerging exceptionalist sense of the United States as a country set apart from the ravages of war was buttressed by the country's new understanding of itself as, in Alan Filreis's words, "the inevitable safe harbor for great art under duress elsewhere."[49]

Just as Stevens assiduously visited exhibitions that featured paintings by European modernists in the 1940s, so Frost's growing willingness to equate himself with figures like Eliot during the 1950s suggests that he had come to recognize by this time the sophisticated manipulation of formalist tropes as a kind of patriotic endeavor. One mark of the technocratic expertise of the United States during this cold war era involved its capacity to appropriate the utopian impulses of modernism as a form of cultural capital, to direct them toward its own national ends. In other words, a willingness to accommodate the indeterminate dynamics of modernist aesthetics became a sure sign of America's cultural superiority to the Soviet Union on the intellectual battlefield of the cold war; whereas the Soviets were disparaged for still favoring what were commonly described as lumbering, anachronistic modes of socialist realism, the Americans prided themselves on preferring a style supposedly "above" politics, a style characterized by a mythic, allusive, and opaque language that drew openly on the prestige accumulated by modernist claims toward universalism.

Given the implicitly nationalist teleology underpinning these cosmopolitan formulas in the post-1945 era, it is not surprising that the growing academic acknowledgment at this time of Frost as a complex poet, someone who was addressing deeper themes than appeared to be the case at first sight, added to the general esteem surrounding him. Richard Poirier's book, *Robert Frost: The Work of Knowing* (1977), might be seen as the culminating account of his poetry within this universalizing context, because it assiduously turns Frost into an emblem of modernism whose texts are constructed through elaborate wordplay and self-canceling rhetoric. Frost, according to Poirier, typically piles up negatives to pretend to hide the very thing he is declaring, and this ensures that his pastoral scenes tend to be underwritten by a confessional subtext of sexual or psychological complication. Frost's work, in this interpretation, represents a play of antithetical signs, a textual field where antagonistic crosscurrents are brought into perpetual circulation, and where aesthetic resolution involves merely that "momentary stay against confusion" guaranteed by the action and reaction of opposite forces.[50] Poirier traces Frost's treatment of poetry as "performance," and he relates his epistemological skepticism to a genealogy of American pragmatism reaching back through Emerson and William James.[51] He also reads Frost in a belated New Critical manner, understanding his structural self-reflexivity to be an internalization of the principle of irony, where no statement can withstand the interrogation of a liberal consciousness committed to the principles of fluidity and open-mindedness. This, of course, constituted something like the official ideology of the United States during this cold war era: the cultural prospect of "freedom" was linked to an ability to see different sides of any particular question, together with a refusal to be coerced dogmatically into accepting any fixed position. Hence, as Eric Cheyfitz and others noted, it is not difficult to see how New Criticism became established as the formalist correlative to American literary nationalism at this time. Indeed, the rapid institutionalization of New Criticism in the postwar American academy trained a generation of future citizens to attend to the subtle interplay of ambiguity and tensions in American culture more generally.[52]

Not coincidentally, it was during this cold war era that Frost's poetic persona came fully "into its own," as he had prophesied in *A Boy's Will*, with his populist skepticism appearing to embody synecdochically that concern for a mythic image of freedom in American culture as a whole. The poem "Skeptic," from the 1947 collection *Steeple Bush*, perfectly enunciates this reflexive, self-ironizing idiom that became associated with the free voice of America in these early cold war years:

> Far star that tickles for me my sensitive plate . . .
> I don't believe I believe you're the last in space,
> I don't believe you're anywhere near the last. (389)

Yet it is also not difficult to see how Frost's poems of this time also refract the neutralizing dynamics of the cold war in the way they disarm ideas or propositions by playing them off against mirror images of themselves. "Two Leading Lights," again from *Steeple Bush*, juxtaposes the sun and moon in a celestial dualism where each comes to define the other.

Again, this represents a classic metaphor of "containment culture," in Alan Nadel's phrase, where the idea of one cosmic force (America, freedom) can be imagined only through a form of binary opposition (the Soviet Union, totalitarianism) that explicitly threatens but implicitly reinforces it.[53]

Much of Frost's most compelling work in this period is organized around this principle of doubleness and repetition, repetition that appears not only in overt thematic patterns—as in "Two Look at Two" (1923)—but also, more surreptitiously, in the formal patterning of a poem like "Something for Hope" (1946), the poem from which *Steeple Bush*'s title was taken:

> At the present rate it must come to pass,
> And that right soon, that the meadowsweet
> And steeple bush, not good to eat,
> Will have crowded out the edible grass.
>
> Then all there is to do is wait
> For maple, birch, and spruce to push
> Through meadowsweet and steeple bush
> And crowd them out at a similar rate . . .
>
> A cycle we'll say of a hundred years.
> Thus foresight does it and laissez-faire,
> A virtue in which we all may share
> Unless a government interferes. (375–76)

As with all classic pastoral, this poem is only nominally about agricultural life. Its more crucial images revolve around conceptions of cyclic time and self-replication, with the internal verbal echoes and regular verse pattern betokening an interlocking, self-contained structure that becomes, in itself, a guarantee of the universe of repetition it is describing. Frost's mode of pastoral order, in other words, is designed as a form of containment, a defense against radically discordant elements that would not acquiesce in the ritualistic exchange of rhyme. By specifically associating the value of government noninterference with this supposedly timeless pattern, Frost enacts a typical hegemonic gesture whereby the cultural is equated with the "natural." The values of American free enterprise are invested accordingly with a mythic status.

This is why Frost's cold war persona so closely identifies poetic order with national identity. A poem, he writes in "The Constant Symbol"

(1946), is "a figure of the will braving alien entanglements." The most significant word here is "alien," with its implication of how "every single poem written regular," as he puts it, replicates the imposition of a moral order designed to confront forces that may be literally or metaphorically foreign. In this essay, Frost deliberately equates aesthetic control with patriotic endeavor, "the way the will has to pitch into commitments deeper and deeper to a rounded conclusion . . . be it in art, politics, school, church, business, love, or marriage."[54] He continued in this overtly political vein throughout the rest of his life, describing himself in 1949 as not a regionalist but a "realmist" who wrote "about realms of democracy and realms of spirit," and proclaiming in 1952 that anyone who disliked nature was probably a communist.[55] The role of public bard also formed the basis of the famous political interventions toward the end of his life: his recital of "The Gift Outright" at Kennedy's inauguration in 1961, and the trip to the Soviet Union in 1962, where he demonstrated his cold war credentials by urging Khrushchev to support a "noble rivalry" between the superpowers, as though politics, like poetry, were a closed system structured around clearly demarcated fields of play.[56]

It was during this later phase of his life, said Lionel Trilling, that Frost became "virtually a symbol of America."[57] The way the poet orchestrated this self-mythologization was by aligning his oracular verse with an aesthetics of abstraction, defined by Philip Fisher in nationalist terms as a mode predicated on the "subtraction of differences." Frost's poems, like Fisher's models of the Cartesian suburb or the style of abstract expressionism, comprise forms of "democratic social space" where repetition and interchangeability become the most crucial markers within the system.[58] A poem like "Something for Hope" is less about New England or any other specific place than about how this self-replicating pastoral object works as a mirror of the larger matrix that encompasses it. In this sense, Frost's poems, through their processes of abstraction, devise a kind of mobile grid through which American readers become free to appropriate these symbols as part of their national iconography. Frost's artistic strategy thus owes less to the phenomenological particularism of William Carlos Williams, say, than to the corporate networks that bound the nation together throughout Frost's career, from mass production in the early years of the twentieth century to the development of freeways and network television after the Second World War.[59] All of these modes of circulation were geared not toward diversity but toward homogeneity, toward self-generation and modular repetition. Thus, the reason Frost's work became so popular in the 1950s was not so much because of its rural nostalgia, but because, paradoxically enough, it seemed so modern. The aesthetics of mechanical reproduction in his poetry formed a precise counterpart to those larger cultural narratives that were being generated throughout the United States in the service of this normative grid of abstraction.

The idea of an American writer choosing deliberately to speak on behalf of his national community goes back as far as Emerson and Whitman, of course. But Frost conceived his mythological role differently, or at least in a more technological way, because his enterprise involved appropriating the engines of mass communication for his own purposes. Rather than enjoying Emerson's faith in an "organic" relation between "the timely man" and national destiny, of the kind outlined in "The Poet" (1844), Frost's reinvention of Emerson's "representative" voice for this age of mass media involved a more astute awareness of the fraught conditions of mechanical reproduction and popular reception.[60] Frost was, in a way, the Warhol of his time, skillfully able to manipulate the iconography of nationalism in the interests of a vigorous self-promotion as he toured college campuses after the Second World War. This kind of circular relationship between spokesperson and community is described by Bourdieu as a form of "political fetishism"; the fetishizing of national identity, for instance, indicates a process through which individuals constitute themselves as part of a group, while at the same time losing control of the group in and through which they are constituted. Bourdieu explains that this exercise of "symbolic" power relies on a "sort of usurpatory ventriloquism, which consists in giving voice to those in whose name one is authorized to speak."[61] From this perspective, the apparent symbiosis between Frost as unofficial poet laureate and the extended circles of his national audience would give the American public an illusion that the orator was speaking on their behalf, despite the fact that his texts emerged from within a fractious ideological condition, and despite the way they project a particular and very partial manner of social control. The "oracle effect," as Bourdieu describes it, consists in that sleight-of-hand whereby the representative figure succeeds in translating himself from history into mythology, thereby seeming to rise above the contingent divisions of material circumstances by presenting himself as "a transcendent moral person":

It is in what I would call the *oracle effect*, thanks to which the spokesperson gives voice to the group in whose name he speaks, thereby speaking with all the authority of that elusive, absent phenomenon, that the function of priestly humility can best be seen: it is in abolishing himself completely in favour of God or the People that the priest turns himself into God or the People. It is when I become Nothing—and because I am capable of becoming Nothing, of abolishing myself, of forgetting myself, of sacrificing myself, of dedicating myself—that I become Everything. I am nothing but the delegate of God or the People, but that in whose name I speak is everything, and on this account I am everything. The oracle effect is a veritable *splitting of personality*: the individual personality, the ego, abolishes itself in favour of a transcendent moral person.[62]

The crucial point to recognize here is how Bourdieu's oracle effect depends on the "splitting of personality." In the earlier romantic vision of Emerson, the seer's task was to express himself "symmetrically and abundantly, not dwarfishly and fragmentarily"; but for Frost, as for Bourdieu, a more impersonal manipulation of fragmented perspectives becomes a necessary part of the enterprise.[63] Frost's symbolic vistas thus incorporate acts of ventriloquism, whereby, within the theater of operations, the idea of freedom is not merely a natural good, but also, more immediately, a performative effect. In this way, Frost's texts work as fields of force through which certain paradoxical divisions are acted out. In "Our Singing Strength" (1923), for instance, the capacity for articulation is said to be intimately entwined with a trope of repression, the censorship of society as well as of self:

> Well, something for a snowstorm to have shown
> The country's singing strength thus brought together,
> That though repressed and moody with the weather
> Was nonetheless there ready to be freed
> And sing the wild flowers up from root and seed. (240)

Freedom in this vision involves a breaking of bonds, the transgressive rupture of that restraint that would smother it. This metaphorically imitates the dynamic of cold war nationalism that could define patriotic liberation only through a binary opposition reinscribing those negative polarities that Frost's poems set out deliberately to repel.

James R. Dawes has written about the psychological investment in transgression in Frost's poems, his interest in flirting with Gothic modes to explore realms of the clandestine and perverse.[64] This is true enough, but it is important to recognize how this irruption of a transgressive idiom also functions in a larger public sphere, because one of the central concerns of Frost's work is the staging of a dialectic between terrain that is off-limits and the purifying forces of light. As a political and cultural issue, as Richard Burt has said, censorship is less about blocking access to forbidden material than about staging just this kind of show trial between integrity and corruption.[65] Hence—and this is a point Bourdieu also makes—it is difficult to define precisely what counts as censorship in any given context, because the realm of the "doxa," or the undisputed, is organized around the internalization of a deeper or "structural censorship."[66] This is exactly the kind of circuit we find played out in Frost's nationalist idiom: constantly, he glimpses some kind of threatening object, only to pull up his drawbridge in a violent act of censorship. His strategies of rhetorical idealism therefore tend to involve preserving boundaries, creating closed systems of various kinds. By appearing to fold in on themselves, these systems create an imaginary state of national security, a technocratic defense against "alien entanglements."[67] The practice of "mending walls" in Frost's poetry is not just about the construction of contingent meanings for pragmatic purposes; it is also linked, critically, to the reproduction of larger social meanings and the systems that support them.

The analogy I want to pursue here is between a political fetishism, which maintains itself through a series of iconographic enclosures and exclusions, and that form of aesthetic fetishism or decadence that, as we have seen, manifests itself as a residual presence within Frost's inclusive modernist style. Jennifer Terry, in theorizing "deviant historiography," emphasizes that the idea of a deviant subject is constructed in relay or relation between hegemonic and marginal discourses, so that transgression should be seen as central to a "narrative history of the *normal*"; concomitantly, one curious thing about Frost's poetic career is the way he takes violent, disturbing material of all kinds and turns it around so that it comes to seem not only acceptable but, bizarrely enough, both a patriotic necessity and an ethical imperative.[68] In this sense, what Lentricchia calls Frost's "ambidextrous ability" to blend high and low cultures might be understood more cynically as a method of division, a means of keeping different spheres separate by pulling them tantalizingly into visible relation before finally putting up the separating screens.⁶⁹ At the same time, though, it is the disturbed, profane subtext of a poem like "Birches" that gives Frost's myths of folksy accessibility their powerful and poignant valence. In other words, his style of cold war modernism in the *Steeple Bush* poems, predicated on the attraction and repulsion of antagonistic opposites, involves a metaphorical externalization and partial suppression of those self-consciously decadent elements that inspired his early work.

The theoretical notion of fetishism involves a process of splintering and substitution, through which the sacralized object comes to signify what is absent to itself. These are precisely the kind of crevices that are opened up in Frost's projections of the "national symbolic order."⁷⁰ On one level, America is represented in his poetry as a kind of extended family, blithely imbibing the mass culture this "Sunday-school paragon," in Malcolm Cowley's phrase, produces on their behalf.⁷¹ A poem such as "Happiness Makes Up in Height for What It Lacks in Length," published in 1942, epitomizes Bourdieu's oracle effect in the way its sibylline, enigmatic style conveys an illusion of primacy, as though the poet were a prophet rising above the turmoil of world war to issue his riddling instructions from the shrine:

> O stormy, stormy world
> The days you were not swirled
> Around with mist and cloud,
> Or wrapped as in a shroud,
> And the sun's brilliant ball
> Was not in part or all
> Obscured from mortal view—
> Were days so very few
> I can but wonder whence
> I get the lasting sense
> Of so much warmth and light.
> If my mistrust is right
> It may be altogether
> From one day's perfect weather,
> When starting clear at dawn
> The day swept clearly on

To finish clear at eve.
I verily believe
My fair impression may
Be all from that one day
No shadow crossed but ours
As through its blazing flowers
We went from house to wood
For change of solitude. (333)

The charismatic effect of this piece derives both from its abstraction—it emanates not from a particular time or place, but from a mythological type—and from its authoritative tone. The clipped lines, as in Emerson's poetry, suggest how the aphoristic style veers away from empirical description toward realms of the transcendent or vatic, with the extended, declaratory title adding to this derealized effect. It evokes not so much a conception of American pastoral as a vision of some primordial, Edenic innocence, a world prior to storm or shadow.

We might compare this prophetic tone to that of an earlier poem, "Once by the Pacific" (1928), which seems to mingle a similar gnomic or riddling quality with a bizarre anthropomorphic childishness:

The shattered water made a misty din.
Great waves looked over others coming in,
And thought of doing something to the shore
That water never did to land before.
The clouds were low and hairy in the skies,
Like locks blown forward in the gleam of eyes.
You could not tell, and yet it looked as if
The shore was lucky in being backed by cliff,
The cliff in being backed by continent;
It looked as if a night of dark intent
Was coming, and not only a night, an age.
Someone had better be prepared for rage.
There would be more than ocean-water broken
Before God's last *Put out the Light* was spoken. (250)

Again, we have an apocalyptic or oracular impulse here, but in this case, the idiom is juxtaposed with picturesque personifications more typical of a child's picture book: waves that "looked over others coming in," clouds "low and hairy in the skies," and so on. By foregrounding his extravagant similes, Frost succeeds in having it both ways: he inscribes a fortuitous cosmic harmony ("it looked as if / The shore was lucky in being backed by cliff"), while at the same time preserving a withdrawn skepticism that refuses to be taken in by such mythological charades. In line with this double-edged impulse, the cloud's hairy "locks" pun on the process of locking in that this poem enunciates, a defensive enclosure or circumscription of meaning. This is, in turn, implicitly contrasted with the imminent fracture of these mythopoeic designs; there is another pun in the penultimate line on "ocean-water *broken*": the breaking of the waves, but also this landscape breaking in upon itself. Such referential duplicity makes the poem's conclusion both domestic and apocalyptic at once, with the divine injunction to eternal darkness becoming comically diminished to the voice of a petty household tyrant.

The primary issue emphasized by these disjunctions and distortions in Frost's poetic world is the strong connections between fetishism and belief. Kaja Silverman, working from a Lacanian psychoanalytic perspective, argues that the "reality" of any given society depends on a "commensurability of penis and phallus, actual and symbolic father," that is to say, between the affective conditions of mastery and its symbolic determinants.[72] Where some kind of tension arises between these two levels of emotional and intellectual investment, belief itself quickly contracts into that fetishistic paraphernalia that constitutes in itself a dark, parodic mirror of all value systems. This is why, as W. J. T. Mitchell has said, there is such an uncomfortable proximity between modernism and fetishism as discursive domains. Modernism, like fetishism, places its faith in the "irrational, timeless power discovered in the exotic arts of the primitive"; this affiliation between the sacred and the secular is mirrored also in "commodity fetishism," described by Mitchell as "the projection of a magical halo onto expensive or well-publicized objects."[73] The modernist compulsion to turn art into a religion, in other words, is disconcertingly shadowed by the parodic cathexis of fetishism, which reduces the spirit of religion itself to a material work of art. Modernism might thus be said to operate along a mythological continuum, with religion as its "highbrow" and fetishism as its "lowbrow" points of reference.

All this helps to explain the way Frost, as an ordinary man's modernist and acclaimed patriot, owed part of his popular success to an uncanny ability to juggle these structures of fetishism, so as to invest the radically disjunct scenarios of modernist consciousness with a more reassuring teleological aura. We have already seen how this pattern works in "Birches," where he appropriates the perverse aestheticism characteristic of Victorian decadence before reintegrating it into the mythopoeic nature of American pastoral. "Directive" (1947) is another of his famous poems that conjoins an aphoristic resolution—"Drink and be whole again beyond confusion" (379)—with narrative displacements and juxtapositions that range from the tortuous to the absurd:

> Back out of all this now too much for us,
> Back in a time made simple by the loss
> Of detail, burned, dissolved, and broken off
> Like graveyard marble sculpture in the weather,
> There is a house that is no more a house
> Upon a farm that is no more a farm
> And in a town that is no more a town. (377)

This rhetoric of paradox, with all of its self-canceling negatives, leads into all kinds of subsequent anomalies, whose logic would appear to be that of the dreamscape rather than that of the pastoral genre in a more traditional sense:

> I have kept hidden in the instep arch
> Of an old cedar at the waterside
> A broken drinking goblet like the Grail
> Under a spell so the wrong ones can't find it,
> So can't get saved, as Saint Mark says they mustn't.
> (I stole the goblet from the children's playhouse.) (379)

It is, as Andrew M. Lakritz notes, not so easy to see how you can steal a goblet that appears to have been abandoned long ago. The narrative of "Directive" cannot be explicated in rational terms, but only in relation to its stylistics of inversion, its predilection for turning things around the other way, where every proposition is rotated into its contrary. Here, again, the goblet of legend is associated with "the children's playhouse," as though belief itself were a form of child's play.[74]

This discursive metamorphosis, in "Birches," "Directive," and other poems, makes for an odd conjunction between the face of social orthodoxy and ethical propriety on the one hand and a stranger, more labyrinthine world on the other. "Directive" is organized like a trompe l'oeil

painting, whose apparently clear-headed conclusion is altogether belied by the circular syntax that has preceded it. Just as Henry James's
twentieth-century writing was influenced by an emerging culture of surrealism, so Katherine Kearns has compared some of Frost's estranged
landscapes to those of Salvador Dali, and it is worth bearing in mind that
"Directive" was published at the height of Dali's fame in the United
States during the late 1940s.[75] Lakritz, thinking along similar lines, has
linked Frost with Marcel Duchamp in their mutual willingness to play
with ready-made forms so as to disturb an audience's preconceived expectations.[76] Indeed, there is a sense in which Duchamp, Dali, and Frost
were all willing to engage with the more banal commodities of popular
culture—the hackneyed conventions of pastoral verse, in Frost's case—in
an attempt iconoclastically to surprise their customers by renegotiating
these formal clichés through gestures of defamiliarization. Frost, like
Dali, walked a tightrope in the 1940s and 1950s between exploiting
commercial models and mounting an intellectual challenge to them; but
the oscillation in the works of these artists between high and low culture
was symptomatic of their attempt to build a bridge between the alienating
aesthetics of modernism and the more accommodating designs of a
popular surrealism.

The perversity of surrealism, as Charles Altieri explains it, involves
taking literally what modernism intends figuratively.[77] By their fetishistic
concentration on surfaces, and by their materialist refusal to sublimate
physical objects into rarefied forms of symbolism, the surrealists left
modernist ideals ironically exposed as the strange chimeras they are.
Birches, from this perspective, would remain just birch trees; a drinking
goblet would always be a childhood toy, a material entity ineligible for
aggrandizement into an emblem of the holy grail. These fetishized objects appear here as ghostly parallels to the poet's invocation of an idealized America infused by the clear light of transcendent design, what
Frost in his poem for Kennedy called a "Gift outright of 'The Gift Outright'" (422). But one peculiar thing about Frost's flirtation with this
kind of popular surrealism is that it seems to run in parallel with, rather
than simply to controvert, the symbolic manifestations of America in his
work. Following the logic of fragmentation in Bourdieu's oracle effect,
whereby material phenomena become credited with a teleological authority, Frost's voice of America appears to requisition these hollowed-
out objects as emblems of national culture. Again, the "ambidextrous"

style of his poetry lies partly in its capacity to slide between highbrow and lowbrow versions of mythography.

To desublimate Frost in this way is to suggest his connections with the commodity culture as well as the political paranoia of the United States in the middle years of the twentieth century. Poirier's modernist interpretation of Frost, as we saw, turned on a critical quest to recover the writer's inner, authentic "work of knowing," highlighting the strands of romanticism, pragmatism, and skepticism that were said to constitute his commitment to a mythic agenda of American freedom in the cold war era. A reading of Frost's work as inflected by popular surrealist aesthetics, however, would lay less stress on the poet's own supposedly individualistic voice and more on the way he constructed a persona appropriate to the homogenizing conditions of the United States in the postwar era. By engaging on a transnational level with the decadent strains of early modernism in his first books of poetry, Frost gave himself an intellectual basis on which to reimagine the corporate systems of cold war America as, in Bourdieu's phrase, a form of "political fetishism." Frost's implicit transnational perspective, in other words, serves to denaturalize his poetry, to indicate how it is based not just on maverick, colloquial patterns of speech, but also, crucially, on elaborately self-enclosed and self-reflecting systems of meaning. Frost's oracle effect involved a process of displacing or virtualizing his own popular poetic idiom, so that he could ventriloquize himself as the abstract voice of a modular, interchangeable America.

If a half-suppressed impulse of decadence gives Frost's early poetry its peculiar power, the institutionalization of political fetishism gives his later work its oracular authority and public force. While Lionel Trilling in 1959 called Frost "virtually a symbol of America," we might turn this around by suggesting that to read the poet in terms of his oracle effect is to understand him rather as a symbol of virtual America, where national identity itself is recast as something approximating a fetishized, derealized phenomenon.[78] To trace the residual logic of fetishism in Frost's poetry is not to suggest that his texts became immobilized in a phase anterior to modernism, but to argue that they come to embody this obstructive material even in their later incarnations, so that the modernist impulse of Frost's work is always shadowed by these dense, inchoate, and disruptive forces, forces that create interference in his aesthetic and symbolic orders. In this sense, it is possible to trace continuities between the more overtly transnational influences, the strands of decadence, that permeate his earlier poetry and the alien subtexts shadowing the fetishized national mythologies that circulate around his later work. It is not difficult to see that Frost was so keen to understand the making of poetry as a replica of the will's engagement with "alien entanglements" because these alien entanglements are so firmly embedded within the structures of his texts themselves. But it is equally important to recognize that, in accordance with Frost's art of paradox and reversal, his conscious projection of American national values was itself another facet of this style of doubleness or diplopia.

## 6

*Virtual Eden:* Lolita,

*Pornography, and the Perversions*

*of American Studies*

At the time when Robert Frost was promoting the virtues of aesthetic, ethical, and political boundaries on national radio, Vladimir Nabokov was writing his own refractory tribute to the iconography of American nationalism. As a native of St. Petersburg and the author of works in Russian and French as well as English, Nabokov would not appear to be the most obvious avatar of American studies in the subject's nationalist phase of the 1950s. My argument, however, is that *Lolita,* which first appeared in 1955, can be seen as symbiotically intertwined with various classic texts of American studies that helped to invent and define the field during the Truman and Eisenhower years. At times, the dream of Eden that permeates Nabokov's narrative impels it toward becoming a parody of the early American studies movement, which harbored within its collective consciousness similar vestiges of an imaginary paradise. More dexterously, though, *Lolita* makes the theoretical parameters of this movement visible, so that Nabokov's novel might more accurately be described as a metafiction of area studies, a text that holds up a mirror to the implicit assumptions of American studies and renders them translucent. Just as the process of metafiction can reilluminate ways in which more traditional artifacts have been constructed, so Nabokov's virtualization of American studies also reflects back on the established boundaries of other national formations and nation-states, foregrounding the contingent status of their supposedly naturalized values and social markers. In particular, by focusing on the cultural reception of *Lolita* in Britain, we see how the book brings into play troublesome questions about the relationships among formal aesthetics, public morality, and social power. Nabokov's perverse reinscription of American studies might, therefore, be seen ironically to highlight the multiple dilemmas involved in circumscribing specific national territories for academic study or political jurisdiction.

In this sense, the formal properties of Nabokov's fiction aptly mirror the formalization of American studies after the Second World War. Although an increasing consciousness of, and popular commitment to, the idea of the United States making up a common culture can be traced back to the 1930s—when, as Warren I. Susman notes, phrases like "an American Way of Life" and "the American Dream" first came into general use—it was not until later that the subject became professionally institutionalized in the American academy.[1] Henry Nash Smith is sometimes said to be the first person awarded a Ph.D. in American studies, at Harvard in 1940, for a dissertation that was to form the basis of his book, *Virgin Land: The American West as Symbol and Myth,* published by Harvard University Press in 1950.[2] The American Studies Association was founded the following year, the same year that Nabokov began writing *Lolita;* he finished his novel in 1953, as Joseph McCarthy was taking charge of the House Un-American Activities Committee and the Rosenbergs were facing execution for allegedly transmitting atomic secrets to the Soviet Union. In both its conception and its execution, then, *Lolita* is a text shaped by the nationalistic contours of cold war America. The narrative itself spans the period from 1947, when the term cold war was first coined, to 1952, the point at which Irving Howe was categorizing this era in the *Partisan Review* as an "Age of Conformity."[3] In the aftermath of the Second World War and the appearance of the Iron Curtain, a great deal of energy—and, of course, U.S. government funding—went into identifying the special characteristics of an American national character, and *Lolita,* for all of its mordant ironies, also participates in this patriotic quest.[4] In the book's representation of Middle America, as Lance Olsen has written, we see "a Norman Rockwell portrait of shady green suburbs atwinkle with children's laughter." Appropriately enough, Rockwell himself told an interviewer in 1959 that he had named his own dog Lolita.[5]

On the face of it, the conjunction of Rockwell's sentimental Americana with Nabokov's multilingual flamboyance might seem incongruous. Writing in 1959, for instance, F. W. Dupee cited with approbation one reviewer's remark that the author's mind "is so original that it might have arrived here by flying saucer."[6] Nevertheless, Nabokov's text positions itself self-consciously to reflect not only his own new nation—the writer and his family had arrived in the United States in 1940—but also the mythologies of that nation, the ways "America" itself was being framed and reduplicated in this cold war era. If we consider how its identity became academically consolidated as "symbol and myth," to use Henry Nash Smith's term, in the first wave of American studies scholarship during the 1950s, the sense in which the iconography of *Lolita* runs in parallel to these institutional formulas is striking. Nabokov himself would have encountered this academic phenomenon at Cornell University, which established an interdepartmental B.A. in American studies in 1950, two years after he began teaching there; by 1957, Robert H. Elias, a member of the English Department who was serving as chair of the Committee on American Studies, was reporting that the "program at Cornell offers unusually rich opportunities for the selection of courses in the various fields related to American Studies" at both the undergraduate and graduate levels.[7] Nabokov continued as a professor at Cornell until 1959, and so his tenure would have run alongside the development of these cross-disciplinary experiments in discursive nationalism.

One obvious coincidence here involves the link between academic projections of the United States as a young nation and Nabokov's affiliation of his prepubescent heroine with the youthful bounties of America itself. In 1955, the year *Lolita* was first published in Paris, Leslie Fiedler produced *An End to Innocence,* a collection of his writings that also included one new essay, "Adolescence and Maturity in the American Novel." This chapter, which was to form the conceptual basis of Fiedler's *Love and Death in the American Novel* five years later, argued that even the "best [American] writers appear unable to mature," so that "their themes belong to a pre-adult world, and the experience of growing old tends to remain for them intractable." Fiedler primarily had in mind characters like Huckleberry Finn and the boyish heroes of Hemingway as he wrote of how "images of childhood and adolescence haunt our greatest works as an unintended symbolic confession of the inadequacy we sense but cannot remedy."[8] Whatever the moral force of Fiedler's cultural critique, his equation of American literature with the innocence of childhood served to reinforce the establishment of youth as a privileged site for the identification of American character in this cold war era. As Leerom

Medovoi has observed, critics such as Ihab Hassan seized on the qualities of adolescent exuberance and "hope" in novels like *The Catcher in the Rye* as typological guarantees of American freedom and mobility, in contrast to the malevolent determinism of Russia's evil empire.[9] Thus, when he pays tribute to Lolita's innocence and declares that he intends "to protect the purity of that twelve-year-old child," Humbert Humbert is, despite himself, perversely participating in that tribute to youthful insouciance that underwrote the nationalist agenda of cold war America.[10]

It is not difficult to locate similar homologies between the self-consciously Americanist idiom of *Lolita* and the discursive framework of American studies in the 1950s. In the same year *Lolita* appeared, R. W. B. Lewis published *The American Adam,* his mythological vision of "the authentic American as a figure of heroic innocence and vast poten-tialities, poised at the start of a new history." For Lewis, America signified "a divinely granted second chance for the human race, after the first chance had been so disastrously fumbled in the darkening Old World"; and though he chastised contemporary citizens for their willingness to abandon that utopian promise by acquiescing in the limitations of what he called the postwar "age of containment," nevertheless Lewis urged his acolytes to move beyond weary irony and skepticism toward that "most fully engaged" mode, with its "odd aura of moral priority over the waiting world," that he associated with activist fictions such as *The Catcher in the Rye, Invisible Man,* and *The Adventures of Augie March.*[11] Again, this can be juxtaposed with the icons of innocence surrounding Lolita: she holds "in her hollowed hands a beautiful, banal, Eden-red apple" (58), before which Humbert finds himself "as helpless as Adam at the preview of early oriental history, miraged in his apple orchard" (71). Toward the end of the novel, after Lolita has absconded with Dick Schiller, Humbert similarly evokes this loss of innocence as he observes mournfully that Schiller's "Adam's apple was large and hairy" (267). While Nabokov travesties the prelapsarian idyll of 1950s America, his parodic impetus here works through the establishment of parallel narratives, whereby the utopian impulse is implicitly acknowledged as well as slyly subverted. Moreover, Lewis's complaint in *The American Adam* against contempo-rary ideas of "positive thinking," which he saw as a form of "fraud-ulence" designed to substitute "economic successes" for "morality," sounds remarkably similar in tone to the sardonic postures assumed by Humbert toward what he calls the "platitudinous" aspects of American mass culture (80).[12] Like Lewis, Humbert—though not necessarily Nabokov—elaborates his dream vision of the American Eden through an effort haughtily to exclude what is merely commercial or vulgar.

Humbert's journey, then, through his "elected paradise" (163) affords an idiosyncratic version of American transcendentalism. "What I had madly possessed," says the narrator, "was not she, but my own creation, another, fanciful Lolita—perhaps, more real than Lolita" (62). In the infamous scene where "Humbert the Hound" masturbates over Lolita on the Haze family couch, we find, bizarrely enough, an echo of Emerson's canonical thought. In Humbert's eyes, "Lolita had been safely solipsized. The implied sun pulsated in the supplied poplars; we were fantastically and divinely alone" (60). This image of an "implied sun" echoes the sixth section of *Nature*, where Emerson valorizes idealism through his philosophical perspective of self-reliance: "It is a sufficient account of that Appearance we call the World, that God will teach a human mind, and so makes it the receiver of a certain number of congruent sensations, which we call sun and moon, man and woman, house and trade. In my utter impotence to test the authenticity of the report of my senses, to know whether the impressions they make on me correspond with outlying objects, what difference does it make, whether Orion is up there in heaven, or some god paints the image in the firmament of the soul?"[13] In Emerson, this epistemology of idealism is linked inextricably with the faculties of individual isolation and so, potentially at least, solipsism. Similarly, Nabokov's personae are constantly attracted to what Vladimir Alexandrov called the "cosmic synchronization" of a putatively transcendent realm. In *Lolita*, though, this projection remains characteristically double-edged and playful, with the author simultaneously evoking and revoking such transcendentalist designs.[14]

These intertextual plays with the legacy of American romanticism manifest themselves all the way through Nabokov's narrative. An early chapter in *Lolita* includes a reference to the establishment of "a weather station on Pierre Point in Melville Sound" (34), thus recognizing obliquely Herman Melville's *Pierre*, another novel about the misfortunes of incest. Edgar Allan Poe, as many critics have observed, is another lingering presence in the text: Humbert attributes his infatuation with Lolita to the repetition of his love for "a certain initial girl-child" (11) by the name of Annabel, like Poe's Annabel Lee, and he teaches the works of "Monsieur Poe-poe," the "poet-poet," in his college classes (44).[15] The sweeping invocation of

America that emerges in Humbert's mad drive through the "crazy quilt of forty-eight states" (149) is also reminiscent of Whitman's national catalogue in *Song of Myself* (Nabokov had used the neologism "waltwhitmanesque" in his earlier *Bend Sinister*); as Fredrick Karl has noted, this quest also coincides with the protean quality of many American novels of the 1950s, whose capacity for extended mobility and spatial displacement embodies a chameleonic energy traditionally attributed to the American romance.[16] On his journey, Humbert stops at "a motel called Poplar Shade in Utah, where six pubescent trees were scarcely taller than my Lolita" (156), thereby alluding covertly to the metaphysical projection of America as, in Henry Nash Smith's phrase, a "virgin land." This is another metaphorical equation that had become a commonplace of American studies during the "myth and symbol" era: in mastering his female victim, Humbert, like Smith's Western pioneers, believes he is capturing the nubile essence of the American continent. On one level, this works as a grotesque parody of the academic endeavors pursued by Smith and his followers, and also illuminates, as in a crazy mirror, that diminution of female consciousness which, as Nina Baym and others have pointed out, silently framed American studies during its "classic" phase of the 1950s.[17] The theoretical transposition of women from active subjects into metaphorical or infantilized objects, implicit in the work of Smith and Lewis, is made ludicrously explicit and literal in the world of *Lolita*. Nabokov's double-edged discourse takes its peculiar valence from faithfully reproducing the logic of these myths promulgated by professional Americanists, before traducing them into uncanny shadows or simulacra of themselves.

Nabokov, then, ingeniously mimes the formal strategies of American studies, organized as it was around the canonical narratives of American romanticism, but he empties out the subject's moral content: the "Eden-red apple" is held punningly in Lolita's "hollowed hands" (58). Similarly, *Lolita* loyally replicates the consumer culture of Eisenhower's America, even while sardonically recasting it in an unfamiliar light. Humbert's comment that there "is a touch of the mythological and the enchanted" in large American department stores (107) echoes the argument of David Potter, in *People of Plenty* (1954), about how the exceptionalist genius of the American people arose directly from their privileged destiny of material abundance. Potter suggested, in particular, that the institution of advertising could be "peculiarly identified with American abundance," as it had become comparable to "the school and the church in the magnitude of its social influence"; his idea was that modern consumers had been educated and disciplined by the rituals of advertising, just as the behavior of congregations had been spiritually regulated by the Puritan church in former times.[18] Potter's strategy, characteristic of Americanist scholarship of this era, involved an iconoclastic transference of "high" into "low" culture and a subsequent revalidation of these less prestigious materials by relating them analogically to more traditional, established academic designs. The conceptual models underwriting these early theoretical moves in the field were the canonical declarations of cultural independence in the mid–nineteenth century: Emerson's perception of banks and tariffs resting "on the same foundations of wonder as the town of Troy, and the temple of Delphi," and Whitman's similarly neoplatonic alignment of epic prophecy and democratic vistas.[19]

Such interplay between scholarly abstraction and popular engagement is just what we find acted out, if on a more grotesque level, in *Lolita*. If Humbert's cerebral aloofness is teased and taunted by the vulgar world all about him, the novel's heroine is represented, in perfect accord with Potter's thesis, as "the ideal consumer": "If some café sign proclaimed Icecold Drinks, she was automatically stirred, although all drinks everywhere were ice-cold" (146). Though Humbert finds her "to be a disgustingly conventional little girl," he manifestly fails to avoid her "dopey-eyed" charms (145), and this exemplifies the disjunction in Nabokov's work between Humbert's sardonic, European snobbery and the text's richer, more bountiful evocation of Middle American life. America here emerges in the margins, as it were, mediated formally by a double helix of irony and duplicity. Through this rhetoric of duplicity, Humbert's dismissive satire refracts consumerist landscapes into those glamorized, fetishized states of objectification he finds so alluring and that ultimately bring about his downfall. In other words, the novel's rampant commodity fetishism—its exuberant lists of advertisements and popular jingles—mirrors, on some level, its implicit sexual fetishism, a mechanism that locks Humbert's relationship with his stepdaughter into an affair of iconography rather than interiority. Just as Potter's people of plenty have been prepared for their rituals of consumption by the institution of American advertising, so Humbert's psyche has been programmed to fixate on Lolita, partly in a compulsive repetition of his earlier love for Annabel, partly as a response to what he sees as the magical qualities of his new environment. From this perspective, "Lola the bobby-soxer" (60) becomes for Humbert synecdochic of the fabulous continent that he, "a brand-new American citizen of obscure European origin" (105), wishes to annex for his own purposes.

Nabokov was always troubled by the notion that *Lolita* might be seen, especially in Europe, as a critical appraisal of the United States.[20] He insisted repeatedly that he felt more at home in America than anywhere else, and, on the evidence of his letters, was a committed cold war American citizen in the sense of generally supporting the FBI and CIA, while believing the anti-McCarthyites did more damage than the Senator from Wisconsin himself. Nabokov's political attitudes toward America were crucially shaped by his traumatic flight from Russia at the time of the Soviet Revolution, and in later years he expressed regret "that 'America' has such a neutral a-political character," believing what was needed instead was more "vigorous political propaganda."[21] Nabokov shared with Robert Frost, that more prominent cold war activist, a conception of national identity centered on formal patterning and aesthetic resolution: Frost's "Stopping by Woods on a Snowy Evening" is cited in *Pale Fire* (1962), where John Shade pays tribute to the doubling and repetition of the poem's closing lines, which appear to him to bind the literal with the metaphysical in a self-mirroring loop of epistemological closure. *Pale Fire*, of course, parodies the 1950s style of American textual scholarship, whose generic patternings and obsessive methods of order become linked with various forms of typological idealism and Christian visions of "spiritual hope."[22] But, like *Lolita*, *Pale Fire* is also implicated in what it parodies, describing a model of aesthetic containment that becomes synonymous, at a structural level, with the ludic designs and self-regulating systems of America itself.

The difference with Nabokov is that he flaunts this paradoxical disjunction between autotelic aesthetic object and pastoral utopia that the authoritarian impulse of Frost attempts partially to suppress or neutralize. Eden for Frost involves a memory of the pasture, a nostalgia for tranquility and wholeness. Eden for Nabokov, on the other hand, is a purely artificial construction, metaphorically linked in Humbert's mind with the brothels he used to frequent in Paris; thinking back to his tryst with Monique, Humbert recalls that the room had a "mirror reflecting our small Eden" (24), a glass that effectively transposed this mock-utopian moment into a reflexive simulacrum of itself. In *Bend Sinister,* the Edenic motif becomes turned on its head and associated specifically with an escape from a climate of repression: the narrator of this text describes the flight from a foreign country to America as a return to Eden, with Eden becoming a location of the imagined future, a phantasmic paradise regained, rather than a memory of the lost past. In *Lolita,* similarly, Nabokov's persona wends his way through the "inutile loveliness" of Western landscapes (150) as well as among the utopian promises of popular advertisements, thus inverting the standard narrative of postlapsarian exile by aesthetically reconstituting America as a virtual Eden, a millennial realm of artifice, within whose fabricated parameters all the turmoils of sublimation might be integrated into a landscape of the sublime. Yet, this virtual Eden remains a fetishized, fragmented object at the same time it is being projected into a national ideal. As Alan Nadel has argued, what came to problematize cold war narratives of formal containment was the irruption of excess, signified by formal doubling and reduplication, into the "monologic discourse" sanctioned by the custodians of state security.[23] Humbert Humbert, true to his ambidextrous heritage, traverses the "crazy quilt" of America on the wrong side of the law. At the end of his journey, he even decides to follow the English custom by switching to the left-hand side of the road, reckoning that because he had disregarded all the other "laws of humanity" he might as well infringe traffic regulations by driving "on the queer mirror side" (298).

Such a denaturalization of Eisenhower's America by the sinister displacement of a "queer mirror" marks Humbert's contribution to the destabilization of cold war ideology. As an American citizen of hybrid European origins—French birth, Swiss father, English mother—he introduces into the New World a sense of the unassimilable and foreign. By refusing to accommodate himself to the laws of his host country, Humbert persists in interpreting its customs as conditional rather than binding. He constantly comments on the arbitrary provisions of American law, noting, for example, how far legal definitions of a "wayward child" in Massachusetts diverge from the practices of Ancient Egypt or Dante's Florence (21). From this vantage point Humbert's mission once again is to aestheticize America: to transform its landscape from the status of a natural environment into a constructed, and therefore reversible, object. In this sense, what one might term the hyperaesthetic aspect of Nabokov's style works brilliantly in the context of *Lolita*. Nabokov said elsewhere that he sometimes felt his "absence of a natural vocabulary" impeded the fluency of his writing, particularly when he was describing commonplace situations: "An old Rolls-Royce," as he put it, "is not always preferable to a plain Jeep."[24] But in *Lolita* this "old Rolls-Royce" is entirely appropriate, because the circumference of the novel encompasses an alien and transgressive universe, whose infractions of plain style are altogether commensurate with its radical subversion of moral probity.

By thus complicating the relationship between aesthetic representation and national security, Nabokov foregrounds the ways libidinal investments turn on conditions of ontological absence, as he transforms both the "nymphet" Lolita and the mythology of America itself into obscure objects of desire. In its classic forms, sublimation of this kind involves what Hans Loewald called "a differentiated unity," whereby cathectic desires become fused with symbolic displacements to bring about "new synthetic organizations" of emotional and philosophical experience. As Loewald puts it: "Sublimation is a kind of reconciliation of the subject-object dichotomy—an atonement for that polarization (the word *atone* derives from *at one*) and a narrowing of the gulf between object world and self."[25] This would also represent the traditional pattern of the conversion narrative, central to cold war constructions of American studies, through which matter is sublimated into spirit and old affections metamorphosed into transcendent new horizons. This is what we find in Crèvecoeur's myth of the melting pot, for example, a paradigmatic image for the school of American studies founded on ideas of national consensus. It is, however, precisely what we do not find in *Lolita*. Although Nabokov's narrative teases us with the idea of a metaphorical relationship between Lolita and America, Humbert Humbert's libidinal quest cannot, ultimately, transform itself into sublimity: he absurdly remains, as he says, "a humble hunchback abusing myself in the dark" (63).

Rather than interpreting his desire for Lolita as synecdochic of American mythology, then, Nabokov's duplicitous narrative leaves its hero stranded as engaged merely with his stepdaughter's seduction. In Jane Gallop's terms, the father who attempts to aggrandize his sexuality into the "objective" status of symbolic law finds his phallic desires unmasked and exposed ironically as a self-pleasuring phenomenon. In thus "dephallicizing the father," Nabokov's work of fiction disentangles the seductive and mythological levels that Humbert, in his self-aggrandizing way, had tried to bring together.[26] Yet, by opening up these divisions, these queer mirrors, the text also reflects back in its "crazy" way on the radically contingent, if not farcical, nature of national mythologies themselves. If Humbert's desire for Lolita is fetishistic, equally fetishistic are the signifying capacities of the nation-state.[27] By desublimating and disavowing Humbert's patriarchal authority, the novel also deconstructs those symbolic valences associated with the foundational era of American studies, suggesting that they can be recognized as mechanical simulacra rather than emblems of mythic or allegorical power: the song of the open road, the pubescent trees of the Virgin West, the Eden-red apple of Adamic innocence.

In this sense, Fiedler was surely right in his 1958 review of *Lolita* to surmise that it had encountered censorship problems "as an irreligious book rather than a pornographic one." Many novels were more sexually explicit, concluded Fiedler, but the peculiarly unsettling quality of Nabokov's work lay in its "blasphemy against the cult of the child" and its skill at parodying concomitant "myths of sentimentality."[28] As if in corroboration of Fiedler's comments, various American critics who have disliked Nabokov have pointed to what they see as his exaltation of ludic form over ethical content; Hugh Kenner, for instance, found the author's style "vindictively hollow," too much of "an intricate game" to invite the reader's empathy or attention.[29] Edmund Wilson, most famously, lambasted the Russian writer's "poses, perversities, and vanities which sound as if he had brought them from the St. Petersburg of the early nineteen-hundreds," a moralistic mode of critique reminiscent of nothing so much as *The Pilgrim's Progress,* where Bunyan puts formalism alongside hypocrisy as equivalent infractions against the plain code of Puritan righteousness.[30] Kenner, committed to "a homemade world," and Wilson, scathing about the exotic proclivities of a foreign culture, both intuit in Nabokov's writing tendencies of disaffiliation which they perceive to be disturbingly un-American.

In *Lolita,* as so often in Nabokov, this foreign quality is mediated through an aesthetic structure that appears paradoxical or oxymoronic. Humbert writes about the frontiers of the open road from his confined space "in legal captivity" (5), just as his tribute to the extended purviews of immortal love is predicated on capturing his stepdaughter, on keeping her closely within his guard. As Karl noted, for all of its emphasis on "spatiality and constant movement," the novel still conveys "a claustral, enclosed feeling."[31] This rhetoric of paradox is reminiscent of the author's earlier works, such as *Invitation to a Beheading* (1938 in Russian), where the execution of Cincinnatus is anticipated in a courtly, ritualistic manner, as though the participants were preparing for a feast. "A beheading or a tryst?" asks the narrator; "Everything merged totally."[32] As in *Lolita*, the prospects of confinement and escape here become mutually interwoven, so that the hero's projections of freedom come to seem less a product of spontaneous desires than of twisted reversals, where what appeared natural has become taboo, and vice versa. Given these structures of paradox, it becomes important to dissociate the tone of inversion or detachment in Nabokov's fictions from the idea of critical or ethical disapproval. In particular, any account of Nabokov and defamiliarization needs to consider not only these vacillations in narrative position, but also that the author was accused of being "foreign" and "unRussian" even when writing in his native tongue back in the 1930s.[33]

It is not, then, just American consumerism that becomes subject to a rhetoric of estrangement in the oxymoronic style of Nabokov's writing. Consequently, to align him with other refugees from Nazi Europe who engaged in radical critiques of American mass culture—Adorno, Horkheimer, Brecht—is misleading. Instead, the author appropriates his structural alienation from America as an ontological image of slippage and loss, a representation of how "exilic consciousness" negotiates the "space of not-being-there," as Emily Apter describes it.[34] Nabokov thus cherishes exilic consciousness as mimetic of a condition in which language and memory are always searching for their lost, ideal other. Slippage, rather than defamiliarization, is Nabokov's great theme: Shklovskij's defamiliarizing mode of *ostranenie* implies an element of rational control over the culture that is being objectified, but the genius of Nabokov's texts involves conjuring up a self-contradictory structure where rationality and obsession meet, where the satirical stance of his narrator finds itself overwhelmed by the emotional forces swirling all around him.[35]

This sense of slippage becomes particularly apparent in the novels Nabokov wrote about the United States. If the narratives he wrote in Europe are more like elaborate and ingenious chess games, the iridescent quality of his American works involves a heightened capacity to juxtapose his metafictional labyrinths with a mordant, plangent mood of insufficiency and ironic absence. In 1967, he remarked to an interviewer that, although he disliked the "Germanic regime of militarism and music" that he associated with Plato's *Republic,* he nevertheless found the Greek philosopher's theory of ideal forms both evocative and appealing: "I am afraid to get mixed up with Plato, whom I do not care for, but I do think that in my case it is true that the entire book, before it is written, seems to be ready ideally in some other, now transparent, now dimming dimension, and my job is to take down as much of it as I can make out and as precisely as I am humanly able to. The greatest happiness I experience in composing is when I feel I cannot understand, or rather catch myself not understanding (without the presupposition of an already existing creation) how or why that image or structural move or exact formulation of phrase has just come to me."[36] Seeing himself as the mediator between a ghostly state of plenitude and a material world of erratic contingency, Nabokov strategically sought out locations of exile that might provide an external correlative to this condition of dislocation. In *Speak, Memory* (1967), he writes that "homesickness has been with me a sensuous and particular matter"; speaking from Switzerland in 1964, he admitted: "I think I am trying to develop, in this rosy exile, the same fertile nostalgia in regard to America, my new country, as I evolved for Russia, my old one, in the first post-revolution years of West-European expatriation."[37]

From this angle, John Haegert's view that "the agent of [Humbert's] undoing is his own inability . . . to participate in the plenitude of American life on its own terms, without some mediating vision of Europe to direct and control it" ignores the fact that, for Nabokov's protagonists, rapture and rupture are necessarily part of the same dynamic process.[38] Zygmunt Bauman theorizes strangeness as that which is "physically near while remaining spiritually remote," understanding it as a force that reveals the limits of liberal pluralism by highlighting that which cannot, ultimately, be transformed or subsumed within an "in-group." "It is not the failure to acquire native knowledge that constitutes the outsider as a stranger," writes Bauman; "it is the existential constitution of the stranger which makes the native knowledge unassimilable."[39] According to this perspective, Nabokov's novels of the 1950s exist in an elusive state of in-betweenness: both homely and unhomely, American and alien, sublime and abject. Their aesthetic intensity derives not from attempting to occlude the difference between American nativism and stylistic misrecognition, as Haegert imagined, but rather from establishing a series of interlocking circuits where these forces rub up against each other, so as to become mutually reinforcing within the same paradoxical cycle.

To recognize how the sublime and the abject are inextricably intertwined in Nabokov's writing is to restore a perverse component in the subliminal field of American studies. In *Powers of Horror,* Julia Kristeva writes of abjection as situated "at the crossroads of phobia, obsession, and perversion," describing it as a liminal phenomenon that disturbs identity and system by its tendency toward the "immoral, sinister, scheming, and shady: a terror that dissembles, a hatred that smiles." Abjection is associated here with psychological divisions and traumatic dislocations; for the exile, the "abject from which he does not cease separating is for him—a *land of oblivion* that is constantly remembered," whose "symptom is the rejection and reconstruction of languages." If we map Kristeva's theoretical matrix onto the crosscurrents of *Lolita,* we see how Humbert's slippery multilingual facility becomes commensurate with the lost love of his youth, for whom Lolita herself represents both a fetishized substitute and a sublime simulacrum. Kristeva also writes of how "religious, moral, and ideological codes" attempt the "purification and repression" of abjection in the name of "the sleep of individuals and the breathing spells of societies"; yet she also suggests that these various catharses or acts of exclusion cannot annihilate the abject, which enjoys a chameleonic capacity to exist alongside, rather than in straightforward opposition to, "Prohibition and Law." In this prismatic light, the duplicitous character of Nabokov's novel can be seen to turn on its infiltration, rather than its refusal, of American mythologies. As Kristeva puts it: "The abject is perverse because it neither gives up nor assumes a prohibition, a rule, or a law; but turns them aside, misleads, corrupts; uses them, takes advantage of them, the better to deny them."[40]

*Lolita* thus runs the exalted or sublime alongside the abject or perverse to suggest how the metanarratives of transcendentalism, as reproduced in the conceptual field of American studies, form but crazy mirror images of Humbert's abject longing for a twelve-year-old nymphet. Nabokov suggests that the idealized "American Adam," as described in stentorian fashion by Lewis in the last year of Eisenhower's first presidential term, is predicated on the same cathectic virtualizations of an imaginary object that we find in Humbert's perverse elegy for Lolita, bedecked as she is in a dress patterned with little red apples. Nabokov accordingly transposes the study of America into a duplicitous rather than unitary area. Whereas Lewis, Marx, and the other founding fathers of American studies sought to reconcile subject and object, fact and symbol into a synthetic and syncretic account of America's fabled promise, Nabokov restores negative and transgressive elements within the circumference of this quest for transcendent sublimity. The seer's eye that in Emerson appears neoplatonically validated finds itself ironized in *Lolita*, where Humbert's drive for absolute power leads him, as he says, to solipsize his stepdaughter and to base his feigned omnipotence on a criminal desire for voyeuristic pleasure and sadistic control. There is in Nabokov's novels something that resembles the spy novel, an immensely popular genre during this cold war era, and here it is as if Humbert Humbert, with his foreign provenance, his doubled-up pseudonym and multiple identities, were in some sense spying on America. As with all good spies, he takes care to camouflage his proclivities by ingratiating himself with the world around him, and it is not until some time has passed that the good citizens of Ramsdale come to realize that Humbert does not subscribe to their pedagogical morality of literature nor their procreative morality of sex.[41]

One of the consequences of this duplicitous, parodic strain in *Lolita* is, as Lionel Trilling observed in 1958, "to throw the reader off balance," to expose him or her to the narrative's peculiar "ambiguity of tone." Trilling noted that it was this "curious moral mobility" that gave the book "its remarkable ability to represent certain aspects of American life."[42] We see here, of course, the New York critic implicitly trying to conscript Nabokov into his liberal imagination, where the absence of dogmatic certainty would supposedly attest to the open-minded characteristics of American national culture. This in itself involves another cold war fiction: the pluralistic indeterminacy of the United States against the totalitarian closure of the Soviet Union. Nevertheless, if we understand this indeterminacy as a form of generic heterodoxy rather than simply a mode of literary ambiguity or liberal tolerance, we can see how *Lolita*'s radical collapsing of aesthetic and moral categories, its tendency to mix up high and low cultures as well as to confound the sublime with the perverse, leads precisely to that point where the reader is caught "off balance," as Trilling so acutely saw. More recently, Rachel Bowlby has written of how *Lolita* embodies a "poetry of advertising," aestheticizing popular culture and creating a milieu where "high and low languages" interfere with each other "in both directions"; this again is suggestive of the stylistic hybridity of a text that cannot easily be situated on either side of any given dividing line that upholds, in its hierarchical domain, the "literary" canon.[43] In this sense, *Lolita,* for all its implicit parodies of the American studies agenda, also participates in that movement's "democratic" attempt to cut across traditional cultural distinctions, to reorganize discursive frameworks so they might appear to emerge heterogeneously from many different facets of the social body.

The problematic nature of *Lolita*'s status as highbrow literature bears directly on the censorship issues that have been associated with the book since its publication in Paris in 1955. The novel's publication history, very briefly, is that Nabokov originally had difficulty placing his manuscript and was relieved when it finally appeared under the imprint of the Olympia Press, run by Maurice Girodais, a publishing house that specialized in risqué and pornographic works. *Lolita* was successfully prosecuted for obscenity in London in 1956, and, at the request of the British Home Secretary, who was concerned about its importation across the English Channel, it was also banned in France in December of that year. In the United States, however, the book was never forbidden: a copy of the Olympia edition was seized by U.S. Customs, but subsequently cleared, leaving the way open for Putnam to publish the novel in 1958. (It continued to be barred in specific locations, however; Cincinnati Public Library, and several others, refused to stock it.) In Britain, meanwhile, *Lolita* had become a cause célèbre after Graham Greene selected it early in 1956 as one of the best novels of the previous year, leading to predictable ripostes from tabloid columnists about how it was "sheer unrestrained pornography . . . the filthiest book I have ever read."[44] While other public figures—notably, Sir Harold Nicolson and Vita Sackville-West—remained violently opposed to the book's publication in Britain, what crucially changed the legal climate was the passage of a revised Obscene Publications Act in 1959, which declared that a work should not be convicted of obscenity if it could be "justified as being for the public good on the ground that it is in the interests of science, literature, art, or learning, or of other objects of general concern." Given this clause of exception for artistic merit, Weidenfeld and Nicolson felt confident enough to publish the book in 1959, when it sold out on publication day.

The following year, the Director of Public Prosecutions sounded out various critical opinions on *Lolita,* but then opted to prosecute *Lady Chatterley's Lover* as a test case for the new law. Lawrence's novel, which had appeared in Penguin paperback, was acquitted in November 1960.[45]

In retrospect, it is not surprising that state prosecutors should have chosen to challenge *Lady Chatterley,* with its more obvious vernacular qualities—"Tha'rt good cunt, though, aren't ter?"—rather than grappling with the more elusive *Lolita.*[46] In his afterword to the novel, Nabokov dismissed modern pornography as a commercialized and entirely predictable operation, stylistically limited to "the copulation of clichés"; but he expressed more sympathy with the kind of "deliberate lewdness . . . with flashes of comedy" that he associated with the French Enlightenment (303). It is this libertine model, intermingling decorum and deviance, that lurks behind *Lolita;* Nabokov, unlike Lawrence, plays with veiled obscenities, imitating some of the classic moves of traditional erotica in the way he teasingly interlaces suggestiveness with conventional restraint. The scene of Lolita playing tennis, for example, incorporates a gamut of oblique sexual allusions within the ludic framework of a sport or game, an idiom that operates reflexively as an image of the author's ingenious purposes: "I suppose I am especially susceptible to the magic of games," he says. "In my chess sessions with Gaston I saw the board as a square pool of limpid water with rare shells and stratagems rosily visible upon the smooth tessellated bottom, which to my confused adversary was all ooze and squid-cloud" (228). There is also one reference in *Lolita* to Lewis Carroll—Humbert at one point makes out "a half-naked nymphet stilled in the act of combing her Alice-in-Wonderland hair" (257)—and, like Carroll, Nabokov enjoys the facility of wrapping up illicit inclinations in a polite and circuitous prose.[47]

It is, of course, this denial of transparent representation and perpetual shift in tone that makes *Lolita* so hard to classify as obscene or otherwise. Its multivalent aspects formally mimic a hybrid, heterogeneous social nexus that disturbs both American conceptions of community and British mystifications of class. *Lolita* was frequently mentioned in the British parliamentary debate on 16 December 1958, which followed the Select Committee Report on Obscene Publications, and every allusion was couched within the framework of this great British discourse on class as MPs tried to decide whether the book should be classified as vulgar or respectable, placed in the category of "pornography" or of "serious works." In the eyes of R. A. Butler, Home Secretary at the time, these two phenomena were as distinct as chalk and cheese, and there could be no argument but that it is the responsibility of government to suppress the former: "We ought to pause for a moment to think why we have a law of obscene publications," he declared. "We are all agreed that the object is to protect from corruption those whose minds are open to immoral influences . . . not to protect the strong, but to protect the relatively weak. That is the necessary and legitimate object of the law."[48] Butler's speech, of course, shows at work the old upper-class paternalism so typical of British governance. The "public good," a term that eventually found its way into the new law, is a phrase much used by the Home Secretary during this debate, as though he and his colleagues possessed some special insight into what was "good" for the public over whom they exercised control.

Nevertheless, Butler's courtly liberal humanism, relatively unusual in the Conservative Party of his day, also sought to create space for what he was pleased to call "genuine" artistry. "I realize," he conceded, "that the aim of those who make this proposal is to ensure that a writer of integrity who expresses the truth as he sees it shall not be liable to prosecution for obscene libel, and that we all want to achieve. The problem is how to secure this without opening a loophole for evil." For "evil" here, read the filthy demands of the swarming masses. In seeking to shore up a binary opposition between the "writer of integrity" and the pornographer, Butler was working unwittingly with a romantic ideology of art, whereby texts are understood not in terms of their cultural production and reception but according to whether they conform to a prior "truth" supposedly located in the author's own mind.[49] Butler was not concerned at all with freedom of thought, with the rights of individual readers, or with equal access to information; instead, he focused exclusively on what he took to be the profundity or otherwise of individual authors. This, of course, is to privilege authorial intention to an extraordinary degree, but it is easy enough to see how such a romantic position would have dovetailed neatly with the social elitism of this Conservative government, which was keen to restrict the general circulation of materials it deemed to be untrustworthy.

Although Butler's theoretical position (if we can call it that) was deeply old-fashioned, even for 1958, it did help to set the standard for this entire debate, both inside and outside Parliament. In the House of Commons,

MPS played at being Leavisite literary critics as they attempted to distinguish genuine art from mere commercial exploitation. The general tone of the debate revolved around the rhetoric of discrimination, with the politicians attempting to negotiate artistic and moral concerns as though they were vying for a place on the editorial board of *Scrutiny*. Nigel Nicolson, for example, assumed an openly ethical and socially prescriptive stance: "*Lolita* deals with a perversion. It describes the love of a middle-aged man for a girl of twelve. If this perversion had been depicted in such a way as to suggest to any reader of middle age or, for that matter, any little girl—could she understand it—that the practices were pleasant and could lead to happiness, I should have had no hesitation in advising my colleagues that we ought not to publish this book. But, in fact, *Lolita* has a built-in condemnation of what it describes. It leads to utter misery, suicide, prison, murder and great unhappiness, both for the man and to the little girl whom he seduces." Like Butler defending the "writer of integrity," Nicolson proposed to salvage *Lolita* by affixing to it an approved interpretation based on moral (and judicial) closure. It is apparent, then, how this controversy over the censorship of *Lolita* in Britain highlights the attempts of political authorities to maintain their traditional forms of order and control. By seeking to find some way to differentiate between "pornography" and "serious works," Harold Macmillan's Conservative government was also attempting implicitly to shore up divisions between social classes, as well as reinforcing a mythical opposition between artistic "spirituality," as one MP described it, and that "which is far coarser."[50]

*Lolita*, however, poses a challenge to these dichotomies of British culture because its hybrid crosscurrents tend to slide around reified social and aesthetic categories of every kind. The novel not only perverts the moral foundations of American studies, but also uses its chameleonic qualities to construct an Americanized version of Englishness, a transatlantic transformation that could not be accommodated easily in the ethical circumference of British society. With his English mother and schooling and his degree in English literature, Humbert fabricates for himself a disconcerting simulacrum of Englishness, as Charlotte Haze notes when she provocatively remarks: "How reserved you are, how 'British.' Your old-world reticence, your sense of decorum may be shocked by the boldness of an American girl!" (68). Clare Quilty, Humbert's double, similarly speaks with a "phoney British accent" (295). From an American perspective, both of these figures might be typecast as Old World agents of corruption, ravagers of America's youthful innocence; but from the British point of view, again, they are playing the dangerous game of hyperaestheticization, imitating forms of culture while emptying out its moral assumptions. Nabokov, who took a degree at Cambridge University, described himself subsequently as having been "an English child," but there is no indication that British politicians in the 1950s were keen to recognize him as one of their own.[51] On the contrary, Nabokov's perpetual subversion of national identity, his capacity to play at being British or American while simultaneously refusing to acquiesce in the more rooted customs of the country, threatened to cock a snook at the established boundaries of the nation-state, which the British government understood, then as now, to be a sine qua non for any efficient maintenance of the law of the land.

In this sense, the allegory of power and control that *Lolita* embodies is reproduced in various discrete national cultures, which can be seen to act as their own kind of Humbert Humbert in the way they attempted to hustle the nymphet out of sight. In the United States, the benchmark obscenity trial of this era, involving the publisher Samuel Roth, was resolved by the Supreme Court in 1957 according to the supreme legal fiction of "the average person, applying contemporary community standards": two grotesque stereotypes that *Lolita*, with its cosmopolitan circumvention of the "average" and the "community," renders simply nonsensical. Historically, censorship in the United States has tended to focus on preserving the sacralized boundaries of particular communities, just as censorship in the United Kingdom has been concerned primarily to police the hierarchical boundaries of social class.[52] *Lolita*'s inscription of a virtual America, however, works against each of these categories. The novel rotates its narrative of the perverse around an axis of the sublime to decenter the familiar icons of the American ideal, while simultaneously deploying this American iconography in juxtaposition with Humbert's English background to produce a discomfitingly unplaceable version of the British gentleman. From this angle, the mixture of levels in *Lolita* evokes the energies of American democracy in such a way as to appear threatening to the more rigid dimensions of British authority. If Nabokov's novel uses its half-British hero to pervert the moral assumptions of America, it equally uses the forces of American heterogeneity to pervert the closed world of British institutions. *Lolita* is not a classic text of traditional American studies because its nationalistic status is dangerously equivocal—neither author nor hero originates from the United States—and because its representation of the American metanarrative of constitutional liberty appears perversely aslant; but it might be a classic text of virtual American studies, because its reconfiguration of a hollowed-out "America" within a transnational network of the simulacrum effectively interrogates the self-preserving model of national identity. By quizzically remapping the legal and political basis of area studies, Nabokov's novel generates a series of crazy mirrors that invite the reader creatively to reimagine the dialectic between local propriety and global dislocation.

This political context of censorship raises other important questions about relationships among *Lolita*, American studies, and the agendas of morality in general. Proponents of American studies as a site for the negotiation of identity politics, a discursive matrix for the reparative representation of particular ethical or ethnic interests, generally find that Nabokov has nothing of interest to say to them. Paul Lauter, for example, in dismissing the "epistemological games constructed by writers like Pynchon, Nabokov, and Barth," chooses to promote instead "other virtues of transparency in structure, of immediacy in language, and of feelings deeply engaged by symbol."[53] It is, accordingly, not altogether surprising to find Nabokov excluded from the *Heath Anthology of American Literature,* of which Lauter is general editor. Conversely, however, it is equally unsurprising that Nabokov should still be taught frequently in American studies programs throughout Europe; in universities in Germany, Denmark, and Switzerland, American literature is of course considered a foreign enterprise, and so there is often a greater emphasis on the problematic relationship between language and culture, with consequently less inclination to assume "transparency in structure" or to equate the construction of American literary narrative with a voice of authenticity. It might, perhaps, seem strange that Nabokov's edgy, parodic idiom should often be regarded in the States as merely a regressive, conservative mode of formalism, although this speaks to a familiar paradox within the indigenous domain of American cultural criticism, whereby the supposedly radical rhetoric of emancipation and renewal in fact forms one of the most traditional gestures in the native lexicon. Comparative in this context too often means simply comparative within the charmed circle of the United States itself, a method that, while it pays scrupulous attention to differential equations of race and gender inside a domestic U.S. context, nevertheless works rigidly to exclude anything that might interfere with the symbolic national apparatus of liberty and liberation on which such foundational assumptions are predicated.[54]

This reflexive reinforcement of domestic agendas is hardly a new phenomenon, of course. Tocqueville wrote back in 1835 that the majority in America "lives in the perpetual utterance of self-applause," and that "there are certain truths which the Americans can learn only from strangers."[55] This kind of language might sound offensively supercilious, typical of a haughty European aristocrat, just as Nabokov's tone seems smug and unsympathetic to some American readers. But Tocqueville's point, like Nabokov's, was not that America enjoys a monopoly on this kind of tautological national narrative, whereby diverse positions find themselves pulled back centripetally toward a consensual center; rather, it was that an observer located on the margins of any given culture is in a better position to see how these majoritarian force fields of containment operate. One crucial aspect of Nabokov's sinistral, transnational style is precisely that it dislocates the apparently "transparent" relationship between narrative and context on which theories of national literature as local mimesis depend. By declining to present a naturalized version of American life, *Lolita* implies ways in which all its values might be reversible.

Indeed, Nabokov's fiction works to disturb preconceptions of what is "natural," not just in relation to questions of national identity, but also with reference to ways in which understandings of broader moral questions can be seen as tied prescriptively to the circumscribed circumstances of particular geographic areas. Those who see *Lolita* as fundamentally unethical tend to regard it as at some level a realist work of fiction, assuming a reflective rather than refractive mirror working as the textual mediator between representation and action. Carol Iannone, for instance, suggests that proponents of modernist aesthetics in general are too willing to regard art as a sacred wood, an entirely separate realm, and are consequently willing to overlook how Lolita herself becomes strategically dehumanized, remaining "in virtual captivity to Humbert through most of the novel."[56] Richard Rorty, similarly, examines the text from a philosophical point of view as an example of sociopathic sadism, noting how Humbert zealously "excludes attention to other people" by inventing a self-enclosed universe whose catastrophe involves a radical failure to acknowledge anything outside itself.[57] Martin Amis, despite being a great admirer of Nabokov, finds *Lolita* "a cruel book about cruelty," with "Humbert's sin" being "biological, a sin against the ordinary," notably in the way he forces his stepdaughter "out of nature . . . insulting and degrading her childish essence."[58] Amis's essentialist reaction, in particular, is tinged with 1990s concerns about child abuse—"the new evil empire," as Laura Kipnis sardonically describes it—anxieties that have brought *Lolita* back into the cultural spotlight.[59] Yet such associations between *Lolita* and the actual practice of child abuse depend on what Frances Ferguson has called a "logic of resemblance" between the "pornographic" narrative and some kind of criminal context.[60] It is precisely this hypothetical circuit of transparency or unmediated representation that Nabokov's radically discontinuous, self-reflexive texts are intent on disrupting. *Lolita*, in other words, does not deal with pedophilia at the level of law or sociology, but at the level of aesthetics and the imagination.

Here, though, is where the subversive potential of "deviant" art really lies. Its most threatening quality, from a political point of view, resides not in any incitement of its audience to imitate specific actions, but in its intimation that such modes of behavior may not, in themselves, automatically be subject to the jealously hegemonic power of national law. Censorship debates are focused, by definition, on the symbolic rather than the social order; the issue is never what actually happens, but what is allowed to be represented. This is why the forces of national government, so keen to patrol borders between literature and pornography and between the different nation-states, have been equally intent on controlling the flows of information in all kinds of directions. As Walter Kendrick puts it, the primary goal of censorship is not to eradicate "obscene" materials but to ensure that the obscene is recognized and demarcated as such, thereby preserving society's moral parameters.[61] There is, consequently, a close affiliation between legal censorship and the academic practice of area studies, because both depend for their efficient operation on the identification of discrete communities, enclosed areas, to which some homogenizing, ethical idea can plausibly be attached. In this light, pornography is threatening not so much as a sign of misogynist dehumanization or bacchanalian revelry, but as a sign of philosophical anarchy: an excess of information, a glut of materials, all of which cannot be safely ordered within the existing frameworks of social knowledge or community practices. This is precisely what we find in *Lolita*: too many words, too many languages, too many possibilities, too much uncomfortable relativism; and this is why the novel stands as a challenge to the established notion of national cultures. Humbert runs through a list of historical sites where his adoration of Lolita would not have seemed out of place—medieval Europe, the East Indies, the Ancient World—and, within the logic of this narrative, we are obliged to believe him.

In his important lecture "The Art of Literature and Commonsense," Nabokov avers that common sense is, precisely, "sense made common," betokening a dull-witted conformity to the given standards of any particular time and place. He drives his point home by appealing directly to the student audience: "It is instructive to think that there is not a single person in this room, or for that matter in any room in the world, who, at some nicely chosen point in historical space-time would not be put to death there and then, here and now, by a commonsensical majority in righteous rage. The color of one's creed, neckties, eyes, thoughts, manners, speech, is sure to meet somewhere in time or space with a fatal objection from a mob that hates that particular tone." Later in this same piece, Nabokov suggests: "Criminals are usually people lacking imagination." Because criminals do not have the power to create an interior universe in keeping with their own particular predilections, he argues, they fall back into a hopeless attempt to reshape worldly events according to their own desires: "Creative imagination . . . would have led them to seek an outlet in fiction and make the characters in their books do more thoroughly what they might themselves have bungled in real life. Lacking real imagination, they content themselves with such half-witted banalities as seeing themselves gloriously driving into Los Angeles in that swell stolen car with that swell golden girl who had helped to butcher its owner. . . . Lunatics are lunatics just because they have thoroughly and recklessly dismembered a familiar world but have not the power—or have lost the power—to create a new one as harmonious as the old."[62] What is significant here is the manner in which Nabokov imagines such a distinct division between thought and action, art and event. On one level, this might be seen as a typical form of modernist idealism, transposing art into an autotelic realm of its own; but, more significantly, this realm also operates for Nabokov as an alternative to historical circumstances, a safe place of escape when, for whatever reason, the banality of everyday common sense fails to measure up to the lively world of the imagination. In these terms, Humbert Humbert as a narrator possesses such a powerful creative imagination precisely because he is such a great criminal. Through erasing the boundaries of common sense, Humbert's imagination invents a world he can live in.

By featuring a duplicitous European who inscribes a hollowed-out version of the American Adam, *Lolita* fails signally to accommodate itself to any form of the national imaginary.[63] Yet, this is where the virtualization of national cultures can reveal their own particular customs and practices within a new, unfamiliar frame. One of the greatest needs of any given culture is to proscribe its own form of abjection, to censor those modes of deviance that the culture itself produces. This is why Victorian England, for instance, whose religion and aesthetics were channeled toward idealizing the figure of the child, was also so censorious about outlawing the forbidden desires that this culture itself had generated.[64] By virtualizing a particular discursive matrix, however, we come to see it as a doubled-up rather than singular construction. By coming at Victorian England from a position of estrangement, we forgo any projection of mythic unity and instead understand Christian philanthropy and child-loving as part of the same paradoxical cycle; similarly, by examining Nabokov's double-crossed virtualization of the American scene, we witness the sublime and the perverse as symbiotic, vacillating aspects of the same culture. The American Adam of Lewis's mythology and the fake Eden of Humbert Humbert's brothel become, ironically, mirror images of each other, complementary reflections of U.S. culture in 1955. This dynamic of reduplication serves to interrogate the boundaries of national identity, to suggest that such identities are always constructed from outside as well as inside their own perimeters, and thus to make the understanding of local conditions a two-way, comparative process. By dismantling the established boundaries of representation and the ethical conventions of common sense, Nabokov's novel interrupts that tautologous circle between area studies and its object of scrutiny, whereby the latter is simply mapped onto the former to show how much the former manifests itself in the latter. *Lolita*, through its bizarre and paradoxical relationship to the host nation, breaks through this tautology to project not only a different America but also a disturbingly different world.

# 7

## Crossing the Water:
## Gunn, Plath, and the Poetry
## of Passage

The momentum behind the development of transatlantic transnationalism in the 1950s came from many different sources. It was, of course, the nightmare of the Nazi regime and the devastation of the Second World War that compelled many European intellectuals, particularly those in Germany, to seek refuge in the United States. Theodor W. Adorno, for example, moved to America in 1938, but he returned to Frankfurt in 1949, having been less than impressed with cultural conditions in Los Angeles. The most famous work of Adorno's West Coast exile was *Dialectic of Enlightenment*, written with Max Horkheimer in 1940 and published in 1947. This profoundly pessimistic treatise describes how, in the eyes of the Frankfurt School, the totalitarian logic of instrumental reason, formerly associated with Hitler's fascism, had crossed the Atlantic and relocated itself amid the commercial and capitalist structures of America. In a subsequent essay on *Brave New World*, the novel originally published by Aldous Huxley in 1932, Adorno interpreted Huxley's dystopian vision specifically as an indictment of the United States; he also said it demonstrated the deplorable need in America for an "intellectual from abroad . . . to eradicate himself as an autonomous being if he hopes to achieve anything or be accepted as an employee of the super-trust into which life has condensed." *Brave New World*, declared Adorno, thus reveals the "virtual transformation of the world into commodities" through its intimation of how "Americanism . . . has taken over the world." This is why, for Adorno, "every intellectual in emigration is, without exception, mutilated": deprived of his own language and history, the displaced thinker finds his own indigenous "knowledge" fatally "sapped."[1]

The complicated situation of the exiles and émigrés who came to the United States during the Nazi years is a topic worthy of separate study, and I do not intend to address it here, except in passing.[2] Nevertheless, one distinction worth making is that Adorno was a true exile, whose move to the United States was forced on him by historical circumstances and did not in any obvious sense involve an act of choice on his part. This correlates with what Fredric Jameson has described as the "nostalgia for centeredness" in Adorno's writing, his modernist and utopian attachment to "unified (if not necessarily organic) form," his longing for the true homeland.[3] Such intense awareness of alienation as a cultural and intellectual phenomenon is different in kind from the experience of a younger generation of expatriates, who moved between countries later in the 1950s. Adorno left America for good in 1953, one year before the arrival from Britain of Thom Gunn, who made a positive decision to go to the United States to join his lover, Mike Kitay, who had been conscripted into the U.S. Air Force. After a brief spell in Texas and a creative writing fellowship at Stanford, where he worked with Yvor Winters, Gunn began teaching at Berkeley in 1958 and has remained in the Bay Area ever since. Gunn was only one of a number of well-known British authors resident in the United States during the 1950s; apart from Huxley, who had moved to California in 1937, the figures with the highest profiles were W. H. Auden and Christopher Isherwood, who both left England in 1939, although Denise Levertov, born in Essex in 1923, also emigrated to the States in 1948. From a technical point of view, Gunn has most in common with the poets, Auden and Levertov, but thematically and psychologically, he is closest to Isherwood, as he himself acknowledged in a 1999 interview when admitting that he had tried to model himself on the California novelist ever since their first meeting in 1955.[4] The purpose of this chapter is to focus on Gunn and Sylvia Plath as two transatlantic poets who began publishing in the 1950s, and whose work was materially influenced by the trajectory of transnational displacement in the years after the Second World War. Plath, of course, went in the opposite direction to Gunn, leaving her native Massachusetts in 1955 to study in England on a Fulbright Scholarship at Cambridge University. She met her future husband, Ted Hughes, at Cambridge, and lived in England for most of the rest of her brief life.

One of the reasons Gunn and Plath were less hostile in principle to transnationalism than was Adorno was the widespread circulation of both intellectual and popular versions of existentialism during the 1950s.

Gunn, even while an undergraduate at Cambridge, looked on his poetry as "the act of an existentialist conqueror, excited and aggressive," and acknowledged that there was "a great deal of raw Sartre" in his second book, *The Sense of Movement,* published in 1957.[5] Plath, similarly, wrote in a journal entry for 1958 that "there are no rules" for the kind of marriage she wanted, so "I must make them up as I go along & will do so."[6] Whereas Adorno cherished a more profoundly integrative conception of the relationship between the individual and society, Gunn and Plath were quite willing, in fact eager, to leave behind the circumstances of their past in order to search for a more fulfilling future. Gunn's early work is suffused with imagery of movement; indeed, the last poem in his first book, *Fighting Terms* (1954), is entitled "Incident on a Journey," and its refrain is a variation on the familiar existentialist idea of "Regretting nothing."[7] Auden developed a similar interest in existentialist theologians such as Reinhold Niebuhr during his years of exile in New York, and this again helped to sustain for him the idea of displacement as an ascetic form of detachment from mere comfort and custom, a spiritually cleansing act arising beneficially out of free moral choice.[8]

For Auden and Gunn, and for Isherwood as well, this existential quest for a new country became closely associated in their minds with the issue of sexual repression and freedom. Until the Wolfenden Report in 1957 recommended that gay sex between consenting adults in private be decriminalized, public opinion in Britain had tended to perceive homosexuality either as an effete upper-class weakness or as something inherently immature and narcissistic. The cultural climate of England in the 1950s was still anxious to extirpate the shades of what was remembered vividly as Nazi evil, and so the representation of an aggressive, lower-middle-class heterosexuality in the works of writers like Kingsley Amis and John Osborne can be seen, among other things, as an attempt to eradicate what they saw as the corrupt posturing of men in uniform by substituting their own brand of earthy common sense.[9] There was, of course, a certain charlatanism in these artistic positions—Osborne, for instance, was later revealed to be bisexual—but they do suggest the extent to which homosexuality, particularly in its public dimensions, became heavily politicized in Britain during the late 1950s. Wolfenden did not change things overnight; in fact, it was to take another ten years before the Sexual Offences Act of 1967 implemented the main recommendations of the Report in Britain. In America, the interaction of state and federal laws created a more variable picture, but the constitutional right to privacy, allied to flourishing gay subcultures in New York City and parts of California, ensured that these British expatriates enjoyed a more emancipated environment than they would have experienced in their home country during this era.

From a British standpoint, then, the virtual America of the 1950s represented a welcome antidote to the pinched, parsimonious circumstances of a Europe still recovering both economically and psychologically from the Second World War. The States appeared to offer the prospect of sexual freedom, material abundance, and limitless personal opportunity in a mobile and classless society.[10] This image of America from abroad as a beacon of liberty was, of course, as much of a chimera in its own way as the carefully crafted myth of the "American Adam" that was being generated in nascent American studies programs in the United States itself at this time. It was, moreover, a chimera that was subsidized directly by the U.S. government. Peter Coleman has written of what he calls a widespread "liberal conspiracy" in the 1950s, on the grounds that the CIA was subsequently exposed as covertly funding the activities of the Congress for Cultural Freedom throughout the world as part of their cold war offensive against communism.[11] The composer Nicolas Nabokov, cousin of Vladimir, was heavily involved in the work of the Congress during its early years and also served as its first secretary-general, and the movement's intellectual "flagship" was the magazine *Encounter*, which first appeared in October 1953 with Irving Kristol and Stephen Spender as founding coeditors; indeed, according to Michael Josselson, the CIA agent with responsibility for the Congress from 1950 to 1967, *Encounter* was considered to be the American intelligence world's "greatest asset."[12]

Kristol's editorial in the first issue of *Encounter*, under the headline "After the Apocalypse," welcomed the demise of "pseudo-prophets" like Hitler, Mussolini, and Stalin, and attempted to equate the new journal with "a love of liberty" and a respect for "literature and the arts as being values in themselves, in need of no ulterior justification." Kristol also made a point here of promoting *Encounter* as "an international magazine, with a British and an American editor."[13] The Congress for Cultural Freedom quickly identified the idea of freedom as their totem and political slogan. In their first "Manifesto," published after their 1950 conference in Berlin, the word appears no less than seventeen times in a document of fourteen brief clauses, with such resonant phrases as "We hold that the historical contribution of any society is to be judged by the extent and quality of the freedom which its members actually enjoy."[14] Looking back from half a century later, it is remarkable how many well-known writers of the time were involved in one way or another with the activities of the Congress: W. H. Auden spoke at conventions in Bombay in 1951 and Paris in 1952, and Allen Tate, Robert Lowell, and Katherine Anne Porter also participated in the Paris festival. The first issue of *Encounter* highlighted transatlantic writing, featuring memoirs by Isherwood and a poem by Auden as well as an article by Spender on American diction and poetry. One of the few writers who declined to publish in the journal was T. S. Eliot, on the grounds that it was, as he put it, so "obviously published under American auspices."[15] Appropriately enough, the last issue of *Encounter* appeared in September 1990, less than a year after the fall of the Berlin Wall had symbolically brought the cold war to an end.

A great deal has been written about the collusion, often uneasy or ambiguous, between American authors and radical political organizations like the Congress of Industrial Organizations in the 1930s; much less has been said about similar interactions between "creative" writers and an institutional politics of liberalism during the 1950s. One obvious explanation for this is that a politics of "freedom" became naturalized as synonymous with the "spirit" of American literature in a symbiotic equation that the communitarian emphasis of the 1930s simply failed to achieve. Nevertheless, neither Coleman's "conspiracy" nor Frances Stonor Saunders's "propaganda" is perhaps quite the right word here, for they imply, as their corollary, a pure dissociation from modes of cultural production that is impossible to imagine. The U.S. government funding of *Encounter* no more invalidates the intellectual projects of that journal than, say, the financial support of the medieval Church could be said to invalidate the architectural grandeur of Chartres Cathedral. In both cases, though, it is important to recognize the way these aesthetic products were framed and informed by a particular kind of cultural context. In the case of *Encounter,* it is particularly relevant to note that the Congress for Cultural Freedom saw the journal as a vital instrument in promoting the image and values of the United States beyond its national boundaries. Specifically, the publication of *Encounter* from London coincided with a new interest in American culture within British university and political life. The British Association for American Studies was formed in 1955, only four years after the equivalent academic organization in the United States, and Marcus Cunliffe, one of the most visible forces in the British Association in its early years, was a frequent contributor to *Encounter.* So, in the early 1960s, was the Cambridge critic Tony Tanner, who dedicated his 1965 study of American literature, *The Reign of Wonder,* to Gunn, and to whom Gunn in turn dedicated his long poem "Misanthropos," published in *Encounter* that same year.[16] Many of the journal's writers on political issues—in particular, Anthony Crosland, another frequent contributor—became identified with "Gaitskellism," the progressive movement on the right wing of the Labour Party in the late 1950s and early 1960s, which largely followed the line put forward by New York intellectual Daniel Bell about the "end of ideology."[17] Crosland and his compeers thus looked to the society of North America as a model for overcoming the supposedly superannuated divisions of the British class war.

Gunn's "On the Move" first appeared in the December 1955 issue of *Encounter,* and his poems in the early collections that treat American popular culture sympathetically—"Elvis Presley," for example, and "The Unsettled Motorcyclist's Vision of His Death"—can be seen as part of this same use of a transatlantic imaginary for iconoclastic, modernizing purposes. "The Unsettled Motorcyclist" evokes the character played by Marlon Brando in *The Wild One,* a film released in the United States in 1953 but banned by the British Board of Film Censors for fourteen years on the grounds that it might lead to youthful delinquency and disorder. By 1957, when *The Sense of Movement* appeared, Gunn was already established in California, and a few poems in this book—"Market at Turk," for instance, set on a San Francisco street corner—reflect his new American world in a close, experiential fashion. More frequently, though, we find in Gunn's poetry of this time a theoretical play with the concept of freedom, its possibilities and limitations, ideas that were simultaneously being explored in different intellectual contexts in the pages of *Encounter.* My point here is not to finger Gunn in some malevolent "liberal conspiracy," but to indicate how the transnational matrix informing his poetry, and that of Plath, developed out of the cultural politics of a specific historical situation.

The involvement of both Gunn and Plath in this politics of transatlantic exile has, perhaps, become blurred by the way they were both subsequently associated more frequently with Ted Hughes than with each other. Plath was, of course, Hughes's first wife, and in a 1962 letter she refers to Gunn as Hughes's "poet-twin," an association confirmed in the public mind by Faber's marketing decision that same year to yoke the *Selected Poems* of Gunn and Huges together in one volume.[18] The following year, Gunn and Hughes were also persuaded by Faber jointly to edit an anthology, *Five American Poets*, featuring writers previously unpublished in England.[19] Nevertheless, there are also strong personal links between Gunn and Plath: he went to lunch with Hughes and Plath at their London home in January 1961 ("a rare, unaffected, kind young chap," she reported to her mother), and earlier they had both been students of English literature at Cambridge, where each was significantly influenced by the teaching of F. R. Leavis, with its strict pedagogical emphasis on the art of close reading.[20] Gunn later wrote that he admired Leavis's ability to go "directly to the texture of poetry . . . risking close scrutiny that entered into the terms of creation," and Plath, after hearing Leavis lecture in 1955, described him as "a magnificent, acid, malevolently humorous little man."[21] But the more general and significant strand to this discussion revolves around the ways Gunn and Plath reformulated existentialism and exile into an aesthetics of transnationalism, a line of argument best illustrated not so much by a comparison of these writers with Hughes but by a distinct contrast with him.

Like Gunn and Plath, Hughes started out reading English at Cambridge, but he soon came to dislike the whole business of literary criticism and switched to archaeology and anthropology for the second part of his degree. Nor was this interest in anthropology and ritual merely a passing phenomenon: apart from two years teaching and traveling with Plath in the United States between 1957 and 1959, Hughes chose consciously to root his life and work in his native country, and his poetry showed an increasing concern to delineate coherent myths of Englishness. In this respect, his appointment to succeed John Betjeman as Poet Laureate in December 1984 represented a natural culmination of his poetic career. The judgment made at that time, by the literary editor of the London *Times,* that Hughes was "without a doubt the most anti-Establishment" figure ever "to have become a court official," can be seen as true in only a very limited sense, for, with his romanticizations of English nature and jeremiads about how England was in danger of losing its soul to the "spiritless materialism" of industrial civilization, Hughes can be seen as quite compatible with a native tradition of radical Protestantism encompassing earlier writers such as Blake, the Brontës, and

D. H. Lawrence.[22] Hughes may not have been exactly courtly in demeanor, but he was certainly patriotic in expression. Moreover, on his death in 1998 there was a concerted effort to incorporate him into a specifically nationalistic tradition of English literature: Hughes was, said Douglas Dunn, "one of the few poets whom it would not be an insult to place alongside Shakespeare," and Valentine Cunningham found him "of comparable stature to Blake or Milton."[23] Such tributes are reminiscent of those paid at the death of a previous Poet Laureate, Tennyson, in 1892, when again there were all kinds of patriotic attempts to inter him in a great tradition of English verse going back to Wordsworth, Keats, and earlier. The French critic Hippolyte A. Taine observed in 1864 that Tennyson had become the nation's favorite poet because he was best able to reflect the Victorian image of their own "elegant and common-sense society," and the same thing might be said about the relationship between Hughes and England in the second half of the twentieth century: he was commonly thought to give expression to a rugged sense of provincial decency, a concern for the country's natural heritage, which became widely equated with the state of the nation itself.[24]

This is not, of course, to deny the darker, more complex aspects of either Tennyson or Hughes, but to suggest that the popular reception of their work accorded with a romanticized sense of patriotic destiny. One exemplification of this nationalist agenda can be seen in the much feted *Birthday Letters* (1998), Hughes's poetic chronicle of his relationship with Plath, which was published shortly before his death. Plath's American identity is represented here as a form of inauthenticity: she is described as "a bobby-sox American," with "long, perfect, American legs" and an "exaggerated American/Grin for the cameras." In this book, it is always English values that make up the assumed moral focus of the narrative and American attributes that are seen as hyperbolic or otherwise off-center. In an attempt to leave behind the innocence of "Red Indian Mickey Mouse America," Hughes portrays the couple retreating into their own English "dreamland," in Devon:

> I wrestled
> With the blankets, the caul and the cord.
> And you stayed with me
> Gallant and desperate and hopeful
> Listening for different gods, stripping off

Your American royalty, garment by garment—
Till you stepped out soul-naked and stricken
Into this cobbled, pictureless corridor
Aimed at a graveyard.[25]

This view in *Birthday Letters* of American culture as a false façade to be stripped away fits precisely with the critical view expressed by Hughes back in 1977: that Plath's "reputation rests on the poems of her last six months."[26] For Hughes, as Jacqueline Rose has remarked, all of Plath's work appears "in terms of a constant teleological reference to *Ariel*," the collection published posthumously in 1965.[27] *Ariel*, as far as Hughes was concerned, is where Plath's real self emerges. Earlier poems, such as those he collected in *Crossing the Water* (1971), were accordingly categorized by him as "transitional" works, stages on the path toward her ultimate, coruscating self-revelation.[28] But one obvious problem with Hughes's interpretation is that it simply reproduces a common nativist myth of English depth and American superficiality. The idea here is that Plath's earlier American poems were cerebral exercises, academic in the derogatory sense, and that it took the primitivist landscapes of England to bring her to a realization of her deeper, more authentic self. In stark outline this trajectory might seem banal enough, but it is essentially the guiding narrative of *Birthday Letters* as well, and it helps to explain why English reviewers have been so enthusiastic about Hughes's last collection: the book is, asserted Cunningham, "unfailingly successful in marking real difference—making distinctions that also indicate where the superiority of Hughes as poet might lie," while reinforcing the sense that "Plath will be turned to more and more merely as a case."[29]

A great deal depends here not just on perspective, but on the way perspective becomes internalized and, consequently, naturalized. Cunningham takes as his standard the iconography of Hughes's "great early poem" "Pike," with its representation of a rural pond embedded "as deep as England."[30] It is against such profundity that he finds Plath's poetry merely neurotic and narcissistic, a typical American "case." Alan Sinfield, though more sympathetic to Plath, takes an opposite tack by proposing to obliterate the whole question of national identity in relation to her work; classifying her as an "international" poet, Sinfield finds it "appropriate to use evidence from Britain and the United States with only occasional discriminations."[31] Such an apparently free-ranging and cosmopolitan approach, however, threatens altogether to dissolve the material conditions of location and context; instead, it echoes earlier, formalist approaches to transatlantic displacement, as manifested in the work of critics of an earlier generation, such as Barbara Everett, who argued that the significance of Auden's move to America had been overplayed on the grounds that emigration was not particularly "important in the fabric of Auden's real life."[32] For Everett, of course, Auden's "real" life was his creative life, the life of his poems, with the cultural circumstances informing their production being only of a very secondary significance. This was the line often taken by comparative literature specialists in the 1950s: that nationalism was a parochial affair and that great writers should aspire toward a "universal" significance in which historical circumstances would, like Lenin's state, simply wither away.[33]

Both Everett's formalism and Sinfield's cosmopolitanism, then, seek to dissociate literature from national identity, whereas Cunningham's more moralistic emphasis works to consolidate such associations by its unspoken equation of aesthetic and nationalistic values. What this transnational critical approach seeks to illuminate, by contrast, is the way social and political aspects of national identity enter into the formal making of poetry. It also highlights the way displaced writers like Gunn and Plath bring such material conditions into the body of their texts through ironic processes of transposition that enable them to render the national imaginary explicit and translucent, rather than, as in Hughes, implicit and deeply inchoate. Gunn and Plath do not simply reflect national traditions, but reflect upon them, projecting the cultural mythologies of Britain and America in a disturbing two-way mirror where each refracts and reveals the outlines of the other.

The image of the mirror, in various configurations, has been central to Gunn's poetry since the 1950s. In *Fighting Terms* and *The Sense of Movement,* his poetic protagonists find themselves in the pincer grip of every kind of dualism: between reason and instinct, between the object signified and the verbal signifier, between an integral and a mirrored or posed self. The mise-en-abîme of "Carnal Knowledge"—"You know I know you know I know you know" (15)—is typical of an uneasy fragmentation that pervades these first two books, whose energy derives to a large extent from the generation of circular, internal tensions. Gunn's early poetry feeds on its own contradictions, is forever trying to accomplish the impossible task of renouncing its own "agnostic irony," as "For a Birthday" puts it (32), by transcending its own linguistic and metaphorical system. But in the next collection, *My Sad Captains* (1961), a marked change of emphasis is apparent. Whereas the motorcyclists in "On the Move," in *The Sense of Movement,* suppress rumination in favor of violent, existential action, the humble creature in "Considering the Snail" from *My Sad Captains* can be read as a witting self-parody of the tough guys seeking belligerently to join "the movement in a valueless world" (40). In contemplating the snail, Gunn is in fact reflecting on his former poetic persona:

> He
> moves in a wood of desire,
>
> pale antlers barely stirring
> as he hunts. I cannot tell
> what power is at work, drenched there
> with purpose, knowing nothing.
> What is snail's fury? (117)

This comic bathos represents the snail as an objectified alternative self. In "Carnal Knowledge," the dislocating irony is tortuously wrapped inside a poem attempting to surmount that irony; in "Considering the Snail," however, Gunn willingly embraces a conception of parody, along with the dualisms inherent in that intertextual form. Dualism implies doubling and division, and so the desire of *Fighting Terms* to erase contradictions and reattain some state of primal unity is now superseded by the poet's recognition of the obdurate nature of ambiguity, fluidity, and open-endedness in a more contingent material world.

One of the functions of this kind of self-parody is to constitute a radical challenge to the formal traditions evoked in Gunn's earlier books, which, in their use of the iambic pentameter to mediate cerebral and sexual dilemmas, looked back mainly to the English metaphysical poets. The first part of *My Sad Captains* consists of poems in classical and regular forms; it revolves on Gunn's established axis of romantic freedom compromised by the circumscriptions of language and civilization, and is prefaced by an epigraph from *Troilus and Cressida:* "The will is infinite and the execution confined, the desire is boundless and the act a slave to limit" (91). The second part takes as its epigraph two sentences from F. Scott Fitzgerald's *The Last Tycoon* (1941), a novel set in California: "I looked back as we crossed the crest of the foothills—with the air so clear you could see the leaves on Sunset Mountains two miles away. It's startling to you sometimes—just air, unobstructed, uncomplicated air" (113). Gunn's choice of Fitzgerald's description of what is "unobstructed" and "uncomplicated" suggests his newfound concern with how "the things themselves are adequate," to quote from "Waking in a Newly Built House," the poem that begins the second part of this collection:

> Calmly, perception rests on the things,
> and is aware of them only in
> their precise definition, their fine
> lack of even potential meanings. (115)

Such "lack of even potential meanings" is characteristic of the crucial shift in emphasis in the overall trajectory of Gunn's work that *My Sad Captains* heralded. As Neil Powell observed, the first poem in this collection, "In Santa Maria del Popolo," refers to Caravaggio's *Conversion of St. Paul*, a painting about the transformation of identity, and "Waking in a Newly Built House" signifies, broadly speaking, the author's conscious decision to affiliate himself henceforth with an American rather than an English poetic tradition.[34]

This attention in "Waking in a Newly Built House" to "things" and "their precise definition" is reminiscent of the aesthetics of William Carlos Williams, on whom Gunn published an essay in *Encounter* in 1965. Here Gunn praised in particular the impulses of authenticity and originality, citing the way the poetry of Williams "embodied a desire that the unknown and unexpressed should not be treated in terms of the already known and expressed."[35] However, the poems in the second half of *My Sad Captains* are written not in the style of free verse associated with Williams, but in syllabics, described by Clive Wilmer as "a form in which arbitrary structure imposes discipline—felt more by the writer than the reader—upon rhythms as unpredictable as those of free verse."[36] One of the best-known exponents of this syllabic art is Marianne Moore, another American model for Gunn's post-1957 style. He subsequently wrote, though, of how he thought Moore's syllabics and free verse "sound exactly alike"; he similarly suggested that in the case of his own verse he found the "virtues" of these forms to be "indistinguishable," with the use of syllabics being "only a way of teaching myself to write free verse."[37]

Nevertheless, in Gunn's 1967 collection, *Touch*, the poet renders thematic this evolution from syllabic to free verse by a conceptual play around the notion of edge and edgelessness. "Confessions of the Life Artist," for instance, is still in syllabics:

> As I support her, so, with
> my magnificent control,
> I suddenly ask: "What if
> she has the edge over me?" (161)

Gunn's artificer here wonders whether the natural life enjoyed by his model might not be superior to the "magnificent control" asserted by his own artistry. The artist creates hard edges, but the model "has the edge" in a metaphorical sense. In *Touch*, therefore, there is a formal progression away from fabricated edges toward a raw edgelessness: "Berlin in Ruins" starts by asserting that the city "has an edge, or many edges" (157), but it then goes on to describe how the fanatical order associated with Berlin's Nazi era has now crumbled away. Moreover, this redundant social order becomes figuratively associated with the "stiff laurel" (158) of Gunn's earlier verse forms, which tend forcibly to be contorted into a classical order, so that this passage away from metrical and syllabic into free verse is equated psychologically with an abandonment of the paraphernalia of violence. The poetry is now directed not toward a sense of movement but, as in the title poem, a capacity to "touch" natural objects:

> What is more, the place is
> not found but seeps
> from our touch in
> continuous creation, dark
> enclosing cocoon round
> ourselves alone, dark
> wide realm where we
> walk with everyone. (169)

*Touch* consciously affiliates itself with a more identifiably American style of free verse which can be traced back to Whitman, and the final poem in this collection is entitled, appropriately enough, "Back to Life."

Here, though, we run into one of Gunn's typical paradoxes, for the idea of returning back to life through the medium of art seems as much a contradiction in terms as the yearning after spontaneous innocence in *Fighting Terms*. Gunn's earliest poems aspire romantically toward a state of preverbal regression, a "time when words no longer help," as "For a Birthday" puts it (32), when the duplicities of language can be cast aside. Whereas in *Fighting Terms* this conflict between mind and body becomes at times quite violent, in *Touch* the poems seem to accept and indeed to welcome such divisions, as they seek with a new openness to explore the aesthetic possibilities of self-contradiction. We find an example of this kind of paradoxical play in "The Kiss at Bayreuth," where the resisting edges of art come up against the unresisting, swaying edgelessness of life:

> Colours drain, shapes blur, resisting,
> details swim together, the mass
> of the external wobbles, sways,
> disintegrating. . . . (156)

We can say, then, that Gunn's poetry of the mid-1960s engages with a conscious process of self-contradiction or self-parody to draw attention to the equivocal status of aesthetic artifice in general. We can say furthermore that the implicit dialectic here between the poet's earlier and later work—the way "Berlin in Ruins" reexamines the imagery of aggression that hovers around *The Sense of Movement*—is another instance of Gunn's exploiting a parodic dualism to focus on how meanings of all kinds become unraveled. By reflecting on his own earlier work, Gunn reveals its transitory, provisional condition; "The Beaters," with its iconography of a "swastika-draped bed," was one of a "dozen poems" omitted by Gunn from his 1993 *Collected Poems* on the grounds of being "stupid or badly written" (489), and there is a sense in which an important impetus for Gunn's work is the process of retrospection and revision, looking back at previous formulations and reimagining them in the light of different circumstances. One of the structural patterns running through Gunn's poetry is this aesthetic of creative destruction, whereby formal scenarios—personal identity, metrical regularity, literary tradition—are reflexively dismantled and renegotiated.

Rather than simply announcing a break between his earlier and later works, therefore, Gunn's American poems often work implicitly to establish intertextual dialogues with their English predecessors. "Words," in the 1971 collection *Moly,* ends up with a clean oxymoron signaling how Gunn's American texts of this period seek to distance themselves from the claustrophobic confines of logical sense:

> I was still separate on the shadow's ground
> > But, charged with growth, was being altered,
> > > Composing uncomposed. (197)

*The Passages of Joy* (1982) similarly includes a poem entitled "Interruption," where the author inspects his own reflection in the glass as he meditates on his latest creative enterprise:

> > . . . what makes me think
> > The group of poems I have entered is
> > Interconnected by a closer link
> > Than any snapshot album's? (378–79)

Gunn's parodic rupturing of his own text in "Interruption" is commensurate with the abrasive open-endedness of *The Passages of Joy* in general, which presents the reader with snapshots of American life—amusement arcades, San Francisco streets—and carefully refuses to annotate, finalize, or affix moral significance. "Sweet Things" foregrounds this strategy of refusal by the way it parodies the speaker's desire for the pseudo-wisdom of sentimental aphorisms designed to protect him from immersion in the world of temporal passage; in this poem, the sweet things of the mind give way to the sweet things of the senses, as epitomized by "lust and energy" (327). Gunn remarked in a 1999 interview that "one should always be happy to be the age one is," and many of his American poems take particular delight in the narrator's position within the world of time and contingency rather than seeking an interpretative position outside of it.[38]

Another poem in *The Passages of Joy*, "Song of a Camera," addresses this rejection of epistemological security from a different technical standpoint:

> > I cut the sentence
> > out of a life
> > out of the story
> > with my little knife . . .
>
> > so that another
> > seeing the bits
> > and seeing how
> > none of them fits

wants to add
adverbs to verbs
A bit on its own
simply disturbs (347)

Note the lack of punctuation here: we find no logical sequence, merely free-floating fragments. And the phrase "A bit on its own / simply disturbs" could be the keynote of *The Passages of Joy* itself, with its random urban landscapes and welcoming embrace of hazard. However, the representation of such haphazardness is never an altogether "natural" process but involves complex questions of style and stylization. "Song of a Camera" is therefore dedicated to, and rhetorically imitates, the art of Robert Mapplethorpe, the gay photographer who became famous in the 1980s for an aesthetics of fetishism, wherein the corporeal part is magnified at the expense of a humanist whole. Mapplethorpe's posed, iconic fragments of the human body involve a provocative displacement of "natural" perspective, and a similar desire to erase the normalizing narratives that provide a conventional frame of reference for any given phenomenon also informs *The Passages of Joy*.

The title of "Song of a Camera" is also a nod to the "I am a Camera" style of Isherwood's Berlin novels, whose "great secret subject," wrote Gunn, is the "degree of separation and . . . degree of identification" experienced by the English narrator, who "realizes just how far he has become part of Berlin." Later in this essay on Isherwood, Gunn described the 1964 novel set in California, *A Single Man,* as resembling *Goodbye to Berlin* in being another book about "expatriates who are of an environment and yet at the same time interestingly separated from it." This idiom of detachment in Isherwood works in with the way his camera technique introduces a mode of impersonality or "transparency," as Gunn put it; but, equally significant, it is also a style of alienation that separates objects and events from their more accustomed contexts and associations.[39] This camera style, as practiced by Isherwood, Mapplethorpe, and Gunn, involves such an intense focus on the estranged particular that the more general matrix traditionally framing that object becomes eliminated, thereby leading to an unusual loss of perspective that serves to denaturalize the province of the familiar. Gunn himself tries something similar with the camera style in *Positives* (1966), the volume in which he provided verses alongside photographs of London by his brother, Ander. *Positives* transforms London into an edgy, existential environment: the patron dozing in a pub is described as "nodding on the brown cracked / American leather of the sofa," as though, like Isherwood in Berlin, Gunn's disaffiliated lens were transforming the capital city into a landscape of menace, with shadows of "American leather" silently disturbing the native somnolence.[40]

This antihumanist dimension to Gunn's poetry, particularly pronounced in the period between the second half of *My Sad Captains* and *The Passages of Joy*, was a source of considerable concern to some of his more traditionalist readers. In his book *The Survival of Poetry* (1970), Martin Dodsworth took exception to what he called a "derivativeness" on Gunn's part, seeing it as the kind of "susceptibility or even submissiveness before other people, and indeed before the world of things" that was intimately connected with the poet's more general themes of domination and submission.[41] Various other English critics frowned on what they called Gunn's "abrogation of human concern" and acquiescence in "the vacant counter-cultural slovenliness of [his] Californian ethic"; they complained of what they perceived as the "narcissism" and faddishness of these poems, their apparently relaxed immersion in the San Francisco gay scene and drug culture; they took issue with what Alan Bold in 1976 described as Gunn's style of "self-indulgent free-association."[42] Reviewing the 1976 volume *Jack Straw's Castle* in the *Times Literary Supplement*, John Bayley raised questions about the dislocated aspects of Gunn's poetic identity by remarking: "Gunn's poetry has often seemed to me to be not quite 'real,' to be, as it were, counterfeiting poetry with a highly accomplished and covertly malignant skill."[43] Looked at in the critical light of British empiricism, all the doubles and mirrorings in Gunn's poetry have tended to create an uncomfortable sense of elusiveness and even fakery. The poet himself, though, has consistently disavowed this romantic dichotomy between "real" and "counterfeiting," preferring to look back instead to the intensely reflexive world of sixteenth- and seventeenth-century poetry: "What we must remember," he wrote in an essay on Ben Jonson, "is that artifice is not necessarily the antithesis of sincerity."[44] For Gunn, as for the Elizabethan sonneteers, the truest poetry is the most feigning. Indeed, we might say that Gunn has constructed an imaginary Elizabethan tradition as a mirror of, and precursor to, his own work; he remarked in a 1995 interview that he looked on a poet like George Herbert as "being a kind of contemporary of mine," an outlook he attributed to having been educated "when the New Criticism was at its height," with its conception of great poetry existing in a timeless present.[45]

The neoplatonic idealism that permeates Gunn's virtual Elizabethan England is actually informed more by American phenomenology than by the empirical, Larkinesque forms that dominated British poetry in the 1960s and 1970s. Despite their apparent looseness of texture, Gunn's sprawling American landscapes rarely appear to be composed merely of accidental phenomena. In *Moly*, he describes the cerebral transformations wrought by LSD in a highly controlled pattern of metrical verse, arguing later that he wanted to lend form to the amorphous, formless experience of taking acid.[46] But the stylistic symmetry here also seems to betoken a world of neoplatonic order, characteristic of the intellectual framework of American transcendentalism, whereby random phenomena are collated around a unifying center.

"Sunlight," the culminating poem in *Moly*, is concerned with this process of reconciling disparate terrestrial phenomena within the universal presence of nature:

> Water, glass, metal, match light in their raptures,
> Flashing their many answers to the one.
> What captures light belongs to what it captures:
> The whole side of a world facing the sun,
>
> Re-turned to woo the original perfection,
> Giving itself to what created it,
> And wearing green in sign of its subjection.
> It is as if the sun were infinite. (223)

"Sunlight" was designated by the author in 1989 as "my favorite poem by myself," and the reciprocal interaction in this poem between the "many" and the "one" is reminiscent of the kind of idealism promulgated by Emerson and Whitman in the nineteenth century and by Stevens in the twentieth.[47] Such idealism is, of course, represented here as hypothetical rather than affirmative: in "Sunlight," the sun appears only "as if" it were infinite, an image compared by the author to a line from Stevens's "Sunday Morning": "Not as a god, but as a god might be."[48] Nevertheless, Gunn here reconsiders his familiar theme of reflexivity in the context of what Emerson would call the "Over-Soul," so that the circulation between different entities, the transition between active and passive modes—"What captures light belongs to what it captures"—becomes more than mere empty mirrorings, because all these fragments are holistically validated by that "original perfection," implying, in secular terms, an essential or apparently "infinite" source of light.[49] (Note that hyphen in "Re-turned," implying a world turning and turning about.) This is not the black mise-en-abîme of "Carnal Knowledge," but rather a mythic justification of an eternal sense of movement, which here becomes redefined as a perpetual oscillation between accident and essence, the many and the one. Such oscillation is reflected formally in the way "Sunlight" alternates lines of ten and eleven syllables, as if to suggest that terrestrial contingencies might always relate to, but can never be entirely subsumed by, the measured order of the iambic pentameter.

In 1986, quoting Ben Jonson's remark that poets should be able to write in many different styles, Gunn talked of his wish to be "a various poet," that is, a writer able to manipulate a variety of technical forms to suit different occasions.[50] This is quite different from the way a poet like Adrienne Rich, for example, simply left behind her formalist structures of the 1950s when she embarked in the feminist 1970s on a style of free verse that she equated with both a personal and artistic "will to change."[51] Gunn, though, moves more flexibly among various idioms, and indeed he takes artistic pleasure in the potential incongruities that can arise from describing one particular landscape through a formal framework normally associated with something quite different. In 1985, for instance, he published "An Invitation from San Francisco to My Brother," a poem with a beady eye for the poor and dispossessed of the Reagan years, which interlaces its iambic pentameters with octosyllabic lines, as if to imply a world not quite in perfect balance:

> By then you will have noticed those
> Who make up Reagan's proletariat:
> The hungry in their long lines that
> Gangling around two sides of city block
> Are fully formed by ten o'clock
> For meals the good Dominicans will feed
> Without demur to all who need.
> You'll watch the jobless side by side with whores
> Setting a home up out of doors. (412)

"An Invitation" might also be said to enjoy a family relationship with England in form as well as content, because its return to the pattern of formal meter and rhyme associated with Gunn's earliest work suggests a shift away from the syllabic forms and free verse that characterized the development of his American style in the late 1960s and 1970s. To oversimplify this argument for a moment: if we see Gunn's free verse as aligned conceptually with America, with risk, and with emancipation from Old World constraints, then his formal verse might be linked, conversely, to a sense of limitation, to traditional European aesthetic models, and (by extension) to an intimation of the pressures of time. Consequently, the renewed emphasis on rhyme and meter in Gunn's poetry of the late 1980s and 1990s could be seen as aesthetically intertwined with its thematic emphasis on chronological sequence. Even in poems such as "Transients and Residents" from *The Passages of Joy* we find Gunn framing the hedonistic urban gay scene within more austere parameters of rhyme and meter, as if to validate the poem's censorious epigraph from Samuel Johnson: "Time hovers o'er, impatient to destroy, / And shuts up all the Passages of Joy." The poem plays off its "parties," "streetboys," and "evenings in the bar" against the shadows of aging and sickness, and in this way the rhyme and meter work as a formal correlative to what Johnson would have recognized as the circumscribed conditions of human mortality. It is not that Gunn simply exploits Johnson's conservative point of view to upbraid this "boisterous" gay culture, but he implies the double-edged perspectives that emerge from pushing its "sense of fun" up against more rigid temporal and philosophical restraints (374–75).

It would be wrong to insist too rigidly on any kind of binary opposition between America and England, for what we encounter more often in Gunn is an internal dialectic, an argument between different cultural modes and formal systems. We see this kind of crosscurrent in the 1988 poem "Words for Some Ash," which describes the disintegration of a human body into "a bag of ash," punning on the word "bound" to signify the way an active leap or bound is itself bound, incorporated, by the inevitable framework of time and death:

> . . . the granules work their way
> Down to unseen streams, and bound
> Briskly in the water's play;

May you lastly reach the shore,
Joining tide without intent,
Only worried any more
By the currents' argument. (472)

The imagery here is of oscillating tides and currents, a "play" of the water that itself implies the linguistic plays and reversals at work within the poem. It is entirely commensurate with the paradoxical cast of Gunn's work that it should be this acknowledgment of mutability, the flow of temporal decay, that is one factor inspiring the poet's return to more formal styles of elegy. As Gunn himself observed in a 1989 interview, one particular "forte" of his writing is "filtering some kind of subject-matter through a form associated with its opposite." He elaborated: "It's as though I'm taking street noises and turning them into a string quartet. I figure that, in that way, one finds out more about the street and one finds out more about the potentiality of the string quartet also."[52] Accordingly, Gunn's transnational style involves in quite a precise way an aesthetics of reversal, whereby the conventions and expectations associated with English literary forms are played off against an American subject matter and vice versa.

Nevertheless, given Gunn's own emphasis on "continuities" in his life and art—"between America and England, between free verse and metre, between vision and everyday consciousness"—it is possible also to see the interpenetration of opposites in these later poems as a confluence of mutually sustaining influences, both a summation and an extension of different postwar poetic traditions.[53] In the 1970s, both Donald Davie and Marjorie Perloff suggested that British poetry and American poetry were not, as Davie put it, "on speaking terms"; but Gunn, who described himself in his *Collected Poems* as having moved from being "an English poet" in his early books to an "Anglo-American" writer later on (489), remains concerned (as Davie was also) to find points of congruence and crossover between these parallel national idioms.[54] This conscious invocation of a hybrid Anglo-American allegiance helps to account for the tone of Gunn's work since *The Passages of Joy*, which emerges out of an increasingly complex, transnational discourse of reverse projection and self-contradiction. In a 1991 essay on Robert Duncan, Gunn remarked on Duncan's "Duplicit Style" as "an active ongoing embrace between contrary meanings"; such reciprocity between alternating positions can also be seen in the poetic tribute "Duncan," which opens the collection *Boss Cupid* (2000):

> He let the divine prompting (come at length)
> Rushingly bear him any way it would
> And went on writing while the Ferry turned
> From San Francisco, back from Berkeley too,
> And back again, and back again. He learned
> You add to, you don't cancel what you do.[55]

This poem is, perhaps, as much about Gunn's own poetry as Duncan's, for the image of the ferry turning backward and forward across the San Francisco Bay could be understood self-reflexively as a metaphor for the way Gunn has been concerned in the 1990s and beyond to shuttle between the styles of English Elizabethan and American objectivist verse.

Gunn's haunting poems about the effects of the AIDS epidemic in San Francisco in *The Man with Night Sweats* (1992) constitute some of the clearest examples of his American subjects finding themselves incorporated within an English Elizabethan framework. For example, in "Courtesies of the Interregnum," first published in 1989, the existential valorization of what is self-defining, risky, and tough finds itself compelled to undertake a negotiation with ancestral limits. The poem pays tribute to a friend stricken with AIDS who "gallantly" maintains his social civility and charm on the path to death; again, it is set in formal rhyme and meter, as though the arbitrary but seemingly inevitable demarcations of these poetic parameters serve as an aesthetic re-creation of the boundaries of mortality. The poem thus formally encompasses that tension between autonomy and submission, between "bravery" and acquiescence in death, which is being described here:

> And he now, athlete-like, triumphs at length,
> Though with not physical but social strength
> Precisely exerted. He who might well cry
> Reaches through such informal courtesy
> To values grasped and shaped out as he goes,
> Of which the last is bravery, for he knows
> That even as he gets them in his grip
> Context itself starts dizzyingly to slip. (477)

"Courtesies of the Interregnum" thus shows Gunn using rhyming iambic pentameters to establish a poetic world of duality and balance where opposites can be played off against each other. Many of his poems of the 1980s and 1990s take up the images of mirroring that have been a discomfiting presence in his writing since *Fighting Terms,* but these later works tend to represent such images of reflection as more like a series of Chinese boxes, whose textual figures of paradox, play, and reversal imply a world where no object or idea can remain undisturbed by its contrary. One example of this is "An Operation" (1991), subsequently collected in *Boss Cupid,* which describes an elaborate undercover sting operation:

> A couple of policemen dressed
> In plain-clothes best,
> Like auto dealers pushing forty,
> Straight and yet sporty,
> Sat, one on show and one confined
> To a room behind
> The storefront rented in pretence . . .
> The hidden cop
> Taped the transactions of the crooks
> Who filled the books
> The other kept, practical, blunt,
> Front of a front.

As the poem develops, this narrative of double-dealing comes to take on a wider conceptual significance. The scene of displacement and reversal becomes a metaphor for larger paradoxes turning on ontological conjunctions of freedom and bondage, a notion addressed explicitly in the more abstract tone of the last stanza:

> And if you wait
> Tilting your chair almost at spill,
> A sort of thrill
> Steals upward to the skin maybe,
> Till you are free
> To stretch within an innocence
> Born from constraints.[56]

That image of the chair tilting, swinging precariously between one possibility and another, epitomizes the way contrary impulses are brought together and sometimes balanced against each other in Gunn's poetic world.

In epistemological terms, such interactions between competing forces result in scenes of perpetual destabilization and radical ambiguity, and in Gunn's later poems these active and reactive forces work on a ludic as well as a thematic level. In *The Man with Night Sweats* and *Boss Cupid*, he blends the phenomenological particularity developed in *The Passages of Joy* and his other "American" works with the styles of self-conscious allegory and traditional meter more typical of his earlier "English" verse. "An Operation" is a good example of this duality, fusing as it does concrete description (the sting operation) with philosophical meditations on paradox toward the end. "Courtesies of the Interregnum" similarly uses the chronometric regularity of poetic form to disrupt the self-possessed quality of phenomenal objects, to introduce within this world of ideal presence a sense of historical objectification and, finally, death. Conversely, the residual phenomenological impulse draws attention to the artificial and ultimately insufficient nature of the allegorical designs that these texts describe. In this way, Gunn specializes in creating self-conscious allegories, allegories that never quite fit together, as in "Cafeteria in Boston" from *The Man with Night Sweats*: "I stomached him, / him of the flabby stomach, / Though it was getting harder to keep down" (452). The focus in this poem swings between the abstract and the physical, between the metaphorical and biological implications of "stomaching" something, with the pun becoming a microcosm of a more general conflict here between the irreducible otherness of the café's tacky "red formica" (452) and the scavenging ambitions of the poet's allegorizing intellect. In this scene, an element of self-parody again intervenes: the technique of shot/reverse shot, familiar from the language of cinema, is turned back on the narrator to make him an object within the landscape he has described. By foregrounding his own aesthetic perspective in this way, the poet self-consciously exposes the fabricated style of his own inventions.

Yet these metaphorical halls of mirrors never involve simple narcissism or the emptier kind of postmodernist gaming. Gunn wrote in 1990 of what he called the complacency of the Language Poets, with their tendency to scoff at " 'subject,' placing the term between quotation marks as if referring to some laughable affectation."[57] His own ludic patterns, by contrast, always seem under threat of being weighed down by heavier purposes; indeed, the piquancy of these playful styles often derives from a sense of friction, from the impression that formal parameters are being imposed on some force that can barely be restrained, that is bursting to get out. Gunn remarked in a 1990 essay how much Elizabeth Bishop used to admire Joseph Cornell's artistic boxes, and he went on to describe how Bishop's poetry, like that of Andrew Marvell, used the idea of a box "to take unmanageable life and make it manageable by reducing it in scale." Gunn added that he himself also considered the box "a wonderful form" for aesthetic expression, comparing this process of miniaturization to "a board-game like Monopoly," which "is oddly comforting in its containment, and yet just as oddly discomfiting in its implications of the excluded. It only hints at what cannot be contained within its limits."[58] Many of Gunn's own recent poems imitate this strategy in the way they cherish formal enclosure and escape from this enclosure simultaneously. In Gunn's world, the idea of liberation depends paradoxically on the idea of confinement.

It is this reconstitution of paradox as an experiential category that links Gunn's cerebral style most obviously with the English metaphysical poets. Gunn has written admiringly about the uses of paradox in the poetry of Fulke Greville, who "never allows his feeling to eliminate his mind," and he said of Ben Jonson: "It is the tornness that he does so well."[59] It is this perception of "tornness," a disorienting sense of being pulled in opposite directions at once, that makes up the characteristic transnational style of Gunn's late work. "The J Car," another mordant elegy from *The Man with Night Sweats* commemorating a friend who died of AIDS, is a superb example of these crossed tensions. More fully realized and embodied than his early "English" poetry, yet also more focused and controlled than much of his "American" work of the 1960s and 1970s, "The J Car" interweaves historical detail and the mirrors of reflection to create a work that is most moving for its very evasion or deflection of emotion. The poem does not in fact specifically mention the AIDS epidemic at all, but describes in meticulous detail a meal shared at a German restaurant shortly before the man's death:

> Finishing up the Optimator beer,
> I walked him home through the suburban cool
> By dimming shape of church and Catholic school,
> Only a few white teenagers about.

After the four blocks he would be tired out . . .
Unready, disappointed, unachieved,
He knew he would not write the much-conceived
Much-hoped-for work now, nor yet help create
A love he might in full reciprocate. (480–81)

Love and work surrender to AIDS. But rather than simply recounting his friend's illness, the narrator displaces that object into a structure of retrospective meditation that is itself framed by the distant impersonality of rhyming iambic pentameters. The symmetry of this rhyme betokens a fatalism that, crossed with the narrator's casual and colloquial tone, produces the kind of dialectic between self-willed freedom and possession by a greater force that is reminiscent of Donne's divine sonnets. Looking back to his poetry of the 1950s, written almost exclusively in iambic pentameter, Gunn observed that his aim at that time was "to be the John Donne of the twentieth century," and oddly enough this ambition now seems to have become realized.[60] Gunn's poetic career has turned full circle: the existential drive for self-definition that helped propel him toward an American poetic idiom has been harmonized with the aesthetic traditions of his British youth.

In 1974, recalling his adolescence in England, Gunn spoke of himself as having a "suburban muse."[61] It is interesting to see how this description in "The J Car" of a "suburban" San Francisco, a landscape of ordered inconsequence and anticlimax, seems to echo the parks and enclosed spaces of his London days, as remembered in earlier poems like "Autobiography" and "Hampstead: The Horse Chestnut Trees." For Gunn, this suburban muse evokes not only a geographic location but also a poetic style and state of mind, an in-between world that is not positively one thing or the other. This suburban landscape appears again in "Patch Work," first published in 1987 and also collected in *The Man with Night Sweats*, where the author implicitly represents his own poetic voice as a "mockingbird" that moves "Above the densely flowering / Suburban plots of May" in deliberately unpretentious fashion, as if acceding to his own marginalization from the symbolic centers of power:

. . . it appears to us
Perched on the post that ends a washing-line
To sing there, as in flight,
A repertoire of songs that it has heard

> —From other birds, and others of its kind—
> Which it has recombined
> And made its own. . . . (427)

Like his suburban mockingbird, Gunn is unafraid of appearing "deriva-
tive," as the poem describes it; like Ben Jonson and the metaphysical
poets, he admires the arts of imitation. Such imitation is not slavish self-
abnegation, but involves the abjuration of romantic individualism and a
turning away from self-deluding quests for pure originality or autonomy.
There is in Gunn's later poems a knowingness, a wry self-mockery,
which places him still in a foreign relation to some aspects of the San
Francisco poetry scene. Gunn's mockingbird acquiesces instead in a
form of limitation, acknowledging that the active will must finally engage
in partnership with aesthetic and ontological boundaries. In particular,
the peculiar poignancy of his later poems lies in the way the narrative
subject seems to be exiled to the margins or suburbs of his own formal
landscape, to become an incidental object within a world he no longer
seeks to transcend or master.

We can glimpse in "The J Car" and "Patch Work," then, a shadow of a
suburban mode that was one of the literary characteristics of the "Movement" group with which Gunn was initially associated in the mid 1950s.[62]
Many critics have charged the Movement writers with a suburban pusil-
lanimity, but Gunn's lasting achievement is to have redefined his native
suburban muse in less confined and particularistic terms, to have transformed it into a more abstract and powerful artistic idiom. Writing in
1990 of Janet Lewis, Gunn observed that one of her poems recalls a scene
from the Michigan of her youth "while writing in the entirely different
landscape of Santa Fe in the early 1920s," thereby creating a "nostalgia . . . containing within its own vigor the germ of a critique against
itself."[63] Although the scenes in *The Man with Night Sweats* are set in
suburban San Francisco rather than suburban London, there is a similar
quality of diplopia or double vision to the landscapes of these poems,
whose recognizably American features are framed within what seems at
times like a curiously Larkinesque milieu. From the quotidian circumstances of "A Blank," for instance, we might almost be back in Larkin's
Hull:

> Watching Victorian porches through the glass,
> From the 6 bus, I caught sight of a friend
> Stopped on a corner-kerb to let us pass. . . . (487)

Like Nabokov, a fellow immigrant writer, Gunn has not been fully accepted into the American literary canon as it has been shaped institutionally since the Second World War. After *The Man with Night Sweats* appeared, Susan Sontag suggested that Gunn was "one of the two or three best poets writing anywhere right now," but still he is not featured in either the Heath or the Norton *Anthology of American Literature,* nor indeed in the 1999 anthology of seventy-six California poets entitled *The Geography of Home: California's Poetry of Place.* He does have a place in the *Norton Anthology of English Literature,* but is represented there by only five early poems, none of which deals explicitly with American materials.[64] Gunn's poetry, then, seems somehow not to be at "home" anywhere. There is still sometimes an inclination in U.S. culture to think of the iambic pentameter as insidiously un-American and antidemocratic, an attitude that goes back to William Carlos Williams's denunciation of the form as a residue of European feudalistic power, the "medieval masterbeat," as he categorized it.[65] It is just this kind of old assumption about what makes up literary nationalism, an assumption harking back to the anthropological persuasions of modernism, that has served to marginalize Gunn from the annals of American literature, even though all of his books except the first were written in the United States and all of them have been manifestly influenced by American concerns. Even Gunn's friend and neighbor, the San Francisco poet August Kleinzahler, remarked that the "tone" of Gunn's poems "is oddly formal to most American poets," that they "certainly don't sound the way Americans speak." For Kleinzahler, this suggests how Gunn "*is* English, after all, even after forty years in the United States."[66]

Unlike Auden and Isherwood, who both took American citizenship in 1946, Gunn has always preferred to retain his status as a resident alien, and so from a legal point of view, if nothing else, this statement is correct. But Kleinzahler's argument that "there's not an aleatory bone in his body" and that Gunn is, aristically speaking, "Handel, not John Cage" would appear to underestimate the extent to which his work has been modulated by his adopted American environment.[67] It also, of course, vividly demonstrates the difficulty of making Gunn's texts line up with the overt or covert agendas of cultural nationalism in general. Despite his own admiration of Gunn's work, Kleinzahler found its style too formalist in orientation to speak naturally to the common expectations of American readers, implying perhaps that his poems sound more "American" to British ears, just as they seem more "British" to Americans. Approaching this question from the other side of the Atlantic, from the radically different vantage point of British cultural materialism, Alan Sinfield criticized Gunn in his poems about AIDS for a reluctance to engage openly with the politics of subcultural resistance.[68] But there is an elusiveness, a refractory element, in Gunn's "duplicit style" that makes him reluctant to conform either to archetypal American myths of freedom or to the British tendency to conflate sexual politics with collective questions of social hierarchy and class conflict. Even in "Epitaph," the memorializing public poem that Gunn wrote to be chiseled in stone at the AIDS Memorial Grove in Golden Gate Park, he elects to place emphasis on individual particularity rather than merely the blander face of identity politics:

> Walker within this circle, pause.
> Although they all died of one cause
> Remember how their lives were dense
> With fine, compacted difference.[69]

Given his own intellectual predilection for "difference," it is not difficult to appreciate the obstacles to interpreting Gunn through any kind of normalizing national narrative. The issue here is not, of course, how we might forcibly insert Gunn's idiosyncratic poetics into any given national tradition, but how his deviations from inherited formats, his infractions of generic orthodoxy, have made his work appear odd and sometimes incomplete to readers who have approached these poems with a certain set of expectations. Gunn's transnational idiom does not involve simply a transcendence of national identity but, rather, a desire to invert and displace nationalistic assumptions, to turn them inside out, so that familiar icons might be reilluminated from an alternative angle of vision. Writing about Allen Ginsberg, for instance, Gunn curiously compared the American beat poet to Edmund Spenser, "that most diffuse of poets," whose exotic appeal in Elizabethan England was, suggests Gunn, analogous to that of Ginsberg in "prim 1950s America." It is not difficult to see what he means: as he says, the charm of both poets "is dependent on the very long-windedness."[70] But this parallel between the orotund Spenser and the maverick Ginsberg is, on the face of it, so incongruous that it takes on the appearance of a conceptual oxymoron, as though Gunn were taking a perverse delight in bringing together quite disparate categories.

To shake loose dogmatic assumptions can, of course, involve its own kind of regenerative moral agenda. Indeed, in an odd kind of way it is possible to imagine Gunn as the successor of those seventeenth-century Englishmen who went out to the New World with a clear moral design, who were weary of the corruption of their homeland and sought to create through transatlantic displacement a renewed sense of community and ethical purpose. Despite his reluctance to attach himself to fixed positions, Gunn has consistently described himself as a socialist, and *The Man with Night Sweats* and *Boss Cupid*, in particular, show his concern with creating and sustaining the values of mutuality in the Bay Area.[71] Sometimes this communal activity is cast within a specifically mythic framework, as in *Moly* or the final poem from *Boss Cupid*, "Dancing David," which envisages a pantheistic participation in the "God-dance" of eros.[72] Sometimes it involves a strong sense of intellectual fellowship with particular writers, as we see from the early poem "To Yvor Winters 1955" to the late poem "To Donald Davie in Heaven." At other times, though, this community is represented in more mundane, everyday terms, as a group of friends helping to support each other through the burdens of illness, death, and loss.

It would be wrong, though, to give the impression of Gunn as an entirely domesticated figure, and the appearance in *Boss Cupid* of "Troubadour," a sequence of "songs" about the mass murderer Jeffrey Dahmer, shows how he is still willing provocatively to explore the kind of juxtaposition of sex and violence that alarmed many of his earlier critics. But most of these later poems about gay culture cherish its consensual, playful, and ordinary aspects, specifically avoiding the kind of masochistic embrace of "destructiveness" or "self-shattering pleasure" that we see in the writings of a different kind of San Francisco gay writer, Leo Bersani.[73] Avoiding Bersani's extremism, Gunn presents himself rather as a survivor, a stoic, who continues to converse with his friends in an eminently civilized fashion. In this sense, he remains a product of English suburbia who, with a plain if extraordinarily subtle common sense, resists the allure of the "end-of-the-world rhetoric" that, as Sontag noted, has come to be associated metaphorically with the AIDS epidemic. Sacvan Bercovitch observed many years ago that the idea of apocalypse, with its glamorous apparatus of catastrophe and violent purification, has always enjoyed a special resonance with Americans, but Gunn has deliberately eschewed such self-immolating romanticism, preferring to confront the great plague with a poetic style more redolent of Elizabethan courtliness and metaphysical wit.[74] His work provides a fine example of how transnational perspectives can modify not just the larger narratives of American literature, but also the manner in which day-to-day life in the United States is represented.

Despite their personal associations, Gunn has never had much time for Plath's writing or for confessional poetry in general. David Fulton has argued that Gunn "is almost wholly English" in his preference for a decorous presentation of personality and sense of "proportion" rather than the tendency of confessional poets to dramatize their own lives, as Gunn himself put it in an essay on Robert Lowell, "endlessly and tediously."[75] It would not be altogether true, though, to suggest that Gunn simply favors neoclassical objectivity over autobiographical extravagance, for, as we have seen, his own poetry plays deliberately with the arts of self-mirroring. In "Jack Straw's Castle," for example, we find the narrator brooding on his imprisonment in a "castle" of the ego:

> why can't I leave my castle
> he says, isn't there anyone
> anyone here besides me
>
> sometimes I find myself wondering
> if the castle is castle at all
> a place apart, or merely
> the castle that every snail
> must carry around till his death (270)

While this mood of solipsism recalls Gunn's earlier work, which despaired of matching internal fantasy with external fact, there is also a consciously ironic stance here through which the poet undermines his image of an enclosed, castellated self. The title itself is an oxymoron: Jack Straw, Gunn points out in the notes to his *Collected Poems,* is defined by the Oxford dictionary as " 'a straw man'; a man of no substance, worth, or consideration" (491), and so, presumably, the last person likely to possess his own castle of bricks and mortar. By interweaving narcissism and self-deprecation in this way, Gunn projects a doubleness of perspective whereby the self-portrait is, as John Ashbery would say, reflected in a convex mirror, repositioned in a more illuminating and playful light.

It is the absence of this kind of perspective that Gunn regrets in the confessional poets, not their focus on individual personality per se. Indeed, it might be possible to argue that the confessional idiom represents for Gunn a threat of the "abject," in Kristeva's sense of that term, a potential psychic dissolution that remains latent within his own work. Abjection, as we saw in relation to Nabokov, implies doubling and division; in Gunn's case, it implies a disturbing shadow self, a solipsistic dejection or infantile nostalgia which his own strategies of artful control are always contending against.[76] *The Man with Night Sweats,* for example, argues intertextually with Robert Lowell's 1964 poem, "Night Sweat," where the Boston poet relates his nocturnal creative activity to regressive memories of childhood:

> always inside me is the child who died,
> always inside me is his will to die—[77]

As we have seen, Gunn's poems about AIDS are particularly resonant for the way they refuse morbid, thanatological consciousness, and so he reworks Lowell's "will to die" into an elliptical, understated description of death as a merely biological occurrence, an event without epistemological significance. Similarly, "The Gas Poker," a 1992 poem about his own mother's suicide, was "modelled," as Gunn put it, on "a Hardyesque kind of poem" to convert the abjection of personal despair into an aesthetic balance of emotional empathy and formal detachment.[78] Consequently, Gunn's poems do not involve a simple negation of the confessional style, but rather its reinscription within a more complex aesthetic framework.

In Plath's poetry, an equivalent sense of detachment emerges not so much through a conscious postmodernist pose, as in Gunn's most polished work, but through a thread of displacement that unravels itself, often in manic and self-subverting ways, throughout her writing. Just as the emergence of reflexive perspectives in Gunn's work coincided with his emigration to the United States, so Plath's poetry was metamorphosed by her transposition from Eisenhower's America to the murkier domain of British culture. Living in England, she wrote home to her mother in 1962, involved enduring six months of "damp and rain and blackness," making her "miss the American snow, which at least makes a new, clean, exciting season out of winter."[79] America in her mind was always associated with what was pristine, translucent, and many of the poems in her first collection, *The Colossus* (1960), share these qualities. Their points of reference are often mythological: Oedipus in "The Eye-

Mote," "Mother Medea in a green smock" in "Aftermath," Aeschylean tragedy in "The Colossus," where "A blue sky out of the Oresteia / Arches above us."[80] But these myths are reminiscent not so much of the classical furies as the archetypal categories of Northrop Frye, whose books, such as *Anatomy of Criticism* (1957), were extremely influential in the American academy during the late 1950s for the way they attempted to impose supposedly timeless categories on the nature of experience.

Many of Plath's American poems of the late 1950s involve a similar strategy of investing proximate landscapes with an abstract or transcendent quality. This ensures that even her more sinister scenes are possessed of a "clean," statuesque element, as in "Mussel Hunter at Rock Harbor":

> I came before the water—
> Colorists came to get the
> Good of the Cape light that scours
> Sand grit to sided crystal. . . . (95)

Despite the ironic attitudes toward the conformist pressures of American culture that emerge strongly in her journals and other prose writings, Plath's early work, in particular, is suffused with American values and attributes. In *The Bell Jar*, first published in 1963 but set in the 1950s, there is a scene where the heroine, Esther Greenwood, unable to decide whether to be a happy housewife or professor or "Olympic lady crew champion," pictures herself beneath a fig tree "starving to death, just because I couldn't make up my mind which of the figs I would choose. I wanted each and every one of them, but choosing one meant losing all the rest."[81] It is a dilemma typical of the Emersonian idealist: the problem of how to accommodate infinite possibility in a postlapsarian world of partial circumstances.

As Jacqueline Rose observed, there has been intense controversy over the "ownership" of Plath ever since her death, with her mother and husband both seeking control of the poet's estate for their own purposes.[82] It is important to recognize that these disputes were not simply personal or financial but involved larger questions about Plath's place in particular cultural traditions. For Aurelia Schober Plath, her daughter remained quintessentially an all-American girl, with *The Bell Jar* being merely a transitory expression of adolescent angst and her suicide in 1963 the result of "some darker day than usual" when she was "temporarily" unable "to be gallant and equal to the life-experience."[83] For Hughes, as we have seen, Plath's darker English voice was her true voice, the voice of experience, and in his terms America became for her a lost "Paradise," the "pre-Adamite" land of "intact childhood," a world of innocence that was fundamentally as illusory as any other Eden.[84] Hughes also recalled with disapprobation that in the late 1950s Plath had been a great admirer of Wallace Stevens—"a kind of god to her"—although he himself had been considerably less enthusiastic about the New England poet's "magniloquence." The implication here is that Hughes eventually succeeded in coaching Plath out of her Stevens obsession into a more solid grasp of the natural world.[85]

This transatlantic conflict over Plath's reputation has also extended into the critical realm. Charles Newman, on behalf of the American academy, sought to associate her with an American "poetic tradition that extends back through Emily [Dickinson] to Anne Bradstreet and Edward Taylor, a tradition in which the imaginative realization of dying is the determining, climactic experience of living."[86] By contrast, the London critic A. Alvarez has written of Plath's "vital decision" to abandon her academic career in the United States; he, like Hughes, portrayed the power of her late work as deriving from a radical, existential break with American cultural traditions, rather than being simply a continuation of them.[87] Indeed, the notable popularity in Britain of American confessional poets—Robert Lowell and John Berryman, as well as Plath—derived in some measure from a sense that they had each left behind the realms of American "abstraction" and taken on the guise of a more personable self. John Bayley, writing in 1977, disparaged the "American blankness" that he saw reproduced in the anonymous poetic terrain of Stevens, but he praised the "good and real" poetry of Lowell and Berryman, who, in training themselves "on European lines," had sought "consciously to *make* themselves," and their poems, more "solid" objects.[88]

Looked at from a transnational point of view, however, it becomes evident that the peculiar intensity of Plath's most incisive work emerges from neither an adherence to American idealist poetics, nor a straightforward conversion to indigenous British romanticism, but rather from the points of transition between these different positions. This is not simply to read the *Ariel* poems in a reductive biographical way, as the product of deracination and exile; it is, though, to suggest how their unsettling aspects are related to a dynamic of interference, a collision between two distinct national traditions, burdened as they each are with the weight of material culture and historical expectation. Plath herself turns these kinds of discrepancies into a thematic issue in "New Year on Dartmoor" (1962), a poem that might be seen as a curious equivalent to Gunn's "Waking in a Newly Built House," published the previous year. However, "New Year on Dartmoor" considers transatlantic displacement from the opposite direction, and the pervasive tone here is one of loss:

> This is newness: every little tawdry
> Obstacle glass-wrapped and peculiar,
> Glinting and clinking in a saint's falsetto. Only you
> Don't know what to make of the sudden slippiness,
> The blind, white, awful, inaccessible slant.
> There's no getting it up by the words you know.
> No getting up by elephant or wheel or shoe.
> We have only come to look. You are too new
> To want the world in a glass hat. (176)

Looking at the rough English landscape through the eyes of an infant, the narrator is taken aback by its "sudden slippiness" and "inaccessible" quality. Objects do not fit into a priori linguistic categories; there is a disconcerting absence of correspondence between mind and world. In the Emersonian, idealist conception of nature, external objects should be linked to an all-seeing eye and to the vistas of human cognition by bonds of analogical similitude; in this new world on Dartmoor, by contrast, everything seems "peculiar," so that the reflexive mirrors of transcendentalism no longer appear valid. This is a world that cannot fit into a "glass hat," and the narrator implicitly aligns herself with the infant as someone who is observing its particularity for the first time.

Whereas Gunn's later poems establish reflection as an informing matrix for aesthetic and ethical value, Plath's poems more often involve reflections that are blank, or, as in "Mirror," that lock the protagonist into the claustrophobic reduplication of an alter ego:

> I am silver and exact. I have no preconceptions.
> Whatever I see I swallow immediately
> Just as it is, unmisted by love or dislike. (173)

One of the recurring motifs in the poems Plath wrote in England over the last few years of her life is precisely this failure of reflexivity: the resistance of a brute material world to the designs of human spirit, the incapacity of metaphor to transform eccentric object into prophetic sign. In "Wuthering Heights" (1961), the landscape of the Yorkshire moors is described through simile rather than metaphor—"The horizons ring me like faggots" (167)—as though the poet were admitting the purely figurative aspect of this conjunction and so, by extension, the power of nature to crush human invention. In the classic New England tradition, Emerson's "transparent eye-ball" positions itself at the center of nature's concentric design: "I am nothing; I see all. The currents of the Universal Being circulate through me."[89] In "Wuthering Heights," on the other hand, the circumference—"Tilted and disparate, and always unstable" (167)—has exceeded the capacity of the eye to regulate it: the "horizons" are heavy, demythologized, deanimated. Hence the dominant tone is one of oppression, with the heavy, empty heavens weighing down upon the speaker:

> The sky leans on me, me, the one upright
> Among all horizontals. (168)

The poem's title evokes all the legends of the Brontës and the English heritage associated with them, and its version of death involves not so much a pathological desire for personal self-extinction as a more intellectualized sense of human perception finding itself overwhelmed by some profoundly atavistic force. "I do not trust the spirit," declares Plath in "Last Words" (172), a poem written just a month after "Wuthering Heights," and her last works range over the primitive country of Britain to argue with the alternative idealization of "spirit" that manifests itself in Emerson, Stevens, and other writers in her native New England tradition.

To see Plath as engaged transnationally with an intellectual demystification of her own transcendentalist legacy is to challenge the popular legend that would simply personify this destructive force and identify it with the character of Hughes himself. My point is that the fragmentation of American idealism in Plath's texts is a much more complex issue, involving a destabilization of national cultures as well as psychological identities. Thomas E. Yingling described Plath as "in the most radical Emersonian tradition, an un-settler," which is partly true; but although Plath's poetic language does perhaps seek to avoid "familiarizing referentiality," it can never altogether achieve this state of pure abstraction or avoid running aground on the world of irreducible matter.[90] Looking at Plath's relationship with Emerson in a more oblique way, Frederick Buell has argued that the exposure of the narrator's pretensions to self-reliance in *The Bell Jar* involves "a sinister caricature of Emerson's ideal," as though Plath were intertextually travestying idealist consciousness.[91] This undertone of aggressive parody emerges clearly in "Tulips," one of the *Ariel* poems, which foregrounds the problematic question of metaphorical correspondence. Whereas this process of correspondence appears to Emerson's Olympian vision as a natural phenomenon, in Plath's poem it manifests itself as more of a twisted, contorted event, with the first half of the line being yoked together uneasily with the second: "Their redness talks to my wound, it corresponds" (161). Throughout *Ariel,* indeed, there is a compulsive return to this theme of arbitrary correspondence and displacement: in "Daddy," the literal father has been knowingly displaced into a Nazi icon—"I thought every German was you"—so that the "model" of "daddy" created by the narrator stands as a memento of her inability to relate to him in a natural manner (223–24). What the Freudians would call psychological displacement operates here in parallel with linguistic forms of displacement, the re-creation of a paternal image through the language of absence and self-conscious analogy. This is why the geographical displacement we see in a poem like "Wuthering Heights," where the narrator gazes with an exile's eye at the unfamiliar Yorkshire moors, is commensurate with the transnational clashes, the jarring incompatibilities between different intellectual traditions, that run throughout *Ariel.* It is also why the assumption that Hughes himself was Plath's destructive "daddy" is so conceptually reductive.

This caricature of transcendental correspondence also offers scope for a kind of surreal playfulness in Plath's representation of common phenomena. In the absence of any proportionate harmony or natural bond between signifier and signified, the objects in her poetic world become crazed, anthropomorphized artifacts:

> The tulips are too red in the first place, they hurt me.
> Even through the gift paper I could hear them breathe
> Lightly, through their white swaddlings, like an awful baby. (161)

Pointing out that her early journals contain a shot-by-shot description of Buñuel's *Un Chien Andalou,* Rose has suggested that a link with surrealist art is "one of the things that is consistently overlooked in the reading of

Plath."[92] In fact, her associations with surrealism have not been entirely neglected: George Steiner in 1967 described "Lady Lazarus" as "a kind of Hieronymous Bosch nursery rhyme" and remarked on the "almost surrealistic wildness of the gesture," and Arthur Oberg in 1978 wrote of "A Birthday Present" as "a surrealistic, sexual-mystical fantasy."[93] Moreover, several critics have commented on her early poems, "Conversation among the Ruins" (1956), "The Disquieting Muses" (1957), and "On the Decline of Oracles" (1957), all of which were directly inspired by Giorgio de Chirico paintings.

It would also be true to say, though, that a more amorphous cultural surrealism, of the kind that permeates Henry James's late writings, runs through much of Plath's work. As with James, this cultural surrealism emanates to a large extent from the fracturing of conventional perspectives, from a skepticism about representational forms predicated on the familiar tropes of allegorical correspondence. Just as James in *The American Scene* plays with the disjunction between America as type and fact, so Plath in "Watercolor of Grantchester Meadows" (1959) envisages England as a doubled-up world, a country reflected "upside down" in the water, whose pictorial inversion mirrors the way it becomes transposed into a "benign / Arcadian green" image of itself (112). That adjective "benign," particularly in its suspended position at the end of a line, hints at something far from benign; partly through the word's medical associations with tumors, "benign" seems to contain in this tantalizing position of enjambment a dialectic between positive and negative, just as these Arcadian meadows are threatened at the end of the poem by cries of rats. As with the trick perspectives used by surrealist artists, we find a kind of double exposure here that links the picturesque with the grotesque.

"Double Exposure" was, in fact, the title of a novel Plath was working on in 1962, and she was, like the surrealists, always interested artistically in the idea of doubles. The title of her honors thesis at Smith College was "The Double in Two of Dostoevsky's Novels," and she wrote to her mother in 1954, when she was working on the thesis, that she was reading "fascinating stuff" by Poe, Hoffman, Freud, and others "about the ego as symbolized in reflections (mirror and water), shadows, twins—dividing off and becoming an enemy."[94] Freud, of course, was appropriated by many of the twentieth-century surrealists, who saw him as writing not just about split personalities in a medical sense but also, more broadly, about split cultures, the fissures and fragmentations that haunt conventional pictures of reality. In Plath's world, such fissures are associated also with transnational displacement. One objective correlative in her poetry for this scene of division is the Atlantic Ocean: the 1960 poem "On Deck" is set at "Midnight in the mid-Atlantic" (142), and there is a significant sense in which all of Plath's late work involves a form of "double exposure," a superimposition of images from either side of the Atlantic divide. The split nature of the poet's cultural allegiance manifests itself in the anamorphic, doubled-up style of her verse, and this suggests again how the intellectual genealogy for transnationalism can be located in surrealism, rather than in the modernist search for cultural purity that underwrote the formation of national identity as a discrete and autonomous phenomenon. In "Black Coat," one of the *Birthday Letters* poems, Hughes specifically describes Plath's tendency toward double focus as a categorical "error," as he equates her "diplopic" projections with a form of personal insincerity or conceptual blurring:

> No idea
> How that double image,
> Your eye's inbuilt double exposure
> Which was the projection
> Of your two-way heart's diplopic error,
> The body of the ghost and me the blurred see-through
> Came into single focus. . . . [95]

Whereas Hughes himself understood the authenticity of objects in terms of their own singular characteristics, Plath, by contrast, was attracted more toward an aesthetics of displacement and transference.

To label Plath a confessional poet, then, is to risk reading her poetry as merely about private breakdown, whereas in fact, she not only constructed an artful rhetorical voice but also embodied within her verse conflicts between different intellectual and poetic traditions. Hughes subsequently wrote of how Plath in the late 1950s was "concentratedly trying to break down the tyranny, the fixed focus and public persona which descriptive or discursive poems take as a norm"; but if she abandoned one "public persona" she quickly assumed another, for the keen contributor to American magazines such as *Mademoiselle* and the *New Yorker* soon came to attach a similar value to her poetry readings on BBC radio.[96] In her last letter to her mother, in February 1963, Plath in fact cited the BBC as a reason she could not return to her homeland: "There is nothing like the BBC in America. . . . I have a chance for three weeks in May to be on the BBC Critics program at about $150 a week, a fantastic break I hope I can make good on."[97] One common assumption about Plath's relationship with both print and broadcast media is that her American market was intellectually trivial and superficial, whereas the BBC at this time was a center of deep moral and artistic seriousness. This is, to say the least, a misleading antithesis: in fact, both the American and the British media offered scope for innovation within certain fairly rigid codes of genteel convention, and Plath's adeptness at dramatizing her own work on the radio effectively emphasizes the self-consciously theatrical aspects of poems like "Lady Lazarus," where the narrator imagines herself acting out a "big strip tease" for the "peanut-crunching crowd" (245). Hughes himself, in a note accompanying the posthumous publication of some of her last works, commented on how her style had shifted from poems "composed slowly, with great deliberation and research," to a less formulaic idiom, and he suggested that this "change . . . can be heard in the inspired and inspiring way she read her later pieces, particularly during the last six months of her life."[98] This led him subsequently to praise her mature poems as "direct, and even plain, speech," as though the radio performances had brought out a quality of oral immediacy inherent in them.[99] The problem with such an interpretation, of course, is that it altogether occludes the performative dimension by straightforwardly equating Plath's voice on the BBC with the voice of her soul. This is not to denigrate the power of these poems, merely to suggest that questions of authenticity or inner revelation are not the right ones to be asking in this context. Much of Plath's later work is about the public performance of despair; it does not necessarily represent its literal embodiment.

Again, one complicating factor here is the subsequent critical battles over Plath's reputation. Alvarez, keen to requisition her as evidence for his own theories on suicide, has been influential in the way *Ariel* has tended to be read as a last, desperate cry from the bunker, rather than, say, an indirect response to political events such as the Cuban Missile Crisis. This crisis, with its serious threat of imminent nuclear war, took place during the last two weeks of October 1962, with its most intense public phase (when Kennedy was issuing ultimatums to Khrushchev) between 22 and 27 October. It was precisely at this time that many of the most famous *Ariel* poems were written, in a frenetic burst of creative activity: "Fever 103°" on 20 October; "By Candlelight" on 24 October; "Ariel" and "Poppies in October" on 27 October; "Nick and the Candlestick" on 29 October, and so on. In her essay "Context," published in *London Magazine* that same year, Plath noted that "the incalculable genetic effects of fallout" was one of the "issues of our time which preoccupy me at the moment," along with "the terrifying, mad, omnipotent marriage of big business and the military in America." She went on to suggest that her poetry was affected by such issues "in a sidelong fashion": "My poems do not turn out to be about Hiroshima," she said, "but about a child forming itself finger by finger in the dark."[100]

Similarly, the *Ariel* poems are not "about" the Cuban Missile Crisis in any positivistic or verifiable sense, but they do approach this subject in, as Plath aptly phrased it, a "sidelong" fashion. In the aftermath of the cold war, it is easy to forget how all-consuming the fear of nuclear catastrophe was for many people at this time, and *Ariel* speaks cogently to this condition of terror and paralysis. The images of "winter" and "night" in "By Candlelight" raise obliquely the specter of a nuclear winter (236), and an ominous air of impending doom hovers over "Nick and the Candlestick":

> Let the mercuric
> Atoms that cripple drip
> Into the terrible well. . . . (242)

Introducing this poem in a BBC reading, Plath remarked that the mother here finds in her baby "a beauty which, while it may not ward off the world's ill, does redeem her share of it" (294). This correlates with a point made by the cultural historian of cold war America, Elaine Tyler May, about how family stability was presented in this era as an antidote to atomic anxieties, as though the womb of domesticity might somehow fortify innocent American families against the invading bomb.[101] Plath always retained the attributes of a cold war American citizen in spite of herself, and "Fever 103°" juxtaposes its nightmare of imminent catastrophe with a series of homely images implying how the world of the nuclear family may find itself smothered by nuclear war. The poem superimposes an image of the scarf that choked Isadora Duncan on its vision of a fatal atomic scarf encircling the globe, a garment that, rather than bringing warmth, is "Choking the aged and the meek" (231).

Many of these *Ariel* pieces were first published in *Encounter* in October 1963, eight months after Plath's death. We can see *Encounter* here performing its customary task of promoting American values abroad, for the rhetoric of extremity and intensity that characterizes these poems appeared, particularly to English readers, as a form of New World directness, a desire to tear the veil of hypocrisy from the brutal modern world. In his influential introduction to *The New Poetry* (1962), Alvarez described "gentility" as "the disease so often found in English culture"; and, though Plath herself was not included in the first edition of this anthology, a growing sense of impatience with insular, Betjemanesque pleasantries strongly influenced the early reception of her work in Britain.[102] Just as the criminal violence of certain films noirs in the 1950s was seen as testifying in a roundabout way to the ideals of American freedom, so the psychological violence of Plath's last poems was seen as the guarantee of an American commitment to authentic anguish rather than polite social mannerism. In an entirely unconscious way, therefore, Plath, like Gunn, became complicit with the particular version of American culture that *Encounter* was promoting: a principled investment in openness and existential freedom, a secession from the bureaucracies of autocratic or paternalistic state control, even at the expense of alienation or death. This is the same valorization of dissent that we see in an earlier, classic cold war text, *The Catcher in the Rye* (1951), whose compulsive form of rebellion was, as Leerom Medovoi has shown, paradoxically intertwined with the very forces of commodification and mass culture it critiqued.[103] In Salinger's text, convention and dissension chase each other's tail in a circular, mutually defining fashion, just as in Plath's poems the acting out of despair becomes a psychological "strip tease" on public radio.

The transnational Plath, then, is a different figure from the one represented by Hughes, not without a certain Anglocentric bias, as retreating from the conformity of Eisenhower's America into the more profound world of her English poems. Hughes was impatient with what he called Plath's "bundles of contradictory and complementary selves," but it is in fact the double exposures of Plath's transnational poetics that make up their refractory, unsettling quality.[104] Several of her poems, from "Channel Crossing" (1956) to "Crossing the Water" (1962), focus on the actual act of traversal, and her work as a whole describes not so much the journey to a particular destination as an unstable oscillation between different points on the compass. Gunn, similarly, takes delight not in a poetry of place but a poetry of passage. As we have seen, the title of his

1982 collection, *The Passages of Joy*, is taken from a poem by Samuel Johnson, "The Vanity of Human Wishes": "Time hovers o'er, impatient to destroy, / And shuts up all the Passages of Joy."[105] Gunn, however, enacts a characteristic revision of the English literary canon as he re-works Johnson's moralistic phrase to suggest not only the joyful passages, or orifices, of the human body, but also both an aesthetic and an ethical appreciation of the idea of passage, metamorphosis, transition. For Johnson, the flow of time tended destructively to annihilate joy, but for Gunn, the flow of time and space contributes positively to it.

There are, of course, numerous ways Gunn and Plath should be seen as very different kinds of poet, both thematically and stylistically. They both, however, experienced an estranged relationship with their native land, an estrangement that came to contribute crucially to the tenor and subtlety of their verse. In a journal entry for 1958, Plath commented that she thought she had "written lines which qualify me to be The Poetess of America (as Ted will be The Poet of England and her dominions)."[106] Hughes, of course, went on to live out this laureate fantasy, cherishing the notion of how his work might come to embody a common psychic investment in cultural homogeneity. The excellence of Gunn and Plath, though, consists precisely in the way their poetry finally eludes such identifications, evoking the lineaments of national identity only to re-flect and reverse them into virtual figures, ghostly specters, perceived as through a glass darkly.

# 8

## Virtual Englands:
## Pynchon's Transatlantic
## Heresies

Partly because of the widespread popularity of *The Crying of Lot 49* (1966), his most accessible and therefore most frequently studied work, the novels of Thomas Pynchon have commonly been associated with the representation of American culture as a conflict between the repressive, authoritarian center and its libertarian fringes. Pynchon's characters seem to inhabit a world of labyrinthine, postmodern mediascapes, without any recognizable point of origin or significance, where the waste material of the commercial world overwhelms more traditional aspects of narrative and subjectivity. In *Lot 49* and in *Vineland* (1990), both set mainly in California, Pynchon's zany West Coast folk take a perverse pleasure in upending old liberal humanist values as they go about their often absurd tasks, while humming jingles like "Meet the Flintstones" or imbibing as background music the theme from *Hawaii Five-O*.

Much Pynchon criticism seeks to relate his work specifically to this indigenous context. Thomas Hill Schaub writes of *The Crying of Lot 49* as emerging out of the climate of the cold war, with its paranoid heroine, Oedipa Maas, having been "schooled in the era of Eisenhower and Foster Dulles," and with her round of television and Tupperware parties testifying to the "numbing narcissism" of life in suburban Los Angeles.[1] Outlining what he sees as the nationalist orientation of Pynchon's agenda from a more philosophical perspective, Richard Poirier argues that a quest hermeneutically to decipher "the systematic conspiracy of reality" links Pynchon's texts with those of classic nineteenth-century writers such as Emerson, Hawthorne, and Melville, all of whom engaged in the "distinctly American vision" of attempting to unravel an order lurking beneath the visible world.[2] Many critics have similarly remarked on the preapocalyptic significance of the number 49 in *The Crying of Lot 49*, writing of how the novel always seems to hover ambivalently on the verge of a final revelation linked to the idea of Pentecost, Greek for "fifty."[3] Others have associated the systematic conspiracies that pervade *Gravity's Rainbow* (1973) with the Watergate era, pointing to the sardonic portrayal of "Richard M. Zhlub" as a small businessman in California, as well as to the epigraph from Nixon himself that opens the fourth section of the book. All of this, argues Stephen Paul Miller, suggests analogies between "Nixon's mid-seventies sense of all-pervasive conspiracy" and the massively overdetermined structures at work throughout Pynchon's novel.[4] Paul Maltby makes a further link between *Gravity's Rainbow* and Pynchon's America by pointing out that Wernher von Braun, the Nazi scientist depicted in the story, was abducted by the CIA at the end of the Second World War and taken to the United States, where he eventually became a naturalized American citizen and, in the 1960s, a leader of the Apollo space program. "It is," writes Maltby, "through allusions to the postwar career of von Braun and the subsequent evolution of his rocket that Pynchon is able to project the fascism of the Third Reich (its militarism and imperialism) onto America."[5]

Without wishing at all to deny the theoretical viability of such analogies, it is also worth emphasizing how much of Pynchon's work is actually set not in America but in England. *Gravity's Rainbow* takes place mainly in London during the final months of the Second World War, in 1944 and 1945, and the heroes of *Mason & Dixon* (1997) are positioned in eighteenth-century Britain, where a good deal of the novel's action takes place. The representation of England and English culture is, therefore, a recurrent, perhaps even a compulsive concern in Pynchon's fiction. From the Foreign Office mandarins grappling with the end of empire in *V* (1963), to the London bureaucrats administering a war economy in *Gravity's Rainbow*, to the class system that frustrates the ambitious protagonists in *Mason & Dixon*, Pynchon's texts work paradoxically to inscribe their vision of a New World by returning continually to the site of the Old. To be sure, Pynchon's virtual Englands are always constructed in a self-consciously fictional fashion: in the 1984 introduction to *Slow Learner*, his collection of early short stories, the author refers to his "old Baedeker trick" of writing about places he has never been, and many of his literary encounters with Englishness seem to involve an elaborate fakery, as his characters assume the costumes and manners of another time and place.[6] One small though not untypical example is the pop group in *The Crying of Lot 49*, The Paranoids, who in these days of Beatlemania have been told by their manager not only to sing with an English accent but to "watch English movies" on television so as to perfect their art of mimicry.[7] As we shall see, however, especially with *Mason & Dixon*, Pynchon develops this "Baedeker trick" in a much more elaborate and extended way in his later writing. By conceptualizing English national identity as an artifice in this way, Pynchon comes implicitly to frame his American "Vineland" in a reversed or virtual projection, defined not so much for what it is as for what it should not be. In his most important work, Pynchon appropriates England so as to define America negatively, as an open space or blank, a land of tantalizingly infinite potential.

At the same time, Pynchon also invokes the circuits of transatlantic exchange to problematize the old teleologies of American exceptionalism. He balances the sanctified iconography of God's chosen land against various global crosscurrents that threaten to ironize, if not engulf, the separatist conditions of his native country's supposed manifest destiny. Various British critics, most notably Deborah L. Madsen, have discussed Pynchon's writing under the rubric of colonialism, arguing that the author in fact "uses the mythology of exceptionalism to offer a critique of . . . America's imperialistic ambitions." For Madsen, the surveyors' effort in *Mason & Dixon* to map a boundary between Pennsylvania and Maryland indicates an attempt to make "the New World conform to the Old," thereby imposing "upon the American wilderness a European worldview, a European metaphysic, that is deadly."[8] Although it is true that this novel contemplates the implications of institutionalizing the North-South divide that shored up the institution of slavery, such a pointed notion of the "European metaphysic" turning out to be "deadly" implies as its correlative a state of exceptionalist innocence or purity that is, I argue, antipathetic to the author's universalist idiom. It is never the case in Pynchon's world that we find straightforward binary oppositions, of the kind that would pit light against dark, colonized against colonizer, America against Europe. This is why nakedly political readings of these novels often seem so flat and reductive; as Leo Bersani has noted, the popular notion of Pynchon as a "hero of the counter-culture," a devotee of "love, anarchy, and randomness," relies on a one-dimensional interpretation whereby the Machiavellian government plots hypothesized in these narratives can all finally be said to be "true." Similarly, Madsen's postcolonial reading of Pynchon in terms of a dialectic between oppression and liberation is predicated on the kind of rigid polarity between "We and They" from which the multivalent, encyclopedic categories of his fiction are always veering away.[9]

This encyclopedic quality highlights one of the crucial paradoxes running through Pynchon's work, which is that he writes about the projection of national identities from an internationalist, universalist perspective. Tony Tanner acutely observed of *V* that it seems in some ways to be "an 'Augustinian' novel about 'Manichaean' people," and these kinds of theological subtexts permeate all of Pynchon's writing.[10] In the Manichaean heresy, which strongly influenced the dualistic impetus of American Puritanism, evil is understood as an autonomous force, equipotential with good; but in the more emollient view of Augustine of Hippo, evil should be seen as a mere privation, the absence of good, not its antithesis. For Augustine, good and evil made up a universal whole; for Manichaeus, on the other hand, they were polar opposites. Although biographical facts about Pynchon's life are notoriously sketchy, we know that he was brought up as a Catholic, with a Catholic mother and Protestant father, and that when he was at Cornell he "went to Mass and confessed, though to what," recalled one of his friends from that time, "would be a mystery."[11] I am not, of course, trying to make Pynchon out to be a closet Jesuit or a true believer; I am suggesting, more broadly, that a cultural legacy of Catholic universalism haunts his writings and tends to deflect them away from both Puritan reifications of evil and exceptionalist idealizations of American national identity. Pynchon represents the United States not as a country that could ever separate itself from the rest of the world, but as only one parish within a larger global network.

In *V*, the reduction of national stereotypes to a kind of performative charade is ironically underlined and heightened by the deliberately international sweep of the novel, which situates national types in comparative relation to each other. Victoria Wren, British by nationality, an ex-convent schoolgirl who now practices "her private, outré brand of Roman Catholicism," is described as having been "recently self-proclaimed a citizen of the world," and Pynchon's narrative valorizes her global perspective through its focus on international relations, espionage, and tourism.[12]

Indeed, tourism is categorized here as a kitschy, lowbrow form of universalism: it is, we are told in Chapter 14, "supranational, like the Catholic Church, and perhaps the most absolute communion we know on earth: for be its members American, German, Italian, whatever, the Tour Eiffel, Pyramids, and Campanile all evoke identical responses from them; their Bible is clearly written and does not admit of private interpretation" (409). Writing of *Gravity's Rainbow*, Edward Mendelson similarly observed that it reflects not just the locale of North America but "a new international culture, created by the technologies of instant communication and the economy of world markets," where information is "the only medium of exchange."[13] *Gravity's Rainbow* furnishes a specific historical context for this dissolution of national identity, relating it to circumstances at the end of the Second World War, when international defense pacts and trade agreements were increasingly superseding any individual nation's illusion of political autonomy: "The Nationalities are on the move. It is a great frontierless streaming out here."[14] Mendelson rightly suggests that this global, encyclopedic impulse positions Pynchon stylistically as the successor to James Joyce, and there is also a resemblance in the way their catholicized forms of universalism render national boundaries permeable and so make national identities appear, as the theologians would say, accidental rather than essential.

This intellectual influence of this cultural Catholicism is at its most self-evident in Pynchon's scattered nonfiction essays, which, because they have not yet been collected in one volume, are rarely read together as a group. He shows a consistent attraction to other writers working out of a similar religious heritage; in the introduction to *Slow Learner*, for instance, he nominates Kerouac's *On the Road* as "one of the great American novels," comparing it to Helen Waddell's *The Wandering Scholars,* an account of rebellious poets in the Middle Ages "who left the monasteries in large numbers and took to the roads of Europe."[15] In a 1992 introduction to the works of Donald Barthelme, he admires Barthelme's specifically "anti-transcendent" humor, his ability "to put us in the presence of something already eerily familiar," his melancholic "combination of grace and disenchantment."[16] Such receptiveness to the idea of an oblique, quotidian "grace" is, of course, shared by Pynchon's own iridescent fiction as well. In a 1993 discussion in the *New York Times* of "Sloth" as one of the "Seven Deadly Sins," Pynchon becomes more overtly theological, citing Aquinas's analysis in *Summa Theologica* of sloth, or "acedia," as a mortal sin involving "defiant sorrow in the face of God's good intentions," a "deliberate turning against faith in anything because of the inconvenience faith presents to the pursuit of quotidian lusts, angers and the rest."[17] And in a 1998 review of Gabriel García Márquez's *Love in the Time of Cholera,* he writes of how Márquez's emphasis on love involves, effectively, an assertion of "the resurrection of the body, today as throughout history an unavoidably revolutionary idea." Thus, writes Pynchon, Márquez's form of "magical realism" produces "works that can even return our worn souls to us"; again, Pynchon here reveals his interest in recovering a form of enchantment, a magic realm that, in however heterodox a manner, works as a counterpoint to the more mundane world of secular affairs.[18]

John A. McClure has written explicitly about "resacralization" in relation to Pynchon; however, I am less concerned with his work's putatively devout qualities than with the ways the philosophical universalism associated with this religious discourse becomes displaced formally into an aesthetic of heterogeneity, an aesthetic that rubs ideologically against established cultural hierarchies.[19] Whereas the essay on Márquez pays tribute to magical realism, Pynchon's rumination on his own artistic methods in the introduction to *Slow Learner* includes a recollection of how, as a young writer, "it was the Surrealists who'd really caught my attention," with their "simple idea that one could combine inside the same frame elements not normally found together to produce illogical and startling effects."[20] This mode of surrealism clearly affected the Latin American magical realists, and I would argue that it also has continued to influence Pynchon throughout his later works, to such an extent that it would make sense to think of him alongside authors with more obvious surrealist allegiances, such as Georges Bataille, rather than simply to place him in the camp of maverick West Coast compatriots like, say, Tom Robbins. Writing of the modern French surrealists, Susan Rubin Suleiman has suggested that in their "refusal of integration and hierarchy and in their pursuit of heterogeneity in all its various forms—from parody to punning to collage," it is possible to see in surrealist texts "an analogue of the pervert's refusal of 'normal' adult sexuality."[21] Pynchon's style is not so conceptually abstract as that of Sollers or Bataille, of course; nevertheless, there is a similar move in his works to explore the idea of heterogeneity and dispersal in order deliberately to undermine the staid manners of a controlled humanist orthodoxy. As Jonathan Dollimore

noted, before Freud commandeered the term for psychoanalytical purposes, the concept of perversion tended to signify theological infraction,
a swerving away from the one source of truth.[22] There is in Pynchon's
texts a specific interest in both forms of perversion: in the idea of heresy
and in heresy's psychological correlative, the sexual fetish. Both of these
categories work as deliberate affronts to liberal norms, and Pynchon's
perverse style might be said to offer an Americanized, democratized
version of Bataille's surrealist idiom in the way it exploits techniques of
disjunction to expose the blinkers of smug social hierarchies and assumptions. Like Bataille, Pynchon is less interested in the social place-
ment of his characters than in exposing them to what Aquinas would
have called the luminous vistas of a universal radiance.

For Pynchon, then, cultural surrealism performs a double function.
On one level, it works as an iconoclastic force, disrupting claims to authority and hierarchical classification. In his 1984 essay "Is It O.K. to Be a
Luddite?" Pynchon inveighed against "a permanent power establishment of admirals, generals and corporate CEO's, up against whom us
average poor bastards are completely outclassed." He added that although "we are all supposed to keep tranquil and allow it to go on," the
convergence of technologies in the forthcoming "data revolution" would
make it "every day less possible to fool any of the people any of the
time."[23] Through their strange and often fabulous juxtapositions, Pynchon's novels react against the negative force of what in *Vineland* is called
"misoneism," a supposedly "deep organic human principle" named by
criminologist Cesare Lombroso after the Greek for "hatred of anything
new."[24] Lombroso, according to Pynchon's novel, proffered in the nineteenth century a "scientific" explanation for criminal behavior, explain-
ing that "the brains of criminals were short on lobes that controlled
civilized values like morality and respect for the law, tending indeed to
resemble animal more than human brains" (272).[25] In this novel, federal
agent Brock Vond is said to be a "devotee" of Lombroso (272), but the
iconoclastic humor of Pynchon's surrealist style works to demystify any
kind of "deep organic human principle" that tries to pass itself off as
eternal truth.

In *Vineland*, Vond is described, in an echo of the "Luddite" essay
published the same year, as having "caught a fatal glimpse of that level
where everybody knows everybody else, where however political fortunes
below might bloom and die, the same people, the Real Ones, remained

year in and year out, keeping what was desirable flowing their way" (276). As a character, however, Vond himself is humanly fallible and not altogether unlikable; with his "naked itch to be a gentleman" (276), he shares the common enough experience of frustrated ambition, and his involvement as a law enforcer with the exponents of "hippie" culture suggests the extent to which these two sides were mixed up with each other, indeed helped to define each other, during the rebellious summers of love in the late 1960s. The romantic involvement here between Vond and Frenesi, daughter of the ex-hippie Sasha, emphasizes the quirky symbiosis in this novel between conservatives and radicals, as does Sasha's lament that, for all its "political incorrectness," she seems to have passed down her own "uniform fetish," "a helpless turn toward images of authority," to her besotted child (83). In fact, the true villains in *Vineland* are not figures like Vond but those called emphatically in capitals by the author "the Real Ones," people who remain, significantly, out of sight. In this regard, there is a telling analogy here with the English monarchy: the Wayvone family are said to own nothing and to receive merely "an annual operating budget from the corporation that owned them," like, as one of them puts it, "the royal family in England" (93). For Pynchon, the invisible elements controlling affairs in corporate America have become, like the royal family, a force whose authority is all the more difficult to challenge because it remains intangible and amorphous. Just as Melville in *Pierre* brings grasping American landowners and the British aristocracy into parallel, so Pynchon here aligns American corporatism with the British monarchy to elucidate the inscrutable will to power of each.

The second way Pynchon exploits cultural surrealism is to reinscribe a vision of America as translucent, exposed to light, not ultimately confined by coercive or repressive influences. In *Vineland*, the television programs, and even some of the commercial outlets—the "Breez-Thru gas station," for instance (4)—take on a kind of magical realist quality, both comic and iconic at once. The book pays tribute to a mythological idea of "Vineland the Good" (322), harking back to the land discovered by the Vikings long before Columbus; it evokes lyrically the "spruces tall and massive" in the redwood forests (377), the "watershed" of the "sacred and magical" California coastline, the "river of ghosts" held to be "exceptional" by the Yurok Indians (186). This knowing reinscription of American exceptionalism emerges antithetically out of what is described in

*Vineland* as a "transpacific" perspective (56): the novel is set in 1984, with President Reagan on the verge of reelection, and in this era of unfettered multinational capitalism America's economic fortunes have become linked inextricably to the fluctuations of the Tokyo Stock Exchange. The transpacific businessman, Takeshi Fumimota, shuttles between Japan and California "for reasons of business connected with the mysterious obliteration of a research complex belonging to the shadowy world conglomerate Chipco" (142), with this deterritorialized world of corporate finance and "Reaganomic ax blades" (90) set in contrast to the "territories of the spirit" found among the buried cultures of Vineland. Pynchon's affective descriptions of land held sacred by the Yurok Indians and old Spanish Jesuit missions bespeak an attachment to the integrity and distinctiveness of place that seemingly is epitomized by the loving last word of the novel, "home" (385).

There is also in *Vineland* a passage that echoes for the Pacific coast what F. Scott Fitzgerald had done for the Atlantic coast at the end of *The Great Gatsby* (1925), when the houses on Long Island seem to "melt away" from Nick Carraway's sight to reveal "the old island here that flowered once for Dutch sailors' eyes—a fresh, green breast of the new world."[26] Like Fitzgerald, Pynchon represents the American shoreline, its national boundary, through a kind of double exposure where myth and history are fused into one:

> Someday this would be all part of a Eureka—Crescent City—Vineland megalopolis, but for now the primary sea coast, forest, riverbanks and bay were still not much different from what early visitors in Spanish and Russian ships had seen. Along with noting the size and fierceness of the salmon, the fogbound treachery of the coasts, the fishing villages of the Yurok and Tolowa people, log keepers not known for their psychic gifts had remembered to write down, more than once, the sense they had of some invisible boundary, met when approaching from the sea, past the capes of somber evergreen, the stands of redwood with their perfect trunks and cloudy foliage, too high, too red to be literal trees—carrying therefore another intention, which the Indians might have known about but did not share. (317)

*Vineland* faces the Pacific Ocean in the same way *Gatsby* is imagined against the Atlantic, and there are clearly elements of elegy and loss in both works. Nevertheless, it would be wrong to see in either novel simply a negative or moralistic impetus, as if to indicate an etiolated idealism finding itself swamped by the corrupting forces of commerce. Instead, both narratives evoke a more indirect conjunction of myth and material- ism, so that everyday life on the West Coast becomes magically—tran- substantiatively, as it were—illuminated in a resplendent light. Again, Pynchon's emphasis is on conjunction, not disjunction. Just as the title of *Gravity's Rainbow* joins together the earth and the sky, so at the end of *Vineland* the heretical nun, Sister Rochelle—a member of an order "never recognized by Rome . . . but persisting with grace and stamina there in California for hundreds of years" (107)—envisages Hell not as a place of separation or eternal damnation, but as a region seek- ing "reunion, with the true, long-forgotten metropolis of Earth Unre- deemed" (383).

One of the prerogatives of Pynchon's heterodox style, then, is to bring into juxtaposition categories conventionally kept apart. A recurring fig- ure in *Vineland* is that of the wave, associated on the most literal level with the College of the Surf in Trasero County, "where the waves were so high you could lie on the beach and watch the sun through them" (204), but also suggesting ways the citizens of the republic become passive "riders" on their country's "technowave, belonging to distant others as surf belonged to the sea" (37). Such objectifications should not be seen simply as a satire on corporate manipulation, because they are also an evocation of "collective being," in Leo Bersani's phrase, implying the shift from an epistemological quest for knowledge to ontological acquies- cence in a corporate state that lies at the heart of Pynchon's fundamen- tally communal project.[27] In *Vineland,* Darryl Louise has been told that eventually "she would discover that all souls, human and otherwise, were different disguises of the same greater being—God at play" (121), and at the climax of the book Jess Traverse performs his annual ritualistic read- ing of a passage from Ralph Waldo Emerson, an extract he had found "quoted in a jailhouse copy of *The Varieties of Religious Experience,* by William James. Frail as the fog of Vineland, in his carrying, pure voice, Jess reminded them, 'Secret retributions are always restoring the level, when disturbed, of the divine justice. It is impossible to tilt the beam. All the tyrants and proprietors and monopolists of the world in vain set their shoulders to heave the bar. Settles forever more the ponderous equator to its line, and man and mote, and start and sun, must range to it, or be pulverized by the recoil'" (369). It is, of course, unusual to cite directly a discursive passage of this length in a work of fiction, but the quotation here is particularly revealing, not only for its castigation of "tyrants and proprietors and monopolists," but also for its faith in a "divine justice" that preserves within nature a finely tuned balance. But it is also important here that Pynchon chooses to refract the words of Emerson and James through the experiences of one of his own reprobate characters, for his concern is not with the promulgation of American transcendentalism or pragmatism in a purely conceptual sense, but rather with the incarnation of these ideas in the lives of his fellow Americans.

It is also appropriate at the end of *Vineland* that Pynchon should choose to cite Emerson, the very exemplar of American cultural self-reliance, for throughout the book there is a subtle but persistent effort formally to mimic the domestic rhythms of everyday speech in the United States. To take just one small example of this method: "Radio weather reports called for a real scorcher, even down in Vineland after the fog burned off" (323). The idiom of this phrase—"called for," "real scorcher"—imitates the idiosyncratic language of the local radio weather report without quoting it directly, as if the narrator had impersonally entered into and was rhetorically embodying the terms of his creation. It is reminiscent of the technique of Joyce in *Dubliners*, where the author indirectly enables his characters to speak for themselves without seeking to diminish them into mere satirical targets. Pynchon's writing, in other words, does not seek so much to advocate the virtues of cultural nationalism as to embody them. Just as Joyce's fiction frames the texture of Irish life within a universalist structure, so Pynchon's novels seek to incorporate the contingencies of America within a larger ontological circumference. The Emersonian impulse here consequently emerges not as an abstract philosophical doctrine but as a nationally specific idiom.

This paradoxical conjunction of nationalism and universalism has left a number of commentators apparently unsure about where Pynchon should be positioned within the tradition of American literature. David Cowart, in an essay on *Mason & Dixon*, seeks to align Pynchon's rejection of the rationalist "pretensions of the Enlightenment" with Thoreau's apocalyptic romanticism, suggesting that a desire to conflate and transcend spatial and temporal dimensions is, as he tentatively puts it, "peculiarly American, perhaps." Later, Cowart describes the quest into uncharted territory in this novel as the incarnation of "an 'American' dream," the quotation marks around "American" indicating the extent to which Cowart himself appears uncomfortable with the categories he is proposing.[28] Tony Tanner, in classifying *Mason & Dixon* as "Pynchon's American Road-novel," also resorts to awkward quotation marks when he hypothesizes: "Perhaps all American literature is a 'story of the West' in one way or another—certainly *Mason & Dixon* is."[29] The discomfort of these critics arises from attempts to impose traditional, canonical categories on a text that cannot so easily be explained in terms of American national narratives. What we find, rather, in *Mason & Dixon*, and in Pynchon's novels generally, is the replication of national identity as a simulacrum, a phenomenon reproduced, precisely, in quotation marks. Just as the characters in these novels are denied interiority or a point of origin, as Bersani noted, so the image of America itself is also hollowed out into a ghostly memory or subjunctive chimera, a simulated reduplication of an absent object.[30] Apart from the anomalous *Crying of Lot 49*, most of Pynchon's works are historical works of fiction set in carefully reconstituted past times: *Mason & Dixon* in the eighteenth century, *Gravity's Rainbow* during the Second World War, *V* in the 1950s, *Vineland* in the Reagan era. It is as if Pynchon's narrator is always looking back, always seeking to memorialize particular aspects of American culture as part of the conceptual topography of the nation. Thus, *Mason & Dixon* is not just a "story of the West," but an exploration of how the westering movement itself contributed to the mythological momentum and theoretical understanding of an American national destiny. But the heroes in this fictional narrative travel south and east as well as west, and their conception of America is entangled inextricably with their experiences of Africa and Britain.

This is not, however, simply to emphasize the self-reflexive dimensions of Pynchon's work, which are obvious enough. It is also to suggest how his novels choreograph what Benedict Anderson called the "grammar of nationalism" within a global framework, where national identity has evolved into something distinct from the legal boundaries of the nation-state.[31] For Anderson, national identity itself has increasingly become an imaginative rather than a social or administrative phenomenon, a fiction preserved in a "long-distance" way, either through the geographical distance of exile or the historical distance of retrospective memory. In *The Spectre of Comparisons*, Anderson writes of nationalism at the end of the twentieth century in terms of back formations, reactions against the contemporary condition of global displacement, although he also traces this paradoxical form of nationalism in the seventeenth-century writings of Mary Rowlandson, who, imprisoned by Indian warriors in Massachusetts, described the country about her as an "English Path" with "English Fields" and "English Cattle." For Rowlandson, in her state of captivity, national identity emerges most sharply through contrast and comparison; it is precisely when she feels most distant from England that she imaginatively reconstitutes its landscapes and values most sharply. In general, New Englanders at this time counted themselves as "English" even if they had never seen the mother country, but what we find in this 1682 *Narrative* is an example of the projection of national identity in response to extreme or disorienting circumstances. For Rowlandson, as for Pynchon, nationalist images thus became what Anderson calls "replicas without originals," specters that maintain a residual and affective hold on the imagination despite—perhaps even because of—the emptying out of their positive experiential content.[32] We know that Pynchon's own ancestors left the county of Essex in England to sail with John Winthrop's party to America in 1630, and all of his writing in some way recapitulates his family's first transatlantic voyage. It gazes on the New World from a comparative perspective, playing off the formation of American national identity against its parallax appearances in transoceanic cultural mirrors.

The international vantage points of Pynchon's work tend not so much toward any abstract form of idealism, then, but rather toward a paradoxical scenario where any given object or idea finds itself played off against its contrary. Pynchon's fiction is specifically transnational rather than postnational, for it seeks not to transcend national identity but to resituate it as a residual category liable to be turned on its head. In *V,* Schoenmaker puts forward the thesis that "correction—along all dimensions: social, political, emotional—entails retreat to a diametric opposite rather than any reasonable search for a golden mean" (103), and *V* formally supports this theoretical process through its continual series of reversals and inversions. David Seed's suggestion that the book's title evokes a symbol for alternatives is therefore a good one, for the idea of contradiction and cross-purposes is endemic in the trajectory of this narrative, particularly in the way it internalizes the structure of fetishism that impels Pynchon's heretical sensibility.[33] In fetish theory, the positions of animate and inanimate objects are reversed, so that, as we see in this novel, the characters' perusal of the tourist guidebook fabricated by Karl Baedeker, with its "inanimate monuments and buildings" (408), supersedes any desire they might actually have to encounter the foreign land itself.[34] Pynchon's narrative associates such "fetish-constructions" with a "Kingdom of Death" (411), representing them as symptomatic of a creeping dehumanization that Tanner and others have seen pervading the landscape of this novel.[35] Yet it is not convincing to equate this structure of fetishism in *V* simply with commodity fetishism or package tourism, nor to explain it away simply in terms of the consumer boom of the Kennedy years, because, in both a comic and a sinister way, it takes this depthlessness to be emblematic of the social and political world more broadly.[36] In this sense, the diminution of the book's title to a mere initial is revealing, for the iconoclastic dimension of *V* involves reducing nearly all national characteristics and identity politics to the status of a fragment or fetish. Thus, the book talks of "the English fetish of respectability" (65) and "fetish about playing cricket" (181), as well as their "taking-on of traditional attitudes which (one suspects) must be latent in all English germ plasm: another loony chromosome along with afternoon tea and respect for the Crown" (438).

The effect of all this is to flatten out national identity into a two-dimensional, depthless construction. Pynchon's idiom of paradoxical reversal subverts cherished icons and conventional modes of behavior by divesting them of any established aura and juxtaposing them instead with what is incongruous, ludicrous or trivial. Carruthers-Pillow of the Foreign Office, for example, is said to feel "in the presence of the most inconsequential chit initialed by the Foreign Secretary much as Moses must have toward the Decalogue God blasted out for him on stone" (458): a bizarre mixing of different levels which, again, burlesques English pomposity by unraveling its preconceptions in terms of psychological compulsion or social conditioning. Hence the fetishistic inversions throughout *V*—the compression of Victoria Wren into her own initial letter, for instance—do not simply betoken cultural entropy, but a radical failure of humanist representation in more general terms. Put another way, one underlying strategy of *V* is to shift the novel of character into the novel of systems, where identity of any kind can be presented only as a kind of hollowed-out, fetishistic ritual: as a craving for respectability, or for playing cricket, or for mimicking English accents (like The Para-

noids) and so on. It is entirely appropriate, therefore, that the author of
*Slow Learner* should have foregrounded his "old Baedeker trick" of describing these cultures from an aesthetic, historical, and geographical
distance, because we are never allowed to experience them as anything
other than fictional entities.[37] Pynchon's own simulacrum of Englishness accordingly mirrors the masquerade of Englishness acted out by
colonial types like Carruthers-Pillow, for whom issues of empire appear
primarily matters of style and aesthetic demeanor.

This characterization of national identity as a form of fetishistic fixation also informs the culture of surveillance and control that pervades
*Gravity's Rainbow*. It has become quite commonplace in criticism of this
novel to associate, as Melvyn New does, imperial colonialism with sadistic sexuality, and so to understand the action of the Second World War
itself as a kind of psychopathological perversion.[38] This is the line also
followed by Paul Fussell in *The Great War and Modern Memory*, when he
talks about the "full appropriate obscenity" with which Pynchon portrays
Brigadier Pudding's coprophiliac interests.[39] On a more mundane level,
though, the book's focus on the austere conditions of Britain in 1944
testifies to that critique of dehumanization that Elaine B. Safer and other
critics have found in Pynchon's view of Western society.[40] One might
suggest, in fact, that this scenario of rationing, propaganda, and disinfor-
mation in wartime Britain gives more historical specificity to the idea of
state surveillance outlined in the labyrinthine networks of *The Crying of
Lot 49*. What in the latter novel appears an elaborate metaphorical con-
ceit, perhaps simply the product of fantasy, manifests itself in *Gravity's
Rainbow* as a more literal condition of daily routine, as the London citizens find every aspect of their activities circumscribed by the imposed
imperatives of an alleged national design. Whereas *V* explores the British imperial character overseas, *Gravity's Rainbow* shows this impulse
trained back on the home country, so that we see "The Firm" exercising
its remote control over the inner and outer lives of its clientele. In *Gravity's Rainbow*, the amorphous London smoke itself seems to become "an
imperial presence that lives and moves" (26). Meanwhile, Jessica Swan-
lake resentfully thinks of how the priggish Jeremy, nicknamed Beaver, "*is
the War, he is every assertion the fucking War has ever made—that we are
meant for work and government, for austerity*"; she is equally scornful
about what she calls "the rationalized power-ritual that will be the coming peace" (177). Britain in the 1940s, in other words, is presented as an

objective correlative for the kind of authoritarian, bureaucratic oppression from which Pynchon's more sympathetic characters are always seeking to escape. Operations in England seem to be conducted by The Firm, which Fussell tells us was a euphemism for the British Special Operations Executive based at Baker Street during the Second World War; but, especially given the sardonic comments about the monarchy in *Vineland*, it seems an appropriate irony that the term is now used as a colloquialism for their organization by members of the British royal family.[41]

This aspect of *Gravity's Rainbow* has received a fair amount of critical attention, of course: the propaganda designed to keep the population in the dark about the v-2 rocket, the role of Pointsman and the White Visitation, the toilet paper stenciled "PROPERTY OF HM GOVERNMENT" (92), the BBC announcer "whose melted-toffee voice has been finding its way for years out . . . of the wireless speakers and into English dreams" (74). Equally repressively, Pirate's sexuality, like that of other characters in this book, has been conditioned through the fetishistic paraphernalia of British culture, which then succeeds in closing its circle of containment by conditioning him also to feel "shame" about it (72). In a diary entry for December 1939, Christopher Isherwood comments on a visit to Los Angeles by Aldous Huxley's brother, Julian, whom Isherwood in his grateful exile describes as "very much the official representative of England at war. Behind his sternness, I thought I could detect a certain puritanical sadism—a satisfaction that the lax peace-days were over, and that we'd all got to suffer."[42] This is the kind of role assumed by Pointsman in *Gravity's Rainbow*: war, we are told, is the "State he'd come to feel a citizen of" (75), and he takes a surreptitious delight in promoting the idea of "Crisis" to reinforce his own hold over the population. It is appropriate that "crisis" can be understood in a sexual as well as political sense, because Pointsman deliberately conflates the two in his quest to consolidate national power (270).

As in *V*, the compulsive behavior of characters like Pointsman suggests not merely their own personal idiosyncrasies, but also the pathological or fetishistic components of the national imaginary in more general terms. As Slavoj Žižek observes, the conventional explanation of fetishism depends on a clear distinction between the object in itself on the one hand and a subjective fixation on some specific aspect of that object on the other. Such commonsense orthodoxies, however, are noticeably absent from Pynchon's world. When a deviant fragment exceeds the pattern or shadow of the conceptual whole in *Gravity's Rainbow*, what we find is a more grotesque scenario where the specter of objective historicism is denied and history itself appears to be compounded of fragments and loose ends. Hence the fetish, argues Žižek, signifies a self-conscious incongruity and violence in the very act of critical interpretation, a recognition of "the paradoxical fact that the dimension of universality is always sustained by the fixation on some particular point."[43] Part of Pynchon's skill in *Gravity's Rainbow* is to destabilize English national culture by theatricalizing it, to link the systematic oppressions of the state with the self-gratifying, libidinal impulses of Pointsman, Brigadier Pudding, and the others, thus transposing the affairs of the nation-state into a fantastic charade. Michael Taussig has written of how the nation-state, like the fetish, "has a deep investment" not only in death, but also in "the death of the consciousness of the signifying function"; yet it is one of Pynchon's triumphs, as Taussig claims it was a triumph of Jean Genet, "to have brought the fetish character of the modern state into a clear and sensual focus."[44] Pynchon, like Genet, reinscribes power as performance, recasts authority as a self-gratifying phenomenon.

One way Pynchon achieves this virtualization of British culture in *Gravity's Rainbow* is by reconfiguring it within a rhetoric of reversal and contingency. Like the character of Ensign Morituri, an officer in the Japanese Navy whose knowledge of Great Britain derives exclusively from propaganda newsreels, Pynchon projects various images of England whose fictional, provisional qualities are never quite suppressed. This, of course, is the old Baedeker trick come round again: we are no more expected to enter into a suspension of disbelief when reading *Gravity's Rainbow* than to imagine *Mason & Dixon* as an authentic eighteenth-century diary. In both cases, the author introduces bizarre or anachronistic references to throw the illusion of mimesis out of kilter, thus foregrounding the metafictional status both of his own texts and of the political scenes they are representing. In this way, *Gravity's Rainbow* textualizes its landscape by intertextual allusions such as "one proper Sherlock Holmes London evening" (14), by its constant references to films (particularly toward the end of the book), and by structural oxymorons such as the framing of the romantic relationship between Jessica and Roger Mexico in the terms of an American comedy: "It was what Hollywood likes to call a 'cute meet,' out in the neat 18th-century heart of downtown Tunbridge Wells" (38).

That anomalous juxtaposition of the genteel English Tunbridge Wells with a brash American "downtown" shows Pynchon's glee in taking established forms or concepts and turning them upside down. On a narrative level, *Gravity's Rainbow* is specifically concerned with the reversal of linear sequences of cause and effect—missiles heard approaching only after they explode, bullets flying out of rather than into bodies, and so on—and these physical properties of equal and opposite reaction can be seen as a discursive correlative to the notion of heresy, which also involves the heterodox process of deviation from established conventions, a reversal of the symbolic order.

The idea of heresy is particularly important in *Gravity's Rainbow*, and again it signifies a deviation from standard practice, a reversal of conventional expectations. In the last few pages of the book, Weissman's Tarot cards turn up the Tower, supposedly "a Gnostic or Cather symbol for the Church of Rome," a symbol that can be "generalized to mean any System which cannot tolerate heresy: a system which, by its nature, must sooner or later fall" (747). This doomed system is also equated explicitly here with the Rocket, itself emblematic of the culture of wartime England. From this angle, *Gravity's Rainbow*, dedicated as it is to the pleasures of heresy, might be seen as Pynchon's twentieth-century rewriting of the heretical discourse produced by his seventeenth-century ancestor, William Pynchon, who in 1650 published *The Meritorious Price of Our Redemption*, a dialogue between a tradesman and a divine. William Pynchon infuriated the authorities in Massachusetts by arguing that the unregenerate in America were also in some sense sanctified because their presence could be seen as a necessary condition of the privileged status enjoyed there by the Puritan elite. Due to the unpopularity of his ideas in America, Pynchon Senior was forced to send his manuscript back to England to be published, but the General Court of Massachusetts acted swiftly to ban any imports of the book, suppressing it on the grounds of being, as they put it, "erronyous and hereticale."[45] Deciding he had outstayed his welcome in the New World, William Pynchon himself decided to quit Massachusetts to return to England shortly afterward. All of this is recounted obliquely in *Gravity's Rainbow* through the story of William Slothrop, Tyrone's fictional ancestor, whose work *On Preterition* is similarly banned by the "Winthrop machine" in Boston (554–55), forcing him to go back to the old country "not in disgrace so much as despondency" (556). The compelling image in *Gravity's Rainbow* of William Slothrop "sailing backward in formation" across the Atlantic with Winthrop's flotilla (204) testifies to the author's conception of a world where all currents operate in reverse motion. For Pynchon, the notion of heresy is inscribed within the function of official doctrine, just as the voyage back becomes symbiotically intertwined with the voyage forth.

The heretical dimension of *Gravity's Rainbow*, like that of *The Meritorious Price of Our Redemption*, thus positions itself specifically around a transatlantic axis, demonstrating clearly why Pynchon's texts need to be understood from a transnational rather than merely a national perspective. The mental and physical traversals of the Atlantic apparent in the works of both Pynchons serve to undermine the singular construction of either community. Winthrop's Boston, like Pointsman's London, is seen as a repository of censorship and oppression, but these narratives of heresy break through such circumscribed boundaries to introduce strains of alternation and opposition into these enclosed spaces. Yet if America appears as the edge of Europe, its reverse image, so Europe itself stands as a counterpart to that "Puritan reflex of seeking other orders behind the visible," as Tyrone Slothrop puts it (188). This is another reason for the English location of *Gravity's Rainbow*, because part of the book's critical heresy involves its rejection of Puritan dualisms and Manichaean contraries. Within the frameworks of orthodox Calvinism, as we have seen, good and evil were polar opposites engaged in an apocalyptic conflict between mutually exclusive categories. Such metaphysical dualism expressed itself through social as well as theological partition, underpinning the sanctified position of Puritan divines as well as their scorn for the less fortunate outcasts of society, and it was these assumptions of special election that William Slothrop and his historical prototype both reacted against. Pointsman, who "can only possess the zero and the one" (55), shares this Calvinist attraction to a rigid, coercive dualism; but Pynchon's text is concerned specifically to yoke opposites together, to fuse categories that might seem mutually antagonistic into some form of paradoxical union. We see this, of course, in the oxymoronic nature of the novel's title, *Gravity's Rainbow*; we infer it also from its last word, "everybody" (760), which presents a secularized version of Catholic universalism, an ontology where different orders of being are brought analogically into relation. The book's guiding image of the rainbow as a multicolored, heterogeneous phenomenon works against the starker outlines of "the Puritan mysteries" (267), whose dominant "ruler," says Slothrop, is the disembodied mode of "Vanitas" or "Emptiness" (268).

For all of Pynchon's famous invisibility as a person, therefore, it might be argued that there is almost too much of an authorial creed lurking behind *Gravity's Rainbow*. The critiques of "the German mania for name-giving, dividing the Creation finer and finer," seem to be impelled by a direct antipathy to the more analytical modes of Protestant philosophy (391), while Säure's argument for Rossini's populism over Beethoven's storming idealism also suggests a typically Catholic hostility toward Romantic forms of imaginative autonomy (440). In the same vein, some explicitly metaphysical terms manifest themselves at the end of the novel, when the narrator talks, for example, about those who "disagree with the terms of the Creation" (729). This Catholic subtext would also help to explain the picturesque evocation of Christmas in the first section of the novel, where images of the Nativity are played off against the darker landscapes of wartime London; it would also illuminate half-ironic images like the sacramental loaves of bread—"They are rising, they are transubstantiated" (368)—that Slothrop encounters when he is in Berlin.

The secular function of such sacramentalism in Pynchon's novels is not to promote any religious orthodoxy, however, but to demystify the political apparatus and covert assumptions of nationalist ideologies. In its review of the novel, for instance, the *Times Literary Supplement* complained that *Gravity's Rainbow* was "very hard to read" because it was such a "democratic novel," a book so "devoid of hierarchy or perspective" that it made "classifying" impossible. Though not imperceptive, this is a typically British reaction exemplifying the challenges posed by the universalist inclinations of Pynchon's work to readers more accustomed to a social and artistic world where everything is kept in its place.[46] When Pointsman is talking to Roger Mexico, who harbors a deep and dark "bitterness" toward England and its "System" (126), he cites Pavlov's belief that "all diseases of the mind could be explained" by what Pavlov called "the ultraparadoxical phase," "the confusion of ideas of the opposite" (90). But whereas Mexico specifically expresses antipathy toward linear sequences of cause and effect (89), it is precisely the fear of such anarchic contradictions that leads Pointsman and his patriotic henchmen to reassert meticulously their love of control. The genius of *Gravity's Rainbow*, though, involves its internalization of these paradoxes and contradictions to empty out the symbolic order, thereby turning the myth of national identity into a mere replica of itself. This reveals, as in a virtual mirror, what Jacqueline Rose has referred to as "the potential insanity" of the national imaginary, the way the "moral life" of "Englishness" itself can be understood as a state of fantasy.[47] The burden of *Gravity's Rainbow* is not so much that English imperialism induces pathological deviance, but that it is, in itself, a form of deviance: a bizarre and fetishistic construction set implicitly against the promise of full embodiment, as witnessed in the ontological plenitude of the "Creation."

Catholicism appears again as a subtext in *Mason & Dixon* (1997), where British traditionalists such as Mr. Swivett complain that, by losing eleven days from their calendar, the nation was being forced to conform to "Catholic Time."[48] Britain, the most antipapal of European countries in this era, was almost the last to fall in with the calendar reform promulgated by Pope Gregory XIII in 1582, which was adopted by Catholic countries in the 1580s and by most of the Protestant world in 1700. A bill was passed in the House of Commons in March 1751 to bring British time into alignment with the rest of Europe, and the act took effect in September 1752, when, in a move that was seen as a victory for enlightenment over custom, eleven days were dropped from the British calendar.[49] Pynchon's narrative keeps looping back to this historical event because his novel is about the regulation and measurement of time as well as space, about the mapping of coordinates that allows any particular entity to be placed in relation to the rest of the world. This is, naturally enough, precisely what the old English aristocrats of the eighteenth century do not want: they are, so we are told, quite indifferent to time, regarding it as no less of a foreign intrusion than the "Nouns Case-Endings" favored by Europeans (195). For these English landowners, the Jesuit ideal of a universalism that recognizes no national boundaries threatens to undermine their entrenched social situation, and this is one reason the King is determined never to allow Jesuit philosophers into British North America.

The Catholic Church has its own imperial agenda, of course, as we see in *Mason & Dixon* through the malevolent efforts of Zarpazo, a Spanish Jesuit otherwise known as the Wolf of Jesus, to eradicate Indian culture from the North American continent. In formal terms, however, Pynchon's text imitates the "Jesuit Telegraph" described here, whose central feature was an eighteenth-century mechanical device stationed in Quebec which, thanks to "giant balloons sent to great Altitudes" and "beams of light focused to hitherto unimagined intensities" (287), enabled operators on many different points on the globe to send and receive messages through making connections among stars in the sky. As Elizabeth Jane Wall Hinds has pointed out, when William Emerson in the novel talks of "a great number of Jesuit Observatories, flung as a Web, all over the World it seems" (223), he is anticipating the World Wide Web on the Internet, another "Marvel of instant Communication" (287), which the global geometry and epistolary exchanges of the Jesuits foreshadow.[50] This indicates the way *Mason & Dixon*, for all of its eighteenth-century apparatus, is a characteristically late twentieth-century novel about transnational crossings and the traversal of stable national boundaries; Pynchon unearths in the world of the Enlightenment a genealogical equivalent to his contemporary concern with global remapping. The multinational settings of this novel, in South Africa as well as England and America, serve again to emphasize what Benedict Anderson has called "the spectre of comparisons," the discourses of parallelism and contrast that draw different countries into an uneasy proximity. In *Mason & Dixon,* as in *Gravity's Rainbow,* we find rhetorical structures of parallax and paradox that hollow out the symbolic order of national identity by forcing discrete entities into juxtaposition with what is situated, both literally and metaphorically, on the other side of the line.

In this sense, the parallel narratives in *Mason & Dixon* perform a similar function to the adoption of the Gregorian Calendar in the name of the harmonization of time, or the globalizing imperatives of the Jesuits: they hold up the mirror to an insular national culture and induce its subjects to reexamine their inherited customs in a transnational light. America operates throughout *Mason & Dixon* as a realm of alterity, a potential fissure in the class system that is seen particularly to permeate English society. We hear of food riots in England, of a mob "small and frail from Hunger, yet possess'd by a Titanic Resentment that provided them the strength" (737), and of a ruling aristocracy that, as the Reverend Cherrycoke records in his "Day-Book," regards "the Mass of the People . . . with suspicion and Contempt" (408). There is a reference early in the book to "Gloucestershire Nabobs" (185), which explicitly links the English social hierarchy with the nation's colonial enterprises in India, and, as outsiders within this system, Mason and Dixon find themselves increasingly resentful of British institutions as the story unfolds. Charles

Mason, the son of a baker, is passed over for the role of Astronomer Royal in favor of the less talented Maskelyne, who has the social advantage of being Clive of India's brother-in-law, and this heightens the antagonism that both he and Jeremiah Dixon come to feel toward their native land. When he is running the line between Pennsylvania and Maryland, Dixon says that West is "for Americans what North is for Geordies, an increasing Likelihood of local Power lying in the Hands of Eccentrics, more independence" (596).

One of the Geordie eccentrics we meet in this novel is Dixon's teacher, William Emerson, whose own interest in the dark arts is also driven by "a passionate Resentment" against English traditions (220). In this light, *Mason & Dixon* might be read as a classic declaration of the values of American independence, a fleshing out of Jefferson's abstract document by a demonstration of how social oppression and class antagonism fueled the drive for personal liberty that became institutionally equated with the new land of the United States. Emerson's philosophical iconoclasm not only prefigures Dixon's own attachment to American values later in the novel, but also foreshadows the rhetoric of cultural liberation promoted by his namesake, Ralph Waldo Emerson, some sixty years later. Tanner, who calls Pynchon "an Emersonian, with shadows," describes this fictional William Emerson as, "among other things, an early English version of Ralph Waldo," and he suggests that the title of the English Emerson's first book, *Fluxions,* points forward to the concern with fluidity and metamorphosis in his American counterpart.[51] Founding Fathers Washington, Franklin, and Jefferson are also given cameo roles to play in Pynchon's novel, thus reinforcing the reader's sense of this as a text that offers a monumental, if typically oblique, version of the birth of a nation. In Pynchon's revised version of American history, it is in fact the English Geordie, Jeremiah Dixon, who comes up with one of the most memorable soundbites to define the New World: at a tavern in Williamsburg one evening, he raises his ale-can "To the pursuit of Happiness," whereupon "a tall red-headed youth at the next table" asks for a pencil and says to Dixon, "You don't mind if I use the phrase sometime?" (395).

This encounter between Dixon and Jefferson is not, of course, meant to be historically plausible. As Hinds has observed, all of Pynchon's incongruities, anachronisms, and punning violations of linguistic decorum are intended to violate conventional aesthetic limits, just as the "subjunctive" terrain of America itself is portrayed as transgressing against traditional boundaries of order and regulation.[52] This is one reason for the author's representation here of the American West in surreal terms: amid the talking dogs and ducks and the tomatoes towering higher than churches, we get an impression of how the world is being turned "inside-out" (706). In other words, the surreal magnifications of the landscape in the last sections of Pynchon's novel testify to the characters' vision of a new world where the miraculous world of nature is coming to supplant older established institutions, making their time-honored conventions seem tired and anodyne by comparison. As these explorers move further into the West, their English methods of empirical science are balked by the advent of the strange and wondrous, the "Revelation, meadow'd to the Horizon," as the Reverend Cherrycoke puts it (7). Desire for the "Eternal West" (671) thus becomes a utopian gesture, associated with "a secret Body of Knowledge,—meant to be studied with the same dedication as the Hebrew Kabbala would demand" (487), and mythologized here, in an echo of Pynchon's earlier novel about the modern American West, as "Vineland the Good" (634).

"We trespass, each day ever more deeply," says Mason, "into a world of less restraint in ev'rything" (608). Etymologically speaking, trespassing, like transgression, involves the crossing of a boundary, and it is easy to see how Mason and Dixon trespass in all senses of that word; that is to say, they help to invent America by crossing the line they themselves have imagined. As in *Gravity's Rainbow*, the notion of heresy becomes significant here; for Americans, heresies are said to "flow like blood in the blood-stream" (522), and these English surveyors become honorary Americans through what is described as their "Ritual of Crossing Over" (56). This "Crossing Over" involves not a mere traversal of the Atlantic, but the propulsion of themselves into a "strange Orbit of Escape from the known World" (383), a known world of familiar English customs. This is one reason Pynchon's text is replete with images of optical reflectors, mirrors, prisms: the Enlightenment emphasis on scientific perspective and on the position of the observer is modulated here into a focus on the inherently doubled-up capacities of knowledge. Consequently, the astronomers' twin telescopes signify their constant oscillation between opposing points of view, and this in turn exemplifies the novel's structure of radical paradox, whereby nothing can be defined except through an inversion of its contrary. If the title of *Gravity's Rainbow* is an oxymoron, the title of *Mason & Dixon* is, equally aptly, a duplex: neither Mason nor Dixon, neither Britain nor America, can be understood except in terms of the other. America, says Cherrycoke, is Britain's "dream . . . in which all that cannot pass in the metropolitan Wakefulness is allow'd Expression." This is, quite literally, a virtual America, in the representation of the country as a "Rubbish-Tip for Subjunctive Hopes, for all that *may yet be true*" (345). In the end, Mason, who had originally been less keen than Dixon on settling in America, chooses to go back there to die; in a last manic surge of energy, he uproots his family and takes them back across the Atlantic Ocean, to the land where, finally, he feels "safe" (772). In a coda that evokes both the future of the continent and a poignant sense of loss, the narrative describes how two of Mason's sons stayed to become Americans, while his wife and younger children opted to return to England. Hence, even at the end of his journey, Mason's line is bifurcated; like Dixon, he finds himself always shuttling mentally between the Old World and the New: "Betwixt themselves, neither feels British enough anymore, nor quite American, for either side of the Ocean. They are content to reside like Ferrymen or Bridge-keepers, ever in a Ubiquity of Flow, before a ceaseless Spectacle of Transition" (713).

The investigation of what Edward Soja calls a "spatial hermeneutic" is, of course, as important to postmodernism as the critique of temporality and historicity was to modernist theory, and in *Postmodern Cartographies* Brian Jarvis argues that Pynchon's texts reflect the ways geographical mapping operates generally as a sign of state repression and hegemonic control.[53] It is certainly possible to see aspects of this in *Mason & Dixon*: the boundary line drawn by the surveyors between North and South is used subsequently to prop up the institution of slavery, and the Quaker Dixon, in particular, feels uneasy about underwriting mechanisms of tyranny in, as he puts it, "the one place we should *not* have found them" (693). Yet the surreal aspects of *Mason & Dixon* imply that, like Pynchon's other works, it is predicated on a systemic loop of excess, where the part refuses to conform to the regulatory structure of the whole. This is another version of the fetishistic aesthetic we saw in *V,* where the fragment overwhelms coherent narrative teleology; it also implies again Pynchon's interest in heresy, in transgressing against established structures rather than simply establishing an antinomian alternative to them. For Bataille, who was similarly interested in heresy, system and excess were mutually intertwined and interdependent: "Il faut le système. Et il faut l'excés"

(The system is necessary. And excess is necessary).[54] Casting himself as a member of the English "Mobility," rather than its nobility, Mason says that what they "love to watch" is "any of the Great Motrices, Greed, Lust, Revenge, taken out of all measure, brought quite past the scale of the ev'ryday world, approaching what we always knew were the Dimensions of Desire" (451). The lineaments of "measure" and "scale" here are para-doxical enablers of "Desire," not impediments to it.

Following this logic of inversion, it is not difficult to see that one of the reasons Pynchon's novel draws up boundary lines is specifically so they can be broken. He meticulously constructs a rhetorical simulacrum of an eighteenth-century world only to take delight in fracturing its linea-ments. Sometimes this takes a comic turn, as with the appearance in Chapter 50 of an ancestor of Popeye: " 'I am that which I am,' helpfully translates a somehow nautical-looking Indiv. With gigantick Free-Arms, and one Eye ever a-Squint from the Smoke of his Pipe" (486). But this emphasis on the rupture of boundaries is not merely a playful phenome-non, because it also betokens a radically egalitarian impetus that seeks, among other things, to overturn the hierarchical divisions of slavery: "Sooner or later," Dixon tells a slave driver in Pennsylvania, "a Slave must kill his Master. It is one of the Laws of Springs" (697). The novel's initial section, set in the Dutch Calvinist community of South Africa, is clearly intended to work in parallel with this consideration of slavery in America; Dixon makes this comparison explicit, in fact, when he points out that the Americans "keep Slaves, as did our late Hosts" (248). The object of such textual mirroring is, once again, to empty out the symbolic order by repositioning it in an alternative, virtualized perspective. Just as the British class system looks different when juxtaposed with the Ameri-can quest for freedom, so American practices of slavery are denatural-ized and magnified through being twinned with the religious and racial discrimination that Mason and Dixon find in Cape Town. In the same way these fictional astronomers engage in "Celestial Trigonometry" (96) to calculate the solar parallax, so Pynchon's readers are invited to bring African slavery and American slavery into an equivalent conceptual par-allax. In this way, slavery, like class discrimination, becomes not simply a question of ingrained local custom and practice, but an area open to transnational illumination.

As in *Gravity's Rainbow*, this defamiliarization of national cultures is symbiotically entwined with a metafictional self-consciousness, which works to textualize the national idiom while at the same time drawing attention to its own aesthetic condition of reversibility. There are many oblique references in *Mason & Dixon* to eighteenth-century English literature and culture—"Mr. Dixon whistling Airs from the Beggar's Opera," for instance (458), and Samuel Johnson's "famous trip to the Hebrides" in 1773 (744)—as if to exemplify how Pynchon's novel is re-creating in pastiche form the traditional mode of picaresque, whose aesthetic features become associated here with the delineation of a particular kind of national identity. *Mason & Dixon* starts off with an image of "a sinister and wonderful Card Table which exhibits the cheaper Wave-like Grain known in the Trade as Wand'ring Heart, causing an illusion of Depth into which for years children have gaz'd as into the illustrated Pages of Books" (5), and this appears synecdochically to anticipate the following 770 pages, which are also concerned with how a tricksy rhetorical idiom can create the stylistic illusion of depth and historical presence. There is, in other words, an internal dialectic in *Mason & Dixon* between illusion and disillusion, presence and absence. The first paragraph of the novel mentions "a Mirror in an inscrib'd Frame" (6), commemorating a farewell ball held by the British in 1777; this mirror emblematically conflates past and present, signifying both the virtual presence of the British in America but also, simultaneously, their subsequent absence.

*Mason & Dixon* thus produces a replica of the British involvement in North America, an aesthetic counterpart to the notion of virtual representation in government that was a source of deep antagonism between Britain and America in the 1760s. This political debate is touched on in the novel, when Mason and Dixon engage in a discussion with Captain Volcanoe while on a visit to New York about the whole nature of representation. At this time, British conservatives put forward the argument that it did not matter that American constituencies were not directly represented at the House of Commons in London, because they were fortunate enough to be indirectly—or "virtually"—represented by exist ing legislators who had the interests of the entire British empire at heart. As so often in Pynchon, this political scenario is also framed within a theological context, as this belief in "Virtual Representation" is compared by Captain Volcanoe to the "Doctrine of Transubstantiation": he says there is "a curious likeness" between the communion host transforming itself into the body of Christ and Members of Parliament from England transubstantiating themselves into embodiments of the "will of the People" (404). By contrast, as Mason argues, the preferred American way involves "*Consubstantiation*—or the Bread and Wine remaining Bread and Wine, whilst the spiritual Presence is reveal'd in Parallel Fashion, so to speak—closer to the Parliament we are familiar with here on Earth, as whatever they may *represent*, yet do they remain, dismayingly, Humans as well" (404). In this sense, as Mason implies, the act of representation itself might be seen as another new American invention: just as Winthrop's Puritans sought through parallel constructions to represent an absent God whom they deemed quite beyond the realms of transubstantiative mediation, so these American revolutionary politicians disavow the efficacy of any mystical body to govern the country, seeking instead to institute a system of accountable representation where those who are present are delegated to act in the place of those who are not.

Representation, of course, is a term with artistic as well as political implications. Indeed, it is not a difficult leap from political representation in America as a mode of institutional absence to the paradoxical interplay between ontological plenitude and systematic displacement in Pynchon's self-consciously alienating representations of British and American culture. Through his radical demystifications of the illusions of political and artistic transparency, the author inscribes America as a crucial signifying absence or gap in the world of Britain. America thus offers a specter of alterity, a virtual mirror, in which Mason and Dixon see the conditions of their old selves reversed. In the light of his works from the 1960s and 1970s, Pynchon has often been thought to write most effectively about paranoia, a theme that has sometimes led to a simplistic reading of him as a countercultural figure who exposes government conspiracies against the common people. But in the paragraph in *Gravity's Rainbow* before the one in which Slothrop famously thinks about the "Puritan reflex of seeking other orders behind the visible," there is a reference to his "recklessness transatlantic" (188), as if to intimate that Pynchon's character would not have been able to make such an identification without the alternative perspective induced by his English exile: "Presto change-o! Tyrone Slothrop's English again!" (204).

Paranoia, then, is not so much a donnée of Pynchon's work as a comparative category within it. Indeed, picking up the Greek prefix *para* (alongside), it might be possible to think of the author more in terms of parallelism or paradox, because his texts do not, like those of the old Puritan divines, keep different categories firmly apart, but bring them into a provocative, if often surreal, juxtaposition. Using a peculiarly ca-tholicized version of his American Puritan heritage, Pynchon's texts, like those of his seventeenth-century ancestor, traverse the Atlantic in a "Ubiquity of Flow," as *Mason & Dixon* puts it (713), to reveal heresies within the established boundaries of national identities. In *Gravity's Rainbow*, Slothrop's journey east leads him to reimagine Puritan elitism and nationalism as a murderous charade; in *Mason & Dixon*, the west-ward journey of the marginalized astronomers induces them mentally to transpose their native England from an empirical into a virtual phenom-enon. Pynchon's iconoclastic universalism thus operates as a form of displacement, emptying out the cathectic substance of established na-tional orders, and playing Britain and America off against each other in order to demystify both. His two major novels consequently have as much to say about British culture as about American, and one aspect of their mordant genius lies in the way they conjure up a comparative Atlantic world as they shuttle backward and forward between both sides of the ocean.

*Virtual Americas:*

*Cyberpastoral, Transnationalism, and*

*the Ideology of Exchange*

Early in 1995, *Wired,* the American magazine dedicated to celebrating the information revolution, published its first British edition. Emblazoned across the cover was a portrait of Thomas Paine, together with one of his famous apocalyptic maxims: "We have it in our power to begin the world over again." Elsewhere in this issue, *Wired* hailed Paine as its newly appointed "Patron Saint," a beacon of libertarian thought whose concern for the empowerment of individual citizens rather than their subjection to oppressive authorities would provide a potential model for the decentralized, anti-institutional forces of global cyberspace.

It is an evocative, even tantalizing, idea, another modulation of those utopian visions that have appeared in different guises throughout modern history, and that often have been associated, in one form or another, with America. In the Renaissance era, as J. H. Elliott has shown, Europeans would dream of the newfound world as a fabulous source of gold and untold wealth, and reluctant Old World cosmographers puzzled over how to fit all the new data from America into their traditional epistemological schemes.[1] No less compelling from their perspective was the appropriation of early America as what Anne McClintock calls "a pornotropics for the European imagination—a fantastic magic lantern of the mind onto which Europe projected its forbidden sexual desires and fears." Depictions of the "discovery" of America by Jan van der Straet and others represent it visually as an eroticized encounter between man and woman, with the "virgin land" figured as a territory to be conquered and "known," in all senses of that word.[2] In the late eighteenth century, such fantasies tended to assume a more social and political aspect, as the salons of Europe came to reimagine America as an external correlative to their romantic aspirations for a new earthly Atlantis. Thus it was that Paine, William Blake, and others aligned their images of paradise regained with projections of the newly emerging nation of the United States: Paine's transatlantic perspective led him to conceive of America as something magnificently other, an escape from the old social obstacles haunting moribund Britain.

In retrospect, it is easy to see how many of the difficulties Paine encountered with Jefferson, Washington, and others arose from his reading of the United States through the lens of alterity, his desire radically to simplify social and political issues in the interests of promulgating his pastoral hypostatization of America as the brave new world. My point is that the conceptual displacements involved in all transatlantic refractions of this kind have the effect of prismatically reconfiguring local cartographies into unfamiliar, estranged patterns. For Paine in 1790, as for British *Wired* in 1995, the United States of America represents not so much a political or historical fact as a virtual reality, a realm of difference poised to interrupt the claustrophobic vistas of Old World life. Conversely, American literary and cultural theory has engaged at different periods with various forms of European philosophy to interrogate the New World's metaphorical premises of liberty and exceptionalism. Again, it is possible to trace this practice back to the eighteenth century, when the influence of Locke, natural science, and other forms of Enlightenment philosophy began to make the separatist formulas of the Puritan "city on a hill" appear increasingly anachronistic. More recently, George Lipsitz has noted that the methodological apparatus of European cultural theory, with its radical refusal of self-authenticating identity, has made it difficult to frame the traditional Americanist question "What is American?" in the same old way.[3] From Adorno and Horkheimer to Foucault, Derrida, and Baudrillard, European approaches to American culture often have served to interrogate the self-reliant romanticism bound up with native forms of idealism, the "Emersonianism," as Ross Posnock represents it, that "remains our most obdurate intellectual reflex, one that often controls and indeed stifles the terms of intellectual debate."[4]

In *Negative Dialectics* (1966), Adorno described "nonidentity" as "the secret *telos* of identification," arguing that alienation and contradiction should be seen as inherent within the terms of identity. The very process of dialectic, he suggests, indicates the "inherent reversibility of the identity thesis" and so "counteracts the principles of its spirit." For Adorno, this dialectical impulse accordingly breaks the "spell" of identification, a spell through which the subject becomes associated with a metaphysical sense of presence that can be traced ultimately to a "theological heritage." In this sense, a redescription of U.S. culture from a position outside what Adorno calls "the magic circle of identitarian philosophy" would have the effect of demystifying the implicitly idealist teleology that gets reproduced through familiar cycles of American exceptionalism.[5] This principle of estrangement could also be seen as commensurate with recent moves to reconstitute the nationalist paradigm of the American literary canon by way of postcolonial discourses concerned with the expression of differential power equations. In a 1993 essay, Amy Kaplan described a familiar strategy of contemporary British studies as the contesting of "an ethnocentric national tradition by decentering it from the postcolonial vantage of commonwealth culture and imperial history," a move compared by Kaplan to the equally familiar effort in American studies since the 1960s to deconstruct "a monolithic American tradition" through a validation of "competing domestic traditions." However, she then suggested that this opposition is becoming complicated by a process of mutual reciprocity and exchange, as British work comes to focus more on "the empire close to home"—in Ireland, and urban immigrant communities—whereas America, by contrast, comes to reconceptualize itself as an "empire" necessarily linked to "other nations in a global system."[6]

My purpose in this book has similarly been to reconsider various American writers from a transnational perspective, seeking to avoid their alignment with such "monolithic" national narratives. By discovering alternative genealogies (such as surrealism) for the disjunctions that can be seen in particular texts, I have attempted to evade that circular explanatory process whereby American literature is validated because of what is said to be its inherently "American" qualities. That is not to say that national identity no longer has any value as a frame for textual analysis; it suggests, however, that this category is urgently in need of updating, and that national identity must be brought explicitly into the frame as an object of scrutiny in itself rather than being accepted uncritically as the donnée for a particular area of study. In recent years, there have been many expressions of discontent with the ways American studies as a subject has conceptualized itself in relation to existing systems of knowledge, and this discontent received its most public voice in Janice Radway's 1998 presidential address to the American Studies Association.[7] As Radway observed on that occasion, the academic nostalgia for some essential, unifying "American" identity now seems to be intellectually impossible; indeed, it may be as much of a chimera as the notorious quest in a previous generation for the "Great American Novel." Within the epistemological framework of poststructuralism, the tropes of myth and typology that supported American literature and American studies in their earliest days have been superseded by the newer idioms of borders and hybridity, leaving an academic discipline founded on the area studies model struggling to achieve what Paul A. Bové describes as "the point of 'exile' in relation to itself and its nationalist projects."[8]

All of this raises crucial questions about the identification and status of American subjects in an international context. How might it be possible academically to recuperate an area originally defined specifically against Eurocentric and transnational modes of cognition?[9] How also would American literature or American studies position itself with regard to cultural studies and other emerging methods of interdisciplinary activity? What might be the rationale for an Americanist agenda in an era when traditional models of nationalist synthesis no longer appear valid?

As we saw in the first chapter, the early developments of American studies in the United States during the late 1940s and 1950s became theoretically interwoven with the languages of nationalism and idealism that supported the American academy during this age of anxiety. Donald E. Pease writes of how even cultural critics like Leslie Fiedler, who were consistently hostile to the conservative conventions of American life at this time, were themselves still ensnared in that cold war rhetoric whereby the American spirit of self-authenticating freedom placed itself in opposition to oppressive forces of ideological tyranny. As a result, American studies in the years after the Second World War tended to reproduce "a consensus criticism of the consensus," in Nina Baym's acerbic phrase.[10] The work of F. O. Matthiessen, Richard Chase, and others may have set itself at an oblique angle to the civic orthodoxies of that time, but in their critical recapitulation of a transcendental ethic of higher freedom they were implicitly endorsing a patriotic version of liberty that became institutionally equated with the idea of America itself.

These transcendental directives became comfortably refurbished within a rhetorical anti-Marxism that expressed itself in sublimated "myth and symbol" formulas appropriate to the Manichaean dualisms of spirit versus matter, freedom versus history, which came to typify American studies during these cold war years.

Such formulations, of course, no longer enjoy currency, and since the 1980s the emerging field of cultural studies, in particular, has been instrumental in restoring a materialist base to the more abstract typologies of American studies. Although cultural studies quickly became assimilated into the American academy, the movement was initially associated with critical methodologies that evolved out of a British Marxist tradition; James Carey, for instance, argues that "British Cultural Studies could be described just as easily and perhaps more accurately as ideological studies, for they assimilate, in a variety of complex ways, culture to ideology."[11] The general effect of this intrusion of British cultural materialism into the domain of the United States was to mount a systematic challenge to the ghosts of American cultural exceptionalism. In 1993, for instance, Fredric Jameson remarked that humanities departments in American universities over the previous few years had been displaying a kind of "anglophilia" with respect to their newfound enthusiasm for cultural studies, an enthusiasm that paralleled the "francophilia" of ten years earlier; the influence of Derrida and his Parisian acolytes had been supplanted by the legacy of Raymond Williams, Stuart Hall, and the Centre for Contemporary Cultural Studies at Birmingham.[12] Jameson wrote of American studies and cultural studies as professional competitors, which, in terms of institutional politics, may indeed have been the case, though many of today's most influential "new Americanists" would see these academic terrains more as a theoretically seamless unit and would seek to deny any substantial conflict of interest between them. My purpose here, however, is not to propose a reconciliation between American studies and cultural studies but to suggest potential sources of friction between them, mutual incompatibilities that can illuminate but also shed an ironic light on each area of study.

To be sure, no contemporary account of American studies can ignore how the subject has been reshaped, as through a triangulation process, by its interaction with the more overtly political dimensions of the cultural studies movement. As a consequence, to pit myths and symbols of freedom against the forces of ideology in the time-honored "American" way no longer appears feasible, for all the reasons Amy Kaplan and others have outlined; it is no longer viable for American literature to seek consummation, as Lionel Trilling in 1946 thought it could (and should), by simply transcending the demystifying imperatives of ideological categories.[13] But this proposition also works in reverse: the matrix of cultural studies is problematized by various residual energies working through forms of American discourse that traditionally have resisted epistemological closure. In his discussion of Emerson and William James, for example, Howard Horwitz seeks to circumvent issues of theory and ideology by associating these terms with some putatively abstract, reified design, a design based, claims Horwitz, on an a priori idealism which then is simply imposed on textual practice. Thus, Horwitz writes of "the inherent redundancy of the term *ideology*," suggesting that it "has positive content only when imbued in advance with an agenda, political or moral, usually both."[14] But I would argue that the opposite of ideology in this context is not simple praxis, nor the more celebrated tradition of American pragmatism, which Horwitz in his way continues, and which could manifestly be said to involve its own kind of (nonconformist) ideology; rather, the opposite of ideology is negative ideology, ideology in an inverted or virtual mode.

This notion of negative ideology owes something to Adorno's conception of negative dialectics, through which identity becomes reversible, with alienation acknowledged as an integral part of its constitutive process. The crucial point about negative ideology, from this angle, is its capacity to describe an ideological matrix that simultaneously welds together ideological formation and its contradiction, thereby indicating "that the concept does not exhaust the thing conceived."[15] In this sense, the anti-ideological stance of Emerson and William James might be said to contain its own ideological formation. Ontologically, Emerson and James can no more resist ideological interpellation than they could resist bodily incarnation; but the strength of their writing arises from the way it succeeds in bracketing ideological concerns, so that it can swerve away into the more active realms of relative autonomy. The concern for freedom of spirit in Emerson and James thus appears not so much a categorical imperative as a perfect simulation; its purchase on the imagination lies in its aesthetic form rather than its truth value. American discourse, then, does not simply overwhelm and cancel ideology; instead, it negotiates ideology's erasure, putting the ideological sign, as it were, into suspension. At stake here is the question of conceiving ideology in negative or aesthetic terms. Just as various styles of theology preserve themselves as signifying practice even when their substantive formulas have been emptied out, so this same logic could be applied to ideology: ideology maintains a powerful signifying charge in a strictly aesthetic sense, a spectral capacity to shape literary and cultural production, even when that ideological framework can no longer function as a metanarrative within which textual issues are ultimately incorporated. From this perspective, aesthetics and ideology come together in a paradoxical, even oxymoronic construction. In fact, American literature in some of its most engaging manifestations might be said to revolve around the aestheticizing of ideology, or ideological aesthetics, whereby the imperatives of national identity are emptied out into fictional performances.

It would be useful here to take a specific example of this ideology of contradiction or exchange. In an incisive essay in which she laments that Jameson's ubiquitous matrix, "the cultural logic of late capitalism," has become as unsubtle and unsatisfactory a formula for explicating cultural events as the old "Elizabethan world picture," Marjorie Perloff tells of hearing a paper by a young British scholar on John Ashbery as the "poet of empire," where Ashbery's poetry was indicted for reproducing the ideologies of colonialism, patriarchy, and so on. Perloff criticizes this account both for its "reductionism" and for what she calls its empirical errors in relation to Ashbery's life and work; however, she acknowledges the possibility of presenting "a good case for Ashbery's poems as representations of the imperial America of the postwar decades," provided it were "made on different and more complex grounds." In particular, writes Perloff, there would be a need to exercise greater caution in dealing with empirical material, "to proceed more inductively than we are currently used to doing, to avoid the imposition of a prior set of theory isms on complicated historical data."[16] It may be difficult not to agree in principle with this wary style of scholarship, yet it is equally difficult to imagine any cultural studies approach to Ashbery as imperialist that, however brilliantly researched and executed, would not find itself caught up in just the same kind of theoretical dilemmas. From a culturalist point of view, Ashbery's self-reflecting surfaces and rhetorical complexities may indeed seem to demand some kind of political grounding, the restoration of a material base whose apparent invisibility constitutes a "significant absence" within these texts; but from the perspective of a critic concerned primarily with American postmodernism, any such prescription would inevitably find itself in turn ludically subject to transposition and displacement by the peculiar convex mirrors of Ashbery's romantic irony.[17]

Although it would be hard to conceive of a cultural studies reading of Ashbery's poetry that would not produce rebarbative tensions of the kind Perloff identifies, it could be argued that these types of jagged intersections perform valuable kinds of intellectual work. Through an openly structured paradox, these transatlantic crosscurrents serve to reposition the aesthetics of American literature not as a mode of autonomy but as a mode of alterity, an antidote to the inward-looking definitions associated with both American studies and cultural studies in their more familiar forms. My point here is that an international angle on American studies can create interference between text and context, thereby disturbing the tautological assumptions that would seek to explain individual events through metanarratives of American consciousness. Again, Adorno in *Negative Dialectics* critiques what he calls the "circle of identification—which in the end always identifies itself alone . . . drawn by a thinking that tolerates nothing outside it." To interrupt this kind of self-perpetuating circuit between identity and interpretation should be seen as one of the key tasks of a virtual American studies.[18]

Such strategic interruptions seem particularly important in view of the fact that scholars working in other fields have noted ways that American studies has become professionally "entrenched," replicating exactly those kinds of academic hierarchies and disciplinary structures with which its interdisciplinary impetus sought initially to quarrel.[19] Citing Tremaine McDowell's manifesto for the establishment of the first American studies program at the University of Minnesota in 1945, Patrick Brantlinger described the identity of American studies in the United States as being founded on the idea of synthesis: McDowell paid homage to "the unity within diversity, the diversity within unity which characterize life in the United States," before declaring that American studies would offer the best "hope . . . for bridging the unnatural gulf which separates the campus from the world outside."[20] In this vision, American studies was perceived as a cross-disciplinary mechanism designed not only to link the humanities and social sciences but also to connect the academy with a more broadly based American culture, thereby undermining the jealously guarded professional boundaries dividing academic interest groups from each other and also from the wider world. Such holistic imperatives gradually became assimilated into standard academic discourse; in terms of academic development, the key time was probably the 1960s, when the dramatic expansion of American studies ran alongside a rapid dissemination of the tenets of structuralism, a well-matched coupling that promoted explanations of American culture in terms of myths and archetypes: the South, the frontier, ethnic or immigrant identity, and so on.

Over the past twenty years, the poststructuralist critique of origins has worked to subvert these older ideals of interdisciplinary synthesis, instituting instead a widespread emphasis on the differential discourses of gender, race, and class. It is not difficult, though, to see how such voices from the margins come to create their own forms of tautology and self-fulfilling prophecy. Indeed, protestations about American ethnic diversity often appear to be predicated on the kind of identity politics that is bound up with transcendental, Emersonian imperatives asserting some self-defining freedom of the human spirit. Paul Lauter, for instance, is a compelling advocate of what he calls the cultural studies "turn" in American studies, by which he means a shift away from the "remote and academic" study of writers like Thoreau and Melville, whose complex works could properly be appreciated only by "learned initiates," toward a much broader domain encompassing popular culture and autobiographical narratives, a domain "within which people engage in those most significant of intellectual ventures, changing or policing the society in which they live."[21] There is no doubt that Lauter is right to point out ways issues of caste and class have helped to shape the American literary canon, and to highlight how the expectations associated with textual practices of " 'high' modernism," for example, worked implicitly to exclude women writers and writers of color.[22] What is less clear, however, is whether by seeking actively to reform the narrow cold war rhetoric that underwrote the equally narrow, technocratic methods of New Criticism, Lauter may not simply be replacing one national narrative based on the idea of patriotic unity with another focused on diversity and multiculturalism. Unity and diversity, though, can easily be recognized as simply differing points on the time-honored American scale of e pluribus unum.[23] In some ways, it seems appropriate that Lauter should keep returning so compulsively to memories of the Yale curriculum in the 1950s to justify this multicultural agenda, because there is an important sense in which he is still adhering to that old Yale model, whereby academic programs are designed to reflect and protect the moral conscience of the nation as a whole.

Exactly how an American national narrative should be constructed—whether through an emphasis on unity or diversity, high culture or low culture—is one thing; whether it should be constructed in this way at all, through a model in which national narratives emerge out of the way citizens "engage" with "the society in which they live," is quite another question. Is it the case, in the migrant and digital conditions of the twenty-first century, that American narratives are the exclusive preserve or prerogative of those who "live" there? Gayatri Spivak, coming at these issues from an Asian American perspective, has written cogently of how these "parochial multicultural debates" in the United States, "however animated, are not a picture of globality," and she accordingly advocates a "Transnational Culture Studies" that might place such transactions more within an "international frame."[24] Again, the point is to break the magic circle between text and context, to hold in suspension those conditions whereby the progressivist formulas of American studies would—naturally, as it were—underwrite a rhetoric of emancipation.

The theoretical dilemma in all of these interdisciplinary undertakings arises out of this mutually defining and apparently naturalized relationship between text and context. Just as the mythic idealism of American studies in the 1950s was entangled inevitably, if paradoxically, with the cultural circumstances of that time, so the more recent paradigms of cultural studies have found themselves interpellated, however reluctantly, within the ideological infrastructure of new market forces.[25] One side of the equation correlates all too symmetrically with the other; textual *langue* implies contextual *parole,* and vice versa. The way multiculturalism has swiftly become institutionalized in the United States echoes the way cultural studies in Britain during the 1980s and 1990s rapidly became an academic commodity, manifestly embedded within systems of exchange and market value. In Britain, the exponential growth of cultural studies was bound up in various ways with the establishment of new universities by the Conservative government of this time, in response to changing social and economic needs; in his 1992 book, *Cultural Populism,* Jim McGuigan analyzed what he described as the increasingly empathic, journalistic tendencies in British academic study of popular culture, the way discussions of soap operas, street fashion, and so on became enthralled by the very phenomena they were seeking to critique.[26] In this sense, Baym's killing phrase for American studies of the 1950s, "a consensus criticism of the consensus," could just as easily be applied to British cultural studies of the 1980s. While seeking to resist institutional structures and subvert traditional academic categories, both American studies and cultural studies in these eras found themselves ever more tangled up within the established formats they attempted initially to displace.

In itself, this is neither particularly surprising, nor an occasion for intellectual outrage. It does, though, help to account for what cultural critic Bill Schwarz in 1994 acknowledged as "the uniformity and predictability of much of the work" being done at that time in cultural studies, the same sense of predictability Perloff complained about in relation to the conference paper on postcolonialism in John Ashbery.[27] This is not, of course, to argue against the many useful ways literature and culture might provocatively and illuminatingly be juxtaposed, but rather to call into question the practice of simply appropriating culture as a "natural" framework to underwrite certain kinds of national narrative, as if there could be a clear, transparent window between text and context, a symbiotic relationship through which one side of the equation validated the other. In this regard, one crucial theoretical problem relates to a general uncertainty within the cultural studies domain about the value and significance of aesthetics. Cultural studies in many of its manifestations still holds to a postromantic distinction between aesthetics and morality, with the result that the ethical and political investments of many of its practitioners lead them to dismiss questions of aesthetic discrimination as merely a residue of the genteel world of fine taste, a world they typically associate with the canonical standards maintained by older, anachronistic styles of literary criticism. In this ritualistic overthrow of the literary by the cultural, as John Guillory has observed, specific philosophical conceptions of the aesthetic tend to become conflated entirely with questions of aesthetic *value*, without adequate reflection on the ways literature itself has developed as a contingent and historical (rather than universal) category.[28] The aesthetic is thus seen simply as, in Anthony Easthope's phrase, the "heart of a heartless world," an extravagance that works to gloss over the harder, more pressing issues of cultural representation and power.[29]

Yet this has led some versions of American literary and cultural criticism into a situation whereby its projects come to involve merely a reinforcement of the familiar. By its sometimes sentimental evocation of what is commonly known, and by its prioritizing of societal ethics over the more disruptive strains of aesthetics, a critical discourse inflected by the concerns of cultural studies runs the risk of locking itself into insular preoccupations where the weight of the ordinary world precludes the possibility of being able to imagine that world differently. This was the critical rationale behind Jameson's 1993 remark that cultural studies often tends to lack "international dimensions": in its concentration on local micronarratives, television soap operas, or whatever, cultural studies sometimes simply replicates the circumscribed ideological parameters of the objects it is representing.[30] To be sure, this is not true of cultural studies in all of its manifestations, and over the past decade there have been many attempts to consider the significance of cultural phenomena beyond the confines of the nation-state. Nevertheless, it remains true that academic explications of American narratives frequently rely on a reified idea of "culture" defined in a highly prescriptive, nationalistic, and inward-looking sense. For instance, Philip Fisher's *Still the New World* (1999) is subtitled *American Literature in a Culture of Creative Destruction,* with that preposition "in" signifying Fisher's belief that American literature can be described within a cultural context mapped out by the nation's "clear stake in newness" and its "permanently unsettled conditions." For Fisher, therefore, the Emersonian idea of utopian promise provides "the natural constitution for an unfinished land," with Frederick Jackson Turner's hypothesis about the American "frontier spirit" being "the single most important historical idea ever proposed by an American intellectual."[31]

The problem here is not that Fisher's aggregation of text and context—interpreting Twain and Whitman in relation to issues of migration, technology, and formal abstraction—may not in itself be useful and suggestive; nor is it necessarily to deny his thesis of U.S. cultural difference. The difficulty comes from Fisher's attempt to essentialize this difference, to reinscribe a version of American exceptionalism predicated on a bounded idea of national culture from which other influences are specifically excluded. Because of the totemic status allotted here to the frontier spirit, for instance, the "intellectual melancholy" of Matthew Arnold and Arnold Schopenhauer is said peremptorily to have no place in the American cultural consciousness.[32] From a traditionalist point of view, there still seems to be a peculiar kind of cultural prestige associated with the identification of a unifying deity, a guiding hand behind American national destiny, even if from an intellectual perspective this whole idea appears increasingly dubious, if not absurd. Indeed, one issue raised by Fisher's treatment of American culture is the extraordinary pertinacity of nationalistic affiliations in the academic marketplace, the political, professional, and indeed emotional energy invested in certain understandings of particular countries or domains. Even some of those who now acknowledge themselves skeptical in principle about formulations of national or regional cultures nevertheless continue in practice to endorse their familiar, comfortable lineaments—sometimes with an ironic aside about their necessarily "fictive" nature.[33] However, transnationalism can more robustly interrogate such foundational assumptions precisely through the way it emphasizes, as Jameson described it, the nexus of interaction between different intellectual or social paradigms linked to particular local formations. Jameson himself, of course, has expressed reservations about the notion of area studies in all of its manifestations, arguing that the very idea of a nation now involves "merely a relational term for the component parts of the world system."[34] These internationalist scenarios, then, comprise the historical situation within which we find that American cultural idealism needs to be relocated within the discursive matrix of a much wider global framework.

One example of this kind of conceptual displacement and reversal can be seen in the work of the American cultural historian T. J. Jackson Lears. Lears's 1981 book about the secularization of religious thought in late nineteenth-century America, *No Place of Grace,* heaps up a mountain of information from a huge variety of cross-disciplinary sources, so that the specific thesis about modernism Lears was working with begins to wobble under the weight of the particular events he describes. The author's preface to the book's 1983 paperback edition is especially revealing in this regard: he writes of his attraction to Gramsci's notion of cultural hegemony, but then cautions that "Gramsci's concept could easily degenerate into a mechanistic approach"; he notes that "Raymond Williams helped some, but my own sense was that cultural transformations were even messier and more complicated than his pioneering work suggested."[35] Gramsci's social formulations had become enormously influential among the British radical intelligentsia after the English translation of his *Selections from the Prison Notebooks* in 1971; in an essay of 1973, for example, Raymond Williams develops the Gramscian notion of hegemony as "deeply saturating the consciousness of a society," and it is this kind of European outlook that pervades Williams's later, more theoretically self-conscious work, such as *Marxism and Literature* (1977).[36] Stuart Hall, similarly, has described the Birmingham Centre for Cultural Studies in the 1970s as being engaged with "what I would call a Gramscian project," defined by Hall as an interrogation of "what Gramsci called 'the national popular': how it was constituted; how it was being transformed; why it mattered in the play and negotiation of hegemonic practices."[37] Such an analysis is designed to scrutinize the limitations of common sense, understood by Gramsci as that traditional wisdom institutionalized and revered by hierarchical custom.

Despite Lears's tributes to Gramsci and Williams, though, his own style of scholarship is predicated ultimately on precisely that idiom of transparency that Gramsci's work itself seeks radically to interrogate. "I went to the sources," Lears writes, "and (taking the advice of a wise mentor) tried to let the sources speak. . . . I worked from history to theory, and I tried to use theory to inform but not imprison my understanding of historical experience."[38] But if the engagement with European forms of ideology is characteristic of recent work by some American cultural historians, so too is the resistance to such formulas; while invoking theoretical concerns, Lears also takes pleasure in the way such patterns become usurped or overtaken by the more random currents of worldly affairs. It is not difficult to see how the notion of letting "the sources speak" for themselves involves its own kind of ideological blind spots, and my purpose here is not to praise Lears's theoretical perspicacity. More straightforwardly, the point is how his idiomatic style of cultural fiction appears an appropriate way to write American studies in what might be called the Whitmanian tradition ("Do I contradict myself? Very well then, I contradict myself. I am large, I contain multitudes"). Lears works out these kinds of paradox further in a 1985 essay for the *American Historical Review*, where he discusses how "the concept of cultural hegemony" has been received reluctantly by American historians. He discovers a "hostility toward Gramsci's work among American historians of all political stripes," an antagonism he associates with the familiar American belief in self-reliance: "The idea that less powerful folk may be unwitting accomplices in the maintenance of existing inequalities runs counter to much of the social and cultural historiography of the last fifteen years, which has stressed the autonomy and vitality of subordinate cultures."³⁹

I do not want to relapse into the obvious snare of oversimplifying what are complex intellectual traditions, of equating the Old World merely with politicized versions of cultural materialism and the New World with more romantic forms of self-determination. What I do want to emphasize is the value associated with a process of mutual mirroring and reversal, whereby Gramsci, for example, is taken out of what is thought to be his "natural" context and made to interact instead with the alien philosophical terrain of the United States. By creating their own negative image of Gramsci—negative not only in the sense of being antipathetic, but also of being displaced and reversed, as in a virtual reality—American historians reveal not only what is in their culture, but also what is not. Significant absences can manifest themselves more apparently in methodological forms than in thematic content; because it is this prism of alterity that reveals what any given culture lacks, the crucial task for any academic matrix is to establish two-way mirrors that can disrupt those self-generating tautologies whereby the answer to any given inquiry is postulated in advance. Such, as I have suggested, has been the case in both American and cultural studies over recent years. But one of the advantages of balancing these areas against each other is to turn them both into ludic images of their opposite, to aestheticize their ideological apparatuses, thereby making them appear provisional rather than necessary constructions.

In October 1988, Stuart Hall and Martin Jacques edited a special issue of *Marxism Today* with the theme of what they called "New Times," an era defined by the conception "that Britain and other advanced capitalist societies are increasingly characterised by diversity, differentiation and fragmentation, rather than that homogeneity, standardization and the economies and organisations of scale which characterised modern mass society."⁴⁰ According to Hall and Jacques, the radical Left in Britain during the 1980s had failed to recognize that Thatcherism and the dynamics of this new environment were not necessarily cognate. Thatcherism, in a classic hegemonic gesture, attempted to align notions of globalization exclusively with its own free market dogmas; but actually, this gradual erosion of the autonomy of nation-states forms part of a much wider process, impelled, as Hall noted, by the "shift . . . to new 'information technologies' from the chemical and electronic-based technologies which drove the 'second' industrial revolution from the turn of the century onwards."[41] In this different kind of situation, nationalism would necessarily be expected to fade in significance as a coherent, organizing principle for thought or practical business of any kind.

Such developments will, of course, eventually come to have important repercussions for the study of culture in nationalist terms. In recent years, the attempt to define American literature as immanently embodying some patriotic spirit has come under fire from various quarters. William C. Spengemann points out that the term American literature was not invented until the 1780s, so that Anne Bradstreet, Edward Taylor, and other supposed harbingers of American romanticism should be seen more as representatives of the "literature of British America"; Peter Carafiol argues that the equation of nineteenth-century transcendentalism with an "American ideal" of self-centered nonconformity involves an extrapolation and secularization of archaic Christian metaphors about the freedom of the "soul."[42] An emphasis on similar kinds of displacement and slippage also characterized work in British cultural studies during the 1990s. The earliest practitioners in this field—Richard Hoggart, E. P. Thompson, Raymond Williams—were all working, in their different ways, with an idealized conception of community as an empowering and socially cohesive force; thus, in *The Long Revolution* (1961), Williams lamented "our own divided time" and sought to "define the theory of culture as the study of relationships between elements in a whole way of life."[43] However, Williams's concentration on "rooted" communities "whose members share an area of common meaning" has been challenged more recently by discourses privileging various forms of mobility and exchange.[44] The widespread critique of essentialism, with its archaic assumptions about ideal social types, has correlated with what Edward Said calls a kind of "traveling theory," which declares itself hostile to "separatism" and to the romantic doctrine that "only in the community, and the purer form of the community, is my salvation."[45]

Such an emphasis on modes of deracination and transposition has strongly influenced the black British scholar Paul Gilroy, who insists on considering North American culture in relational and postcolonial terms, as one node along an axis that also encompasses Africa and Europe. Gilroy, who studied with Hall at the Centre for Contemporary Cultural Studies, is more concerned to represent America as a figure of interruption, a means of disturbing any "narrowly ethnic definition of racial authenticity" or the "purity of cultures" on either side of the Atlantic.[46] He consequently takes issue with what he sees as the traditional "racism and ethnocentrism" of English cultural studies, citing in particular the tendencies of E. P. Thompson and Raymond Williams to construct mythographies of British cultural identity from which blacks were systematically omitted.[47] Gilroy seeks instead to correlate black culture in Britain with American black protest movements, just as, conversely, he uproots characters like W. E. B. Du Bois and Richard Wright from their reified, canonical situation within an African American tradition by inscribing their work within less familiar European intellectual contexts. Gilroy's affiliation with the field of cultural studies, broadly defined, has militated against any investment on his part in the particular qualities of American national identity; indeed, *The Black Atlantic* specifically takes issue with what he calls "the nationalist focus which dominates cultural criticism," describing this as something that creole forms should react against. This specifically materialist analysis serves to demystify any romantic conception of "race," "people," or "nation," suggesting instead that cultures are formed from heterogeneous strands linked to "the persistent crisscrossing of national boundaries."[48] In *Against Race* (2000), Gilroy develops the logic of his antiessentialist position still further, arguing controversially that there is a political continuum between attempts to define racial identity and the logic of fascism. Linking the consolidation of racial typology both with the modernist quest for origins and the old "biblical stories of nation-building," Gilroy advocates instead a philosophical cosmopolitanism that would "battle against revitalized fascisms, nationalism, regionalism, fundamentalism, and particularism."[49]

The lukewarm response to *Against Race* in America, particularly by comparison with the rapturous reception accorded to *The Black Atlantic*, throws into relief some of the inevitable tensions incumbent on a transnational approach to the study of the United States emanating from the anti-idealist premises of British cultural materialism. Although *Against Race* eventually hypothesizes its own version of global idealism linked to the "planetary humanism" of figures like Bob Marley, its concern not only to demystify racial and ethnic categories (as in *The Black Atlantic*) but, more radically, to renounce them entirely created a distinct sense of unease among those on both sides of the Atlantic for whom such categories retain a promise of identification and community.[50] In her review in the African American journal *Callaloo,* for example, Neeta Bhasin commented: "I'm not entirely convinced that the notion of a strategic engagement with the idea of essentialism is not a useful one or that we are even ready to give up solidarities based on race in this particular moment."[51] What needs to be emphasized here, then, are the mutual antagonisms, as well as sources of illumination, involved in dynamic exchanges of this kind between different intellectual traditions. Although it is true that the more aggressively secular narratives of cultural studies have made valuable interventions in the Americanist field, reconfiguring its traditionally idealist assumptions within a discursive matrix of ideological materialism, it is also true that a scholar like Gilroy, emerging out of a cultural studies base, has brought back to his native field significant aspects of American mobility, particularly in the way he has focused on repressed histories of transatlantic displacement as a means to interrogate superannuated conceptions of the Volk. In this respect, it might be argued that American studies continues to exercise as much intellectual influence on cultural studies as the other way around, although it should be emphasized that this approach involves an internationalist slant on the study of the United States, which bears little relation to—indeed, in Gilroy's case, is frankly hostile to—the nostalgia for national, regional, and ethnic particularisms that still lingers in many aspects of the American studies movement.

One way of examining this trajectory of reciprocal interaction and exchange is to consider how the academic directions of Stuart Hall's work have developed. Like C. L. R. James some twenty years earlier, Hall came to England from the Caribbean in the 1950s with a particular interest in American culture. Before moving into sociology in the 1960s, his professional expertise had been in more traditional areas of American literature: the topic of his Oxford Ph.D. thesis, never completed, was the international theme in Henry James, and his first teaching experience was on the American novel.[52] After his move to the Centre for Contemporary Cultural Studies at Birmingham in 1964, Hall became less well-disposed toward American society, whose structural idealism he came to see as erasing social and political contradictions in support of an all-encompassing "American world-cultural hegemony." Specifically, Hall at this time critiqued the "scientific" functionalism of American sociology, which was "integrative in perspective" and could conceive of deviations from "the model of the American dream" only in terms of "dysfunctions" and "tension management."[53] This, of course, represented America's typical version of itself during the cold war era: celebrating itself as a pluralist society, a category constantly counterposed to the malevolent states of totalitarianism, the United States generally succeeded in smothering dissent by incorporating such energies within the grand metanarrative of its national imaginary. In 1986, Hall was still speaking of the "historical amnesia characteristic of American culture," its uncanny capacity to sublimate material events into atemporal forms of myth.[54]

Yet the "New Times" argument, dating from 1988, marks an important shift in Hall's attitude toward America. By dissociating the fluidities of information and representation and the mobility of capital from any necessary affiliation with the ideologies of Thatcher or Reagan, Hall opened up the possibility of socialist agendas committed to diversity and difference. In exploring ways of organizing society other than through monolithic systems of state power, Hall acknowledged the value of reconstructing discourses on ethnicity in new, more sophisticated forms: "By 'ethnicity,' " he wrote, "we mean the astonishing return to the political agenda of all those points of attachment which give the individual some sense of 'place' and position in the world, whether these be in relation to particular communities, localities, territories, languages, religions or cultures."[55] In a 1992 interview, Hall remarked on how this American conception of ethnic difference has helped to prize open some of those differences that have remained latent rather than overt in the European context: "Western Europe did not have, until recently, any ethnicity at all. Or didn't recognize it had any. America has always had a series of ethnicities, and consequently, the construction of ethnic hierarchies has always defined its cultural politics."[56]

Concomitant with this emphasis on ethnic positioning, we find an increased attention to questions of citizenship and individual rights, causes that have been associated with America since the days of Thomas Paine. As Hall observed, the radical Left in Britain has tended to dismiss issues of rights as a liberal fraud: formal rights of liberty, so the argument runs, do not guarantee those more substantive rights of self-determination that could be produced only through a redistribution of wealth and a reorganization of social class. Yet, as central governments in Britain anxiously responded to the "new times" of cultural diversification with ever more repressive attempts to define some homogeneous national identity, so pressure began to grow for what Hall called "a new balance—a new settlement—between liberty and equality."[57] Organizations such as Charter 88 emphasized the need to circumscribe the authority of the state to guarantee constitutionally the legal rights of British subjects; in a 1993 essay Hall specifically argued the need to dissociate legal notions of citizenship from more affective understandings of cultural identity, such as those favored by earlier cultural critics like Raymond Williams.[58] In *Culture and Society*, Williams had disparaged the idea of "society" as a bourgeois notion, a means whereby social life is reduced, as he says, to "a merely neutral area, or an abstract regulating mechanism"; Williams contrasted this, of course, with his more positive version of "culture," based not just on the law but on "the need to think and feel in common terms."[59] Hall's own essay, however, is more cognizant of subcultures, racial frictions, and other forms of social diversity. Rather than seeking to reconstruct some mythical synthesis, Hall suggested that "the capacity to *live with difference*" is destined to be "the coming question of the twenty-first century." Accordingly, he continued, there is a need to "transform the language of citizenship to new historical circumstances . . . far from collapsing the complex questions of cultural identity and issues of social and political rights, what we need now is *greater distance between them*. We need to be able to insist that rights of citizenship and the incommensurabilities of cultural difference are respected and that *the one is not made a condition of the other*" (Hall's italics).[60] For example, blacks in Britain do not necessarily need to be assimilated or integrated into the community—whatever that might mean—but they do need a passport.

This more legalistic definition of community could be related to what Samuel Taylor Coleridge called "civilization" rather than "culture."[61] It displaces the romantic projection of emotional unity between subject and object, self and surroundings, and opts to work instead with an acknowledged dualism between elective affinities on the one hand and a necessary but radically demystified public sphere on the other. Accordingly, Hall's emphasis on differential networks rather than cultural homogeneity hollows out the old myths of plenitude and imaginary identification, seeking instead to reinscribe the study of culture as a site of alternation and alterity. From this perspective, Hall's academic career has in some sense gone full circle: having started off analyzing the interplay between America and Europe in Henry James's novels, he now seeks to reconstitute what one might call the exchange value of the United States within a European matrix of cultural studies. To put this another way, the United States crucially appears to Europe at the beginning of the twenty-first century as a signifier rather than a signified, a global power whose strategic interventions now center around the fields of information and representation rather than military force. The mobility of these designs overlaps with a virtual image of America, which emerges significantly as the nexus of international media and communication, a space outside the framework of Raymond Williams's old "rooted" settlements.[62]

Rhetorical invocations of American space, of course, go back at least as far as Frederick Jackson Turner. Again, my purpose here is not simply to relapse into traditional invocations of the American sublime; nor am I seeking to valorize a transnational system of exchange based on what Rob Wilson calls "democratic and marketplace myths of reciprocity": the idea that the United States, while supposedly engaged in a free trade of intellectual and economic property, is actually seeking to bolster its position of global dominance through an uneven weighting of these transactions.[63] As we have seen, the politics sustaining the national identity of the United States is fantastically flexible—e pluribus unum—and to cast a virtual reflection that would displace not only the old myths of national unity but also parallel narratives of diversity and local identification is to risk interrupting that circuit of reciprocity through which the American national imaginary is constituted. My suggestion is, therefore, that these transatlantic dialogues might establish a conceptual network whose para-tactical divisions involve not merely the ideological demystification of American "freedom" but its radical aestheticization. It is an *aesthetics* of liberty that is at stake here: not a pure or transcendent freedom, which would be an ideological impossibility, but a virtual image of liberty, its simulacrum. American studies and cultural studies both have traditionally engendered their own imagined community, but in tracing the friction and dissonance between these diverging models we witness the anachronistic nature of nationalist ideals and the heterogeneity of "functionally differentiated" societies in our contemporary era.[64]

At the beginning of the twenty-first century, national identity, like other forms of organic or mythic identity, discovers itself to be decentered and fissured, leaving the Americanist field vulnerable on two fronts: prone to the charge that any area-based organization of knowledge, particularly one centered around a conception of the nation-state, belongs to an earlier phase of cognitive mapping; and uncomfortably aware of how, within this revised transnational grid, America's symbolic points of reference—freedom, individualism, and so on—have themselves become manifestly liable to deconstruction through their repositioning within a larger global framework where all ideologies become relative. Yet the comparative perspective implicit in this partition position also has the effect of locating ideology in an aesthetic light, rather than seeking to prioritize it as an all-encompassing metanarrative useful for its truth value. From this point of view, America is valuable not for what it might be in itself, but for the interference it creates in others; accordingly, the academic terrains of American literature and American studies must increasingly involve analysis of how the United States interfaces with other world cultures. Over the past half century, it has been notoriously difficult to define Americanist areas as discrete domains without falling back into the intractable enigmas of nationalism or essentialism; but it is easier to see how American studies might work as a virtual discipline, a means of disrupting the self-enclosing boundaries of other areas, whether academic disciplines or geographic territories, by its projections of dislocation and difference.

As we saw when discussing Nabokov in chapter 6, a different kind of rhetorical space was evoked by critics such as R. W. B. Lewis in the 1950s to incorporate narratives of American literature into an idealized topos of American pastoral. Such equations of nature and nation have constituted one of the most common strategies in constructions of national identity on both sides of the Atlantic. In his 1991 book, *Romantic Ecology*, British critic Jonathan Bate attempted to dismiss what he perceived as narrowly ideological ways of reading the celebrant of the Lake District, William Wordsworth, seeking instead to reconstitute the Victorian way of appreciating him as a poet with a religious "faith in the perfectibility of mankind." For Bate, Wordsworth's vision of an "unmediated, unalienated relationship with nature" anticipates the concerns of contemporary green activists, that "the earth is a single vast ecosystem which we destabilize at our peril."[65] In *Achieving Our Country* (1998), Richard Rorty also cited with approbation the pedagogical example of Wordsworth in his chapter on the "inspirational value of great works." Wordsworth's apotheosizing of the familiar appeared in Rorty's eyes a necessary counterbalance to what he called the "profoundly antiromantic" and "depressing" stance of academics like Fredric Jameson and A. J. Ayer, who, specializing in professional demystification, have failed to share the American philosopher's belief that "the ability to shudder with awe is the best feature of human beings." Rorty's concern actively to engage a poetics of attachment to national situations and localized forms of praxis moves him to quote directly from Wordsworth's *Prelude:* "What we have loved / Others will love, and we will teach them how."[66]

Of particular concern here is the mutual interest of both Bate and Rorty in appropriating pastoral scenarios to underwrite their national political agendas. This process of projection involves what Homi K. Bhabha has called the "recurrent metaphor of landscape as the inscape of national identity," where the spirit of place is found to be invested with particular kinds of symbolic meanings.[67] It is this latter view of nature as a subliminal construction, a way of organizing reality, that provides the framework for Catherine L. Albanese's 1990 book, *Nature Religion in America,* where she traced the cluster of symbols and beliefs associated with the idea of nature in American culture from the seventeenth century through to the present day:

> Amerindian immersion in nature lives on in a traditionalist version as well as in a New Age incarnation that is decidedly eclectic. Puritan/Calvinist awe at the violent wilderness and respect for its negative forces thrives in the work of some contemporary nature writers. Republican apotheosis of nature in a politicized ideology ranges through the present-day environmental movement, for example, as it manifests itself in the "Greens" and in ecofeminism. Transcendentalists prosper in the general harmonial-metaphysical dialectic of New Age religion and in the special case of Goddess religion. And physical religion persists in vibrational medicines that range from the contemporary laying on of hands to the quest for purity in food. All told, the recapitulating pieties move freely together, mixing and matching, bowing to new partners in a quantum dance of religious syncretism.[68]

To be sure, this account of the natural realm in U.S. culture is itself highly synchronic, glossing over the many variations among these different phenomena. Nevertheless, as a historian of civil religion in America, Albanese is well placed to observe with a certain amount of skepticism ways in which the idea of nature has been repackaged for various political or commercial ends. She discusses how to call a substance "natural" is to promote its sales in marked ways, an argument that anticipates Andrew Ross's observation that the idea of nature was commandeered in the early 1990s by popular figures like Kevin Costner and linked to a reactionary promotion of the virtues of frugality and simplicity, the climate of "Just say no."[69] Albanese's thesis also fits with the historical analysis undertaken by Roderick Nash in *Wilderness and the American Mind*, where he writes of how environmentalists like Aldo Leopold in the 1920s understood the wilderness as a correlative to idealized forms of American culture, enjoying the characteristics of what Leopold called "vigorous individualism" and "lack of subservience to stiff social forms." This was a line also promoted by Supreme Court Justice William O. Douglas in 1960, when he described the wilderness as the ultimate source of American liberal, democratic traditions and, therefore, essential to the nation's constitutional traditions of life, liberty, and the pursuit of happiness.[70]

The last chapter in Albanese's work is appropriately entitled "Recapitulating Pieties: Nature's Nation in the Late Twentieth Century," a phrase that echoes the title given to a posthumous collection of Perry Miller's essays which appeared in 1967. Miller in fact used the term "nature's nation" in his essay "The Romantic Dilemma in American Nationalism," first published in the *Harvard Theological Review* in 1955. Unlike Bate or Rorty, though, Miller was less an advocate for the natural world than an intellectual historian of it; just as he wrote about New England Puritanism from the perspective of an atheist, so he used a comparative, cosmopolitan method to interrogate the significance of nature within the discursive framework of nineteenth-century American culture. One of the essays reprinted in this book is a 1961 piece called "Thoreau in the Context of International Romanticism," which argues against the view of Thoreau as merely a local observer of nature and considers him instead alongside European writers such as Goethe and, once again, Wordsworth. For Miller, then, this natural world was primarily an intellectual construction, a corollary, in fact, to the Puritan codification of the New England environment that he wrote about in his earlier work.[71] What Miller would have wanted theoretically to resist is the kind of sacralization of place that has inspired work in both environmental and area studies over recent years; indeed, these latter fields might be seen as to some extent conceptually commensurate, as they have involved the identification of certain privileged spaces that have tended then to become associated with ideas of plenitude or mutual interdependence. In *The Idea of Culture* (2000), Terry Eagleton recalled Raymond Williams many years ago describing ecology as "the study of the interrelation of elements in a living system," and Eagleton accurately observed that this can be seen as "interestingly close" to Williams's definition of culture, which was similarly concerned with the continuity across time of certain national traditions.[72]

This interest in various forms of mythic totality is one reason why both "romantic ecology," in Bate's phrase, and American studies have returned compulsively to the nineteenth century as their site of epistemological value. In *Residues of Justice* (1996), Wai-chee Dimock points out that "the discourse of part and whole was very much a standard trope in the nineteenth century, a regular feature of its social critique." Tracing this idea of "part and whole" through Karl Marx's notion of the alienation of the self as well as the discourses of unity and division in Emerson and Thoreau, Dimock argues that the particular vision of justice that is a legacy of this nineteenth-century vision of wholeness has been counterproductive in many different ways; instead, she expresses interest in hypothesizing what she calls "a nonintegral conception of reason . . . more heterogeneous, more responsive to contrary possibilities."[73] Such contrariness would, of course, be antipathetic to someone like Bate, whose vision of Wordsworth's "pastoral poetry" as possessing the "permanent enduring power" of an "evergreen language" works as a simple synecdoche for what he takes to be the eternal glories of English literature as a whole.[74] But it would also serve to cast a quizzical eye on the identification of nature and nation within an American pastoral tradition, not just in the obvious classic examples like that of F. O. Matthiessen—whose justly famous 1941 book, *American Renaissance,* equates the spirit of transcendentalism with a version of cultural nationalism—but also in more recent critical work, where ideas of pollution and "toxic discourse" are linked to an ethic of purification that recycles the cultural Puritanism of Thoreau in a new way.[75]

Just as the rhetorical idealization of American nature underwrote the cold war fiction of the 1950s, so its more recent modulation into a politics of the environment has continued to shore up definitions of American literature and American studies into the twenty-first century. Yet such environmental writing, while explicitly internationalist and concerned with the fate of the globe, is often implicitly nationalist and concerned with issues of simplification and transcendence in a way that connects very obviously (as Albanese has suggested) with certain time-honored American ideals. As we saw in the first chapter, Lawrence Buell's work disdains the more practical questions of environmental politics and seeks to discover within nature some kind of philosophical remedy for "the pathologies that bedevil society at large."[76] Again, it is the way American nature is requisitioned for transcendent purposes that is of particular interest here; rather like Stanley Cavell—or even, perhaps, more distantly, William James—Buell's version of environmentalism involves an extrapolation of the New England intellectual tradition into a variety of religious experience whose circumference is decidedly local. The ideological inflections of this particular agenda become more self-evident once we bring to mind cultural figures who cannot be fit into its theoretical parameters. Andy Warhol, to take an obvious if extreme example, always refused to have anything to do with recycling or environmental protection because he was opposed in principle to the moral agendas of frugality, particularly the ways they have become encumbered with what Andrew Ross has called "the evangelical spirit that is the apocalyptic house style of so much environmental writing."[77] Similarly, in his 1997 novel, *Underworld*, Don DeLillo associates his national narrative not with purification but with waste: "Waste," says the book's narrator, "is the secret history, the underhistory, the way archaeologists dig out the history of early cultures, every sort of bone heap and broken tool, literally from under the ground." Waste for DeLillo signifies a kind of ontological limitation, in keeping with the thread of medievalism, the sense of memento mori, that runs all through his narrative: "We were the Church Fathers of waste in all of its transmutations," recalls the Italian American hero at another point.[78] To accuse DeLillo's psychological characterizations of lacking "inner life" is to miss their point, which involves precisely the emptying out of spirit into matter, the flattening of etiolated ideals into the glories of garbage.[79] If American culture for Thoreau is signified by its aspirations toward regeneration and purity, American culture for DeLillo is signified by its degeneration into the effluvia of consumer rituals, such as the detritus of the baseball games he chronicles here with such fondness. Too often, as in the opinions of Justice Douglas, the American wilderness is made to stand as an antithesis to what is taken to be the Orwellian uniformity of mass culture. But this, of course, is merely to privilege a certain version of liberalism without considering how its ethical compulsions are linked, philosophically as well as etymologically, with particular ethnic circumstances.

This is not, of course, to argue against the usefulness or desirability of a politics of nature on its own terms, but to suggest that the potential benefits of such interventions often get overlaid with an awkwardly moralistic and sometimes ethnocentric component. Such ethnocentrism becomes all the more disagreeable when it attempts to suppress its own partial perspectives in the name of advancing a universal truth. In his fine book, *Nature's Economy*, Donald Worster specifically cautions against the easy identification of ecological doctrines with ethical imperatives, as he works through different ways the matrix of nature has been conceptualized, from the Arcadian sentiments of Gilbert White to the more pessimistic scientific formulas of Charles Darwin. Nor does Worster shy away from links between organic versions of ecology as concerned with the interrelation of all natural things and the politics of fascism in the middle of the twentieth century; indeed, he discusses how, not coincidentally, such organicist theories began to fall into disrepute among academic ecologists soon after the trauma of the Second World War.[80] These intellectual homologies between organicism and fascism are an awkward business to negotiate, but Worster's cautious and pluralistic approach seems more convincing than the argument in *Romantic Ecology*, where Bate attempts to defend himself against Anna Bramwell's charge that "the greenest political party of our century has been the Nazis" by claiming that it is the local quality of English poetry, its penchant for the "naming of places," "that allows for a differentiation between love of the land and love of the fatherland."[81] Even more problematically, Bate suggested in 1996 that "criticism will only reach maturity when it ceases to be apologetic about the sacredness of things," and he called for more attention to the work of the later Heidegger, who assaulted conceptions of use value in "The Question Concerning Technology." Bate concluded, with what might be described as a nice understatement: "If we are to follow the later Heidegger into the Black Forest, we will have to tread very carefully: the political fallout will be bloody."[82]

My purpose here is not, of course, simplistically to conflate the organic aspects of either environmentalism or area studies with the blood-and-thunder versions of organicism that characterized fascist ideologies in the middle of the twentieth century. What I do suggest is that standard liberal assumptions of an absolute antithesis between these movements should be seen as dubious, because intellectually they are much more closely intertwined with each other than they might at first appear. As we have seen, Gilroy has written about the thematic continuities between modernism and fascism in their mutual quest for racial origins and collective identities in the earlier part of the twentieth century, and Eric Cheyfitz has observed that F. O. Matthiessen's idealization of the "imperial male body" in *American Renaissance* introduces in that text an "unexamined contradiction between the imperial and the democratic." By extolling the idea of America as an incarnation of the natural, by implying a similar kind of organic structure within the human body and the body of the state, Matthiessen's work, according to Cheyfitz, comes dangerously close to endorsing the principles of a fascism that his "democratic sublime" officially rejected.[83] Let us be quite clear: this is not to imply in any way that Matthiessen was a closet fascist; indeed, we know about his profoundly socialist commitments and sympathies. It is, though, to suggest on a more abstract level the uncomfortable proximity between investment in a particular nation-state, bounded both geographically and politically, and the "imperial" logic that as Kwame Anthony Appiah has observed, is often implicated in the idea of a "national common culture."[84] Such analogies are evoked explicitly in *Dialectic of Enlightenment,* first published by Theodor W. Adorno and Max Horkheimer in 1947, where the German exiles described how the brutal logic of instrumental reason, previously associated in their eyes with the political regime of Hitler, had traversed the Atlantic and embedded itself among the commercial marketplaces of America. Adorno and Horkheimer thus found that the holistic impetus of modernity's utopian or dystopian systems had migrated west, moving from an overtly repressive state apparatus in their native Germany to one that was more insidiously so in the United States: "Abstraction," they wrote, which is "the tool of enlightenment, treats its objects as did fate, the notion of which it rejects: it liquidates them."[85]

One important aspect of the work of Adorno and Horkheimer is the way their critique of American values emerges from a specifically transnational perspective. Indeed, the force of their antifascist analysis derives from their detachment from locality: in 1947, they belonged to the world of neither Germany nor America, they had a stake in neither the political nor the natural environment. Whereas for Rorty engagement with one's native land is an ethical imperative, for Adorno and Horkheimer disengagement and alienation were equally crucial political choices. It is precisely this mode of displacement that can offer another way of practicing American studies, one that empties out indigenous assumptions and twists them around in a new way. In *Achieving Our Country*, Rorty peremptorily advises the American cultural Left "to forget about Baudrillard's account of America as Disneyland—as a country of simulacra— and to start proposing changes in the laws of a real country, inhabited by real people who are enduring unnecessary suffering."[86] Such a pragmatic style of political activism might seem, on the face of it, full of plain common sense, but one of the risks of such supposedly demystified perspectives is a potential blindness to the sense of disturbance within symbolic orders that transnational modulations necessarily produce. In his major work, *Philosophy and the Mirror of Nature* (1980), Rorty advocates the wholesale abandonment of the idea of knowledge as reflection, and disavows the figure of a "Glassy Essence" that might contain secret knowledge to which humans would strive to gain access through quasi-spiritual metaphors of illumination and sight. Rather than seeking wisdom in this academic "Mirror of Nature," Rorty puts forward a more historicist understanding of meaning as radically contingent, and he accordingly nominates as "the three most important philosophers" of the twentieth century Wittgenstein, Dewey, and Heidegger.[87]

But if Wittgenstein speaks to the positivist impulse in Rorty's project and Dewey to its strand of social liberalism, the presence of Heidegger in this trio suggests ways in which Rorty's "Philosophy without Mirrors" cannot, finally, occlude the ghosts of transcendence. In the tradition of William James and other luminaries of American pragmatism, Rorty tries to clear away the distorting categories of reflection and refraction and engage more immediately with what he takes to be the existential processes of "living."[88] Without wishing to oversimplify Rorty's sophisticated argument, it is worth highlighting how his move to suppress mirror theory, which he associates with antiquated scholastic modes of thought, works in direct contrast to the emphasis in this book on ways phenomena become projected, inverted, and reduplicated. My argument is that one of the characteristics of American idealist philosophy over the past two hundred years has been a tendency creatively to forget its own epistemological status, to imagine itself—naturally, as it were—as the center of its own world, rather than seeing itself positioned in an oblique or belated relation to larger global networks. Whereas Rorty wants to eliminate this epistemological mirror to naturalize the standing of his own specifically "American" philosophy, this book has attempted to dislocate such assumptions precisely by reilluminating the cracked, crazy mirrors within whose purview all American discourse finds itself framed. Again, the parallel with Heidegger is striking here: Adorno, who generally despised Heidegger's work, said the Nazi sympathizer shrouded his transcendental leanings in a language of authenticity, an "absolutized immanence" authorized by a "posture of consciousness," and the same thing might be said of Heidegger's admirer, Rorty.[89] In both cases, the intense dedication to a particular national community derives ultimately not only from the value placed on the experiential, but also from endowing the idea of existential consciousness with something like the status of metaphysical identity. This does not, of course, make Rorty a fascist any more than Matthiessen, but it does raise some troublesome questions about the grounding of American national narratives on phenomenological versions of "nature."

It is not only the United States that is made different by the deployment of these curved mirrors. One of the points made by Baudrillard is that because of America's "mythical power throughout the world," other geographical areas such as Europe can no longer be understood simply on their own integral terms; to understand Europe, according to Baudrillard, one needs to start with America.[90] In this sense, American studies should be seen as involving not just domestic agendas, but also those points of intersection and crossover where the United States interfaces with the wider world. In her book *Virtualities*, Margaret Morse points out that the term "cybernetics" derives from the Greek *cyber*, meaning "steersman," and therefore, by extension, feedback; following this logic, it is, I think, possible to see how a virtual American studies categorized in terms of feedback systems and loops of communication has more contemporary relevance than the old model of a sacred land, a model that has more in common with the romantic teleologies of the nineteenth century.[91] The point here, simply enough, is that the natural and the national are both fluctuating, highly contested categories that have traditionally attempted to suppress their own arbitrary status by equating themselves with each other. It is this kind of romantic epistemology that has bequeathed to us the notion of "nature's nation," as we read the phrase today, whereby nature is the primary and nation the secondary term, so that nature, as it were, bestows its favors on the nation. One of the purposes of a virtual American studies would be to invert this syntax, to avoid reproducing such tautologies by foregrounding instead the construction of a subject predicated on division and disjunction. Rather than that quest for mythic integrity and interdisciplinary coherence that drove American studies scholarship during its heyday of the 1950s and 1960s, a virtual American studies should be organized around a more general idiom of dislocation and estrangement, serving to interrogate not only the boundaries of the nation-state, but also the particular values associated explicitly or implicitly with it. Virtual American studies would accordingly be predicated on the reversed grammar of nation's nature, where a native country projects its own images of the natural to accommodate particular ideological designs.

To talk of American studies in postnational terms, then, may be premature, for the nation has not yet ceased to be meaningful as a category of affiliation and analysis. To talk of the subject in transnational terms, however, is to acknowledge the necessity for Americanists both inside and outside the United States to rearticulate their field dialogically and comparatively. In *Underworld*, DeLillo's narrator talks about the pertinence of "seeing things twice," of breaking down phenomenological integrity to conscript objects and events into a cycle of connections; not coincidentally, the novel's final image for this process is the Internet, where simulation becomes all-encompassing and the personal god is metamorphosed into a personal computer.[92] As Žižek observed in *The Plague of Fantasies*, one of the most disconcerting facets of cyberspace is the way it "merely radicalizes the gap constitutive of the symbolic order." Moreover, as Žižek went on to suggest, the symbolic order itself can be equated with a virtual reality: "(symbolic) reality always—already was 'virtual,' that is to say: every access to (social) reality has to be supported by an implicit phantasmic hypertext."[93] Following this logic, the potential of cyberpastoral could be seen as implicit within all pastoral forms. Cyberpastoral, that is to say, opens up the crevices between nature and nation, indicating the inherently unstable relationship that always already exists between geographic location and symbolic meaning. Such a definition of cyberpastoral might be seen as continuous in significant ways with the more traditional conception of American pastoral outlined by Leo Marx, who, as we saw in the first chapter, has consistently emphasized its artificial and generic style, its emphasis on complex forms of withdrawal from society rather than any "literal representation of the nonhuman world."[94] In this sense, cyberpastoral might be said to highlight those aspects of displacement and exchange inherent in more traditional pastoral modes.

This argument involves neither the utopian claims for virtual reality as a potential state of unadulterated freedom, as advanced by Sadie Plant and others, nor the other side of that coin, which is the dystopian vision of it as perpetual incarceration, a digital space complicit with the American corporate world as well as with the techniques of military surveillance from which it originated.[95] The focus here is on those points where cyberpastoral meets pastoral, where transnationalism intersects with a spectral nationalism, and with the paradoxes that are introduced into each system as a consequence of these reversed perspectives. The many challenges to American exceptionalism on theoretical grounds since the 1960s have not been able to erase altogether residual attachments to the national symbolic as a source of cultural significance, whether through romantic ecologies of the Wordsworthian type or through forms of resistance to the impact of globalization. The bumper sticker "Think Global, Act Local"—which might be described as a folksy version of Emerson's famous image of the transparent eyeball in the way it attempts unproblematically to align immediate object with transcendent idea—simply passes over ways in which national identity continues to be a third point in a triangulation process that mediates and complicates relations between the particular and the universal. There have been many examples recently of the way transnational capitalism, in Terry Eagleton's words, "fosters by way of reaction cultures of defensive solidarity": the anti-European movement in Britain, the increasing visibility of patriotic groups and nativist allegiances in the United States, and indeed the revival of nationalist parties in many countries throughout the world.[96] Nor do such animosities between the local and the global manifest themselves merely in right-wing or fundamentalist reactions, as we see from the establishment of such organizations as the Transnational Resource and Action Center, a radical group based in San Francisco that actively campaigns against the partnership between transnational corporations and the United Nations and that seeks to defend "universal labor, environmental and human rights in this age of globalization."[97] In the days after the attacks on New York City and Washington, D.C., in September 2001, there was a more general desire in the United States to relapse nostalgically into simpler forms of patriotism, with music television stations featuring sentimental, down-home videos by John Cougar Mellencamp and the like, as if to exemplify Eagleton's thesis that it is the potential erasure of the functional framework underpinning national identity that engenders, by way of reaction, an increasingly anxious attachment to its popular symbolic forms. These attacks themselves represented a particularly bleak example of American cultural apparatus being appropriated and turned back against itself, with the rapid global circulation of people, technology, and capital creating an inherently unstable situation where, unlike in the cold war era, a national enemy cannot be positioned as geographically remote or intrinsically foreign.

The implications of these issues are too far-reaching for discussion here, but the challenge to studies of national culture is simply this: that it no longer makes sense to circumscribe geographic or academic areas in the ways they were defined a generation ago. Area studies in the twenty-first century should involve not just the production of local and experiential perspectives, but an interrogation of boundaries between the local and the global, the national and the transnational, to analyze how these tensions and frictions are being played out in many different parts of society. If the study of American culture is to resituate itself in that contentious domain where the national intersects with the transnational, its interventions will be at their most pointed where the sources of resistance are at their most stubborn.

# NOTES

## 1
## Virtual Subjects: Transnational Fictions
## and the Transatlantic Imaginary

1  *Webster's Ninth New Collegiate Dictionary* (Springfield, MA: Merriam-Webster, 1989), 1317. Webster dates "virtual focus" from 1704, "virtual image" from 1859.

2  Henry James, *The American Scene* (1907), ed. Leon Edel (Bloomington: Indiana UP, 1968), 34.

3  Nina Baym, *Novels, Readers, and Reviewers: Responses to Fiction in Antebellum America* (Ithaca, NY: Cornell UP, 1984), 242.

4  Ann Douglas, *Terrible Honesty: Mongrel Manhattan in the 1920s* (New York: Farrar, Straus and Giroux, 1995), 3.

5  Barbara Eckstein, "Ethnicity Matters," *American Literary History* 7 (1995): 579.

6  Philip Fisher, "Democratic Social Space: Whitman, Melville, and the Promise of American Transparency," *Representations* 24 (1988): 60–101, and *Still the New World: American Literature in a Culture of Creative Destruction* (Cambridge, MA: Harvard UP, 1999), 33–55; Rob Kroes, *If You've Seen One, You've Seen the Mall: Europeans and American Mass Culture* (Urbana: U of Illinois P, 1996), 107.

7  D. H. Lawrence, *Studies in Classic American Literature* (1923, rpt. Harmondsworth, England: Penguin, 1971), 7.

8  Malcolm Bradbury, *The Modern American Novel* (Oxford: Oxford UP, 1983), 157.

9  David Damrosch, "Literary Study in an Elliptical Age," in *Comparative Literature in the Age of Multiculturalism*, ed. Charles Bernheimer (Baltimore: Johns Hopkins UP, 1995), 128–30.

10 Regenia Gagnier, " 'The Disturbances Overseas': A Comparative Report on the Future of English Studies," *Victorian Literature and Culture* 27 (1999): 471.

11   Paul Jay, "Beyond Discipline? Globalization and the Future of English," *PMLA* 116 (2001): 42.

12   Zygmunt Bauman, "Strangers: The Social Construction of Universality and Particularity," *Telos* 78 (1988–1989): 19.

13   For one classic interpretation of American literature from this position, see Hugh Kenner, *A Homemade World: The American Modernist Writers* (New York: Knopf, 1975).

14   Guenter H. Lenz, "'Ethnographies': American Culture Studies and Postmodern Anthropology," *Prospects* 16 (1991): 22.

15   Arjun Appadurai, *Modernity at Large: Cultural Dimensions of Globalization* (Minneapolis: U of Minnesota P, 1996), 17, 46.

16   For a discussion of "myth and symbol" criticism in American studies, see Alan Trachtenberg, "Myth and Symbol," *Massachusetts Review* 25 (1984): 667–73, and Donald E. Pease, "New Americanists: Revisionist Interventions into the Canon," *boundary 2* 17, no. 1 (spring 1990): 1–37.

17   Bill Readings, *The University in Ruins* (Cambridge, MA: Harvard UP, 1996), 12.

18   J. Hector St. John de Crèvecoeur, *Letters from an American Farmer and Sketches of Eighteenth-Century America*, ed. Albert E. Stone (New York: Viking Penguin, 1981), 70; Ernest Samuels, ed., *The Education of Henry Adams* (Boston: Houghton Mifflin, 1973), 343.

19   Northrop Frye, "The Archetypes of Literature" (1951), in *Criticism: Major Statements*, 3d ed., ed. Charles Kaplan and William Anderson (New York: St. Martin's Press, 1991), 504.

20   Raymond Williams, "Base and Superstructure in Marxist Cultural Theory," *New Left Review* 82 (Nov.–Dec. 1973): 10. For Jameson's view of the tensions between national and international situations, see "The State of the Subject (III)," *Critical Quarterly* 29, no. 4 (1987): 24–25.

21   Jacques Derrida, *Specters of Marx: The State of the Debt, the Work of Mourning, and the New International* (1993), trans. Peggy Kamuf (New York: Routledge, 1994), 169, 91.

22   Samuels, *The Education of Henry Adams*, 380–81.

23   Ernest Renan, "What Is a Nation?" in *Becoming National: A Reader*, ed. Geoff Eley and Ronald Grigor Suny (New York: Oxford UP, 1996), 52.

24   E. J. Hobsbawm, *Nations and Nationalism since 1780: Programme, Myth, Reality* (Cambridge, England: Cambridge UP, 1990), 182.

25   Derrida, *Specters of Marx*, 79.

26   Immanuel Wallerstein, "The National and the Universal: Can There Be Such a Thing as World Culture?" in *Culture, Globalization, and the World-System: Contemporary Conditions for the Representation of Identity* (Basingstoke, England: Macmillan/State University of New York at Binghamton, 1991), 104.

27   Appadurai, *Modernity at Large*, 3.

28   Paul Smith, *Millennial Dreams: Contemporary Culture and Capital in the North* (London: Verso, 1997), 10.

29  Fredric Jameson, "Notes on Globalization as a Philosophical Issue," in *The Cultures of Globalization,* ed. Fredric Jameson and Masao Miyoshi (Durham, NC: Duke UP, 1998), 72, 75.

30  Masao Miyoshi, "A Borderless World? From Colonialism to Transnationalism and the Decline of the Nation-State," *Critical Inquiry* 10 (1993): 744, 731–32, 747.

31  For the classic statement of how national formations were constructed in the modern era, see Benedict Anderson, *Imagined Communities: Reflections on the Origin and Spread of Nationalism* (London: Verso, 1983).

32  William James, *Writings 1902–1910* (New York: Library of America, 1987), 1179, 1168, 1159. On James's debt to Emerson, see Jonathan Levin, *The Poetics of Transition: Emerson, Pragmatism, and American Literary Modernism* (Durham, NC: Duke UP, 1999), 45–56.

33  Mark C. Taylor, *About Religion: Economies of Faith in Virtual Culture* (Chicago: U of Chicago P, 1999), 168–201.

34  David M. Potter, *People of Plenty: Economic Abundance and the American Character* (Chicago: U of Chicago P, 1954).

35  Leo Marx, "Pastoralism in America," in *Ideology and Classic American Literature,* ed. Sacvan Bercovitch and Myra Jehlen (Cambridge, England: Cambridge UP, 1986), 56; Henry David Thoreau, *Walden* (1854), ed. J. Lyndon Shanley (Princeton, NJ: Princeton UP, 1971), 210–22.

36  William James, *The Varieties of Religious Experience: A Study in Human Nature* (New York: Longmans, Green and Co., 1902), 189, 257, 206, 217.

37  R. W. B. Lewis, *The American Adam: Innocence, Tragedy and Tradition in the Nineteenth Century* (Chicago: U of Chicago P, 1955), 9, 5–6; Lawrence Buell, *The Environmental Imagination: Thoreau, Nature Writing, and the Formation of American Culture* (Cambridge, MA: Harvard UP, 1995), 143–79.

38  Lewis, *The American Adam,* 1, 9. On the Puritan "evangelizing" strain in Buell's work, see Leo Marx, "The Full Thoreau," *New York Review of Books,* 15 July 1999, 44–48.

39  Thoreau, *Walden,* 49.

40  Linda Hutcheon, *A Theory of Parody: The Teachings of Twentieth-Century Art Forms* (New York: Methuen, 1985), 61.

41  Appadurai, *Modernity at Large,* 16.

42  Emily Apter, *Continental Drift: From National Characters to Virtual Subjects* (Chicago: U of Chicago P, 1999), vii, 18–19, 20.

43  Ibid., 106.

44  Werner Sollors, "Introduction: After the Culture Wars; or, From 'English Only' to 'English Plus,'" in *Multilingual America: Transnationalism, Ethnicity, and the Languages of American Literature* (New York: New York UP / Longfellow Institute, 1998), 3, 7; Rob Wilson, "Goodbye Paradise: Global/Localism in the American Pacific," in *Global/Local: Cultural Production and the Transnational Imaginary,* ed. Rob Wilson and Wimal Dissanayake (Durham, NC: Duke UP, 1996), 313.

45   See, for instance, Jay, "Beyond Discipline?" 42–43.

46   *The Life and Writings of Frederick Douglass*, vol. 2, ed. Philip S. Foner (New York: International Publishers, 1950), 2:203.

47   See, for instance, Edward Watts, *Writing and Postcolonialism in the Early Republic* (Charlottesville: UP of Virginia, 1998); Lawrence Buell, "American Literary Emergence as a Postcolonial Phenomenon," *American Literary History* 4 (1992): 411–42; Paul Giles, *Transatlantic Insurrections: British Culture and the Formation of American Literature, 1730–1860* (Philadelphia: U of Pennsylvania P, 2001).

48   Julia Kristeva, *Nations without Nationalism*, trans. Leon S. Roudiez (New York: Columbia UP, 1993), 33, 50, 16.

49   Mitsuhiro Yoshimoto, "Real Virtuality," in Wilson and Dissanayake, *Global/Local*, 111.

50   See Laura Kipnis, *Bound and Gagged: Pornography and the Politics of Fantasy in America* (New York: Grove Press, 1996), 3–63, and Chapter 6 below.

51   Robert Markley, "Boundaries: Mathematics, Alienation, and the Metaphysics of Cyberspace," in *Virtual Realities and Their Discontents*, ed. Robert Markley (Baltimore: Johns Hopkins UP, 1996), 67, and "Introduction: History, Theory, and Virtual Reality," in *Virtual Realities and Their Discontents*, 2. For Sadie Plant's optimistic view of how global telecommunications are "undermining both the pale male world and the patriarchal structures of the south and east, bringing unprecedented economic power to women writers and multiplying the possibilities of communication, learning, and access to information," see her essay "On the Matrix: Cyberfeminist Simulations," in *Cultures of Internet: Virtual Space, Real Histories, Living Bodies*, ed. Rob Shields (London: Sage, 1996), 181.

52   Donald Morton, "Birth of the Cyberqueer," *PMLA* 110 (1995): 375.

53   Markley, "Boundaries: Mathematics, Alienation, and the Metaphysics of Cyberspace," 70, 73.

54   Samuel Taylor Coleridge, *Biographia Literaria* (1817), in *The Portable Coleridge*, ed. I. A. Richards (New York: Viking, 1950), 518; Rob Shields, "Introduction: Virtual Spaces, Real Histories, and Living Bodies," in *Cultures of Internet*, 7.

55   N. Katherine Hayles, *How We Became Posthuman: Virtual Bodies in Cybernetics, Literature, and Informatics* (Chicago: U of Chicago P, 1999), 7.

56   Ibid., 10.

57   See, for instance, Jeffrey Louis Decker, "Dis-Assembling the Machine in the Garden: Antihumanism and the Critique of American Studies," *New Literary History* 23 (1992): 281–306.

58   Donna J. Haraway, *Modest_Witness@Second.Millennium.FemaleMan©Meets_Oncomouse™: Feminism and Technoscience* (New York: Routledge, 1997), 268–70.

59   McKenzie Wark, *Virtual Geography: Living with Global Media Events* (Bloomington: Indiana UP, 1994), 43, 28.

60   Margaret Morse, *Virtualities: Television, Media Art, and Cyberculture* (Bloomington: Indiana UP, 1998), 185, 25.

61 Appadurai, *Modernity at Large*, 19, 158–59, 172.

62 John Carlos Rowe et al., introduction to *Post-Nationalist American Studies*, ed. John Carlos Rowe (Berkeley: U of California P, 2000), 1. For an analysis of how "the temporal dimension of the postnational sits in uneasy tension with a critical dimension that would activate a process of disengagement from the whole nationalist syndrome," see Donald Pease, "The Politics of Postnational American Studies," *European Journal of American Culture* 20, no. 2 (2001): 87.

2

*Narrative Reversals and Power Exchanges:
Frederick Douglass and British Culture*

1 William L. Andrews, *To Tell a Free Story: The First Century of Afro-American Autobiography, 1760–1865* (Urbana: U of Illinois P, 1986), 103. On "the link between language and power," see also Valerie Smith, *Self-Discovery and Authority in Afro-American Narrative* (Cambridge, MA: Harvard UP, 1987), 4.

2 Joseph Fichtelberg, *The Complex Image: Faith and Method in American Autobiography* (Philadelphia: U of Pennsylvania P, 1989), 148, 116–17.

3 Frances Smith Foster, *Witnessing Slavery: The Development of Ante-bellum Slave Narratives* (Westport, CT: Greenwood Press, 1979), 15; Gerald Fulkerson, "Exile as Emergence: Frederick Douglass in Great Britain, 1845–1847," *Quarterly Journal of Speech* 60 (Feb. 1974): 73. For the view that the 1830s and early 1840s were the high point of transatlantic abolitionism, which had passed its peak by the time Douglass arrived in Britain in 1845, see David Turley, *The Culture of English Antislavery, 1780–1860* (London: Routledge, 1991), 197.

4 Frederick Douglass, "West India Emancipation," in *The Civil War, 1861–1865*, vol. 3 of *The Life and Writings of Frederick Douglass*, ed. Philip S. Foner (New York: International Publishers, 1952), 134–35.

5 Frederick Douglass, "West India Emancipation," speech delivered 4 August 1857, in *Pre-Civil War Decade, 1850–1860*, vol. 2 of *The Life and Writings of Frederick Douglass*, ed. Philip S. Foner (New York: International Publishers, 1950), 428. Garrison's interest in the British movement for emancipation in the West Indies dates to the late 1820s, when he was editor of *The Genius of Universal Emancipation*. On the quarrel over women's role in the antislavery movement, see Howard Temperley, *British Antislavery, 1833–1870* (London: Longman, 1972), 89–90.

6 Henry Louis Gates Jr., introduction to *The Slave's Narrative*, ed. Charles T. Davis and Henry Louis Gates Jr. (New York: Oxford UP, 1985), xvi.

7 Charles Dickens, *American Notes* (1842), ed. John S. Whitley and Arnold Goldman (Harmondsworth, England: Penguin, 1972), 271.

8 Frederick Douglass, "Remarks at Soiree in Honor of Messrs. Douglass and Buffum, Paisley, Scotland, March 1846," in *Supplementary Volume, 1844–1860*, vol. 5 of *The Life*

and Writings of Frederick Douglass, ed. Philip S. Foner (New York: International Publishers, 1975), 35–36.

9   Philip S. Foner, introduction to Early Years, 1817–1849, vol. 1 of The Life and Writings of Frederick Douglass (New York: International Publishers, 1950), 72.

10  William S. McFeely, Frederick Douglass (New York: Norton, 1991), 139; Richard Bradbury, "Frederick Douglass and the Chartists," in Liberating Sojourn: Frederick Douglass and Transatlantic Reform, ed. Alan J. Rice and Martin Crawford (Athens: U of Georgia P, 1999), 169–86.

11  Waldo E. Martin Jr., The Mind of Frederick Douglass (Chapel Hill: U of North Carolina P, 1984), 41. On Griffiths, see John R. McKivigan, "The Frederick Douglass–Gerrit Smith Friendship and Political Abolitionism in the 1850s," in Frederick Douglass: New Literary and Historical Essays, ed. Eric J. Sundquist (Cambridge, England: Cambridge UP, 1990), 208.

12  Julia Griffiths, "Letters from the Old World," Douglass' Monthly, July 1859, 107.

13  Julia Griffiths, "Letters from the Old World," Douglass' Monthly, Jan. 1863, 772.

14  Frederick Douglass, "Change of Opinion Announced," in Life and Writings, 2:155–56.

15  Frederick Douglass, "The Constitution and Slavery," in Life and Writings, 1:361–67.

16  Eric J. Sundquist, To Wake the Nations: Race in the Making of American Literature (Cambridge, MA: Harvard UP, 1993), 89.

17  Frederick Douglass, Narrative of the Life of Frederick Douglass, in Autobiographies (New York: Library of America, 1994), 8, 58–59; subsequent page references to the 1845 Narrative are to this edition and are cited parenthetically in the text as N.

18  Russ Castronovo, Fathering the Nation: American Genealogies of Slavery and Freedom (Berkeley: U of California P, 1995), 199–200.

19  Gregory S. Jay, "American Literature and New Historicism: The Example of Frederick Douglass," boundary 2 17 (spring 1990): 226.

20  Robert B. Stepto, From Behind the Veil: A Study of Afro-American Narrative (Urbana: U of Illinois P, 1979), 21.

21  Cynthia S. Hamilton, "Frederick Douglass and the Gender Politics of Reform," in Rice and Crawford, Liberating Sojourn, 77; Fulkerson, "Exile as Emergence," 72.

22  Theodore Weld, American Slavery As It Is: Testimony of a Thousand Witnesses (New York: American Anti-Slavery Society, 1839), 115; see also Robert S. Levine, Martin Delany, Frederick Douglass, and the Politics of Representative Identity (Chapel Hill: U of North Carolina P, 1997), 102.

23  Dickens, American Notes, 283.

24  David Van Leer, "Reading Slavery: The Anxiety of Ethnicity in Douglass's Narrative," in Sundquist, Frederick Douglass: New Literary and Historical Essays, 132; Deborah E. McDowell, "In the First Place: Frederick Douglass and the Afro-American Narrative Tradition," in Critical Essays on Frederick Douglass, ed. William L. Andrews (Boston: Hall, 1991), 201–3.

25  On the opposition between sentimentality and theatricality, see Karen Halttunen,

*Confidence Men and Painted Women: A Study of Middle-Class Culture in America, 1830–1870* (New Haven: Yale UP, 1982), 153–90.

26  Audrey A. Fisch, " 'Negrophilism' and British Nationalism: The Spectacle of the Black American Abolitionist," *Victorian Review* 19 (winter 1993): 33, 24. On the general links between sex and violence in nineteenth-century popular culture, see David S. Reynolds, *Beneath the American Renaissance: The Subversive Imagination in the Age of Emerson and Melville* (New York: Knopf, 1988), 211–24; and Ronald Pearsall, *The Worm in the Bud: The World of Victorian Sexuality* (London: Weidenfeld and Nicolson, 1969), 364–92.

27  Slavoj Žižek, *The Plague of Fantasies* (London: Verso, 1997), 82, 92–93, 73.

28  Frederick Douglass, *My Bondage and My Freedom* (1855), in *Autobiographies*, 366, 367; further references are to this edition and are cited parenthetically in the text as *BF*.

29  See McFeely, *Frederick Douglass*, 182. Typically, Griffiths induced Douglass in 1852 to write his only work of pure fiction, "The Heroic Slave," as part of *Autographs for Freedom*, an anthology designed to raise money for the antislavery cause. Based on the life of Madison Washington, "The Heroic Slave" appropriately represents the African American protagonist as beholden to British political liberty on two separate occasions. After his successful flight to Canada in 1840, the narrative persona of Washington writes: "I nestle in the mane of the British lion, protected by his mighty paw from the talons and beak of the American eagle"; after the 1841 rebellion on board the *Creole*, the ship is guided by Washington into the "British port" of Nassau, in the Bahama Islands, where the American slaves are set free. Ronald Takaki, *Violence in the Black Imagination: Essays and Documents*, rev. ed. (New York: Oxford UP, 1993), 56, 73.

30  Sundquist, *To Wake the Nations*, 121–22.

31  John Carlos Rowe, "Between Politics and Poetics: Frederick Douglass and Postmodernity," in *Reconstructing American Literary and Historical Studies*, ed. Günter H. Lenz, Hartmut Keil, and Sabine Bröck-Sallah (Frankfurt am Main: CampusVerlag, 1990), 198–99.

32  Paul Gilroy, *The Black Atlantic: Modernity and Double Consciousness* (London: Verso, 1993), 59.

33  Herman Melville, *Moby-Dick, or The Whale*, ed. Harrison Hayford, Hershel Parker, and G. Thomas Tanselle (Evanston, IL: Northwestern UP/Newberry Library, 1988), 6.

34  Carla L. Peterson, "Capitalism, Black (Under)development, and the Production of the African-American Novel in the 1850s," *American Literary History* 4 (1992): 562, 579.

35  William Wells Brown, *Clotel; or, The President's Daughter*, ed. William Edward Farrison (New York: University Books/Carol, 1969), 188.

36  Levine, *Martin Delany, Frederick Douglass*, 4–6.

37  Frederick Douglass, "The Key to *Uncle Tom's Cabin*," in *Life and Writings*, 2:241.

38  Frederick Douglass, "To My American Readers and Friends," in *Life and Writings*, 2:463.

39  Frederick Douglass, "The Meaning of July Fourth for the Negro," speech delivered

5 July 1852, in *Life and Writings*, 2:203. (An extract from this speech was published as an appendix to *My Bondage and My Freedom* under the title "What to the Slave Is the Fourth of July?")

40  Kwame Anthony Appiah, "Cosmopolitan Patriots," *Critical Inquiry* 23 (1997): 617–39.

41  Douglass to Garrison, 29 September 1845, in *Life and Writings*, 1:121.

42  Douglass to Garrison, 26 February 1846, in *Life and Writings*, 1:141.

43  Douglass, "Farewell Speech to the British People," in *Life and Writings*, 1:212.

44  Dickens, *American Notes*, 284; Thomas Carlyle, "Chartism," in *Critical and Miscellaneous Essays*, 5 vols. (1839; rpt. London: Chapman and Hall, 1899), 4:137, 164, 179.

45  Thomas Carlyle, "Occasional Discourse on the Nigger Question," in *Critical and Miscellaneous Essays*, 4:353, 364.

46  Thomas Carlyle, "Shooting Niagara: And After?" in *Critical and Miscellaneous Essays*, 5:5–7.

47  Ibid., 5:21.

48  Thomas Carlyle, "Signs of the Times," in *Critical and Miscellaneous Essays*, 1:82.

49  Benjamin Disraeli, *Sybil, or The Two Nations*, ed. Thom Braun (Harmondsworth, England: Penguin, 1980), 214, 317.

50  Elizabeth Gaskell, *North and South*, ed. Dorothy Collin (Harmondsworth, England: Penguin, 1970), 42, 195, 291, 512, 395.

51  The "condition of England" question was also aired widely in the United States. See Marcus Cunliffe, *Chattel Slavery and Wage Slavery: The Anglo-American Context, 1830–1860* (Athens: U of Georgia P, 1979), 14–15.

52  Gaskell, *North and South*, 515.

53  On Gaskell and Norton, see A. B. Hopkins, *Elizabeth Gaskell: Her Life and Work* (London: John Lehmann, 1952), 362–63. On the response of Cobden and Bright to the American Civil War, see Donald Read, *Cobden and Bright: A Victorian Political Partnership* (London: Edward Arnold, 1967), 218–29. On the role of the *Times*, see Ephraim Douglas Adams, *Great Britain and the American Civil War* (London: Longmans, 1925), 2:293–99.

54  Harriet Jacobs, *Incidents in the Life of a Slave Girl* (1861), introduction by Valerie Smith (New York: Oxford UP, 1988), 277.

55  Catherine Gallagher, *The Industrial Reformation of English Fiction: Social Discourse and Narrative Form, 1832–1867* (Chicago: U of Chicago P, 1985), 4–12.

56  Theodore W. Allen, *The Invention of the White Race. Volume 1: Racial Oppression and Social Control* (London: Verso, 1994), 178.

57  Douglass to Garrison, May 23, 1846, in *Life and Writings*, 1:167.

58  McFeely, *Frederick Douglass*, 280; Philip S. Foner, *British Labor and the American Civil War* (New York: Holmes and Meier, 1981), 60.

59  "The Missing Link," *Punch*, 18 March 1862, 165; quoted in L. Perry Curtis Jr., *Apes and Angels: The Irishman in Victorian Caricature*, rev. ed. (Washington, DC: Smithsonian

Institution Press, 1997), 100. On the contribution of anthropology to racist thinking at this time, see Christine Bolt, *Victorian Attitudes to Race* (London: Routledge and Kegan Paul, 1971), 93.

60  Allen, *The Invention of the White Race*, 1:28, 159.

61  Frederick Douglass, "The Douglass Institute," in *Reconstruction and After*, vol. 4 of *The Life and Writings of Frederick Douglass*, ed. Philip S. Foner (New York: International Publishers, 1955), 179.

62  Frederick Douglass, "The Position of the British Government toward Liberty," in *Life and Writings*, 4:266–68.

63  Frederick Douglass, "Speeches at Anti-Colonization Mass Meeting of Colored Citizens of City of New York, April 23, 1849," in *Life and Writings*, 5:123.

64  Frederick Douglass, "The Present Condition and Future Prospects of the Negro People," in *Life and Writings*, 2:249.

65  Frederick Douglass, "Colored Americans, and Aliens—T. F. Meagher," in *Life and Writings*, 5:365.

66  Stefan Collini, *Public Moralists: Political Thought and Intellectual Life in Britain, 1850– 1930* (Oxford: Clarendon Press, 1991), 187. This emphasis on manly valor may also have contributed to Douglass's choice of his surname, taken from the Scottish warrior in Walter Scott's poem "The Lady of the Lake," on the prompting of Nathaniel Johnson in 1846. See George Shepperson, "Frederick Douglass and Scotland," *Journal of Negro History* 38 (July 1953): 307–21.

67  Frederick Douglass, *Life and Times of Frederick Douglass, Written by Himself* (1893), in *Autobiographies*, 1017. Further references are to this edition and are cited parenthetically in the text as *LT.*

68  Richard Hardack, "The Slavery of Romanism: The Casting Out of the Irish in the Work of Frederick Douglass," in Rice and Crawford, *Liberating Sojourn*, 124.

69  Frederick Douglass, "The Douglasses Abroad," in *Life and Writings*, 4:122–23.

70  Hardack, "The Slavery of Romanism," 118, 125.

71  Priscilla Wald, *Constituting Americans: Cultural Anxiety and Narrative Form* (Durham, NC: Duke UP, 1995), 20.

72  Fichtelberg, *The Complex Image*, 154. For a view of Douglass's "ideology" as "thoroughly inconsistent, usually opportunistic, and always self-serving," see Wilson J. Moses, "Where Honor Is Due: Frederick Douglass as Representative Black Man," *Prospects* 17 (1992): 179.

73  Hardack, "The Slavery of Romanism," 134, 127.

74  Gillian Beer, *Darwin's Plots: Evolutionary Narrative in Darwin, George Eliot and Nineteenth-Century Fiction* (London: Routledge and Kegan Paul, 1983), 50.

75  Eric J. Sundquist, "Introduction: The Country of the Blue," in *American Realism: New Essays*, ed. Eric J. Sundquist (Baltimore: Johns Hopkins UP, 1982), 7.

76  Peter F. Walker, *Moral Choices: Memory, Desire, and Imagination in Nineteenth-Century American Abolition* (Baton Rouge: Louisiana State UP, 1978), 247; George M. Fred-

rickson, *The Black Image in the White Mind: The Debate on Afro-American Character and Identity, 1817–1914* (1971; rpt. Hanover, NH: UP of New England; Wesleyan UP, 1987), 108. For Emerson's association of hybridity with degeneration, see H. L. Malchow, *Gothic Images of Race in Nineteenth-Century Britain* (Stanford: Stanford UP, 1996), 184.

77  Walker, *Moral Choices*, 261. For another view of how the psychological and political ambivalence of Douglass was rooted "in his very mulattoness—his racial ties to both white and black," see Takaki, *Violence in the Black Imagination*, 18.

78  On the association of nineteenth-century Irish Americans with both black and white cultures, see Noel Ignatiev, *How the Irish Became White* (New York: Routledge, 1995).

79  Terry Eagleton, *Heathcliff and the Great Hunger: Studies in Irish Culture* (London: Verso, 1995), 125, 132, 9.

80  Russel B. Nye, *William Lloyd Garrison and the Humanitarian Reformers* (Boston: Little, Brown, 1955), 96–97.

81  For a discussion of this episode, see Wilson J. Moses, "Dark Forests and Barbarian Vigor: Paradox, Conflict, and Africanity in Black Writing before 1914," *American Literary History* 1 (1989): 639.

## 3
## *"Bewildering Intertanglement":*
## *Melville's Engagement with British Tradition*

1  Myra Jehlen, introduction to *Herman Melville: A Collection of Critical Essays*, ed. Myra Jehlen (Englewood Cliffs, NJ: Prentice-Hall, 1994), 3.

2  Hershel Parker, "Historical Note," in *Moby-Dick; or, The Whale*, by Herman Melville, ed. Harrison Hayford et al. (Evanston, IL: Northwestern UP, 1988), 732. Subsequent page references to this edition appear in the text.

3  Herman Melville, *Correspondence*, ed. Lynn Horth (Evanston, IL: Northwestern UP, 1993), 724; Parker, "Historical Note," 739.

4  Melville, *Correspondence*, 764.

5  For Masefield's response, see Hershel Parker and Harrison Hayford, eds., Moby-Dick as Doubloon: Essays and Extracts (1851–1970) (New York: Norton, 1970), 124. Barrie recommends *Typee* and *Omoo* in a letter to the Dutch novelist Maarten Maartens on 20 November 1893. See *Letters of J. M. Barrie*, ed. Viola Meynell (London: Peter Davies, 1942), 28.

6  D. H. Lawrence, *Studies in Classic American Literature* (1923; rpt. Harmondsworth, England: Penguin, 1971), 139, 154.

7  Quoted in Parker and Hayford, Moby-Dick as Doubloon, 159–60.

8  E. M. Forster, *Aspects of the Novel*, ed. Oliver Stallybrass (Harmondsworth, England: Penguin, 1962), 130, 126, 171.

9  W. H. Auden, *The Enchafèd Flood; or, The Romantic Iconography of the Sea* (London: Faber, 1951), 67, 122.

10  Quoted in Parker and Hayford, Moby-Dick *as Doubloon*, 136.

11  Herman Melville, "Hawthorne and His Mosses," in *The Piazza Tales and Other Prose Pieces, 1839–1860*, ed. Harrison Hayford et al. (Evanston, IL: Northwestern UP, 1987), 247–48.

12  Quoted in Watson G. Branch, ed., *Melville: The Critical Heritage* (London: Routledge and Kegan Paul, 1987), 228.

13  Michael Paul Rogin, *Subversive Genealogy: The Politics and Art of Herman Melville* (New York: Knopf, 1983), 48–59.

14  Robert W. Johannsen, introduction to *Manifest Destiny and Empire: American Antebellum Expansionism*, ed. Sam W. Haynes and Christopher Morris (College Station: U of Texas at Arlington/Texas A&M UP, 1997), 5.

15  Herman Melville, *Typee: A Peep at Polynesian Life*, ed. Harrison Hayford, Hershel Parker, and G. Thomas Tanselle (Evanston, IL: Northwestern UP, 1968), 258.

16  Leon Howard, "Historical Note," in Melville, *Typee*, 290; Hershel Parker, *Herman Melville: A Biography. Vol. 1, 1819–1851* (Baltimore: Johns Hopkins UP, 1996), 443.

17  Edward L. Widmer, *Young America: The Flowering of Democracy in New York City* (New York: Oxford UP, 1999), 195–96.

18  Lawrance Roger Thompson, *Melville's Quarrel with God* (Princeton, NJ: Princeton UP, 1952). On this topic, see William V. Spanos, *The Errant Art of* Moby-Dick: *The Canon, the Cold War, and the Struggle for American Studies* (Durham, NC: Duke UP, 1995).

19  C. L. R. James, *Mariners, Renegades and Castaways: The Story of Herman Melville and the World We Live In*, rev. ed. (London: Allison and Busby, 1985), 121, 35.

20  C. L. R. James, *American Civilization*, ed. Anna Grimshaw and Keith Hart (Cambridge, MA: Blackwell, 1993), 13.

21  "Literary Executor's Afterword," in James, *American Civilization*, 334.

22  James, *Mariners, Renegades and Castaways*, 76.

23  James, *American Civilization*, 132.

24  Lawrence Buell, "Melville and the Question of American Decolonization," *American Literature* 64 (1992): 233.

25  David M. Potter, *The Impending Crisis, 1848–1861*, ed. Don E. Fehrenbacher (New York: Harper and Row, 1976), 250.

26  Herman Melville, *Journal of a Visit to London and the Continent, 1849–1850*, ed. Elanor Melville Metcalf (London: Cohen and West, 1949), 68.

27  Nathaniel Hawthorne, *The English Notebooks*, ed. Randall Stewart (New York: Modern Language Association of America, 1941), 433.

28  Herman Melville, *Journal of a Visit to Europe and the Levant*, ed. Howard C. Horsford (Princeton, NJ: Princeton UP, 1955), 56, 209, 267.

29  Ross Posnock, "The Politics of Nonidentity: A Genealogy," *boundary 2* 19, no. 1 (spring 1992): 37.

30  Homi K. Bhabha, *The Location of Culture* (London: Routledge, 1994), 12, 162.

31  Herman Melville, *Redburn: His First Voyage*, ed. Harrison Hayford et al. (Evanston, IL:

Northwestern UP, 1969), 133. Subsequent page references to this edition appear in the text.

32  Herman Melville, *Mardi, and a Voyage Thither,* ed. Harrison Hayford et al. (Evanston, IL: Northwestern UP, 1970), 176. Subsequent page references to this edition appear in the text.

33  Richard H. Brodhead, "*Mardi:* Creating the Creative," in Jehlen, *Herman Melville,* 39.

34  Merrell R. Davis and William H. Gilman, eds., *The Letters of Herman Melville* (New Haven: Yale UP, 1960), 79.

35  Melville, "Hawthorne and His Mosses," 244.

36  Jonathan Arac, *Commissioned Spirits: The Shaping of Social Motion in Dickens, Carlyle, Melville, and Hawthorne* (New Brunswick, NJ: Rutgers UP, 1985), 156.

37  Thomas Carlyle, *Sartor Resartus,* ed. Kerry McSweeney and Peter Sabor (Oxford: Oxford UP, 1987), 146, 196. Subsequent page references to this edition appear in the text.

38  Melville, *Journal of a Visit to London,* 39.

39  John Carlos Rowe, *Through the Custom-House: Nineteenth-Century American Fiction and Modern Theory* (Baltimore: Johns Hopkins UP, 1982), 24, 193.

40  Leo Bersani, *The Culture of Redemption* (Cambridge, MA: Harvard UP, 1990), 146.

41  Ibid., 153.

42  Quoted in Robin Sandra Grey, "Surmising the Infidel: Interpreting Melville's Annotations on Milton's Poetry," *Milton Quarterly* 26 (1992): 108.

43  William S. Ament, "Bowdler and the Whale: Some Notes on the First English and American Editions of *Moby-Dick,*" *American Literature* 4 (1932): 39–46.

44  Quoted in Branch, *Melville: The Critical Heritage,* 255, 260, 257, 288.

45  Leon Howard, "Historical Note," in *Pierre; or, The Ambiguities,* by Herman Melville, ed. Harrison Hayford et al. (Evanston, IL: Northwestern UP, 1971), 379. Subsequent page references to Melville's narrative appear in the text.

46  Henry James, "The Art of Fiction" (1884), in *The House of Fiction,* ed. Leon Edel (London: Rupert Hart-Davis, 1957), 24.

47  F. R. Leavis, *The Great Tradition: George Eliot, Henry James, Joseph Conrad* (1948; rpt. Harmondsworth, England: Penguin, 1962), 178.

48  Hershel Parker, "Melville and the Berkshires: Emotion-Laden Terrain, 'Reckless Sky-Assaulting Mood,' and Encroaching Wordsworthianism," in *American Literature: The New England Heritage,* ed. James Nagel and Richard Astro (New York: Garland Press, 1981), 65; Herman Melville, *White-Jacket; or, The World in a Man-of-War,* ed. Harrison Hayford et al. (Evanston, IL: Northwestern UP, 1970), 40.

49  Robert Weisbuch, *Atlantic Double-Cross: American Literature and British Influence in the Age of Emerson* (Chicago: U of Chicago P, 1986), 13, 41; Hershel Parker, "Historical Supplement," in *Clarel: A Poem and Pilgrimage in the Holy Land,* by Herman Melville (Evanston, IL: Northwestern UP, 1991), 645.

50  Ruth Christiani Brown, "*The French Lieutenant's Woman* and *Pierre:* Echo and An-

swer," *Modern Fiction Studies* 31 (1985): 115–32; Richard Gray, " 'All's o'er and ye know him not': A Reading of *Pierre*," in *Herman Melville: Reassessments*, ed. A. Robert Lee (London: Vision, 1984), 132.

51  Melville, *The Piazza Tales and Other Prose Pieces*, 296. Subsequent page references to these diptychs are taken from this edition and appear in the text.

52  Geoffrey Sanborn, *The Sign of the Cannibal: Melville and the Making of a Postcolonial Reader* (Durham, NC: Duke UP, 1998), 26.

53  Ibid., 115.

54  Herman Melville, *Israel Potter: His Fifty Years of Exile*, ed. Harrison Hayford et al. (Evanston, IL: Northwestern UP, 1982), 27. Subsequent page references to this edition appear in the text.

55  F. O. Matthiessen, *American Renaissance: Art and Expression in the Age of Emerson and Whitman* (New York: Oxford UP, 1941), 491, 493.

56  Carolyn L. Karcher, *Slavery over the Promised Land: Slavery, Race, and Violence in Melville's America* (Baton Rouge: Louisiana State UP, 1980), 104.

57  Melville, "Benito Cereno," in *The Piazza Tales*, 50. Subsequent page references to Melville's narrative are taken from this edition and appear in the text.

58  Louise J. Kaplan, *Female Perversions: The Temptations of Emma Bovary* (New York: Doubleday, 1991), 43.

59  Jonathan Arac, "Narrative Forms," in *The Cambridge History of American Literature. Volume 2, Prose Writing, 1820–1865*, ed. Sacvan Bercovitch (Cambridge, England: Cambridge UP, 1995), 607.

60  R. W. B. Lewis, afterword to *The Confidence-Man: His Masquerade*, by Herman Melville (New York: New American Library, 1964), 263. See also Gary Lindberg, *The Confidence Man in American Literature* (New York: Oxford UP, 1982).

61  Herman Melville, *The Confidence-Man: His Masquerade*, ed. Harrison Hayford, Hershel Parker, and G. Thomas Tanselle (Evanston, IL: Northwestern UP, 1984), 42, 118. Subsequent page references to this edition appear in the text.

62  Shirley M. Dettlaff, "Ionian Form and Esau's Waste: Melville's View of Art in *Clarel*," *American Literature* 54 (1982): 213, 216.

63  Matthew Arnold, "General Introduction to *The English Poets*," quoted in William B. Dillingham, *Melville and His Circle: The Last Years* (Athens: U of Georgia P, 1996), 95.

64  Matthew Arnold, *The Poems of Matthew Arnold*, ed. Kenneth Allott (London: Longmans, 1965), 492; Walter E. Bezanson, "Melville's Reading of Arnold's Poetry," *PMLA* 69 (1954): 385.

65  Dillingham, *Melville and His Circle*, 34–35.

66  Herman Melville, *Clarel: A Poem and Pilgrimage in the Holy Land*, ed. Harrison Hayford, Hershel Parker, and G. Thomas Tanselle (Evanston, IL: Northwestern UP, 1991), 350. Subsequent page references to this edition appear in parentheses in the text.

67  Melville, *Correspondence*, 121.

68  Newton Arvin, "Melville's *Clarel*," *Hudson Review* 14 (1961): 299; Andrew Hook,

"Melville's Poetry," in *Herman Melville: Reassessments,* ed. A. Robert Lee (London: Vision, 1984), 181; Robert Penn Warren, "Melville's Poems," *Southern Review* NS 3 (1967): 817–18.

69   Dettlaff, "Ionian Form and Esau's Waste," 223.

70   Quoted in Bezanson, "Melville's Reading of Arnold's Poetry," 368–69, 380–84.

71   Melville, *Correspondence,* 492.

72   Bezanson, "Melville's Reading of Arnold's Poetry," 388.

73   Richard Harter Fogle, "Melville's Poetry," *Tulane Studies in English* 12 (1962): 83.

74   William C. Spengemann, "Melville the Poet," *American Literary History* 11 (1999): 599–600, 605.

75   Bezanson, "Melville's Reading of Arnold's Poetry," 376.

76   Arnold, *Poems,* 186.

77   Melville, "Hawthorne and His Mosses," 243.

78   Park Honan, *Matthew Arnold: A Life* (London: Weidenfeld and Nicolson, 1981), 479; Matthew Arnold, "Emerson," in *Philistinism in England and America: The Complete Prose Works of Matthew Arnold,* ed. R. H. Super (Ann Arbor: U of Michigan P, 1974), 175.

79   Andrew Marvell, *The Complete Poems,* ed. Elizabeth Story Donno (Harmondsworth, England: Penguin, 1972), 75, 98.

80   Herman Melville, *Billy Budd Sailor (An Inside Narrative),* ed. Harrison Hayford and Merton M. Sealts Jr. (Chicago: U of Chicago P, 1962), 128, 55. Subsequent page references to this edition appear in the text.

81   Brook Thomas, *Cross-Examinations of Law and Literature: Cooper, Hawthorne, Stowe, and Melville* (Cambridge, England: Cambridge UP, 1987), 212.

82   For a discussion of Billy Budd as "a sado-masochistic drama" concerned with "the sexual attraction between power and powerlessness," see Robert K. Martin, *Hero, Captain, and Stranger: Male Friendship, Social Critique, and Literary Form in the Sea Novels of Herman Melville* (Chapel Hill: U of North Carolina P, 1986), 107–8.

83   Eve Kosofsky Sedgwick, *Epistemology of the Closet* (Berkeley: U of California P, 1990), 109.

84   Barbara Johnson, "Melville's Fist: The Execution of Billy Budd," *Studies in Romanticism* 18 (1979): 585.

85   Andrew Delbanco, *Required Reading: Why Our American Classics Matter Now* (New York: Farrar, Straus and Giroux, 1997), 22, x.

86   Lawrence, *Studies in Classic American Literature,* 139.

87   Quoted in Frederick R. Karl, *Joseph Conrad: The Three Lives* (London: Faber, 1979), 615.

4
*"Changed and Queer": Henry James and the Surrealization of America*

1   T. J. Clark, *Farewell to an Idea: Episodes from a History of Modernism* (New Haven: Yale UP, 1999), 407, 7.

2  Wanda Corn, *The Great American Thing: Modern Art and National Identity, 1915–1935* (Berkeley: U of California P, 1999), 31–32, 80.

3  D. H. Lawrence, *Studies in Classic American Literature* (1923; rpt. Harmondsworth, England: Penguin, 1971), 7.

4  T. S. Eliot, "Little Gidding," in *The Complete Poems and Plays of T. S. Eliot* (London: Faber, 1969), 194.

5  Quoted in Dickran Tashjian, *Skyscraper Primitives: Dada and the American Avant-Garde, 1910–1925* (Middletown, CT: Wesleyan UP, 1975), 49.

6  Roger Shattuck, *The Banquet Years: The Arts in France, 1885–1918* (London: Faber, 1959), 238–39; Peter Nicholls, *Modernisms: A Literary Guide* (Basingstoke, England: Macmillan, 1995), 291.

7  Charles Altieri, "Surrealist 'Materialism,'" *Dada/Surrealism*, no. 13 (1984): 95.

8  James Clifford, *The Predicament of Culture: Twentieth-Century Ethnography, Literature, and Art* (Cambridge, MA: Harvard UP, 1988), 9; Robin Walz, *Pulp Surrealism: Insolent Popular Culture in Early Twentieth-Century Paris* (Berkeley: U of California P, 2000), 4–6.

9  Walz, *Pulp Surrealism*, 45.

10  Quoted in George Wickes, *Americans in Paris* (Garden City, NY: Doubleday, 1969), 126.

11  Shattuck, *The Banquet Years*, 228; Apollinaire quoted in Corn, *The Great American Thing*, 60.

12  Quoted in Alan Young, *Dada and After: Extremist Modernism and English Literature* (Manchester, England: Manchester UP, 1981), 48–49.

13  Leon Edel and Lyall H. Powers, eds., *The Complete Notebooks of Henry James* (New York: Oxford UP, 1987), 350, 358.

14  Georg Lukács, "The Ideology of Modernism," in *The Meaning of Contemporary Realism*, trans. John Mander and Necke Mander (London: Merlin Press, 1963), 37.

15  F. O. Matthiessen, *Henry James: The Major Phase* (New York: Oxford UP, 1944); Robert Hughes, *The Shock of the New: Art and the Century of Change*, 2d ed. (London: Thames and Hudson, 1991), 51; Maya Slater, trans., *Three Pre-Surrealist Plays: The Blind (Les Aveugles); Ubu the King (Ubu roi); The Mammeries of Tiresias (Les Mamelles de Tirésias)* (Oxford: Oxford UP, 1997).

16  Roger Shattuck, introduction to *Selected Works of Alfred Jarry*, ed. Roger Shattuck and Simon Watson Taylor (New York: Grove, 1965), 19.

17  Alfred Jarry, *The Supermale: A Modern Novel*, trans. Barbara Wright (London: Cape, 1968), 7–9.

18  J. H. Matthews, *The Imagery of Surrealism* (Syracuse, NY: Syracuse UP, 1977), 9.

19  W. H. Auden, introduction to *The American Scene*, by Henry James (New York: Scribner's, 1946), xi; Matthews, *The Imagery of Surrealism*, 9.

20  Walter Benjamin, *Reflections: Essays, Aphorisms, Autobiographical Writings*, ed. Peter Demetz, trans. Edmund Jephcott (New York: Schocken, 1978), 179, 189.

21  Margaret Cohen, *Profane Illumination: Walter Benjamin and the Paris of Surrealist Revolution* (Berkeley: U of California P, 1993), 11.

22 Ross Posnock, *The Trial of Curiosity: Henry James, William James, and the Challenge of Modernity* (New York: Oxford UP, 1991), 151, 284, 191. Benjamin's phrase comes from his essay "On Some Motifs in Baudelaire" in *Illuminations: Essays and Reflections*, ed. Hannah Arendt (New York: Schocken, 1969), 176.

23 Posnock, *The Trial of Curiosity*, 189, 24, 103.

24 Ezra Pound, "Provincialism the Enemy" (1917), in *Selected Prose, 1909–1965*, ed. William Cookson (London: Faber, 1973), 159; T. S. Eliot, "On Henry James" (1918), in *Henry James: Critical Assessments*, ed. Graham Clarke (Mountfeld, England: Helm Information, 1991), 304; Richard Poirier, *A World Elsewhere: The Place of Style in American Literature* (New York: Oxford UP, 1966), 211.

25 Clark, *Farewell to an Idea*, 7.

26 John Carlos Rowe, *The Other Henry James* (Durham, NC: Duke UP, 1998), 93.

27 Henry James, *The Tragic Muse*. In *The Novels and Tales of Henry James, New York Edition: Vols. 7 and 8* (New York: Scribner's, 1909), 2.371; 1.260.

28 Rowe, *The Other Henry James*, 4; Elaine Showalter, *Sexual Anarchy: Gender and Culture at the Fin de Siècle* (New York: Viking, 1990), 3.

29 Sheldon M. Novick, introduction to *Henry James and Homo-Erotic Desire*, ed. John R. Bradley (Basingstoke, England: Macmillan, 1999), 11.

30 John R. Bradley, "Henry James's Permanent Adolescence," in Bradley, *Henry James and Homo-Erotic Desire*, 66; Richard Ellmann, "Henry James among the Aesthetes," in *along the riverrun: Selected Essays* (London: Hamish Hamilton, 1988), 134. On James and homosexuality, see also Fred Kaplan, *Henry James: The Imagination of Genius. A Biography* (London: Hodder and Stoughton, 1992).

31 Henry James, preface to *What Maisie Knew, In the Cage, The Pupil*. In *The Novels and Tales of Henry James, New York Edition: Vol. 11* (New York: Scribner's, 1909), vi.

32 Henry James, *The Lesson of the Master, The Death of the Lion, The Next Time and Other Tales*. In *The Novels and Tales of Henry James, New York Edition: Vol. 15* (New York: Scribner's, 1909), 109. Subsequent page references to this edition are cited in the text.

33 For the 1890 edition, see Henry James, *The Tragic Muse* (Harmondsworth, England: Penguin, 1978), 177; for the New York edition, see James, *The Tragic Muse*, 1.260.

34 Henry James, *Letters: Volume 3, 1883–1895*, ed. Leon Edel (Cambridge, MA: Harvard UP, 1980), 482.

35 Quoted in Roger Gard, ed., *Henry James: The Critical Heritage* (1982; rpt. London: Routledge, 1997), 256–57.

36 James, *What Maisie Knew, In the Cage, The Pupil*, 11.419. Subsequent page references are cited in the text.

37 Rowe, *The Other Henry James*, 176.

38 Hugh Stevens, "Queer Henry *In the Cage*," in *The Cambridge Companion to Henry James*, ed. Jonathan Freedman (Cambridge, England: Cambridge UP, 1998), 132.

39 On the sexual scandals of the 1890s, see Richard Dellamora, *Masculine Desire: The Sexual Politics of Victorian Aestheticism* (Chapel Hill: U of North Carolina P, 1990),

194; Suzanne Nalbantian, *Seeds of Decadence in the Late Nineteenth-Century Novel: A Crisis in Values* (New York: St. Martin's Press, 1983), 1–17.

40  Henry James, *A Small Boy and Others* (London: Macmillan, 1913), 362–64.

41  Adeline R. Tintner, *Henry James's Legacy: The Afterlife of His Figure and Fiction* (Baton Rouge: Louisiana State UP, 1998), 259–67. On Demuth's friendship with Duchamp, see Tashjian, *Skyscraper Primitives*, 55–56, 209.

42  Corn, *The Great American Thing*, 194–96, 239.

43  Showalter, *Sexual Anarchy*, 112; Gard, *Henry James: The Critical Heritage*, 317, 337; Eve Kosofsky Sedgwick, *Epistemology of the Closet* (Berkeley: U of California P, 1990), 182–212.

44  Michael Moon, A Small Boy and Others: *Imitation and Initiation in American Culture from Henry James to Andy Warhol* (Durham, NC: Duke UP, 1998), 24.

45  Letter to William James, 29 October 1888, *Letters*, 3:244.

46  Benjamin, "The Image of Proust," in *Illuminations*, 205, 208, 211.

47  "As an American novel that is not immediately distinguishable, on the basis of sub-ject, style, argument, genre, or theme, from many of its European counterparts, *The American* calls into question the very idea of American literature." See William C. Spengemann, introduction to *The American*, by Henry James (Harmondsworth, En-gland: Penguin, 1981), 12–13. See also William C. Spengemann, *A Mirror for Ameri-canists: Reflections on the Idea of American Literature* (Hanover, NH: UP of New En-gland, 1989), 161.

48  Henry James, *The Wings of the Dove*. In *The Novels and Tales of Henry James, New York Edition: Vols. 19 and 20* (New York: Scribner's, 1909), 1.131. Subsequent page refer-ences to this edition are cited in the text.

49  Michael Moon, "Sexuality and Visual Terrorism in *The Wings of the Dove*," *Criticism*, 28 (1986): 432.

50  Mark Seltzer, *Henry James and the Art of Power* (Ithaca, NY: Cornell UP, 1984), 108, 167–68, 148.

51  Henry James, "Emile Zola," in *Notes on Novelists, with Some Other Notes* (London: Dent, 1914), 30.

52  Georges Bataille, *Erotism: Death and Sensuality* (1957), trans. Mary Dalwood (San Francisco: City Lights, 1986), 141.

53  Dickran Tashjian, *A Boatload of Madmen: Surrealism and the American Avant-Garde, 1920–1950* (New York: Thames and Hudson, 1995), 105.

54  Teresa de Lauretis, *The Practice of Love: Lesbian Sexuality and Perverse Desire* (Bloom-ington: Indiana UP, 1994), 269.

55  Moon, "Sexuality and Visual Terrorism," 438. See also Eve Kosofsky Sedgwick, "Is the Rectum Straight? Identification and Identity in *The Wings of the Dove*," in *Tendencies* (New York: Routledge, 1994), 73–103.

56  Henry James, *The Golden Bowl*. In *The Novels and Tales of Henry James, New York Edition: Vols. 23 and 24* (New York: Scribner's, 1909), 1.3.

57 On the "postcolonial" characteristics of *The Golden Bowl*, see Margery Sabin, "Henry James's American Dream in *The Golden Bowl*," in Freedman, *The Cambridge Companion to Henry James*, 206–7.

58 Henry James, "Occasional Paris," in *The Art of Travel: Scenes and Journeys in America, England, France and Italy from The Travel Writings of Henry James*, ed. Morton Dauwen Zabel (1958; rpt. New York: Freeport, 1970), 213–14.

59 Quoted in Robert M. Crunden, *American Salons: Encounters with European Modernism, 1885–1917* (New York: Oxford UP, 1993), 283.

60 Henry James, *The Ambassadors*. In *The Novels and Tales of Henry James, New York Edition: Vols. 21 and 22* (New York: Scribner's, 1909), 1.4. Subsequent page references to this edition are cited in the text.

61 Maud Ellmann, " 'The Intimate Difference': Power and Representation in *The Ambassadors*," in *The Ambassadors, by Henry James: An Authoritative Text. The Author on the Novel. Criticism*, 2d ed., ed. S. P. Rosenbaum (New York: Norton, 1994), 504, 512–13.

62 Julie Rivkin, "The Logic of Delegation in *The Ambassadors*," *PMLA* 101 (1986): 823.

63 Quoted in Van Wyck Brooks, *The Pilgrimage of Henry James* (London: Cape, 1928), 138.

64 Bataille, *Erotism*, 109.

65 Henry James, *The American Scene*, ed. Leon Edel (Bloomington: Indiana UP, 1968), 14. Subsequent page references to this edition are cited in the text.

66 Walz, *Pulp Surrealism*, 32.

67 Stephen Spender, *Love-Hate Relations: A Study of Anglo-American Sensibilities* (London: Hamish Hamilton, 1974), 94.

68 Patricia McKee, *Producing American Races: Henry James, William Faulkner, Toni Morrison* (Durham, NC: Duke UP, 1999), 39.

69 Sara Blair, *Henry James and the Writing of Race and Nation* (Cambridge, England: Cambridge UP, 1986), 5; Leon Edel, *Henry James: The Master, 1901–1916* (London: Rupert Hart-Davis, 1972), 284.

70 Michael Seidel, *Exile and the Narrative Imagination* (New Haven: Yale UP, 1986), 134, 144.

71 Philip Horne, *Henry James and Revision: The New York Edition* (Oxford: Clarendon P, 1990), 49–50.

72 Slavoj Žižek, *The Sublime Object of Ideology* (London: Verso, 1989), 99.

73 Henry James, *Letters: Volume 4, 1895–1916*, ed. Leon Edel (Cambridge, MA: Harvard UP, 1984), 355; Edel, *Henry James: The Master*, 287, 295.

74 James, *Letters*, 4:357; Edel, *Henry James: The Master*, 294.

75 James, *Letters*, 4:355; Edel, *Henry James: The Master*, 294.

76 Martha Banta, "Men, Women, and the American Way," in Freedman, *The Cambridge Companion to Henry James*, 25.

77 Sara Blair, "Realism, Culture, and the Place of the Literary: Henry James and *The Bostonians*," in Freedman, *The Cambridge Companion to Henry James*, 152.

78  Slavoj Žižek, *The Plague of Fantasies* (London: Verso, 1997), 104.

79  Beverly Haviland, *Henry James's Last Romance: Making Sense of the Past and the American Scene* (Cambridge, England: Cambridge UP, 1997), 215.

80  Walter Benn Michaels, *The Gold Standard and the Logic of Naturalism: American Literature at the Turn of the Century* (Berkeley: U of California P, 1987), 218–21.

81  Alvin Langdon Coburn, *Alvin Langdon Coburn, Photographer: An Autobiography*, ed. Helmut Gernsheim and Alison Gernsheim (New York: Praeger, 1966), 58.

82  James, preface, *The Golden Bowl*, 1.xi. On James and photography, see Ralph F. Bogardus, "The Photographer's Eye: Henry James and the American Scene," *History of Photography* 8, no. 3 (1984): 179–86, and *Pictures and Texts: Henry James, A. L. Coburn, and New Ways of Seeing in Literary Culture* (Ann Arbor, MI: UMI Research Press, 1984). For a contrasting view of James as hostile to the "mechanical" art of photography, see Stanley Tick, "Positives and Negatives: Henry James vs. Photography," *Nineteenth Century Studies* 7 (1993): 69–101. For the more reasonable suggestion that James distinguished among different types of photography, abhorring the popularity of Kodaks on the mass market but admiring the "pioneers of art photography," see Peter Rawlings, "A Kodak Refraction of Henry James's 'The Real Thing,' " *Journal of American Studies* 32 (1998): 459–60.

83  Nancy Armstrong, *Fiction in the Age of Photography: The Legacy of British Realism* (Cambridge, MA: Harvard UP, 1999), 251–52, 246.

84  Henry James, "The Jolly Corner," in *The Altar of the Dead, The Beast in the Jungle, The Birthplace and Other Tales*. In *The Novels and Tales of Henry James, New York Edition: Vol. 17* (New York: Scribner's, 1909), 435. Subsequent page references to this edition are cited in the text.

85  Julia Kristeva, *Strangers to Ourselves* (1989), trans. Leon S. Roudiez (New York: Columbia UP, 1991), 195.

86  Cohen, *Profane Illumination*, 135.

87  Marianne Oesterreicher-Mollwo, *Surrealism and Dadaism* (Oxford: Phaidon, 1979), 13.

88  Jean-Paul Sartre, *What Is Literature?* (1948), trans. Bernard Frechtman (London: Methuen, 1950), 139.

89  Frederick M. Dolan, *Allegories of America: Narratives, Metaphysics, Politics* (Ithaca, NY: Cornell UP, 1994), 2–5.

90  André Breton, *Nadja* (1928), trans. Richard Howard (New York: Grove Weidenfeld, 1960), 52.

91  Tashjian, *A Boatload of Madmen*, 66–90.

92  Clifford, *The Predicament of Culture*, 146.

93  Tashjian, *Skyscraper Primitives*, 49; Corn, *The Great American Thing*, xvi–xix.

94  Quoted in Fernand Ouellette, *Edgard Varèse* (1966), trans. Derek Coltman (London: Calder and Boyars, 1973), 56.

95  Wickes, *Americans in Paris*, 267–68; Henry Miller, *Tropic of Cancer* (1934; rpt. Lon-

don: Granada, 1965), 169, 23. Miller also wrote a perceptive essay on Varèse, finding in his music a "sense of violation, of sacrilege," which he associated with a representation of "society" as "one interrupted dissonance for which no resolving chord will ever be found." See "With Edgard Varèse in the Gobi Desert," in *The Air-Conditioned Nightmare* (1945; rpt. London: Heinemann, 1962), 152, 155.

96  Miller, *Tropic of Cancer*, 256.

97  Louis-Ferdinand Céline, *Journey to the End of the Night* (1932), trans. Ralph Manheim (London: John Calder, 1988), 54. Subsequent page references to this edition are cited in the text. For the links between Miller and Céline, see Alice Kaplan and Philippe Roussin, "Introduction: Céline, USA," *South Atlantic Quarterly* 93 (1994): 199–204.

98  Raoul R. Ibargüen, "Céline, Miller, and the American Canon," *South Atlantic Quarterly* 93 (1994): 489.

99  J. Gerald Kennedy, *Imagining Paris: Exile, Writing, and American Identity* (New Haven: Yale UP, 1993), 172.

100  Djuna Barnes, *Nightwood* (1937; rpt. New York: New Directions, 1961), 45–46. On the representation of bisexuality in *Nightwood*, see Marjorie Garber, *Vice Versa: Bisexuality and the Eroticism of Everyday Life* (New York: Simon and Schuster, 1995), 159–60.

101  Blair, *Henry James and the Writing of Race and Nation*, 20.

102  James Joyce, *A Portrait of the Artist as a Young Man*, ed. Richard Ellmann (London: Cape, 1968), 207.

103  W. G. Rogers, *Gertrude Stein Is Gertrude Stein Is Gertrude Stein* (New York: Crowell, 1973), 3, 205.

104  Walter Benn Michaels, *Our America: Nativism, Modernism, and Pluralism* (Durham, NC: Duke UP, 1995), 83.

105  Margaret Morse, *Virtualities: Television, Media Art, and Cyberculture* (Bloomington: Indiana UP, 1998), 182.

106  Eliot, "On Henry James," 309.

107  Fredric Jameson, *The Political Unconscious: Narrative as a Socially Symbolic Act* (Ithaca, NY: Cornell UP, 1981), 222.

108  For James's view of Lawrence, see his essay "The New Novel" (1914), in *Notes on Novelists*, 252. He heard Frazer lecture at the Royal Institution, 16 March 1915; *Complete Notebooks*, 417. He visited the Post-Impressionist Exhibition in London in 1912; Virginia Woolf, *Roger Fry: A Biography* (London: Hogarth, 1940), 180. He took his nieces to the Scott Cinema, London, on 12 May 1914; *Complete Notebooks*, 399. For his dependence on the telephone in his Carlyle Mansions flat—"I myself rest upon the telephone as upon my nurse's lap in infancy"—see Kaplan, *Henry James: The Imagination of Genius*, 545.

109  Pierre A. Walker, ed., *Henry James on Culture: Collected Essays on Politics and the American Social Scene* (Lincoln: U of Nebraska P, 1999), 151.

## 5
## From Decadent Aesthetics to
## Political Fetishism: The "Oracle Effect"
## of Frost's Poetry

1   Pierre Bourdieu, *Language and Symbolic Power,* ed. John B. Thompson, trans. Gino Raymond and Matthew Adamson (Cambridge, MA: Harvard UP, 1991), 211, 138.

2   Ezra Pound, "Robert Frost (Two Reviews)," in *Literary Essays of Ezra Pound,* ed. T. S. Eliot (Norfolk, CT: New Directions, 1954), 382–86. Pound's review of *North of Boston* was first published in *Poetry* (Dec. 1914).

3   Frank Lentricchia, *Modernist Quartet* (Cambridge, England: Cambridge UP, 1994), 51.

4   Marjorie Perloff, "Modernist Studies," in *Redrawing the Boundaries: The Transformation of English and American Literary Studies,* ed. Stephen Greenblatt and Giles Gunn (New York: Modern Language Association of America, 1992), 170.

5   Mark Richardson, *The Ordeal of Robert Frost: The Poet and His Poetics* (Urbana: U of Illinois P, 1997), 95.

6   Andreas Huyssen, *After the Great Divide: Modernism, Mass Culture, Postmodernism* (Bloomington: Indiana UP, 1986), vii.

7   Antoine Compagnon, *The Five Paradoxes of Modernity* (1990), trans. Franklin Philip (New York: Columbia UP, 1994), 4.

8   Richard Gilman, *Decadence: The Strange Life of an Epithet* (New York: Farrar, Straus and Giroux, 1979), 139.

9   Lawrance Thompson, *Robert Frost. The Early Years: 1874–1915* (New York: Holt, Rinehart and Winston, 1966), 165, 173–74.

10  Robert Frost, *The Poetry of Robert Frost,* ed. Edward Connery Lathem (New York: Holt, Rinehart and Winston, 1969), 14. Subsequent page references for Frost's poetry are taken from this edition and are cited in the text.

11  Algernon Charles Swinburne, *The Complete Works. 1: Poetical Works,* ed. Edmund Gosse and Thomas James Wise (London: Heinemann, 1925), 199.

12  Peter Nicholls, *Modernisms: A Literary Guide* (Basingstoke, England: Macmillan, 1995), 61.

13  T. S. Eliot, "Swinburne as Poet" (1920), in *Selected Essays,* 3d ed. (London: Faber, 1951), 323–27; Nicholls, *Modernisms,* 195.

14  On the negative image of Swinburne among male modernists, see David Bromwich, *A Choice of Inheritance: Self and Community from Edmund Burke to Robert Frost* (Cambridge, MA: Harvard UP, 1989), 199. For H.D.'s more positive evaluation, see Cassandra Laity, "H.D. and A. C. Swinburne: Decadence and Sapphic Modernism," in *Lesbian Texts and Contexts,* ed. Karla Jay and Joanne Glasgow (New York: New York UP, 1990), 217–40.

15  Quoted in Lawrance Thompson, *Robert Frost. The Years of Triumph: 1915–1938* (New York: Holt, Rinehart and Winston, 1970), 620.

16  Robert Frost, *Selected Letters*, ed. Lawrance Thompson (New York: Holt, Rinehart and Winston, 1964), 79. For a discussion of this point, see William H. Pritchard, *Frost: A Literary Life Reconsidered* (Amherst: U of Massachusetts P, 1993), 77.

17  Robert Frost, "The Figure a Poem Makes," in *Robert Frost on Writing*, ed. Elaine Barry (New Brunswick, NJ: Rutgers UP, 1973), 126.

18  Frost, *Selected Letters*, 20, 104.

19  Thomas Hardy, *The Collected Poems* (London: Macmillan, 1930), 137.

20  Thomas Hardy, *The Life and Work of Thomas Hardy*, ed. Michael Millgate (Athens: U of Georgia P, 1985), 350; Richard D. McGhee, " 'Swinburne Planteth, Hardy Watereth': Victorian Views of Pain and Pleasure in Human Sexuality," in *Sexuality and Victorian Literature*, ed. Don Richard Cox (Knoxville: U of Tennessee P, 1984), 83–107.

21  John R. Reed, *Decadent Style* (Athens: Ohio UP, 1985), 77, 80.

22  Robert Frost, *The Letters of Robert Frost to Louis Untermeyer* (London: Cape, 1964), 47.

23  Frost, *Selected Letters*, 80.

24  For a discussion of modernist uses of Victorian poetics, see Carol T. Christ, *Victorian and Modern Poetics* (Chicago: U of Chicago P, 1984), 144.

25  For an analysis of how American modernism came to associate the formation of national identity with a nativist rejection of other cultures, see Walter Benn Michaels, *Our America: Nativism, Modernism, and Pluralism* (Durham, NC: Duke UP, 1995), 83. On Williams's desire to escape British influences, see Michael North, *The Dialect of Modernism: Race, Language, and Twentieth-Century Literature* (New York: Oxford UP, 1994), 157.

26  Philip Rahv, "The Taste of Nothing," *New Masses*, 4 May 1937, 32–33. *Nightwood*, though set in Paris, was written mostly in England; see J. Gerald Kennedy, *Imagining Paris: Exile, Writing, and American Identity* (New Haven: Yale UP, 1993), 221.

27  Quoted in Richardson, *Ordeal of Robert Frost*, 123.

28  On the "Build Soil" controversy, see Stanley Burnshaw, *Robert Frost Himself* (New York: George Braziller, 1986), 42–57. The poem was subsequently published in *A Further Range* (1936). In 1958, Frost talked of the Soviet system as a complement to the American model—"two great ideas—who's to say they're not both valid?"—which again suggests his concern for the shape rather than the substance of political philosophies. See Edward Connery Lathem, ed., *Interviews with Robert Frost* (New York: Holt, Rinehart and Winston, 1966), 189.

29  Lionel Trilling, "A Speech on Robert Frost: A Cultural Episode," *Partisan Review* 26 (1959): 451.

30  Michael Warner, introduction to *Fear of a Queer Planet: Queer Politics and Social Theory*, ed. Michael Warner (Minneapolis: U of Minnesota P, 1993), xxi; Karen L. Kilcup, " ' "Men Work Together," I Told Him from the Heart': Frost's (In)delicate Masculinity," *ELH* 65 (1998): 732.

31  Frost tended to associate homosexuality with British culture, claiming he had never heard of female homosexuality before his visit to England in 1911, where he "read of

them . . . in a series of articles by the heads of the famous public schools—Rugby, Eton, etc." See Kilcup, "Men Work Together," 747.

32  Frost, *Selected Letters*, 89.

33  Ibid., 73–74. In a review of *North of Boston* in the *American Review of Reviews* (April 1915), Sylvester Clarke picked up on this subtext of estrangement and nostalgia: "One almost marvels that such a book, so vividly true to New England scenes and cháracters, could have been created across the water . . . But it was this intense home-longing which visualized his themes." Quoted in Linda Wagner, *Robert Frost: The Critical Reception* (N.p.: Burt Franklin, 1977), 23.

34  Richard Wilbur, *Responses: Prose Pieces, 1953–1976* (New York: Harcourt Brace Jovanovich, 1976), 113.

35  Robert Frost, "On Emerson," *Daedalus* 88 (1959): 717–18.

36  Quoted in Wagner, *Frost: The Critical Reception*, 67.

37  Robert Crawford, "Robert Frosts," *Journal of American Studies* 20 (1986): 219–20. On "The Subverted Flower," see Richard Poirier, *Robert Frost: The Work of Knowing*, 2d ed. (Stanford: Stanford UP, 1990), 57–58.

38  Katherine Kearns, *Robert Frost and a Poetics of Appetite* (Cambridge, England: Cambridge UP, 1994), 5, 188.

39  Jürgen Habermas, *A Theory of Communicative Action. Volume 2: Lifeworld and System: A Critique of Functionalist Reason*, trans. Thomas McCarthy (Cambridge, England: Polity Press, 1987).

40  For a discussion of this point, see Craig Calhoun, "Introduction: Habermas and the Public Sphere," in *Habermas and the Public Sphere*, ed. Craig Calhoun (Cambridge, MA: MIT Press, 1992), 6.

41  Thompson, *Frost: The Years of Triumph*, 318.

42  Gorham B. Munson, *Robert Frost: A Study in Sensibility and Good Sense* (New York: George H. Doran, 1927), 113–14.

43  Frost, "The Figure a Poem Makes," 126.

44  Raymond Williams, *The English Novel from Dickens to Lawrence* (London: Chatto and Windus, 1970), 119.

45  Lentricchia, *Modernist Quartet*, 51.

46  Quoted in Lawrance Thompson and R. H. Winick, *Robert Frost: The Later Years, 1938–1963* (New York: Holt, Rinehart and Winston, 1976), 223, 244.

47  John F. Lynen, *The Pastoral Art of Robert Frost* (Nw Haven: Yale UP, 1960), 43.

48  Huyssen, *After the Great Divide*, 169.

49  Soby quoted in Alan Filreis, *Wallace Stevens and the Actual World* (Princeton, NJ: Princeton UP, 1991), 57, 51.

50  The first edition of *Robert Frost: The Work of Knowing* was published by Oxford University Press in 1977. In his foreword to the second edition, John Hollander wrote that Poirier's book had modernized Frost, after his reputation "had confused a whole critical generation" (Poirier, *Robert Frost*, xii).

51  Poirier, *Robert Frost*, 330. There is particular emphasis on this "Emersonian-pragmatist" (325) tradition in the author's afterword to the second edition (315–38).

52  Eric Cheyfitz, "What Work Is There for Us to Do? American Literary Studies or Americas Cultural Studies?" *American Literature* 67 (1995): 847. On this point, see also Terry Eagleton, "The Idealism of American Criticism," *New Left Review* 127 (May–June 1981): 53–65.

53  Alan Nadel, *Containment Culture: American Narratives, Postmodernism, and the Atomic Age* (Durham, NC: Duke UP, 1995).

54  Robert Frost, "The Constant Symbol," in Barry, *Robert Frost on Writing*, 129.

55  Lathem, *Interviews with Robert Frost*, 124, 132.

56  Thompson and Winnick, *Frost: The Later Years*, 320.

57  Trilling, "A Speech on Robert Frost," 448.

58  Philip Fisher, "Democratic Social Space: Whitman, Melville, and the Promise of American Transparency," in *The New American Studies: Essays from Representations*, ed. Philip Fisher (Berkeley: U of California P, 1991), 72.

59  For an analysis of how freeways, television, and other systems of mass communication "are not merely similar in form" but are "constructed to interact in mutually reinforcing ways," see Margaret Morse, "An Ontology of Everyday Distraction: The Freeway, the Mall, and Television," in *Logics of Television: Essays in Cultural Criticism*, ed. Patricia Mellencamp (Bloomington: Indiana UP, 1990), 193–221.

60  R. W. Emerson, "The Poet," in *The Collected Works of Ralph Waldo Emerson, 3. Essays: Second Series*, ed. Alfred R. Ferguson and Jean Ferguson Carr (Cambridge, MA: Harvard UP, 1983), 14, 21, 4.

61  Bourdieu, *Language and Symbolic Power*, 204, 211.

62  Ibid., 211.

63  Emerson, "The Poet," 22.

64  James R. Dawes, "Masculinity and Transgression in Robert Frost," *American Literature* 65 (1993): 297–312.

65  Richard Burt, "Introduction: The New Censorship," in *The Administration of Aesthetics: Censorship, Political Criticism, and the Public Sphere* (Minneapolis: U of Minnesota P, 1994), xviii.

66  Bourdieu, *Language and Symbolic Power*, 138.

67  In 1956, for instance, Frost provided for radio listeners to the National Association of Educational Broadcasters network his own allegorical reading of "Mending Wall": "The point being, you see, that even when you can't see any reason for them, you've got to have boundaries, you've got to have nations. If you have internationalisms, you've got to have nations to be international between." See Michael E. Cornett, "Robert Frost on Listen America: The Poet's Message to America in 1956," *Papers on Language and Literature* 29 (1993): 426.

68  Jennifer Terry, "Theorizing Deviant Historiography," *differences* 3, no. 2 (summer 1991): 71.

69  Lentricchia, *Modernist Quartet*, 107.

70  On national identity as an imaginary construction, see Donald E. Pease, "National Identities, Postmodern Artifacts, and Postnational Narratives," *boundary 2* 19, no. 1 (1992): 5.

71  Malcolm Cowley, "Frost: A Dissenting Opinion," *New Republic*, 11 Sept. 1944, 312.

72  Kaja Silverman, *Male Subjectivity at the Margins* (New York: Routledge, 1992), 42.

73  W. J. T. Mitchell, *Picture Theory: Essays on Verbal and Visual Representation* (Chicago: U of Chicago P, 1994), 236.

74  Andrew M. Lakritz, *Modernism and the Other in Stevens, Frost, and Moore* (Gainesville: UP of Florida, 1996), 115. On the significance of self-parody and childishness in Frost's later poetry, see Jan B. Gordon, "Robert Frost's Circle of Enchantment," in *Modern American Poetry: Essays in Criticism*, ed. Jerome Mazzaro (New York: David McKay, 1970), 60–92.

75  Kearns, *Frost and a Poetics of Appetite*, 186.

76  Lakritz, *Modernism and the Other*, 188.

77  Charles Altieri, "Surrealism and Materialism," *Dada/Surrealism* 13 (1984): 94.

78  Trilling, "A Speech on Robert Frost," 448.

6
### Virtual Eden: Lolita, Pornography, and the Perversions of American Studies

1  Warren I. Susman, "The Thirties," in *The Development of an American Culture*, ed. Stanley Coben and Lorman Ratner, 2d ed. (New York: St. Martin's Press, 1983), 221.

2  Lawrence Buell, commentary on "Can 'American Studies' Develop a Method?" by Henry Nash Smith, in *Locating American Studies: The Evolution of a Discipline*, ed. Lucy Maddox (Baltimore: Johns Hopkins UP, 1999), 13.

3  Howard Temperley and Malcolm Bradbury, "War and Cold War," in *Introduction to American Studies*, ed. Malcolm Bradbury and Howard Temperley (London: Longman, 1981), 253, 255.

4  Philip Gleason, "World War II and the Development of American Studies," *American Quarterly* 36 (1984): 343–58.

5  Lance Olsen, Lolita: *A Janus Text* (New York: Twayne, 1995), 72; Lynn Spiegel, "High Culture in Low Places: Television and Modern Art, 1950–1970," in *Disciplinarity and Dissent in Cultural Studies*, ed. Cary Nelson and Dilip Parameshwar Gaonkar (New York: Routledge, 1996), 319.

6  F. W. Dupee, "*Lolita* in America," *Encounter* 12 (Feb. 1959): 31.

7  Robert H. Walker, *American Studies in the United States: A Survey of College Programs* (Baton Rouge: Louisiana State UP, 1958), 30–31.

8  Leslie Fiedler, *An End to Innocence: Essays on Culture and Politics* (Boston: Beacon Press, 1955), 193, 209.

9 Leerom Medovoi, "Democracy, Capitalism, and American Literature: The Cold War Construction of J. D. Salinger's Paperback Hero," in *The Other 1950s: Interrogating Midcentury American Icons*, ed. Joel Foreman (Urbana: U of Illinois P, 1997), 259.

10 Vladimir Nabokov, *Lolita* (London: Weidenfeld and Nicolson, 1959), 63. Subsequent page references to this edition are cited in the text.

11 R. W. B. Lewis, *The American Adam: Innocence, Tragedy, and Tradition in the Nineteenth Century* (Chicago: U of Chicago P, 1955), 1, 5, 198–99.

12 Ibid., 197–98.

13 R. W. Emerson, "Nature," in *The Collected Works of Ralph Waldo Emerson, 1: Nature, Addresses, and Lectures,* ed. Alfred R. Ferguson (Cambridge, MA: Harvard UP, 1971), 29.

14 Vladimir E. Alexandrov, *Nabokov's Otherworld* (Princeton, NJ: Princeton UP, 1991), 48.

15 On the significance of Poe in *Lolita,* see Martha Banta, "Benjamin, Edgar, Humbert, and Jay," *Yale Review* 60 (1971): 532–49.

16 Vladimir Nabokov, *Bend Sinister* (London: Weidenfeld and Nicolson, 1972), 83; Frederick R. Karl, *American Fictions, 1940–1980* (New York: Harper and Row, 1983), 224.

17 Henry Nash Smith, *Virgin Land: The American West as Symbol and Myth* (Cambridge, MA: Harvard UP, 1950). For Nina Baym's critique of these assumptions, see "Melodramas of Beset Manhood: How Theories of American Fiction Exclude Women Authors," *American Quarterly* 33 (1981): 123–39. For a further critique of how sexual and national narratives became conflated in the portrayal of journeys over American "'virgin' territory," see Elizabeth Freeman, "Honeymoon with a Stranger: Pedophiliac Picaresques from Poe to Nabokov," *American Literature* 70 (1998): 866.

18 David M. Potter, *People of Plenty: Economic Abundance and the American Character* (Chicago: U of Chicago P, 1954), 167.

19 R. W. Emerson, "The Poet," in *The Collected Works of Ralph Waldo Emerson, 3: Essays, Second Series* (Cambridge, MA: Harvard UP, 1983), 21–22.

20 Alfred Appel Jr., "The Road to *Lolita,* or the Americanization of an Emigré," *Journal of Modern Literature* 4 (1974): 8.

21 Vladimir Nabokov, *Selected Letters, 1940–1977,* ed. Dmitri Nabokov and Matthew J. Bruccoli (London: Vintage, 1990), 557, 494–95.

22 Vladimir Nabokov, *Pale Fire* (London: Weidenfeld and Nicolson, 1962), 223.

23 Alan Nadel, *Containment Culture: American Narratives, Postmodernism, and the Atomic Age* (Durham, NC: Duke UP, 1995), 191.

24 This remark came in a 1967 interview with the *Paris Review,* reprinted in Vladimir Nabokov, *Strong Opinions* (New York: McGraw-Hill, 1973), 106.

25 Hans W. Loewald, *Sublimation: Inquiries into Theoretical Psychoanalysis* (New Haven: Yale UP, 1988), 24, 13, 20.

26 Jane Gallop, *The Daughter's Seduction: Feminism and Psychoanalysis* (Ithaca, NY: Cornell UP, 1982), xv, 77.

27  Michael Taussig defines "State fetishism" as that "peculiar sacred and erotic attraction, even thraldom, combined with disgust, which the State holds for its subjects." See "*Maleficium*: State Fetishism," in *Fetishism as Cultural Discourse*, ed. Emily Apter and William Pietz (Ithaca, NY: Cornell UP, 1993), 218.

28  Leslie A. Fiedler, "The Profanation of the Child," *The New Leader*, 23 June 1958, 29.

29  Hugh Kenner, *A Homemade World: The American Modernist Writers* (London: Marion Boyars, 1977), 211, 219.

30  Quoted in Brian Boyd, *Vladimir Nabokov: The American Years* (London: Vintage, 1992), 78.

31  Karl, *American Fictions*, 224.

32  Vladimir Nabokov, *Invitation to a Beheading*, trans. Dmitri Nabokov (London: Weidenfeld and Nicolson, 1960), 60.

33  This point is made in Jane Grayson, *Nabokov Translated: A Comparison of Nabokov's Russian and English Prose* (Oxford: Oxford UP, 1977), 2.

34  Emily Apter, "Comparative Exile: Competing Margins in the History of Comparative Literature," in *Comparative Literature in the Age of Multiculturalism*, ed. Charles Bernheimer (Baltimore: Johns Hopkins UP, 1995), 86, 93.

35  In 1970, Nabokov specifically took issue with an attempt critically to explicate his work within this Russian formalist matrix, arguing: "What doesn't make strange, estrange, strangify in a book, if the author is a genuine artist? No, leave those terms alone. Avoid textbook truth"; quoted in Peter Lubin, "Kickshaws and Motley," *Triquarterly* 17 (winter 1970): 203. This negative view of "textbook truth" was one reason Nabokov fell out with Roman Jakobson, doyen of structural linguistics, when the latter was a professor at Harvard. Nabokov tended to link these academic theories of formalism and defamiliarization with the mechanistic formulas associated in his mind with life behind the Iron Curtain, and he complained about what he took to be the Czech scholar's "excessive devotion to totalitarian countries" (*Selected Letters*, 216).

36  Nabokov, *Strong Opinions*, 69.

37  Vladimir Nabokov, *Speak, Memory: An Autobiography Revisited* (London: Weidenfeld and Nicolson, 1967), 250; Nabokov, *Strong Opinions*, 49.

38  John Haegert, "Artist in Exile: The Americanization of Humbert Humbert," *ELH* 52 (1985): 785.

39  Zygmunt Bauman, "Strangers: The Social Construction of Universality and Particularity," *Telos* 78 (winter 1988–1989): 9, 18–19.

40  Julia Kristeva, *Powers of Horror: An Essay on Abjection* (1980), trans. Leon S. Roudiez (New York: Columbia UP, 1982), 45, 4, 8, 45, 209, 16, 15.

41  On the way Lolita appeared "to disrupt the system of private freedom and public obligations informing U.S. Cold War ideology," see Frederick Whiting, "The Strange Particularity of the Lover's Preference: Pedophilia, Pornography, and the Anatomy of Monstrosity in *Lolita*," *American Literature* 70 (1998): 834. Whiting discusses per-

ceived analogies at this time between espionage and sexual subversion: "In much the same fashion that political enemies threatened to penetrate the government, sexual others threatened to infiltrate the home" (836).

42  Lionel Trilling, "The Last Lover: Vladimir Nabokov's *Lolita*," *Encounter*, 11 Oct. 1958, 19.

43  Rachel Bowlby, *Shopping with Freud* (London: Routledge, 1993), 67–68.

44  Quoted in Olsen, *Lolita: A Janus Text*, 15–18.

45  John Sutherland, *Offensive Literature: Decensorship in Britain, 1960–1982* (Totowa, NJ: Barnes and Noble, 1982), 18–19.

46  D. H. Lawrence, *Lady Chatterley's Lover*, ed. Michael Squires (Cambridge, England: Cambridge UP, 1993), 177.

47  Nabokov's intimate knowledge of *Alice in Wonderland* would have come from his Russian translation of the novel, published in Berlin in 1923.

48  "Obscene Publications," in *Parliamentary Debates (Hansard)*, Fifth Series 597 (1958–59), 1004, 994.

49  "Obscene Publications," 1001–2. In the terms of this debate, Butler's willingness to accommodate "truly creative work" inclined him toward the liberal position proposed more vigorously by Roy Jenkins, then Labour M P for Birmingham, Stechford. A substantial number of Conservative M P s were opposed to any change in the law.

50  "Obscene Publications," 1048–49, 1040.

51  Nabokov, *Strong Opinions*, 81.

52  Walter Kendrick, *The Secret Museum: Pornography in Modern Culture* (New York: Viking Penguin, 1987), 201. Since the 1950s, the significance of "community standards" in determining the parameters of obscenity in the United States has become gradually less evident, as the constitutional emphasis on freedom of expression has tended to override such local interests. The 1997 decision by the Supreme Court to guarantee immunity for Internet Service Providers against prosecution by state or local governments is one example of this. The case also exemplified the various difficulties at the end of the twentieth century associated with the demarcation of particular geographical areas for judicial purposes, circumferences that both the methodologies of area studies and the mechanisms of state censorship have traditionally relied on. Of course, this erasure of protective boundaries has also left the Internet (and other modes of production, such as television) increasingly vulnerable to commercial exploitation by multinational corporations and other international media interests.

53  Paul Lauter, *Canons and Contexts* (New York: Oxford UP, 1991), 77.

54  For a fuller discussion of this point, see Paul Giles, "Reconstructing American Studies: Transnational Paradoxes, Comparative Perspectives," *Journal of American Studies* 28 (1994): 344–47.

55  Alexis de Tocqueville, *Democracy in America*, trans. Francis Bowen, introduction by Alan Ryan (London: Everyman, 1994), 265. Tocqueville's discussion of "the unlimited power of the majority" comes in book 1, chapter 15.

56 Carol Iannone, "From *Lolita* to *Piss Christ*," *Commentary*, Jan. 1990, 54.

57 Richard Rorty, *Contingency, Irony, and Solidarity* (Cambridge, England: Cambridge UP, 1989), 165.

58 Martin Amis, "*Lolita* Reconsidered," *Atlantic Monthly*, Sept. 1992, 110, 117–18.

59 Laura Kipnis, *Bound and Gagged: Pornography and the Politics of Fantasy in America* (New York: Grove Press, 1996), 5.

60 Frances Ferguson, "Pornography: The Theory," *Critical Inquiry* 21 (spring 1995): 690.

61 Kendrick, *The Secret Museum*, 219–20.

62 Vladimir Nabokov, *Lectures on Literature*, ed. Fredson Bowers (London: Weidenfeld and Nicolson, 1980), 372, 376.

63 For an analysis of how "the field-Imaginary of American Studies" inscribes a particular version of national consensus, folding the area studies model back into a form of ideological hegemony, see Donald E. Pease, "New Americanists: Revisionist Interventions into the Canon," *boundary 2* 17, no. 1 (spring 1990): 1–37.

64 On this point, see James R. Kincaid, *Child-Loving: The Erotic Child and Victorian Culture* (New York: Routledge, 1992), 3, 198.

7

*Crossing the Water:*
*Gunn, Plath, and the Poetry of Passage*

1 Theodor W. Adorno, *Prisms* (1967), trans. Samuel and Shierry Weber (Cambridge, MA: MIT Press, 1981), 98, 101, 99, and *Minima Moralia: Reflections from Damaged Life* (1951), trans. E. F. N. Jephcott (London: New Left Books, 1974), 22.

2 On this topic, see, for example, Anthony Heilbut, *Exiled in Paradise: German Refugee Artists and Intellectuals in America, from the 1930s to the Present* (New York: Viking, 1983); Martin Jay, *Permanent Exiles: Essays in the Intellectual Migration from Germany to America* (New York: Columbia UP, 1985); Stephanie Barron, *Exiles and Emigrés: The Flight of European Artists from Hitler* (New York: Abrams/Los Angeles County Museum of Art, 1997).

3 Fredric Jameson, *Late Marxism: Adorno, or, The Persistence of the Dialectic* (London: Verso, 1990), 244.

4 James Campbell, *Thom Gunn in Conversation with James Campbell* (London: Between the Lines, 2000), 53. This is the transcript of an interview first broadcast on BBC Radio 3 in May 1999. Gunn has also paid tribute to Auden as a poet who influenced him "profoundly" when he was "about nineteen or twenty," adding: "He's not an influence I've gone back to, however." See "Thom Gunn: The Art of Poetry LXXII," *Paris Review*, no. 135 (1995): 149–50.

5 Thom Gunn, "My Life Up to Now," in *The Occasions of Poetry: Essays in Criticism and Autobiography*, ed. Clive Wilmer (London: Faber, 1982), 173, 177.

6 *The Journals of Sylvia Plath, 1950–1962*, ed. Karen V. Kukil (London: Faber, 2000), 412.

7 Thom Gunn, *Collected Poems* (London: Faber, 1993), 33. Subsequent page references to Gunn's poems are taken from this edition and cited in the text.

8 Peter Conrad, *Imagining America* (London: Routledge and Kegan Paul, 1980), 195–97. For the general influence of Niebuhr on the development of American liberalism in the late 1940s and early 1950s, see Thomas Hill Schaub, *American Fiction in the Cold War* (Madison: U of Wisconsin P, 1991), 10–13.

9 On this issue, see Alan Sinfield, *Literature, Politics and Culture in Postwar Britain* (Berkeley: U of California P, 1989), 65, and Gregory Woods, *A History of Gay Literature: The Male Tradition* (New Haven: Yale UP, 1998), 294.

10 On British views of the United States in the 1950s, see Malcolm Bradbury, "How I Invented America," *Journal of American Studies* 14 (1980): 115–35, and Robert Lawson-Peebles, "Dean Acheson and the Potato Head Blues; or, Some British Attitudes to America and Its Literature," *Prospects* 15 (1990): 1–21.

11 Peter Coleman, *The Liberal Conspiracy: The Congress for Cultural Freedom and the Struggle for the Mind of Postwar Europe* (New York: Free Press/Macmillan, 1989).

12 Quoted in Frances Stonor Saunders, *Who Paid the Piper? The CIA and the Cultural Cold War* (London: Granta Books, 1999), 166.

13 Irving Kristol, "After the Apocalypse," *Encounter* 1, no. 1 (Oct. 1953): 1.

14 Quoted in Coleman, *Liberal Conspiracy*, 250.

15 Quoted in Saunders, *Who Paid the Piper?* 186.

16 Thom Gunn, "Misanthropos," *Encounter* 25, no. 2 (Aug. 1965): 19–25.

17 Daniel Bell, *The End of Ideology: On the Exhaustion of Political Ideas in the Fifties* (Glencoe, IL: Free Press, 1960).

18 Sylvia Plath, *Letters Home: Correspondence, 1950–1963*, ed. Aurelia Schober Plath (London: Faber, 1975), 442.

19 Thom Gunn and Ted Hughes, eds., *Five American Poets* (London: Faber, 1963). The five poets represented are Edgar Bowers, Howard Nemerov, Hyam Plutzik, Louis Simpson, and William Stafford.

20 Plath, *Letters Home*, 405.

21 Thom Gunn, "Cambridge in the Fifties" (1977), in *The Occasions of Poetry*, 160; Plath, *Letters Home*, 186.

22 Robert Richman, "A Crow for the Queen," *New Criterion* 3, no. 6 (Feb. 1985): 91; Egbert Faas, "Ted Hughes and *Crow*," *London Magazine* 10 (Jan. 1971): 9.

23 "Praise for a Colossus of Literature," *Guardian*, 30 October 1998, 5.

24 Quoted in John D. Jump, ed., *Lord Alfred Tennyson: The Critical Heritage* (London: Routledge, 1967), 272.

25 Ted Hughes, *Birthday Letters* (London: Faber, 1998), 39, 15, 3, 89, 122.

26 Ted Hughes, introduction to *Johnny Panic and the Bible of Dreams, and Other Prose Writings*, by Sylvia Plath (London: Faber, 1977), 13.

27 Jacqueline Rose, *The Haunting of Sylvia Plath* (London: Virgao, 1991), 73.

28 Paul Alexander, *Rough Magic: A Biography of Sylvia Plath* (New York: Viking, 1991), 348–49.

29  Valentine Cunningham, "For Better or Verse," *Times Higher Education Supplement*, 27 Nov. 1998, 20–21.

30  Ted Hughes, *Lupercal* (London: Faber, 1960), 57.

31  Sinfield, *Literature, Politics and Culture in Postwar Britain*, 208–9.

32  Barbara Everett, "Auden Askew," *London Review of Books*, 2 Dec. 1981, 5.

33  For the association of comparative literature with an attempt "to overcome national prejudices and provincialisms" and to attain "an international perspective which envisages a distant ideal of universal literary history and scholarship," see René Wellek, "The Name and Nature of Comparative Literature," in *Discriminations: Further Concepts of Criticism* (New Haven: Yale UP, 1970), 36.

34  Neil Powell, "Real Shadow: Gunn and Caravaggio," *Agenda* 37, nos. 2–3 (1999): 57 62.

35  Thom Gunn, "William Carlos Williams," *Encounter* 25, no. 1 (July 1965): 67. Several of Gunn's early American poems were also first published in this journal, including "Flying above California" and "Telegraph Avenue," in *Encounter* 16, no. 3 (Mar. 1961): 3–5.

36  Clive Wilmer, "Definition and Flow: A Personal Reading of Thom Gunn," *PN Review* 5, no. 3 (1978): 52.

37  Thom Gunn, "Three Hard Women: H.D., Marianne Moore, and Mina Loy" (1988), in *Shelf Life: Essays, Memoirs and an Interview* (London: Faber, 1994), 40. Gunn recalled in 1999 that "the person whose syllabics were of greatest interest to me was my old friend, Donald Hall" (Campbell, *Thom Gunn in Conversation*, 45).

38  Campbell, *Thom Gunn in Conversation*, 55.

39  Thom Gunn, "Christopher Isherwood: Getting Things Right" (1990), in *Shelf Life*, 186, 196, 182.

40  *Positives: Verses by Thom Gunn, Photographs by Ander Gunn* (London: Faber, 1966), 42.

41  Martin Dodsworth, "Thom Gunn: Poetry as Action and Submission," in *The Poetry of Survival: A Contemporary Survey*, ed. Martin Dodsworth (London: Faber, 1970), 196.

42  Colin Falck, "Uncertain Violence," *New Review* 3, no. 32 (Nov. 1996): 37–41; Ian Hamilton, "The Call of the Cool," *Times Literary Supplement*, 23 July 1982, 782; Alan Bold, *Thom Gunn and Ted Hughes* (Edinburgh: Oliver and Boyd, 1976), 78.

43  John Bayley, "Castles and Communes," *Times Literary Supplement*, 24 Sept. 1976, 1194.

44  Thom Gunn, "Ben Jonson" (1974), in *The Occasions of Poetry*, 111.

45  "Thom Gunn: The Art of Poetry LXXII," 148.

46  Brendan Bernhard, "Boss Cupid's Poet: The Good Life and Hard Times of Thom Gunn," *LA Weekly*, 17–23 Nov. 2000; 10 June 2001 ⟨http://www.laweekly.com/ink/00/52/wls-bernhard.shtml⟩.

47  Gunn made this remark when introducing a reading of "Sunlight" on BBC Radio 3, 3 Sept. 1989.

48  "Thom Gunn: The Art of Poetry LXXII," 167.

49  R. W. Emerson, "The Over-Soul," in *The Collected Works of Ralph Waldo Emerson*, 2:

*Essays, First Series*, ed. Alfred R. Ferguson and Jean Ferguson Carr (Cambridge, MA: Harvard UP, 1979), 159–75.

50  Graham Fawcett, "Thom Gunn's Castle," BBC Radio 3, 4 Mar. 1986.

51  Adrienne Rich, *The Will to Change: Poems, 1968–1970* (New York: Norton 1971).

52  *Poet of the Month: Thom Gunn*, interview with Clive Wilmer, BBC Radio 3, 3 Sept. 1989; transcribed in Clive Wilmer, *Poets Talking: The 'Poet of the Month' Interviews from BBC Radio 3* (Manchester, England: Carcanet, 1994), 5.

53  Gunn, "My Life Up to Now," 184.

54  Julian Gitzen, "Transatlantic Poets and the Tradition Trap," *Critical Quarterly* 25, no. 2 (summer 1983): 53.

55  Thom Gunn, "Adventurous Song: Robert Duncan as Romantic Modernist," in *Shelf Life*, 144, 146; Thom Gunn, *Boss Cupid* (London: Faber, 2000), 3.

56  Gunn, *Boss Cupid*, 20–21.

57  Thom Gunn, "Fever in the Morning: Jim Powell" (1990), in *Shelf Life*, 121.

58  Thom Gunn, "Outside of the Box: Elizabeth Bishop" (1990), in *Shelf Life*, 77–78.

59  Thom Gunn, "Fulke Greville" (1968), in *The Occasions of Poetry*, 75; Gunn, "Ben Jonson," 114.

60  Quoted in Thom Gunn, *Contemporary Authors*, New Revision Series 33 (1991): 196.

61  Thom Gunn, "My Suburban Muse" (1974), in *The Occasions of Poetry*, 153–56.

62  Blake Morrison, *The Movement: English Poetry and Fiction of the 1950s* (Oxford: Oxford UP, 1980), 57–64.

63  Thom Gunn, "As If Startled Awake: The Poetry of Janet Lewis," in *Shelf Life*, 68.

64  Sontag quoted in Bernhard, "Boss Cupid's Poet"; Christopher Buckley and Gary Young, eds., *The Geography of Home: California's Poetry of Place* (Berkeley: Heyday Books, 1999); M. H. Abrams and Stephen Greenblatt, eds., *Norton Anthology of English Literature*, 7th ed. (New York: Norton, 2000), 2:2576–79. The poems included here are "Considering the Snail," "A Map of the City," "Black Jackets," "My Sad Captains," and "From the Wave."

65  William Carlos Williams, "The American Spirit in Art," *Proceedings of the American Academy of Arts and Letters*, 2d series, 2 (1952): 59. See also Mike Weaver, *William Carlos Williams: The American Background* (Cambridge, England: Cambridge UP, 1971), 87.

66  August Kleinzahler, "The Plain Style and the City," *Agenda* 37, nos. 2–3 (1999): 44.

67  Ibid., 47.

68  Alan Sinfield, "Thom Gunn and the Largest Gathering of the Decade," *London Review of Books*, 13 Feb. 1992, 16–17, and *Cultural Politics: Queer Reading* (London: Routledge, 1994), 76–81.

69  Gunn, *Boss Cupid*, 44.

70  Thom Gunn, "A Record: Allen Ginsberg's Life" (1989), in *Shelf Life*, 100, 107.

71  Gunn described himself as a socialist in response to a question at a poetry reading at Portland State University, Oregon, April 1989, and again in an interview in January

1999 (Campbell, *Thom Gunn in Conversation*, 20). In a June 1957 letter to *London Magazine*, Gunn wrote that "political engagement has nothing to do with literary merit"; however, according to Blake Morrison, Gunn is "the one Movement poet to have moved not from the communal towards the individual, but from the individual towards the communal" (Morrison, *The Movement*, 291, 276).

72  Gunn, *Boss Cupid*, 114.

73  Leo Bersani, *The Freudian Body: Psychoanalysis and Art* (New York: Columbia UP, 1986), 20, 51. For the representation of AIDS in various American poets, see Deborah Landau, " 'How to Live. What to Do.' The Poetics and Politics of AIDS," *American Literature* 68 (1996): 193–225. Landau contrasts Gunn's "reticent" tone (204) with the more "explicitly polemical" style of writers such as Paul Monette (201).

74  Susan Sontag, *AIDS and Its Metaphors* (New York: Farrar, Straus and Giroux, 1989), 86; Sacvan Bercovitch, *The American Jeremiad* (Madison: U of Wisconsin P, 1978).

75  David Fulton, " 'Too Much Birthday Cake': Gunn and the English Resistance to American Confessional Verse," *Symbiosis* 3 (1999): 41, 47–48.

76  Julia Kristeva, *Powers of Horror: An Essay on Abjection* (1980), trans. Leon S. Roudiez (New York: Columbia UP, 1982).

77  Robert Lowell, *For the Union Dead* (London: Faber, 1965), 68.

78  Quoted in Fulton, " 'Too Much Birthday Cake,' " 51.

79  Plath, *Letters Home*, 446.

80  Sylvia Plath, *Collected Poems*, ed. Ted Hughes (London: Faber, 1981), 114, 129. Subsequent page references to Plath's poetry are taken from this edition and cited in the text.

81  Sylvia Plath, *The Bell Jar* (London: Faber, 1966), 80.

82  Rose, *Haunting of Sylvia Plath*, 65–113.

83  Quoted in Plath, *Letters Home*, 500.

84  Hughes, *Birthday Letters*, 186.

85  Thomas West, *Ted Hughes* (London: Methuen, 1985), 43.

86  Charles Newman, "Candor Is the Only Wile: The Art of Sylvia Plath," in *The Art of Sylvia Plath: A Symposium*, ed. Charles Newman (London: Faber, 1970), 26.

87  A. Alvarez, *The Savage God: A Study of Suicide* (London: Weidenfeld and Nicolson, 1971), 19.

88  John Bayley, "A Poet Insufficiently Himself?" *New Review* 4, no. 43 (Oct. 1977): 12.

89  R. W. Emerson, "Nature," in *The Collected Works of Ralph Waldo Emerson, 1: Nature, Addresses, and Lectures*, ed. Alfred R. Ferguson (Cambridge, MA: Harvard UP, 1971), 10.

90  Thomas E. Yingling, *AIDS and the National Body*, ed. Robyn Wiegman (Durham, NC: Duke UP, 1997), 154, 157.

91  Frederick Buell, "Sylvia Plath's Traditionalism," in *Critical Essays on Sylvia Plath*, ed. Linda W. Wagner (Boston: Hall, 1984), 153.

92  Rose, *Haunting of Sylvia Plath*, 140. In a journal entry for 1956, Plath also talks about "an absorbing if oversimplified surrealist movie," *Rêves à Vendre*, at the Studio

Montparnasse in Paris, "a sequence of dreams inspired by artists like Max Ernst, Man Ray, Ferdinand Léger, Calder and Marcel Duchamp: a mixture of droll . . . and disturbing" (*Journals of Sylvia Plath*, 560).

93  George Steiner, "Dying Is an Art," in Newman, *The Art of Sylvia Plath*, 217; Arthur Oberg, *Modern American Lyric: Lowell, Berryman, Creeley, and Plath* (New Brunswick, NJ: Rutgers UP, 1978), 142.

94  Plath, *Letters Home*, 146. On the significance of doubles in Plath's work, see Linda W. Wagner, introduction to *Critical Essays on Sylvia Plath*, 17.

95  Hughes, *Birthday Letters*, 103. For a discussion of "Black Coat" in relation to the reception of *Birthday Letters*, see Sarah Churchwell, "Secrets and Lies: Plath, Privacy, Publication and Ted Hughes's *Birthday Letters*," *Contemporary Literature* 42, no. 1 (spring 2001): 132–33.

96  Ted Hughes, "Notes on the Chronological Order of Sylvia Plath's Poems," in Newman, *The Art of Sylvia Plath*, 191.

97  Plath, *Letters Home*, 498.

98  Sylvia Plath, "Ten Poems," *Encounter* 22, no. 4 (Oct. 1963): 45.

99  Hughes, "Notes on the Chronological Order of Sylvia Plath's Poems," 195.

100  Sylvia Plath, "Context" (1962), in *Johnny Panic and the Bible of Dreams*, 92.

101  Elaine Tyler May, "Explosive Issues: Sex, Women, and the Bomb," in *Recasting America: Culture and Politics in the Age of Cold War*, ed. Lary May (Chicago: U of Chicago P, 1989), 163.

102  A. Alvarez, "Introduction: The New Poetry, or Beyond the Gentility Principle," in *The New Poetry*, ed. A. Alvarez, 2d ed. (Harmondsworth, England: Penguin, 1966), 32.

103  Leerom Medovoi, "Democracy, Capitalism, and American Literature: The Cold War Construction of J. D. Salinger's Paperback Hero," in *The Other Fifties: Interrogating Midcentury American Icons*, ed. Joel Foreman (Urbana: U of Illinois P, 1997), 276.

104  Quoted in Rose, *Haunting of Sylvia Plath*, 105.

105  Samuel Johnson, *The Complete English Poems*, ed. J. D. Fleeman (New Haven: Yale UP, 1971), 89.

106  *Journals of Sylvia Plath*, 360.

8

## Virtual Englands:
### Pynchon's Transatlantic Heresies

1  Thomas Hill Schaub, *American Fiction in the Cold War* (Madison: U of Wisconsin P, 1991), 190.

2  Richard Poirier, "The Importance of Thomas Pynchon," in *Mindful Pleasures: Essays on Thomas Pynchon*, ed. George Levine and David Leverenz (Boston: Little, Brown, 1976), 28–29.

3 Edward Mendelson, "The Sacred, the Profane, and *The Crying of Lot 49*," in *Pynchon: A Collection of Critical Essays*, ed. Edward Mendelson (Englewood Cliffs, NJ: Prentice-Hall, 1978), 134–35.

4 Stephen Paul Miller, *The Seventies Now: Culture as Surveillance* (Durham, NC: Duke UP, 1999), 202.

5 Paul Maltby, *Dissident Postmodernists: Barthelme, Coover, Pynchon* (Philadelphia: U of Pennsylvania P, 1991), 195–96.

6 Thomas Pynchon, *Slow Learner: Early Stories* (1984; rpt. London: Random House/Vintage, 1995), 21.

7 Thomas Pynchon, *The Crying of Lot 49* (1966; rpt. London: Pan/Picador, 1979), 17.

8 Deborah L. Madsen, *American Exceptionalism* (Edinburgh: Edinburgh UP/British Association for American Studies, 1998), 152, 155–56.

9 Leo Bersani, "Pynchon, Paranoia, and Literature," *Representations* 25 (1989): 103, 101, 108.

10 Tony Tanner, *City of Words: A Study of American Fiction in the Mid–Twentieth Century* (London: Jonathan Cape, 1971), 156. Tanner qualified his opinion by adding that "the novelist is clearly inwardly affected by the Manichaeanism of his characters" (156).

11 Jules Siegel, "Who Is Thomas Pynchon . . . and Why Did He Take Off with My Wife?" *Playboy*, Mar. 1977, 122.

12 Thomas Pynchon, *V* (1963; rpt. London: Pan/Picador, 1975), 167–68. Subsequent page references to this edition are cited in the text.

13 Edward Mendelson, "Gravity's Encyclopaedia," in Levine and Leverenz, *Mindful Pleasures*, 165, 258, 178.

14 Thomas Pynchon, *Gravity's Rainbow* (New York: Viking, 1973), 549. Subsequent page references to this edition are cited in the text.

15 Pynchon, *Slow Learner*, 7.

16 Thomas Pynchon, introduction to *The Teachings of Don B.: Satires, Parodies, Fables, Illustrated Stories, and Plays of Donald Barthelme*, ed. Kim Herzinger (New York: Random House/Turtle Bay Books, 1992), xvii–xviii. For a discussion of cultural Catholicism in Barthelme and Kerouac, see Paul Giles, *American Catholic Arts and Fictions: Culture, Ideology, Aesthetics* (Cambridge, England: Cambridge UP, 1992), 375–93, 405–24.

17 Thomas Pynchon, "Nearer, My Couch, to Thee," *New York Times Book Review*, 6 June 1993, 3, 57.

18 Thomas Pynchon, "The Heart's Eternal Vow," *New York Times Book Review*, 10 Apr. 1988, 47, 49.

19 John A. McClure, "Postmodern/Post-Secular: Contemporary Fiction and Spirituality," *Modern Fiction Studies* 41 (1995): 144.

20 Pynchon, *Slow Learner*, 20.

21 Susan Rubin Suleiman, *Subversive Intent: Gender, Politics, and the Avant-Garde* (Cambridge, MA: Harvard UP, 1990), 150.

22  Jonathan Dollimore, *Sexual Dissidence: Augustine to Wilde, Freud to Foucault* (Oxford: Clarendon Press, 1991), 131–47.

23  Thomas Pynchon, "Is It O.K. to Be a Luddite?" *New York Times Book Review*, 28 Oct. 1984, 40–41.

24  Thomas Pynchon, *Vineland* (Boston: Little, Brown, 1990), 272–73. Subsequent page references to this edition are cited in the text.

25  For a discussion of the "discourse of Lombrosian criminal anthropology," see William Greenslade, *Degeneration, Culture and the Novel, 1880–1940* (Cambridge, England: Cambridge UP, 1994), 88–119.

26  F. Scott Fitzgerald, *The Great Gatsby*, ed. Matthew J. Bruccoli (Cambridge, England: Cambridge UP, 1991), 140.

27  Bersani, "Pynchon, Paranoia, and Literature," 113, 107.

28  David Cowart, "The Luddite Vision: *Mason & Dixon*," *American Literature* 71 (1999): 350, 352.

29  Tony Tanner, *The American Mystery: American Literature from Emerson to DeLillo* (Cambridge, England: Cambridge UP, 2000), 226, 231.

30  For a discussion of how the novel "performs incompleteness in a complicated and discreetly moving way," see Michael Wood, "Pynchon's *Mason & Dixon*," *Raritan* 17, no. 4 (1998): 129–30.

31  Benedict Anderson, *The Spectre of Comparisons: Nationality, Southeast Asia, and the World* (London: Verso, 1998), 26.

32  Ibid., 58, 61, 26.

33  David Seed, *The Fictional Labyrinths of Thomas Pynchon* (Basingstoke, England: Macmillan, 1988), 115.

34  For a good overview of fetish theory, see the first chapter in Emily Apter, *Feminizing the Fetish: Psychoanalysis and Narrative Obsession in Turn-of-the-Century France* (Ithaca, NY: Cornell UP, 1991), 1–14.

35  "The book is full of dead landscapes of every kind—from the garbage heaps of the modern world to the lunar barrenness of the actual desert" (Tanner, *City of Words*, 157).

36  "Written during the consumer boom of the Kennedy years, *V* reveals a society where the space of personal meaning has been largely occupied by the signifying power of commodities" (Maltby, *Dissident Postmodernists*, 133).

37  Pynchon, *Slow Learner*, 21.

38  Melvyn New, "Profane and Stencilled Texts," *Georgia Review* 33 (1979): 404.

39  Paul Fussell, *The Great War and Modern Memory* (New York: Oxford UP, 1975), 328.

40  Elaine B. Safer, *The Contemporary American Comic Epic: The Novels of Barth, Pynchon, Gaddis, and Kesey* (Detroit: Wayne State UP, 1989), 82.

41  Fussell, *The Great War and Modern Memory*, 328–29.

42  Christopher Isherwood, *Diaries, Volume 1: 1939–1960*, ed. Katherine Bucknell (1996; rpt. London: Random House/Vintage, 1997), 58.

43  Slavoj Žižek, *The Plague of Fantasies* (London: Verso, 1997), 104.

44 Michael Taussig, "*Maleficium:* State Fetishism," in *Fetishism as Cultural Discourse,* ed. Emily Apter and William Pietz (Ithaca, NY: Cornell UP, 1993), 246, 240.

45 David D. Hall, "Readers and Writers in Early New England," in *A History of the Book in America. Volume 1: The Colonial Book in the Atlantic World,* ed. Hugh Amory and David D. Hall (Cambridge, England: Cambridge UP / American Antiquarian Society, 2000), 128.

46 "Waiting for the Bang," *Times Literary Supplement,* 16 Nov. 1973, 1389.

47 Jacqueline Rose, *States of Fantasy* (Oxford: Clarendon Press, 1996), 67.

48 Thomas Pynchon, *Mason & Dixon* (New York: Henry Holt, 1997), 192. Subsequent page references to this edition are cited in the text.

49 Robert Poole, *Time's Alteration: Calendar Reform in Early Modern England* (London: University College London Press, 1998), 103–20.

50 Elizabeth Jane Wall Hinds, "Sari, Sorry, and the Vortex of History: Calendar Reform, Anachronism, and Language Change in *Mason & Dixon,*" *American Literary History* 12 (2000): 203.

51 Tanner, *American Mystery,* 236–37.

52 Hinds, "Sari, Sorry, and the Vortex of History," 190–92; Tanner, *American Mystery,* 224.

53 Edward W. Soja, *Postmodern Geographies: The Reassertion of Space in Critical Social Theory* (London: Verso, 1989), 2; Brian Jarvis, *Postmodern Cartographies: The Geographical Imagination in Contemporary American Culture* (London: Pluto, 1998), 51–52.

54 Quoted in Julian Pefanis, *Heterology and the Postmodern: Bataille, Baudrillard, and Lyotard* (Durham, NC: Duke UP, 1991), 86.

9

*Virtual Americas: Cyberpastoral, Transnationalism,*
*and the Ideology of Exchange*

1 J. H. Elliott, *The Old World and the New* (Cambridge, England: Cambridge UP, 1970), 11, 14.

2 Anne McClintock, *Imperial Leather: Race, Gender and Sexuality in the Colonial Contest* (New York: Routledge, 1995), 22.

3 George Lipsitz, "Listening to Learn and Learning to Listen: Popular Culture, Cultural Theory, and American Studies," *American Quarterly* 42 (1990): 622.

4 Ross Posnock, "Assessing the Oppositional: Contemporary Intellectual Strategies," *American Literary History* 1 (1989): 148. Since 1980, Derrida's role in shaping American poststructuralism has been particularly prominent, as has Foucault's influence on critical styles of New Historicism, dating from his days at Berkeley.

5 Theodor W. Adorno, *Negative Dialectics* (1966), trans. E. B. Ashton (New York: Seabury P, 1973), 149, 142, 172, 169, 177.

6 Amy Kaplan, " 'Left Alone with America': The Absence of Empire in the Study of

American Culture," in *Cultures of United States Imperialism,* ed. Amy Kaplan and Donald E. Pease (Durham, NC: Duke UP, 1993), 18.

7   Janice Radway, "What's in a Name? Presidential Address to the American Studies Association, 20 November 1998," *American Quarterly* 51 (1999): 1–32.

8   Paul A. Bové, *In the Wake of Theory* (Hanover, NH: UP of New England, 1992), 63.

9   On American studies as a reaction against "Eurocentric forms of study," see Paul Lauter, " 'Versions of Nashville, Visions of American Studies': Presidential Address to the American Studies Association, October 27, 1994," *American Quarterly* 47 (1995): 187.

10  Donald E. Pease, "Leslie Fiedler, the Rosenberg Trial, and the Formulation of an American Canon," *boundary 2* 17, no. 1 (1990): 155–98; Nina Baym, "Melodramas of Best Manhood: How Theories of American Fiction Exclude Women Authors," *American Quarterly* 33 (1981): 129.

11  James W. Carey, *Communication as Culture: Essays on Media and Society* (Boston: Unwin Hyman, 1989), 97.

12  Fredric Jameson, "On 'Cultural Studies,' " *Social Text* 34 (1993): 47.

13  See his critique of V. L. Parrington and Theodore Dreiser, reprinted as "Reality in America" in Lionel Trilling, *The Liberal Imagination: Essays on Literature and Society* (London: Secker and Warburg, 1951), 3–21.

14  Howard Horwitz, *By the Law of Nature: Form and Value in Nineteenth-Century America* (New York: Oxford UP, 1991), 251.

15  Adorno, *Negative Dialectics,* 5.

16  Marjorie Perloff, "Empiricism Once More," *Modern Language Quarterly* 54 (1993): 130–31. Perloff refers here to Fredric Jameson, *Postmodernism: or, The Cultural Logic of Late Capitalism* (Durham, NC: Duke UP, 1991).

17  For the standard account of how determinate absences shape literary texts, see Pierre Macherey, *A Theory of Literary Production,* trans. Geoffrey Wall (London: Routledge and Kegan Paul, 1978).

18  Adorno, *Negative Dialectics,* 172.

19  On the theoretical difficulties associated with American studies, see Giles Gunn, *The Culture of Criticism and the Criticism of Culture* (New York: Oxford UP, 1987), 147. For the view that "American Studies has not had the influence on other disciplines that one might expect and has produced an interdisciplinary subfield rather than a reorganization of knowledge," see Jonathan Culler, *Framing the Sign: Criticism and Its Institutions* (Norman: U of Oklahoma P, 1988), 8.

20  Patrick Brantlinger, *Crusoe's Footprints: Cultural Studies in Britain and America* (New York: Routledge, 1990), 28.

21  Scott McLemee, "A Star of American Studies (or Is That 'Un-American Studies'?)," *Chronicle of Higher Education,* 15 June 2001, 12–13. See also Paul Lauter, *From Walden Pond to Jurassic Park: Activism, Culture, and American Studies* (Durham, NC: Duke UP, 2001).

22  Paul Lauter, "Little White Sheep, or How I Learned to Dress Blue," *Yale Journal of Criticism* 8, no. 2 (1995): 108, and "Caste, Class, and Canon," in *Feminisms: An Anthology of Literary Theory and Criticism*, rev. ed., Robyn R. Warhol and Diane Price Herndl (Basingstoke, England: Macmillan, 1997), 129–50.

23  On the ironies associated with e pluribus unum in relation to arguments over the literary canon, see William C. Spengemann, "E Pluribus Minimum," *Early American Literature* 29 (1994): 276–94.

24  Gayatri Chakravorty Spivak, *Outside in the Teaching Machine* (New York: Routledge, 1993), 279, 262.

25  For the classic statement of how "Ideology interpellates individuals as subjects," see Louis Althusser, "Ideology and Ideological State Apparatuses (Notes towards an Investigation)," in *Essays on Ideology* (London: Verso, 1984), 1–60. On the complicity of cultural studies with global capitalism, see Slavoj Žižek, "Multiculturalism, or The Cultural Logic of Multinational Capitalism," *New Left Review* 225 (Sept.–Oct. 1997): 28–51, and *The Ticklish Subject: The Absent Centre of Political Ontology* (London: Verso, 1999), 218.

26  Jim McGuigan, *Cultural Populism* (London: Routledge, 1992), 5. For a longer analysis of the position of cultural studies in Britain, see Paul Giles, "Virtual Americas: The Internationalization of American Studies and the Ideology of Exchange," *American Quarterly* 50 (1998): 523–47.

27  Bill Schwarz, "Where Is Cultural Studies?" *Cultural Studies* 8 (1994): 387.

28  John Guillory, *Cultural Capital: The Problem of Literary Canon Formation* (Chicago: U of Chicago P, 1993), 265–73.

29  Anthony Easthope, *Literary into Cultural Studies* (London: Routledge, 1991), 13.

30  Jameson, "On 'Cultural Studies,' " 49.

31  Philip Fisher, *Still the New World: American Literature in a Culture of Creative Destruction* (Cambridge, MA: Harvard UP, 1999), 5, 17, 7.

32  Fisher, *Still the New World*, 17.

33  In relation to the American South, see, for instance, Richard Gray, *Southern Aberrations: Writers of the American South and the Problems of Regionalism* (Baton Rouge: Louisiana State UP, 2000), 500.

34  Jameson, "On 'Cultural Studies,' " 50.

35  T. J. Jackson Lears, *No Place of Grace: Antimodernism and the Transformation of American Culture, 1880–1920*, 2d ed. (New York: Pantheon, 1983), xiii.

36  Raymond Williams, "Base and Superstructure in Marxist Cultural Theory," in *Problems in Materialism and Culture: Selected Essays* (London: Verso, 1980), 37.

37  Stuart Hall, "The Emergence of Cultural Studies and the Crisis of the Humanities," *October* 53 (summer 1990): 17–18.

38  Lears, *No Place of Grace*, xii–xiii.

39  T. J. Jackson Lears, "The Concept of Cultural Hegemony: Problems and Possibilities," *American Historical Review* 90 (1985): 573.

40 Stuart Hall and Martin Jacques, introduction to *New Times: The Changing Face of Politics in the 1990s* (London: Verso, 1989), 11.

41 Stuart Hall, "The Meaning of New Times," in *New Times*, 118.

42 William C. Spengemann, *A Mirror for Americanists: Reflections on the Idea of American Literature* (Hanover, NH: UP of New England, 1989), 26; Peter Carafiol, "The Constraints of History: Revision and Revolution in American Literary Studies," *College English* 50 (1988): 605.

43 Raymond Williams, *The Long Revolution* (London: Chatto and Windus, 1961), 287, 46.

44 Raymond Williams, *Culture and Society, 1780–1950* (London: Chatto and Windus, 1958), 325; Williams, *The Long Revolution*, 31.

45 Edward Said, *The World, the Text, and the Critic* (Cambridge, MA: Harvard UP, 1983), 241; Anne Beezer and Peter Osborne, "Orientalism and After: An Interview with Edward Said," *Radical Philosophy* 63 (1993): 28. This disagreement between Williams and Said over the nature of community was highlighted in their dialogue at the Institute of Education, London, in 1986, where Said described "the whole problematic of exile and immigration" as "the great modern or, if you like, postmodern fact, the standing outside of cultures." See "Media, Margins and Modernity: Raymond Williams and Edward Said," in Raymond Williams, *The Politics of Modernism: Against the New Conformists*, ed. Tony Pinkney (London: Verso, 1989), 196.

46 Paul Gilroy, *The Black Atlantic: Modernity and Double Consciousness* (London: Verso, 1993), 27, 7.

47 Paul Gilroy, "Cultural Studies and Ethnic Absolutism," in *Cultural Studies*, ed. Lawrence Grossberg, Cary Nelson, and Paula Treichler (New York: Routledge, 1992), 190, 192.

48 Gilroy, *The Black Atlantic*, 6, 34–35.

49 Paul Gilroy, *Against Race: Imagining Political Culture beyond the Color Line* (Cambridge, MA: Harvard UP, 2000), 102, 75.

50 Ibid., 131, 2.

51 Neeta Bhasin, review of *Against Race*, by Paul Gilroy, *Callaloo* 23, no. 3 (2000): 1151.

52 Stuart Hall, *Critical Dialogues in Cultural Studies*, ed. David Morley and Kuan-Hsing Chen (London: Routledge, 1996), 498; Hall, "The Emergence of Cultural Studies and the Crisis of the Humanities," 13.

53 Stuart Hall, "Cultural Studies and the Centre: Some Problematics and Problems," in *Culture, Media, Language: Working Papers in Cultural Studies, 1972–79* (London: Hutchinson/Centre for Contemporary Cultural Studies, University of Birmingham, 1980), 23, 20.

54 Hall, *Critical Dialogues in Cultural Studies*, 133.

55 Hall, "The Meaning of New Times," 133.

56 Hall, *Critical Dialogues in Cultural Studies*, 466.

57 Stuart Hall and David Held, "Citizens and Citizenship," in *New Times*, 173, 184.

58 Stuart Hall, "Culture, Community, Nation," *Cultural Studies* 7 (1993): 360.

59   Williams, *Culture and Society*, 325.

60   Hall, "Culture, Community, Nation," 360–61.

61   Quoted in Raymond Williams, *Keywords: A Vocabulary of Culture and Society* (N.p.: Fontana/Croom Helm, 1976), 48–50.

62   Williams, *Culture and Society*, 325.

63   Rob Wilson, "Exporting Christian Transcendentalism, Importing Hawaiian Sugar: The Trans-Americanization of Hawai'i," *American Literature* 72 (2000): 541.

64   For Jürgen Habermas, one of the characteristics of the modern "functionally differentiated society" is precisely that it "cannot be adequately grasped by holistic concepts" of communal identity. Hence he casually dismisses yearnings for older forms of national identity as "kitsch." See Jürgen Habermas, "Further Reflections on the Public Sphere," in *Habermas and the Public Sphere*, ed. Craig Calhoun (Cambridge, MA: MIT Press, 1992), 436; Peter Dews, ed., *Autonomy and Solidarity: Interviews with Jürgen Habermas*, rev. ed. (London: Verso, 1992), 179.

65   Jonathan Bate, *Romantic Ecology: Wordsworth and the Environmental Tradition* (London: Routledge, 1991), 29, 40.

66   Richard Rorty, *Achieving Our Country: Leftist Thought in Twentieth-Century America* (Cambridge, MA: Harvard UP, 1998), 125, 129, 134.

67   Homi K. Bhabha, *The Location of Culture* (London: Routledge, 1994), 143.

68   Catherine L. Albanese, *Nature Religion in America: From the Algonkian Indians to the New Age* (Chicago: U of Chicago P, 1990), 154–55.

69   Ibid., 197; Andrew Ross, *The Chicago Gangster Theory of Life: Nature's Debt to Society* (London: Verso, 1994), 16–17, 100.

70   Roderick Nash, *Wilderness and the American Mind*, rev. ed. (New Haven: Yale UP, 1967), 188, 248–49.

71   Perry Miller, *Nature's Nation* (Cambridge, MA: Harvard UP, 1967), *The New England Mind: The Seventeenth Century* (New York: Macmillan, 1939), and *The New England Mind: From Colony to Province* (Cambridge, MA: Harvard UP, 1953).

72   Terry Eagleton, *The Idea of Culture* (Oxford: Blackwell, 2000), 134.

73   Wai-chee Dimock, *Residues of Justice: Literature, Law, Philosophy* (Berkeley: U of California P, 1996), 60, 9.

74   Bate, *Romantic Ecology*, 18.

75   Lawrence Buell, "Toxic Discourse," *Critical Inquiry* 24 (1998): 639–65.

76   Lawrence Buell, *The Environmental Imagination: Thoreau, Nature Writing, and the Formation of American Culture* (Cambridge, MA: Harvard UP, 1995), 2.

77   Ross, *The Chicago Gangster Theory of Life*, 13.

78   Don DeLillo, *Underworld* (New York: Scribner, 1997), 791, 102.

79   Buell, "Toxic Discourse," 663.

80   Donald Worster, *Nature's Economy: A History of Ecological Ideas* (1977; rpt. Cambridge, England: Cambridge UP, 1985), 330–31.

81   Bate, *Romantic Ecology*, 11.

82 Jonathan Bate, review of *The Environmental Imagination*, by Lawrence Buell, *ANQ* 9, no. 2 (spring 1996): 56.

83 Eric Cheyfitz, "Matthiessen's *American Renaissance:* Circumscribing the Revolution," *American Quarterly* 41 (1989): 354–55.

84 Kwame Anthony Appiah, "Cosmopolitan Patriots," *Critical Inquiry* 23 (1997): 632.

85 Theodor W. Adorno and Max Horkheimer, *Dialectic of Enlightenment*, trans. John Cumming (London: Verso, 1979), 13.

86 Rorty, *Achieving Our Country*, 99.

87 Richard Rorty, *Philosophy and the Mirror of Nature* (Oxford: Blackwell, 1980), 43, 86, 5.

88 Ibid., 357, 61.

89 Adorno, *Negative Dialectics*, 106, 112. See also Fredric Jameson, *Late Marxism: Adorno, or, The Persistence of the Dialectic* (London: Verso, 1990), 9.

90 Jean Baudrillard, *America* (1986), trans. Chris Turner (London: Verso, 1988), 116.

91 Margaret Morse, *Virtualities: Television, Media Art, and Cyberculture* (Bloomington: Indiana UP, 1998), 14.

92 DeLillo, *Underworld*, 155, 813.

93 Slavoj Žižek, *The Plague of Fantasies* (London: Verso, 1997), 143.

94 Leo Marx, "The Full Thoreau," *New York Review of Books*, 15 July 1999, 45. Marx's classic account of American pastoral is *The Machine in the Garden: Technology and the Pastoral Ideal in America* (New York: Oxford UP, 1964).

95 For a dystopian view of digital technology as entirely complicit with American capitalism, epitomized by the way an American Express advertisement portrays itself as a "virtual credit space," see Ken Hillis, *Digital Sensations: Space, Identity, and Embodiment in Virtual Reality* (Minneapolis: U of Minnesota P, 1999), 198.

96 Eagleton, *The Idea of Culture*, 63. On the revival of nationalism, see also Benedict Anderson, *The Spectre of Comparisons: Nationalism, Southeast Asia, and the World* (London: Verso, 1998), 58–74.

97 Upendra Baxi, visiting professor of law at New York University and former vice chancellor of the University of Delhi, quoted in a press release from the Transnational Resource and Action Center, 12 Mar. 1999.

# INDEX

Blake, William, 63, 188, 189, 255
Bourdieu, Pierre, 127, 147–49, 154–55
Bourne, Randolph, 134
Bové, Paul A., 257
Bradbury, Malcolm, 3
Bradstreet, Anne, 215, 269
Bréton, André, 90, 101, 106, 118; *Nadja*, 119
Bright, John, 38
British Association for American Studies, 186–87
Britten, Benjamin, 50
Brontë, Emily, 188, 217
Brown, William Wells, 32–33
Buell, Lawrence, 12–14, 54, 279
Buñuel, Luis, 121, 218
Burke, Edmund, 81
Butler, R. A., 174–75

Calvinism, 58, 59–60, 83, 243, 276. *See also* Puritanism
Capitalism, 9–14, 37–38, 120, 122, 162–63, 182, 281, 285, 328 n.95
Carafiol, Peter, 269
Caravaggio, Michelangelo Merisi da, 193
Carlyle, Thomas, 36–37, 41, 44–45, 57, 59, 60
Carroll, Lewis, 173
Catholicism, 42–43, 279; and Pynchon, 228–31, 242–46
Cavell, Stanley, 279
Céline, Louis-Ferdinand, 122–23
Censorship, 17, 63, 78, 101, 187; and Frost, 127, 139, 149; and Nabokov, 172–77, 179, 181. *See also* Obscenity
Central Intelligence Agency (CIA), 164, 185
Centre for Contemporary Cultural Studies, 258, 267, 269–71
Chance, 117–19
Chartism, 24
Chase, Richard, 257
Cheyfitz, Eric, 144, 281
Christianity, 7–8, 10, 11, 13, 20, 164, 181, 184, 251–52; and Douglass, 25, 27, 32,

46; and Melville, 59, 75, 76–80. *See also* Calvinism; Catholicism; Protestantism; Puritanism
Civil War. *See* American Civil War
Clark, T. J., 88, 94
Clarkson, Thomas, 23
Class, 16, 18, 39, 58, 69, 72, 262; and Gunn, 185, 187, 210; and Nabokov, 173–75; and Pynchon, 226, 246–47
Clifford, James, 90
Cobbett, William, 39
Cobden, Richard, 38
Coburn, Alvin Langdon, 115–16
Cocteau, Jean, 91
Cold War, 6, 10, 52–53, 186, 225, 257–58, 262, 272, 278, 286; and Frost, 127, 143, 145, 148, 150, 155; and Nabokov, 158–60, 165–66, 171; and Plath, 221–22
Coleridge, Samuel Taylor, 18, 273
Colonialism, 5, 15, 75, 256, 260; and Pynchon, 226–27, 239, 245–46. *See also* Postcolonialism
Confessional Poetry, 212–13
Congress for Cultural Freedom, 185–86
Conrad, Joseph, 86
Cornell, Joseph, 206
Cowley, Malcolm, 150
Crèvecoeur, J. Hector St. John de, 7, 166
Crosland, Anthony, 187
Cuban Missile Crisis, 221–22
Cultural Studies, 257–58, 262–65, 270–71, 274
Cunliffe, Marcus, 187
Cybernetics, 18–19
Cyberspace, 15, 17–18, 125. *See also* Internet

Dadaism, 91, 120
Dali, Salvador, 154
Damrosch, David, 5
Dante (Dante Alighieri), 138, 142
Darwin, Charles, 43–44, 77, 280
Davie, Donald, 202, 211
Decadence, 94; and Frost, 127, 129–36, 149–50, 153, 155–56

Fussell, Paul, 239, 240
Frye, Northrop, 7, 214

Gagnier, Regenia, 5
Garrison, William Lloyd, 23–27, 29, 30, 34,
    36, 45, 46, 291 n.5
Gaskell, Elizabeth, 37–38, 39, 46
Gender, 18, 23, 86, 139, 177, 262; and
    James, 96, 97; and *Lolita*, 159, 162; and
    Modernism, 123, 124, 131. *See also*
    Homosexuality
Genet, Jean, 241
Gilroy, Paul, 269–71, 281; *Against Race*,
    270–71; *Black Atlantic*, 31, 270
Ginsberg, Allen, 210
Globalization, 5–7, 9–10, 74, 177, 228,
    268, 274–75, 283, 285–86
Goethe, Johann Wolfgang von, 17, 142, 277
Gramsci, Antonio, 266–68
Greenberg, Clement, 120
Greene, Graham, 172
Greville, Fulke, 206
Griffiths, Julia, 24–25, 30, 46, 293 n.29
Guillory, John, 264
Gunn, Thom, 1, 16, 183–213, 223–24;
    "Beaters," 195; "Berlin in Ruins," 194,
    195; *Boss Cupid*, 203–5, 211; "Cafeteria in
    Boston," 205; "Carnal Knowledge," 191–
    92, 200; "Confessions of the Life Art-
    ist," 194; "Considering the Snail," 192;
    "Courtesies of the Interregnum," 203–
    5; "Dancing David," 211; "Duncan," 203;
    "Epitaph," 210; *Fighting Terms*, 184, 191–
    92, 195, 204; "For a Birthday," 192, 195;
    "Gas Poker," 213; "Incident on a Jour-
    ney," 184; "In Santa Maria del Popolo,"
    193; "Interruption," 196; "Invitation
    from San Francisco to My Brother,"
    200–201; "Jack Straw's Castle," 212; "J
    Car," 206–8; "Kiss at Bayreuth," 195;
    *Man with Night Sweats*, 203–8, 211, 213;
    "Market at Turk," 187; "Misanthropos,"
    187; *Moly*, 195, 199, 211; *My Sad Cap-
    tains*, 192, 198; "On the Move," 187;
"Operation," 204–5; *Passages of Joy*,
    196–98, 201–2, 223; "Patch Work,"
    207–8; and politics, 210–11, 319 n.71;
    *Positives*, 197–98; *Sense of Movement*,
    184, 187, 191–92, 195; "Song of a Cam-
    era," 196–97; "Sunlight," 199–200;
    "Sweet Things," 196; and syllabics, 193–
    94; "To Donald Davie in Heaven," 211;
    "To Yvor Winters, 1955," 211; *Touch*,
    193–95; "Transients and Residents,"
    201; "Troubadour," 211; "Unsettled Mo-
    torcyclist's Vision of His Death," 187;
    "Waking in a Newly Built House," 193,
    216; "Words," 195; "Words for Some
    Ash," 201

Habermas, Jürgen, 140, 327 n.64
Hall, Stuart, 258, 267–68, 271–74
Haraway, Donna, 19
Hardy, Thomas, 132–33, 213
Harland, Henry, 96
Hawthorne, Nathaniel, 47, 48, 50, 55, 59,
    80, 225; *Marble Faun*, 79–80
Hayles, N. Katherine, 18–19
Hegel, G. W. F., 17
Heidegger, Martin, 280, 282–83
Hemingway, Ernest, 123, 124, 128, 159
Herbert, George, 198
Herder, Johann Gottfried von, 17
Hobsbawm, Eric, 8
Hoggart, Richard, 269
Holbein, Hans, 103
Homosexuality, 62, 82–83, 95–97, 136,
    184–85, 206–7, 211, 308 n.31. *See also*
    Gender
Horkheimer, Max, 168, 182, 255, 281–82
Horne, Philip, 108
Horwitz, Howard, 259
Hughes, Ted, 183, 187–91, 215, 217–18,
    221, 223; *Birthday Letters*, 189–90, 220;
    "Pike," 190; as Poet Laureate, 188–89,
    223
Hutcheon, Linda, 13
Huxley, Aldous, 182, 183, 240

Huxley, Julian, 240
Huyssen, Andreas, 129, 142

Iannone, Carol, 178
Imperialism. *See* Colonialism
Internet, 246, 284, 314 n.52. *See also* Cyberspace
Ireland, 36–43, 45, 256
Irving, Washington, 51
Isherwood, Christopher, 183–84, 186, 197–98, 208, 240
Ivory, James, 99, 303 n.44

Jacobs, Harriet, 39
Jakobson, Roman, 313 n.35
James, Alice, 96, 110
James, C. L. R., 53, 271
James, Henry, 3, 47, 64, 88–119, 125–26, 127, 219, 271; *Ambassadors*, 103–5; *American Scene*, 2, 92, 93, 103, 105–15, 116, 125, 219, 274; "Beast in the Jungle," 98; "Death of the Lion," 95–96; *Golden Bowl*, 102, 109, 116; "In the Cage," 97; "Jolly Corner," 116–17; "Occasional Paris," 102–3; "Question of the Mind," 126; *Small Boy and Others*, 93, 98; *Tragic Muse*, 94–96; "Turn of the Screw," 97, 98; *What Maisie Knew*, 95; *Wings of the Dove*, 100–102, 118
James, William, 96, 99, 104, 132, 144, 259, 279, 282; *Pragmatism*, 11, 93; *Varieties of Religious Experience*, 11, 12, 234–35; "World of Pure Experience," 11
Jameson, Fredric, 8, 9–10, 126, 183, 258, 260, 265, 266, 276
Jarry, Alfred, 92
Jay, Paul, 5
Jefferson, Thomas, 18, 247, 255
Jewett, Sarah Orne, 10
Johnson, Lionel, 134
Johnson, Samuel, 61, 84, 201, 223, 251
Jonson, Ben, 198, 200, 206, 208
Joyce, James, 123, 124, 136, 138, 141, 229, 235

Kaplan, Amy, 256, 259
Kaplan, Louise J., 73
Kendrick, Walter, 179
Kennedy, John F., 146, 221, 238
Kenner, Hugh, 6, 167, 288 n.13
Kerouac, Jack, 229
Kipnis, Laura, 179
Kleinzahler, August, 208
Kristeva, Julia, 16–17, 117, 121, 170, 213
Kristol, Irving, 185

*Ladies' Home Journal*, 3
Larkin, Philip, 199, 208
Lauter, Paul, 177, 262–63, 324 n.9
Lautréamont, Comte de [pseud. For Isidore Ducasse], 89, 92
Lawrence, D. H., 126, 189; *Lady Chatterley's Lover*, 173; *Studies in Classic American Literature*, 3, 49, 61, 86, 89
Lears, T. J. Jackson, 266–68
Leavis, F. R., 64, 175, 188
Lenz, Guenter H., 6
Leopold, Aldo, 277
Levertov, Denise, 183
Lewis, R. W. B., 60, 162, 275; *American Adam*, 12–14, 19, 160, 170–71, 181, 185
Liberalism, 10, 19, 93–94, 140, 169, 272–73, 277, 280–82, 316 n.8; and American Studies, 120, 171, 186–87; in nineteenth century, 37–38, 42
Lincoln, Abraham, 25, 42
Lipsitz, George, 255
Locke, John, 255
Lombroso, Cesare, 231
Lowell, Robert, 186, 212, 213, 215
Lukács, Georg, 91
Lynch, David, 99

Madsen, Deborah L., 227–28
Magical Realism, 230, 232
Manifest Destiny, 51, 75, 86
Man Ray, 91, 120, 320 n.92
Mapplethorpe, Robert, 197
Markley, Robert, 17–18

Márquez, Gabriel García, 230
Marvell, Andrew, 81, 206
Marx, Leo, 12, 171, 284–85
Masefield, John, 49
Matisse, Henri, 126
Matthiessen, F. O., 92, 93, 257; *American Renaissance*, 52–53, 55, 278, 281
McCarthy, Joseph, 158, 164
McClintock, Anne, 254
McDowell, Tremaine, 261–62
McLuhan, H. Marshall, 35
Melville, Gansevoort, 51, 55
Melville, Herman, 1, 15, 47–87, 161, 225, 262; "Benito Cereno," 72–73; *Billy Budd*, 15, 50, 80–85, 86; *Clarel*, 55, 76, 77–80; *Confidence-Man*, 74–76, 85; "Hawthorne and His Mosses," 50–51, 59, 80, 85; *Israel Potter*, 70–72; *Mardi*, 58–59, 81; *Moby-Dick*, 32, 49–50, 52, 53, 59–64, 67, 72, 86–87, 142; *Omoo*, 49, 50, 69; "Paradise of Bachelors and the Tartarus of Maids," 55, 68–69; *Pierre*, 64–68, 86, 161, 232; "Poor Man's Pudding and Rich Man's Crumbs," 68, 69; *Redburn*, 50, 55, 56–58; "Two Temples," 70; *Typee*, 49, 50, 51–52, 55, 69; *White-Jacket*, 51, 55, 65, 84
Merchant, Ismail, 99, 303 n.44
Michaels, Walter Benn, 115, 125
Miller, Henry, 121–23
Miller, Perry, 7–8, 277
Milman, Lena, 96
Milton, John, 62–63, 138, 189
Mitchell, W. J. T., 152
Miyoshi, Masao, 10
Monarchy, 41, 61, 65–66; and Pynchon, 232, 238, 240
Montesquieu, Baron de la Brède et de, 17
Moon, Michael, 99, 100, 102
Moore, Marianne, 193
Morse, Margaret, 20, 125, 283
Morton, Donald, 18
Multiculturalism, 262–63. *See also* Cultural Studies; Ethnicity

Munson, Gorham B., 141
Myth and Symbol, 1, 3, 7, 14, 19, 89, 257–58, 272, 284; and Frost, 142, 145; and Nabokov, 159, 162

Nabokov, Nicolas, 185
Nabokov, Vladimir, 1, 3, 157–81, 208, 213, 275; "Art of Literature and Commonsense," 180; *Bend Sinister*, 162, 165; *Invitation to a Beheading*, 168; *Lolita*, 1, 14–15, 16, 157–81; *Pale Fire*, 164; *Speak, Memory*, 168
Nadeau, Maurice, 90
Nash, Roderick, 277
New Criticism, 144, 199
Nicholls, Peter, 89, 131
Niebuhr, Reinhold, 184
Nietzsche, Friedrich, 129
Nixon, Richard M., 226
Norton, Charles Eliot, 38

Obscene Publications Act (U.K.), 172–73, 314 n.49
Obscenity, 101, 314 n.52; and Douglass, 27–28, 29; and Melville, 63–64; and Nabokov, 172–73, 176, 179. *See also* Censorship
O'Connell, Daniel, 36, 39
Odger, George, 40
Oregon Question, 51, 52
Osborne, John, 184
O'Sullivan, John L., 51

Pacific Rim, 15, 233
Paine, Thomas, 81, 254, 255, 272
Pastoralism, 12–14, 164, 275–80, 284–85; and Frost, 130, 136, 139–40, 144–46, 151, 153–54
Pater, Walter, 94
Pease, Donald E., 257, 291 n.62, 315 n.63
Perloff, Marjorie, 128, 202, 260–61, 264
Phillips, Wendell, 26, 30
Photography, 107, 115–16, 305 n.82
Picabia, Francis, 120, 121

Picasso, Pablo, 126

Plant, Sadie, 17–18, 285, 290 n.51

Plath, Aurelia Schober, 214–15

Plath, Sylvia, 183–84, 187–91, 212–24; "Aftermath," 214; *Ariel*, 190, 215–16, 218, 221–22; and the BBC, 220–21; *Bell Jar*, 214, 218; "Birthday Present," 219; "By Candlelight," 222; "Channel Crossing," 223; *Colossus*, 213–14; "Context," 222; "Conversation among the Ruins," 219; *Crossing the Water*, 190, 223; "Daddy," 218; "Disquieting Muses," 219; "Double Exposure," 219; "Eye-Mote," 213–14; "Fever 103°," 222; "Lady Lazarus," 219, 221; "Last Words," 217; "Mirror," 216; "Mussel Hunter at Rock Harbor," 214; "New Year on Dartmoor," 216; "Nick and the Candlestick," 222; "On Deck," 220; "On the Decline of Oracles," 219; "Tulips," 218; "Watercolor of Grantchester Meadows," 219; "Wuthering Heights," 216, 218

Plato, 17, 60, 83, 125, 131, 137, 199; and Nabokov, 163, 169, 171

Poe, Edgar Allan, 48, 161, 219

Poirier, Richard, 94, 143–44, 155, 225

Popular Culture, 120, 262, 263; and Douglass, 27, 293 n.26; and Frost, 146–47, 155, 310 n.59, 310 n.67; and Nabokov, 161–65, 171–72; and Pynchon, 225, 250; and Surrealism, 90–91

Porter, Katherine Anne, 186

Posnock, Ross, 93–94, 255

Postcolonialism, 16, 20–21, 54, 56, 228, 256. *See also* Colonialism

Potter, David M., 12, 54, 162–63

Pound, Ezra, 93–94, 123, 128, 134

Pragmatism, 259, 282; and Frost, 132, 143, 155; and Henry James, 93–94, 101, 114, 125

Pre-Raphaelites, 139

Protestantism, 12–13, 188, 228, 244, 245

Psychoanalysis, 97, 152, 166–67, 231

Puritanism, 276–78; and Pynchon, 228, 242–44, 252–53. *See also* Calvinism

Pynchon, Thomas, 1, 177, 225–53; *Crying of Lot 49*, 225–27, 236, 239; *Gravity's Rainbow*, 226, 229, 234, 236, 239–45, 246, 248, 250, 252, 253; "Is It O.K. to Be a Luddite?" 231; *Mason & Dixon*, 18, 20, 226, 227, 236, 241, 245–53; "Nearer, My Couch to Thee," 229–30; *Slow Learner*, 226, 239; *V*, 226, 228–29, 236, 237–39, 240; *Vineland*, 225, 231–35, 236, 248

Pynchon, William, 242–43

Queer theory, 82, 136; and James, 97, 99, 100, 102

Race, 2, 16, 18, 22–46, 86, 107–8, 114, 177, 262, 269–71. *See also* Slavery; Ethnicity

Radway, Janice, 257

Rahv, Philip, 120, 134–35

Readings, Bill, 7

Reagan, Ronald, 200–201, 233, 236, 272

Renan, Ernest, 8

Rich, Adrienne, 200

Rockwell, Norman, 158

Roman Catholicism. *See* Catholicism

Roosevelt, Theodore, 110–11

Rorty, Richard, 178, 277, 282; *Achieving Our Country*, 275–76, 282; *Philosophy and the Mirror of Nature*, 282–83

Rose, Jacqueline, 190, 214, 218, 245

Rosenfeld, Paul, 98

Ross, Andrew, 277, 279

Rossetti, Dante Gabriel, 47, 139

Rowe, John Carlos, 31, 61–62, 95

Rowlandson, Mary, 237

Said, Edward, 269, 326 n.45

Salinger, J. D., 160, 223

Salt, Henry S., 48, 85

Sartre, Jean-Paul, 119, 184

Schopenhauer, Arnold, 83, 265

Paul Giles is Reader in American Literature at the University of
Oxford. He is the author of *Transatlantic Insurrections: British Culture
and the Formation of American Literature, 1730–1860* (Pennsylvania,
2001); *American Catholic Arts and Fictions: Culture, Ideology, Aesthetics*
(Cambridge, 1992); *Hart Crane: The Contexts of "The Bridge"*
(Cambridge, 1986).

Library of Congress Cataloging-in-Publication Data
Giles, Paul.
Virtual Americas: transnational fictions and the transatlantic
imaginary / Paul Giles.
p. cm. — (New Americanists)
Includes index.
ISBN 0-8223-2954-9 (cloth : alk. paper)
ISBN 0-8223-2967-0 (pbk. : alk. paper)
1. American literature—History and criticism. 2. Great
Britain—Foreign public opinion, American. 3. National characteristics,
American, in literature. 4. Literature, Comparative—English and
American. 5. Literature, Comparative—American and English.
6. Nationalism and literature—United States. 7. United
States—Relations—Great Britain. 8. Great Britain—Relations—United
States. 9. Americans—Great Britain—History. 10. United States—In
literature. I. Title. II. Series.
PS159.G8 G53 2002    810.9'3273—dc21    2002003057